To my friend Dr. Frank D'Elia

Best Regards

Frank A. Bayh

23 Jan 2006

A Party of Mad Fellows

Reverend William Corby C.S.C. Chaplain of the 88th New York Veteran Volunteer Infantry. Later President of the University of Notre Dame.

A Party of Mad Fellows

The Story of the Irish Regiments in the Army of the Potomac

Frank A. Boyle

Morningside
1996

ISBN: 0-89029-329-5

Morningside House, Inc.
260 Oak Street, Dayton, Ohio 45410
1-800-648-9710
Fax: 513-461-4260

DEDICATION

To the following who stand for all the men
of the Irish regiments in the
Army of the Potomac

Sergeant Jeremiah Boyle, 69th Pennsylvania.
Killed at Gettysburg, July 3, 1863.

Private John Francis Boyle, 69th Pennsylvania.
Killed at Gettysburg, July 3, 1863.

And for my cousins in World War II

Thomas F. Brennan, Radarman 3/C.
Killed on *USS Bunker Hill*, May 12, 1945.

PFC James J. Dennehy, 314th Infantry.
Killed at St. Lo, July 3, 1944.

Brave
Generous
Handsome

CONTENTS

Illustrations/Maps 8
Foreword 9
Introduction 13
Chapter One: The Fiery Cross 17
Chapter Two: The First Battle 41
Chapter Three: The Brigadier 53
Chapter Four: The Peninsula 81
Chapter Five: Week of Battle 113
Chapter Six: Summer Interlude 159
Chapter Seven: The Harvest in Maryland 175
Chapter Eight: Sprigs of Boxwood 203
Chapter Nine: Celebrations and Supplications 233
Chapter Ten: Springtime in a Wilderness 241
Chapter Eleven: Gettysburg 261
Chapter Twelve: Entr'acte 299
Chapter Thirteen: The Month of Blood 319
Chapter Fourteen: The War Becomes a Siege 367
Epilogue 389
Appendix A: Battle Honors of the Irish Regiments 391
Appendix B: General Officers Associated with the Irish
    Regiments 395
Appendix C: Colonels of the Irish Regiments 397
Appendix D: The Relics of the Irish Regiments 401
Appendix E: "The Irish Division" 403
Appendix F: Letters Home 405
Appendix G: The Brave Colonel James P. McManon at Cold
    Harbor 407
Appendix H: The Notre Dame Connection 409
Bibliography 411
Index 421

ILLUSTRATIONS

Rev. William Corby ii
Brig. Gen. Michael Corcoran 19
Brig. Gen. Thomas Francis Meagher 25
Col. Edward Cass 35
Col. Robert Nugent 55
Maj. Gen. James P. Shields 59
Col. Patrick Robert Guiney 128
Col. St. Clair A. Mulholland 197
Col. Richard Byrnes 207
Col. Patrick Kelly 252
Col. Dennis O'Kane 284
Brig. Gen. Thomas A. Smyth 313
Col. Matthew Murphy 344
Col. James McMahon 356
Bvt. Maj. Gen. James P. McIvor 384

MAPS

First Manassas: Early phase 45
First Manassas: battle on Henry House Hill 46
The Army of the Potomac moves on Richmond, spring
    1862 83
The Battle of Williamsburg 90
The battles of the Peninsular Campaign 98
The Battle of Gaines' Mill 123
The road network east of Richmond 135
The Battle of Glendale 139
The Battle of Malvern Hill 153
The Battle of Antietam: The Struggle for the Bloody Lane . 191
The Battle of Fredericksburg: The Irish Brigade attacks Marye's
    Heights 216
First Division, Second Corps in the Wheatfield at
    Gettysburg 269
The 69th Pennsylvania fights in the Angle at Gettysburg ... 282
Battles of the Overland Campaign, May 3 - June 12, 1864 320
Grant moves to the James River, June 12-16, 1864 363

FOREWORD

Many historians have written that the Civil War was the single, most definitive act in American history. Its outcome determined the supremacy of the Federal government in Washington, that there would be an indussoluble Union of the States, and that chattel slavery would disappear from those States where it had been legal. Throughout history civil wars have always been bitter and hard-fought affairs, and the American Civil War was especially so. The battles were many and desperate and involved so many new techniques of warfare that they require explanation to those who are approaching the war for the first time.

This book is about the experiences of a number of Irish-American citizens who were relative newcomers to the United States. It will be helpful to define some terms at the start so that military neophytes will have a better understanding of the organization of the army, and how it was commanded.

The Civil War soldier went off to battle as a member of a military unit, usually an infantry or cavalry regiment or an artillery battery. The basic unit, the regiment, was, in most cases, organized by the home state at the behest of the central government of either side. When first mustered in, the regiment consisted of approximately one thousand men divided into ten companies. A colonel was in command of a regiment, assisted by a lieutenant colonel and a major. In the beginning, each company was commanded by a captain, aided by two lieutenants and several sergeants and corporals.

In most cases four regiments composed a brigade, properly commanded by a brigadier general. I say "properly" because in both Union and Confederate armies this was more honored in the breach than in the observance. If a brigadier was struck down in battle or incapacitated by sickness, his successor in command usually was the senior colonel in point of service of the four in the brigade. Whether or not this arrangement persisted for very long depended on how quickly the higher command reacted. It might continue the arrangement, or it might find another officer with more capacity or experience to take over.

Several brigades made up a division, usually three, but sometimes more, sometimes less. This higher formation should have been commanded by a major general. Again because of circumstance, this was often not the case in the Union army.

Several infantry divisions made up a corps, and several corps made up the Army of the Potomac, or any of the other armies, both Union and Confederate. In the campaign on the Peninsula, Gen. George B. McClellan, the commander of the Army of the Potomac, had roughly 100,000 men organized in five corps, each of which was composed of two divisions. At the division and corps level there were also attached artillery, engineers, and other supporting services. The cavalry was also organized in regiments, however, instead of companies the horsemen were subdivided into troops and squadrons. Their higher formations, like the infantry, were in brigades and divisions.

As the war continued, the original thousand men in an infantry regiment suffered battle casualties, sickness and disease, and were, correspondingly, decreased. At the time of Gettysburg, in July 1863, after two years of war, most infantry regiments were down to three or four hundred men. The Federal government in Washington never developed a replacement system to keep the veteran organizations at peak strength. Instead, new regiments were formed, for the most part untrained and undisciplined, and put into battle. These soldiers who would have profited from associating with veterans were condemned to repeat the mistakes of the early days.

At the aforementioned Battle of Gettysburg, the Army of the Potomac had experienced two years of hard service and many battles. It had, roughly, the same number of soldiers that McClellan had on the Peninsula, but was now organized in seven infantry corps and one cavalry corps. In May 1864, at the start of Lt. Gen. Ulysses S. Grant's Overland Campaign against

Gen. Robert E. Lee, the army was re-organized into three infantry corps and a cavalry corps. It numbered about 125,000 men as opposed to 85,000 men at Gettysburg.

Infantry soldiers on both sides usually were armed with rifled muskets which were muzzle loaders. A good soldier could get off two to three shots per minute. The weapons had an effective range of five hundred yards and could inflict terrible wounds when firing the soft lead bullet, which was usually of 58 caliber, that is the bullet was 0.58 inches in diameter at the base. One of the great soldiers of history, Napoleon Bonaparte, said that any soldier's chief struggle was not with the enemy, but with hardship. The outdoor life in all kinds of weather, constant marching, and insufficient food, in effect the physical struggle to stay alive, was a tremendous challenge to the human organism. In the Civil War the American soldier saw all of these challenges at close hand, fought an intransigent foe, whether Union or Confederate, and emerged from the cauldron bloody, but unbowed, richer for having served with like human beings in a common cause. Though the South was conquered in the end, it must not be held that the soldiers who had given their all were, in their own eyes, depreciated. They had done all that men can do. Though the North won and restored the Union, there was little triumphalism among the fighting men who survived. That was left for the opportunists, political and economic, who always settle like birds of carrion on the spoils of every war.

ACKNOWLEDGEMENTS

To all who helped me with this book:

My wife and family who have been most supportive and have put up with all manner of invasions of their time and patience. My friends of the Old Lincoln Civil War Society of Philadelphia and the Round Table that sprang from it: Bob Connor, John Bloom, Larry Dixon, Ken Holt, Sande Kartman, Bill Klammer, John Swered, Bev Arthur (deceased), George Cain (deceased), Dave Gottlieb (deceased), Dr. Russ Green (deceased). The curator of the Civil War Museum and Library, Philadelphia, Pennsylvania, Steve Wright; both John Costellos, senior and junior, of the "Old Baldy" Civil War Round Table; Bill Rose of Company D, 69th Pennsylvania Reenactors; Michael Kane of Pittsburgh; Ben Maryniak of the Buffalo Round Table; Frank O'Reilly of Fredericksburg National Military Park; J. Michael Priest, author of *Antietam: The Soldier's Battle*; D. Scott Hartwig of Gettysburg National Military Park; John Dennis Clark (deceased), the historian of the Philadelphia Irish, who drove me to write this book; and the ladies of the Norwood Public Library who have been of great help and encouragement to me: Jane Lloyd, Eileen Baker, Mary Ellen Deasey, Nancy Phillips, Doris Baker, and Dee Howells. Any errors in this book are mine. If there is worth in it, a good deal of the credit should go to them.

I would also like to thank the following:

Yale University Library Collections for permission to quote from a letter of Alexander Stewart Webb to hid father in the Alexander Stewart Webb Collection. The Civil War Museum and Library, Philadelphia for permission to reproduce a letter from Gen. John R. Brooke to Bvt. Maj. Gen. St. Clair Mulholland in the Mulholland Collection. Little, Brown & Company for permission to quote from *Grant Takes Command by Bruce Catton*. Funk & Wagnalls Company for permission to quote from *Diary of a Union Lady: The Diary of Maria Lydig Daly*, edited by H. E. Hammond. Doubleday & Company for permission to quote from *A Stillness at Appomattox* by Bruce Catton.

INTRODUCTION
A PARTY OF MAD FELLOWS

A few miles north and east of Richmond, Virginia, on June 2, 1862, a young war correspondent surveyed the surging waters of the Chickahominy River as it roiled around the supports of what the Army of the Potomac called the Grapevine Bridge. Although the sun was out in full force, the river valley was awash with the heavy run-off of the torrential rains of two days ago which had spread over the tidewater lowlands and turned them into a quagmire. The Grapevine Bridge itself still stood, although the platform was under water, and the supports moved in the flow and groaned, as though ready to give way at any instant.

In the woods bordering the north shore of the Chickahominy long lines of supply wagons and ambulances were wedged nose to tailboard. So narrow were the corduroy approaches to the bridge and so fathomless the swamp on either side that the horse-drawn caravans could go neither forward nor back. From the south side of the river came the muted sound of a dying battle. Fair Oaks-Seven Pines Battle had been fought on the two preceding days south of here. As George A. Townsend, correspondent of the New York *Herald*, sat his horse surveying the scene, the walking wounded of that battle streamed from the south shore up to the bridge, hoping the span would hold their weight. They waded through the water covering the floor of the bridge, stepping from log to log. Gaining the north bank of the river, they were wet from head to foot and bleeding from their wounds. They brought the unwelcome news that their comrades, who were still fighting in the tangled woods, needed food and ammunition.

The commander of the Army of the Potomac, Gen. George B. McClellan, and his staff rode up directly in front of the war correspondent and tried the bridge which quickly sank beneath them. The whole dripping lot of them floundered back to the north side, presenting to the troops the welcome sight of higher authority with a wet bottom. At least it demonstrated a community of interest. The correspondent thought that Little Mac was growing heavy and, as he came to shore, noticed that he shook himself like a dog.

It was all very interesting to George Albert Townsend who had pulled all kinds of tricks to get this close to the fighting of May 31-June 1, 1862. And yet he wished to get even closer. Leaving his horse with a drummer boy, he took off his clothes down to the skin, and holding them over his head, set out on the precarious bridge. He nearly made it over without mishap. But the gods of journalism deserted him in the end and he landed in the muck of the swamp, clothes and all. He dried himself off using his underwear, dressed, and set off southward.

After a half hour's walk he came to an unpainted frame mansion where an elderly gentleman sat on a porch sipping a julep and talking with a sturdy Union officer of decidedly Irish features. As Townsend approached, the officer said to him, "Bloodanowns! And where have ye been? Among the hogs, I think!" But then he helped the reporter to get cleaned up, gave him a julep, and sent his own servant for the reporter's horse. The officer further informed the scribe that he, Townsend, was known to him as a reporter for the *Herald*, since before the war the officer had been the coroner's surgeon in New York and was familiar with the representatives of the press.

"In short," wrote Townsend, later, "we became familiar directly . . . his name was O'Ganlon, Quartermaster of Meagher's Irish Brigade, Sumner's Corps. . . . He proposed to send me to the field, with a note of introduction to the General, and another to Colonel Baker, of the New York 88th (Irish), who could show me the lines and relics of battle, and give me the lists of killed, wounded, and missing. I repaired to his room, and arrayed myself in a fatigue officer's suit, with clean underclothing, after which, descending, I climbed into his saddle, and dashed off, with a mettlesome, dapper pony."[1]

And so a representative of the great American press, one who had been raised in poverty in rural Delaware, the son of a carpenter who doubled as a Methodist preacher on Sundays,

1. George A. Townsend, *Campaigns of a Non-Combatant* (New York: Blelock and Company, 1866), p. 128 ff.

came to meet the Irish Brigade on the day after their first experience of battle. Later he was to write of them:

> Every adjunct of the place was strictly Hibernian. The emerald green standard entwined with the red, white and blue; the gilt eagles on the flagpoles held the Shamrock sprig in their beaks; the soldiers lounging on guard, had "69" or "88" the numbers of their regiments, stamped on a green hat-band; the brogue of every county from Down to Wexford fell upon the ear. . . . When anything absurd, forlorn, or desperate was to be attempted, the Irish brigade was called upon. But, ordinarily, they were regarded, *as a party of mad fellows*, more ornamental than useful, and entirely too clannish and factious to be entrusted with power.[2]

There is a note of wonder in Townsend's piece. What were these Irishmen doing in Virginia fighting in America's war? He met their wounded, some of them with freshly amputated limbs, and talked with a burial party interring some of the Confederate dead. But one cannot escape the fact that, although he had been treated with great hospitality by O'Ganlon and everyone else in the Irish Brigade, Townsend did not feel at home. Later he dined with Col. Joshua Owen, the Welshborn commander of the 69th Pennsylvania Volunteers, an Irish regiment from Philadelphia, which was not a part of the Irish Brigade. Townsend mistakenly identified Owen as being in the Irish Brigade and called him the most consistent and intelligent officer in it. Still later he was assured by Capt. Rufus Pettit of Battery B, New York Light Artillery, that one American was worth ten Irish in a fight. Townsend's relief is evident.

Townsend was an extremely straightforward example of the nineteenth century American. For him, the Irish of the Famine, hurled up on the shore of America, were strangers to be kept at arms-length. They were to be used, not embraced. Finally, they were not to be spoken well of, ever. And they have not been, since 1867 when David Powers Conyngham published *The Irish Brigade and Its Campaigns*. Until now.

2. *Ibid.*, p. 130. Italics added.

15

What manner of soldiers were these Irish, here in the Promised Land? That is the question we will examine. Were they warriors or caricatures? George Townsend's mind was already made up.

So was Rufus Pettit's. So was that of many an American. It is time to see whether or not they were right or wrong. In all, twelve regiments of the Army of the Potomac were known as "Green Flag Regiments," that is, they were composed of Irish immigrants or their immediate descendants. How well did they fight for their adopted country? That is the question we will examine.

CHAPTER ONE
THE FIERY CROSS

Congress was not in session on Inauguration Day, 1861, when Lincoln stood before Chief Justice Roger B. Taney and swore to defend the Constitution and uphold the Union of the several states. It was not in session six weeks later in the very vitals of crisis. The president was the sole architect of policy in the fateful spring of 1861. Until Franklin D. Roosevelt placed the government squarely in the middle of the economy, there was no challenge to Lincoln's broad interpretation of the powers of the presidency. During the Spring of 1861 he could say with as good reason as Louis XIV, "I am the State." For *Lincoln* blockaded the southern ports, *he* refused to allow the Confederacy an existence, and, finally, *he* welded the national sentiment and purpose together by calling out the militia of the states. As befits a lawyer, the language and basis of these tocsins is clearly within the legal code.

In the latter case, for instance, the calling out of the militia, there is a prior act of Congress cited for authority; all the whereases and the commas are in the right places. The entire piece breathes the dignity and majesty of constituted authority, and by its very tone it intimidates those constitutional lawyers who have questioned its legality "to suppress said combinations and to cause the laws to be duly executed."[1]

There was no question from the North. Such a yell had greeted the news of Sumter as only mingled anger, sorrow, and exaltation could draw. There was no loyal opposition. Lincoln's great rival and close friend, Stephen Douglas, conferred with him for two hours, and on leaving the White House issued a statement endorsing the president's policy whole-heartedly.

---

1. United States War Department, *War of the Redbellion: A Compilation of the Official Records of the Union and Conferderate Armies*, 70 vols. in 128 parts (Washington, D.C.: Government Printing Office, 1880-1901), series 3, vol. 1, p. 67. Hereafter cited as *OR.*

The governors of the loyal states turned to the state militias and issued the marching orders. There then ensued a magnificent chaos. The best-intentioned got in each other's way, the unknowing fell down in the press and were trodden, and the lukewarm were turned and borne on by the tide, helpless and squirming. It was the people's war.

Lincoln called for 75,000 men to enlist for a period of three months, and far more than that number wished to join this force for one reason or another. It was later said that the three-months men were not as good soldier material as those who signed up for three years in the summer that followed. The early ones, it was claimed, were the unemployable, the idle, and the adventurous. The later soldiers were the solid props of society, worthy men, actuated by patriotism and lofty ideals. Their original inertia was caused only by a time lag during which they wound up their affairs, being men of property and substance. This downgrading of the early men did not include some of the "crack" militia regiments which by judicious use of political influence managed to get accepted in the first call.

It did not include, for instance, the 7th New York State Militia, composed of the flower of the city. The tailored gray uniforms and white gloves of the 7th went down to the nation's capital in the early days and did a certain amount of guard duty. At the end of thirty days this "crack" regiment went home, and, except for short periods of home-guard activity, was not seen outside its armory walls again. These men were the rich, landed, knowledgeable section of society. They saw no bloodshed, had no thirty-mile a day hikes, and gained only a slight acquaintance with hardtack and beans; such regiments went home during the summer of 1861, were regaled with banquets and oratory, and disappeared into the booming war economy. American society made a distinction between these men, the "better people" and the canaille who would bleed and die. There is a good example of this in a letter from Governor Andrew of Massachusetts to the War Department on April 18,

Divers persons of military experience are enlisting soldiers into the militia with my consent and with a view to U.S. service. The men will be of a hardy class,

18

Michael Corcoran
Colonel, 69th New York State Militia, Brigadier General,
United States Volunteers.
Organizer and commander of the Corcoran Legion.

19

more used to exposure than the volunteer militia commonly are, since our companies in peace are mostly made up of the best citizens.[2]

On April 25 the governor was more explicit,

> Will you authorize the enlistment here and mustering into the U.S. service here of Irish, Germans, and other tough men, to be drilled and prepared here for service? We have men enough of such description, eager to be employed, sufficient to make three regiments.[3]

The governor is here only expressing the Calvinist theory of "the elect" or "the better people" which holds that those favored by God automatically inherit the earth and its fruit. The others, that is "the non-elect," also inherit the earth, in this particular frame of reference, at least enough of it to cover their bones after the din of battle.

Meanwhile, what of these "other, tough men?" Were they at all backward in offering their bodies to the Republic? Did they hold in their memories the scenes of a few years back when the nativists had scourged them? Perhaps they had short memories, or perhaps they were susceptible to the sound of drum and fife. Certainly, they needed the money. But perhaps they had some dawning consciousness of the duties of a citizen whether or not they were of the "better class."

In New York City there were other militia regiments in addition to the 7th Regiment of the state militia. Some were recruited from the volunteer fire companies, some from the immigrants of German birth and background, and then there was the 69th New York State Militia, formed ten years before from the Irish immigrants and their progeny. Seven months before, this regiment had made headlines all across the United States. Queen Victoria's son, Edward, Prince of Wales, the heir to the throne of the British Empire, had come to Canada to pay a state visit. President James Buchanan invited the Prince to come across the border and tour the nation that had risen from the former British colonies.

2. *Ibid.*, p. 86.
3. *Ibid.*, p. 112.

The Prince made a tour of American cities and was well received by all, until his entourage arrived in New York. There Michael Corcoran, the colonel of the 69th New York, said he would not have his regiment turn out to parade for the royal visitor. Corcoran had a flimsy excuse ready. The regiment had already paraded twleve times in a twelve-month period, thus fulfilling the requirements of the law. Against a direct order from the state authorities, Corcoran continued his course and the 69th did not march, whereupon the state authorities prepared a court martial for him. But the day the Prince left the city, the news of the autumn elections was back on the front page of the newspapers. Politics, the principal sport of the American nation, was of particular interest that year. In New York City there were a lot of Irish voters, politicians, hangers-on, and so forth to consider. They were the largest voting bloc in the most vibrant city in the nation, and even though most of them were indifferent toward the Prince of Wales rebuff by Corcoran, the power structure of the city decided not to exacerbate matters. Months went by and there was no court martial. No one seemed surprised.

Then came the national election in which Abraham Lincoln emerged as the sixteenth president of the nation. South Carolina seceded from the Union, and the Cotton States, Georgia, Alabama, Mississippi, Louisiana, also seceded and formed a new nation called the Confederate States of America. With all of that going on, Michael Corcoran disappeared into oblivion. But there was more. The *Star of the West* was fired on when it tried to resupply Fort Sumter in Charleston, then Fort Sumter itself was fired on. Suddenly there was a war on. Regiments were needed with colonels to lead them. Even Michael Corcoran and the 69th New York. All sorts of strange and weird happenings were taking place. Senators and congressmen were suddenly putting on the uniforms of generals and striking military poses.

A good example is what happened to the court-martial of Michael Corcoran which was dealt with in the following:

Special Orders, No. 9.
First Division, N.Y.S.M.,
New York, April 20, 1861.

21

In pursuance of Special Orders, No. 58, from General Headquarters, the Court-martial detailed for the trial of Colonel Corcoran, of the Sixty-ninth Regiment, is dissolved, and the charges dismissed; and Colonel Corcoran is directed forthwith to resume the command of his regiment.

By order of

Major-General Charles W. Sandford[4]

Corcoran celebrated his return to grace with a general order which ended,

The commandant feels proud that his first duty, after being relieved from a long arrest, is to have the honor of promulgating an order to the regiment to rally to the support of the Constitution and laws of the United States.[5]

About a month before the above action a famous war correspondent of the London *Times*, one William Howard Russell, was in New York City and witnessed the St. Patrick's Day parade, held that year on the 18th of March because the 17th was a Sunday. In the framework of the time he was not an unbiased recorder of the doings of the Irish, being subject to the opinions and prejudices of the ascendancy. But he should not be dismissed on that account. He had been in the Crimea and had straightforwardly reported the failures and shortcomings of the British army.

. . . I struggled with a friend through the crowd which thronged Union Square. Bless them! They were all Irish, judging from speech, and gesture, and look; for the most part decently dressed, and comfortable, evidently bent on enjoying the day in spite of the cold. . . . Imagine Broadway lined for the long miles of its course by spectators mostly Hibernian, and the

4. David P. Conyngham, *The Irish Brigade and Its Campaigns* (New York: William McSorley & Co., 1867), p. 20.
5. *Ibid.*, p. 21.

22

great gaudy stars and stripes, waving in all directions, whilst up its centre in the mud march the children of Erin.

Here comes the 69th N. Y. State Militia Regiment—the battalion which would not turn out when the Prince of Wales was in New York, and whose Colonel, Corcoran, is still under court martial for his refusal. Well, the Prince had no loss, and the Colonel may have other besides political reasons for his dislike to parade his men.

The regiment turned out, I should think, only 200 or 220 men, fine fellows enough, but not in the least like soldiers or militia. The United States uniform which most of the military bodies wore, consists of a blue tunic and trousers, and a kepi-like cap, with "U.S." in front for undress. . . . The absence of facings, and the want of something to finish off the collar and cuffs, render the tunic very bald and unsightly. Another band closed the rear of the 69th, and to eke out the military show, which in all was less than 1,200 men, some companies were borrowed from another regiment. . . . A good deal of what passes for national sentiment, is in reality dislike to England and religious animosity.

"Was there any man of eminence in that procession," I asked. "No; a few small local politicians, some wealthy store-keepers, and beer-saloon owners perhaps; but the mass were of the small bourgeoisie. Such a man as Mr. O'Conor, who may be considered at the head of the New York bar for instance, would not take part in it."[6]

So wrote the good Mr. Russell. If he seems too harsh on the Irish, it must be remembered that the British army was at this time the most rainbow-hued force in the world, and a Hussar officer in all his glory was a sight to behold. The Empire was at high tide and the workaday American army blue, especially

6. William H. Russell, *My Diary North and South*, 2 vols. (London: Bradbury and Evans, 1863), 1:136.

23

when it adorned the brawny frame of an Irishman, looked like very small beer indeed. So a good part of his detraction can be blamed on the quartermaster department of the army, but most of it belongs to that insularity that the top-dog Englishman carried within himself around the clock. In justice it must be remarked that the St. Patrick's Day parade would not compare with guard mount at the Horse Guards. Neither would most other American military parades.

Michael Corcoran certainly carried a double load. With others he had helped found the Fenian Brotherhood in 1858. This was a physical force group bent on bringing about the freedom of Ireland from England. To support this idea the more militant ones were enrolled in a quasi-military group called the "Phoenix Brigade," named after the legendary bird which arose from its own ashes. The force was on call for some fortuitous happening overseas which would take them home to strike a blow for that longed-for freedom. Now, in the springtime of decision, John O'Mahony, the chief officer of the Brotherhood, was absent from the country. That made Corcoran the acting chief officer, and raised all sorts of problems, not the least of which was that the Confederacy was not the foe the Fenians most desired to strike. The 69th Regiment, the Phoenix Brigade, and all the others had been raised to be used one day in the liberation of Ireland. Now the plans of Corcoran and the Fenian Brotherhood were upset by this unlooked for war.

On Sunday, April 21, Corcoran addressed the New York Circle of the Brotherhood. He commanded all who were not members of the state militia, and so bound to a period of service, to hold themselves aloof from the war. They were to reserve themselves for the cause to which they were already pledged. In case that looked like disloyalty to the United States, he went on to say that there were ten times as many Irishmen not enrolled in the Brotherhood who wanted to join the 69th; therefore there was no need to deplete Ireland's ranks to fill America's. But, he added, if any of his brother Fenians were determined to go to war, it was preferable that they go with their own countrymen than to have their service go unappreciated and their national identity lost among strangers. On the next day he issued a circular to every circle of the Brotherhood.

Thomas Francis Meagher
Brigadier General, United States Volunteers
Organizer and commander of the Irish Brigade

25

6 Centre Street, New York,
April 22d, 1861.

My Dear Sir,—A sudden emergency calls me for
a time from the duty entrusted to me by Mr. O'Mahony.
The call is so imperative that I must obey whatever
consequences may follow. . . .

I am leaving in great spirits and hope. My last
wish and most ardent desire is that the organization
should be preserved in its strength and efficiency,
and that every man will do his whole duty. We will
not be the worse for a little practice, which we engage
in, with the more heart because we feel it will be
serviceable on other fields.[7]

Six thousand men had shown a desire to enlist in the 69th to
fill 1,000 slots. Due to some mishap, 1,800 were actually
enrolled by the morning of April 22 when Corcoran received
the following order:

Colonel Corcoran will embark his regiment to-
morrow, viz., between ten and eleven o'clock, on
board the James Adger, Pier No. 4 North River, not
exceeding one thousand men, all told.

Charles W. Sandford, Major-General.[8]

The 800 extra looked on themselves as betrayed. What
manner of war was this where the true-blue Irish were to be
kept from glory by a stupid War Department regulation? But
there was no help for it on the day the 69th marched away.
Within a week however the State of New York proposed to the
War Department that the Empire State furnish thirty-eight
regiments of soldiers in addition to the seventeen regiments
summoned for three months of service. The thirty-eight additional regiments would be enlisted for two years unless
sooner discharged. One of these, the 37th, the Irish Rifles,

7. Michael Cavanagh, *Memoirs of General Thomas Francis Meagher*
(Worcester, Massachusetts: The Messenger Press, 1892), p. 371.
8. Conyngham, *The Irish Brigade*, p. 20.

would offer martial employment for those who had not been accepted for the 69th.

Among those who had watched the St. Patrick's Day Parade, in addition to William Russell, was one Thomas Francis Meagher who had recently returned from a trip to Central America. Far from the disgust which welled up in Russell's breast was the sentiment evoked in Meagher's. Although a fervent Irish Nationalist, Meagher was not a member of the Fenian Brotherhood and, indeed, had repulsed the overtures made to him by James Stephens a few years before. Maybe it was the sight of all the green banners waving in the wind and the ordered ranks of marching men. In any case Meagher decided to raise a regiment for the Phoenix Brigade, as the military arm of the Brotherhood was called.[9]

It may seem curious that he would help an organization of which he was not a member. In fact he regarded it as presumptuous himself and suggested that it would be better for all concerned if he received a formal invitation to do so. It was hardly likely that the Brotherhood would refuse. Meagher was the most prominent Irishman in New York, one who could influence people by word and example. He was a real live survivor of the Revolution of 1848, one who had been sentenced to a life term on the Island of Tasmania, from which he had escaped to America in 1852. He had considerable gifts as well. His enemies admitted he could talk well and effectively, even if they did not always care for his message. The message, interestingly enough, was not delivered in an Irish brogue, but in the cultivated tones of the famous English Jesuit public school at Stonyhurst, where his father, a prosperous merchant, had sent him.

In America Meagher had not as yet made a definite mark in journalism or law. He was on the Irish banquet circuit and appeared in several Eastern cities giving speeches about the glories of Erin and the perfidy of the ancient foe. He had managed to marry an "American" lady, Elizabeth Townsend, whose father had protested the match and did not care at all for his son-in-law.[10] For the Fenians who cared nothing for the

9. Cavanagh, *Memoirs of Thomas Meagher*, p. 365.
10. *Ibid.*, p. 345.

cloak of respectability, even scorned it, Meagher's amorphous career in America was no black mark against him. Their target was the following he could command.

So, early in April 1861, young Michael Cavanagh, Secretary to John O'Mahony, Head-Center of the Brotherhood, came to see Meagher to assure him that a formal invitation would be extended to him to raise a regiment for the Phoenix Brigade. Meagher was much pleased. He was leaving that evening for a speaking engagement in Connecticut, and on his return he would accept the written invitation and begin recruiting. Then the talk turned to national events. Sumter had not been fired on as yet, but the situation of the garrison was commonly discussed in every home in the country. There was no doubt of Meagher's sympathies; they were with the South. Only that day he had a vigorous argument on the matter with his father-in-law, an ardent Republican. Later in the morning in Delmonico's Restaurant when a young man denounced the Southern viewpoint, Meagher replied ". . . I tell you candidly and plainly that, in this controversy, my sympathies are entirely with the South!"[11]

While Meagher was in Connecticut, the firing on Fort Sumter took place. Upon his return on April 22, he called at the office of the Brotherhood where Cavanagh handed him the proclamation of the Phoenix Brigade to raise a regiment. As they stood there discussing the matter, Lt. Col. Robert Nugent of the 69th Regiment entered the office and inquired of him, "Well, Mr. Meagher? What do you think of affairs now?" Meagher replied, "I do not know what to think of them; I never saw such a change in public opinion as has taken place during the past week. I feel like one carried away by a torrent. The whole cry is 'The Flag! The Flag!'" He paused and then continued, "Damn them! that didn't let that flag alone." Nugent, under orders to leave for Washington on the morrow, observed how deeply Meagher was moved, and said, "As you feel that way, Mr. Meagher, perhaps you might take a notion of coming with us?" After a moment's reflection, Meagher answered, "I do not know but I might." Apparently this was a revelation to both Nugent and Cavanagh who recorded the conversation. As Nugent left, he remarked, "You'll think this

11. *Ibid.*, p. 368.

over, Mr. Meagher!" To which Meagher answered, "I will think of it." When they were alone, the astonished Cavanagh asked him if he meant what he said; such a reversal of opinion seemed to be beyond belief.[12]

In answer, Meagher almost went into a soliloquy as he examined his own thought processes for the first time.

> Yes! I did mean it—for, looking at every aspect of the question, I do not see what better course I could take. Duty and patriotism alike prompt me to it. The Republic, that gave us an asylum and an honorable career,—that is the mainstay of human freedom, the world over—is threatened with disruption. It is the duty of every liberty-loving citizen to prevent such a calamity at all hazards. Above all is it the duty of us Irish citizens, who aspire to establish a similar form of government in our native land. It is not only our duty to America, but also to Ireland. We could not hope to succeed in our effort to make Ireland a Republic without the moral and material aid of the liberty-loving citizens of these United States. That aid we might rely upon receiving at the proper time. But *now*, when all the thoughts, energies, and resources of this noble people are needed to preserve their own institutions from destruction—they cannot spare either sympathy, arms, or men, for any other cause.
>
> Another thought forces itself upon me in connection with the hopes we entertain for Ireland. It is a moral certainty that many of our countrymen who enlist in this struggle for the maintenance of the Union will fall in the contest. But, even so; I hold that if only one in ten of us come back when this war is over, the military experience gained by that *one* will be of more service in a fight for Ireland's freedom than would that of the entire ten as they are now.[13]

12. *Ibid.*, p. 369.
13. *Ibid.*

There was never a better exposition of the split-mindedeness of the Fenian mentality. Even here in the deepest difficulty of America, the idea of Ireland's ultimate freedom must never be abandoned. And the efforts of Irish-Americans for the Union were to be placed in a bank of goodwill so that at some future day they may be drawn against. There was something more there. America was not the bad father-image to the Fenians that England represented. It was instead a son or daughter-image embodying all the virtues and good qualities to which the Irish had never been allowed to become accustomed. For America there was love and affection, hope and trust.

But in the background there was the older, ineradicable devotion to the homeland. For Meagher and Corcoran and the other Fenians, there was no conflict between the Mother-image of Ireland and the daughter-image of America. The myth of America was simply so powerful, so limitless in its concept and in its direction that it swallowed up the older impulse. It was precisely in this division of affection that the nativists saw a club with which to belabor the Irish. For the Irish their historical experience simply reinforced their feeling for the new homeland.

On the very next day after Meagher's exegesis, the 69th New York State Militia went off to the war, and the entire Hibernian population turned out to bid them good-bye. Corcoran, who had not been well, led the column with Meagher and Judge Charles Daly attending him. When the marchers reached the pier where the steamer waited to take them to Annapolis, Maryland, a near-riot broke out. It seemed as though everyone who was bidding farewell suddenly came to the realization that this might be a last one. The crowd stampeded and it took herculean efforts to sort out the soldiers from their friends. Finally, the steamer edged away from the pier and set out.

Meagher had also found a way to be part of the scene. A body of cavalry was nominally attached to the 69th, called the Brigade Lancers. It was this group whose appearance had excited the mirth of William Howard Russell on St. Patrick's Day. Since they were to be left at home, there was an opening for an additional company. Soon placards covered New York saying,

Young Irishmen to arms!
To arms Young Irishman!
Irish Zouaves.

One Hundred young Irishmen—healthy, intelligent and active—wanted at once to form a Company under command
of Thomas Francis Meagher
To be attached to the 69th Regiment NYSM. No applicant under eighteen or above thirty-five will be enrolled into the company. Application to be made at 36 Beekman street every day, between the hours of 10 AM and 5 PM.[14]

It took just two days to register the necessary number, but the State of New York did not muster them in for a month. They were off for Washington on May 23 to join the regiment, and on the following day passed over Aqueduct Bridge into Virginia. There on Arlington Heights they constructed a fort as laid out by the engineers, 650 feet by 450 feet. The engineers calculated that it would take 3,000 men three weeks to raise the ramparts. The strongbacks of the 1,200 Irish did it in one. They had the honor of a visit by their president, Abraham Lincoln, who was full of affability and badinage. Corcoran wanted to name the fort after the Secretary of State William Seward, but the War Department vetoed that and directed that it be called after himself. There is a photograph of Corcoran standing on the ramparts gazing off into the distance with ten of his officers posed around one of the 8-inch howitzers below.[15] Ten recent West Point cadets had been given to him as drillmasters and they went to the work of whipping the troops into shape with a vengeance.

During the elections of 1860 the *New York Times* had commented on the qualifications of one of the candidates as follows:

The Tammany Hall nominee for this office is Colonel John McCunn, a native of Londonderry, Ire-

14. *Ibid.*, p. 378.
15. Francis T. Miller, ed., *The Photographic History of the Civil War*, 10 vols. (New York: Review of Reviews Company, 1911), 5:76-77.

land, now in his 35th year. Until very recently he
was in partnership with Judge Moncrief having
been educated in the law offices of Charles
O'Conor. Without entering into the reasons for
McCunn's unpopularity with the legal profession, it
is believed that a great majority of the lawyers on
Manhattan Island will vote against him. This will
make little difference as he has received the Mozart
endorsement and will be elected by a fifteen to
twenty thousand majority.[16]

So this ornament of the bar, John McCunn, proved the *Times*
to be a sorrowfully accurate prophet. For some years he had
been identified with the 75th Regiment, NYSM, but that
regiment had passed out of existence in 1856. On April 21,
while Corcoran addressed the Fenian Brotherhood as we
have seen, the old officers of the 75th led by Judge McCunn
met at Hibernian Hall and adopted the following:

> Resolved, That we organize the 75th Regiment to
> serve as a Zouave Corps forthwith, and tender our
> services to the Governor of the State.[17]

Within a week six companies had nearly filled their quotas
and were drilling at the Eagle Drill Rooms under Captains
John Kavanagh, John Burke, and others. McCunn had left
for Washington with the 69th since he was carried on the
rolls as one of three "Engineer" officers. There seems a
strong possibility that there was some tension between him
and Corcoran, and the chance to lead a regiment of his own,
under officers loyal to himself, must have been irresistible.
A private committee headed by the ubiquitous Judge Charles
Daly formed a finance group to keep the men of the new
regiment clothed and fed until the number of men on the
roster would justify New York in mustering them into service.

16. *New York Times*, October 17, 1860, "Candidates for the Bench."
17. A. Milburn Petty, "History of the 37th Regiment, New York Volunteers,"
Journal of the American Irish Historical Society, vol. 33 (1934): 101.

Early in May the regiment went into quarters in the vicinity of 95th Street and Broadway, the men sleeping in a building formerly used as a "German Assembly and Dance Room" where they were supplied with straw and blankets. The officers lived at home. Two companies recruited in Cattaraugus County, Company H from the little town of Allegany, and Company I from Ellicottsville,were assigned to the regiment while it was encamped there. The men of this contingent were mostly American-born with a sprinkling of Germans and Irish. Surgeon William O'Meagher pointed out that since everyone was an American citizen "all harmonized well."[18]

The 75th became the 37th Regiment, New York Volunteer service when the State Militia Board adopted this resolution:

> Resolved, that the companies commanded by the following captains: O'Connor, Doran, Kavanagh, McHugh, Murphy, Busch, Harmon, Clarke, and Peckham be organized into a regiment to be numbered No. 37 and an election of officers be held thereon.[19]

This was the first Irish organization to be accepted for service outside the state militia regiments and the first to be accepted for long-term service of two or three years, rather than the three-months asked for by the Lincoln administration. The green flag carried by the 37th still hangs in the state capitol in Albany with the legend, "The First Regiment of Irish Volunteers In the Field." The later fame of the Irish Brigade and the Corcoran Legion should not rob the 37th of its proud claim. It was indeed the first Irish regiment of volunteers mustered into the service of the United States.

McCunn marched his men down to the barracks on the Battery the following day where they were sworn in by Colonel Samuel Hayman of the 7th U.S. Infantry. He must have liked what he saw for later, when Judge McCunn was retired to civilian life, Hayman asked for and received the command of the 37th. Uniforms were issued on June 21, and a silk regimen-

18. *Ibid.*, p. 102.
19. *Ibid.*

33

tal flag was presented on behalf of the merchants of New York on the following day. Captain McHugh's sister, Mary, came through with guide colors embroidered by herself of "most costly green silk." On June 23 the 37th, led by the Cecilian Band, marched to Pier 1, North River, and boarded the *Atlas*. Father Peter Tissot of St. John's College (now Fordham University) went along as chaplain.[20]

Another Irish regiment served in the three-month service, the 24th Pennsylvania. As might be expected it came from Philadelphia, and in its militia existence was the 2nd Regiment, Second Brigade, Philadelphia County Militia. In 1861 there were two drawbacks to its acceptance for service, its lack of numbers and its commanding officer, Col. Patrick W. Conroy. The first reason was soon taken care of by opening recruiting offices all over the City of Brotherly Love. The second was more formidable. Maj. Gen. George Cadwalader, the division commander, simply could not stand the sight of Conroy, and even when the regiment was fully recruited he would not accept it. The 24th finally got off dead-center through the good offices of their brigadier, Col. John Miles. He persuaded Conroy to resign and recommended as his successor Joshua T. Owen, a Welsh-born lawyer. Of the new enlistees "a number of these represented other nationalities, including what are called straight-out Americans. Every religious denomination of Christianity was represented, even including the Society of Friends of whom there were at least two. There were also several of the Jewish persuasion." Company K was recruited in Wilmington, Delaware, by Capt. Thomas Smyth. He was to be the last Union general killed in the ensuing war.[21]

Fighting against their fellow-Americans would not be a novel experience for Company C, the second oldest Irish militia company in the United States. In 1844 as the Hibernia Greens it had engaged a nativist mob in defence of St. Philip Neri's Church during the riots. On more than one occasion the 24th, nee the 2nd Regiment, had heard the jeers of the nativists

20. *Ibid.*, pp. 103-4.
21. Michael Kane, "The Irish Lineage of the 69th Pennsylvania Volunteers," *The Irish Sword, The Journal of the Military History Society of Ireland*, vol. 18, no. 27 (Winter 1991): 184.

Edward Cass
Colonel, 9th Massachusetts Volunteer Infantry
Mortally wounded at Malvern Hill

as they marched through the city. Often they had been pelted with bricks and stones.

Now they were off to Chambersburg, Pennsylvania, where a seventy-one-year-old general born in the County Tyrone was scratching together the Pennsylvania militia division. Robert Patterson was the richest man in Philadelphia, and he had the difficult job of blocking off the northern end of the Shenandoah Valley from the newly formed Confederate army.[22]

As a result of the ascension of a Know-Nothing administration to power in 1855, the Irish militia companies of Massachusetts were legally disbanded. One of these companies was the Columbian Artillery whose members had sworn never to bear arms while the watchword was "Proscription!" Now the watchword was "The Union!" and never would the other be used again. The former commander of the Columbians, Thomas Cass, after a large meeting in their Jackson Club Room, proposed to Governor Andrew that an Irish regiment be formed. Six companies were recruited in Boston and it was considered only just and right that the members of the Columbian Artillery would form Company A. Company B was called the Otis Guards after Mrs. Harrison Otis, the wife of one of the Brahmins who was sympathetic to the Irish. Company C was the Douglas Guards for the Honorable Stephen Douglas and Company D was the Meagher Guards after Thomas Francis. Company E was named for Cass and Company F for George McClellan when he became famous. The companies from Salem, Marlboro, and Milford were named for the Irish patriots, Lord Edward Fitzgerald, Wolfe Tone, and Thomas Davis. Company K was from Stoughton and honored its own town.

For its early training the regiment encamped on Long Island in Boston harbor. The officers were commissioned by Governor Andrew on May 3, and at that time the regiment was numbered the 13th Massachusetts Volunteer Militia, a designation that lasted for all of thirty-eight days. On June 11 the regiment was mustered into the service of the United States for three years as the 9th Massachusetts Volunteers. There was a

22. Robert Patterson, *A Narrative of the Campaign of the Valley of the Shenandoah in 1861* (Philadelphia: Sherman and Company, printers, 1865).

great deal of trouble at the muster-in. All of the officers commissioned by the Commonwealth had been elected to their posts by the rank-and-file, but some of these did not meet with the approbation of Colonel Cass. On muster day he deposed the captain and first lieutenant of Company D and appointed new men in their places. The men of the company thereupon refused to serve under the newcomers and gave in only after extensive parleying. There was also a new captain and second lieutenant in Company E; when the old captain made no murmur about stepping down to first lieutenant, a growing hostility in the ranks was stilled.

It almost looked as though Cass had some animus against the MacNamara family in Company E. Michael was deprived of the captaincy and James was removed completely as second lieutenant. In later years a third brother was appointed to write the regimental history, and it is evident that the wound never healed in the heart of Daniel. Had Cass foreseen what would happen he might have taken a more conciliatory attitude. He died a heroic death in battle, but it is recorded with perfunctory notice. Apparently, the MacNamaras did not forget the affront to their honor.

After six weeks of hard drill and training the 9th landed at Long Wharf in Boston and paraded up State Street through an immense throng of their friends, relatives, and countrymen. At the state house, Governor Andrew was waiting for them holding in his hands the state flag of Massachusetts. Their color guard already bore the national colour and the Green flag. Since the occasion merited a speech, John Andrew was equal to the occasion.

> Mr. Commander, I thank you and . . . this splendid regiment . . . which the Commonwealth of Massachusetts is proud to register among the first six regiments of its volunteer contingent. . . . The progress of the enlistment of your men and the appointment of the time of your departure have been the subject of the deepest solicitude. . . . a majority, if not all of your command derive their origin, either by birth or directly by descent from another country than this. To you and all your soldiers, from all the inhabitants of this land today

begins an indebtedness which it will take long to discharge, and by future generations will you be remembered. . . . I now put into your hands . . . the State ensign of this Commonwealth. . . . when you look on this venerable ensign you can remember your wives and families in Massachusetts. . . . In the utmost confidence in your patriotism and valor we send you forth as citizens of Massachusetts assured that her honor will never be disgraced by the countrymen of Emmet and O'Connell.[23]

At the close of the ceremony the 9th passed down Beacon Street and through the Charles Street Gate onto Boston Common. It was a touch that gave a deep soul satisfaction to every Irishman in Boston. Twenty-four years before the Yankees had shown their contempt for the Irish when six militia companies had refused to drill with the newly formed Montgomery Guards, and there were many among those who rimmed the field who remembered the melancholy event. Now after all that had happened to them here in the Land of the Bean and the Cod, here was a triumph, here was a victory. All of the "better class" had turned out to see the show. Never did the 9th Massachusetts march so well, drill so precisely, or look so impressive. The hearts of the Boston Irish lifted in rapture. Then the troops went back to Long Island for one more day. The transports would embark them on the morrow.[24]

Now the first Irish regiments were formed and moving out into the current of men who converged on the interface that separated the Union and the Confederacy. To Washington went the 37th and 69th New York and the 9th Massachusetts; the 24th Pennsylvania moved into Hagerstown, Maryland.

None of this recruiting and mustering was done painlessly. The Irish have always been a contentious race, quick to take offense when personal worth is questioned. And, of course, it was questioned endlessly as the troops gathered and the winnowing out of officers and enlisted men occurred. A slight

23. Daniel G. MacNamara, *The History of the Ninth Regiment Massachusetts Volunteer Infantry* (Boston: E. B. Stillings and Co., 1899), p. 23.
24. *Ibid.*, pp. 1-27.

instance of that was seen in the clash between Colonel Cass and the MacNamara family in the 9th Massachusetts. Such an imbroglio probably took place in every one of the Irish regiments a thousand times over. Almost every one of those lately starving peasants from Mayo and Donegal fancied himself as good as any man who ever put on a saber. In addition, there was the interface between the Irish and the state authorities. It turned out that it took lions to lead men who were to be lions in battle. Lambs as officers would simply not do at all. In the background there was the Fenian Brotherhood to be reckoned with, determined that the Irish contribution should stand out and be banked against the need in the future when America would be asked to back a new rising in the Old Country. All in all it was not a simple process, but one of never-ending complexity. Dr. William Burton of Western Illinois University did a thorough study in *Melting Pot Soldiers* of the webs that were wound round them, and much gratitude should be extended to him for a balanced and judicial account.[25]

25. William L. Burton, *Melting Pot Soldiers* (Ames, Iowa: Iowa State University Press, 1988), pp. 112-54.

CHAPTER TWO
THE FIRST BATTLE

If ever a battle should not have been fought, it was that sanguinary contest known to some as First Bull Run and to others as First Manassas. The largest military forces ever put into the field by the American nation came together in the rolling countryside almost within earshot of the capitol. Gen. Winfield Scott afterwards maintained that he, as commander-in-chief, should have been either shot or hanged for sending out such a poor excuse for an army as carried the national colours on that occasion. Foreign military experts who were there described it as a fiasco of armed mobs. Actually, for a first battle, the men on both sides did not do all that badly. And as for strategy, Irwin McDowell's flanking movement was a very good one, and, except for a few breakdowns, could have been successful. It is interesting to speculate that his opponent, P. G. T. Beauregard, contemplated a mirror image maneuver, but was about three steps behind McDowell in timing.

July in the Potomac Valley can be an unbearably hot experience, especially for the Union soldiers who were engaged in digging the walls and bastions for the fortifications of the capital. They might better have employed their time in practice marches and marksmanship, two military necessities. But the seat of government must be protected at all costs, and a ring of forts was thrown up. On the Virginia side, the 69th NYSM turned from digging to close-order drill with the help of their cadets from West Point. One of the visitors to Fort Corcoran was William Howard Russell, who had made such slighting reference to the 69th after observing it in the St. Patrick's Day parade. He thought that the camp had been neatly laid out inside the fort with pine boughs sheltering the tents from the sun. Then he noticed a small door like the entrance to an icehouse, half buried in the ground which one

41

soldier was showing to a friend. A sergeant came running up. "Dempsey," he called, "Is that you going into the 'magazine' wid yer pipe lighted?" Russell lost all interest in Fort Corcoran and rode hastily away.[1] Halfway through the sultry days of July an air of purpose began to possess the Northern host. More regiments marched over the bridges to Virginia, along with trains of supply wagons and, more ominously, army ambulances.

The pressure on McDowell to do something came from Congress, the abolitionists, the Democrats, the Republicans, the press and, of course, the president himself. The picture of Lincoln as a benign, noble father image who regularly pardoned army sentinels for sleeping on duty neglects that side of him which kept the Union armies driving at the South for four years. Even old General Scott, who had a pretty good idea of how unorganized and green the Unionists were, could not hold out against all that importunity forever.

On July 16 the order came to move, and the comic-opera days of the War of 1812 were repeated all over again. Brigades were formed on the way to Centerville for the first time, and divisions the day after that, made by command and not by organization. Not one of the Northern commanders had ever handled a brigade. Only one of the three division commanders, Col. Samuel P. Heintzelman, had ever even seen a battle. Just before giving the "Forward march!" Corcoran found that his boys were brigaded with the 13th New York, the 79th New York, and the 2nd Wisconsin. Their brigadier was a West Pointer who had been most recently employed by a St. Louis streetcar company and before that by a Louisiana military academy. He was red-headed, quick-tempered, and had something to learn about commanding volunteer soldiers. Much later his name would resound as one of the successful Union triumvirate, William Tecumseh Sherman.[2]

It should also be mentioned that prior to the start of the march there had been some disaffection among the troops as to their term of service. The guardhouse lawyers felt that they

---

1. Margaret Leech, *Reveille in Washington 1860-1865* (New York: Harper and Brothers, 1941), p. 93.
2. Lloyd Lewis, *Sherman: Fighting Prophet* (New York: Harcourt, Brace, and Company, 1932), p. 169.

had entered service on April 14, since that was the day that Lincoln had called out the militia for three months. Three calendar months were over on July 13 and mutterings were heard. These men had been away from home for ninety days, they had performed ditch-digging daily and never a Rebel had they seen. If this was a war it did not seem like the one they had signed up for. So Corcoran had his designated orator, Meagher, speak to the grumblers. The Sword Man had not lost his touch. First, he blunted their arguments by agreeing that it was hot and that the work had been heavy; then, he rounded into form. "Are you not Irishmen?" he asked, "the hardest men in all the world?" Well, then, why all this blather? So by conciliation and challenge the grumbling was put aside, and the march to Manassas continued. Not everyone felt that way in the Army of Northeastern Virginia. In the column was the 4th Pennsylvania, whose term of service expired on July 20, the eve of battle. In spite of the earnest pleas of McDowell and the top brass, the regiment turned around when Centerville was reached, and marched back to Washington for muster-out, with the opening roar of battle sounding behind them.

McDowell had further organized his forces on the march into five divisions. Four were led by regular army officers and the fifth was led by a veteran of the Connecticut militia, Daniel Tyler, who was sixty years old and had been out of the army since 1834. Sherman's brigade was placed under Tyler and in the scheme of things worked out by McDowell the mission assigned to this division was important and challenging. Tyler was to move down the Centerville-Warrenton Pike aiming directly for what was thought to be the left of the Confederate position. As this was taking place, two other Union divisions were to make a wide swing to the west and fall upon the exposed flank of the Southerners. There was a sketchy road system on which to carry out this program, one that was very ambitious for a raw army and untrained staff. Had it not been for an excellent Confederate commander, Nathan G. "Shanks" Evans, the scheme might have worked and the war shortened immeasurably.

As dawn broke on Tyler's men, they took up position on either side of the Centerville Pike and spread out in fields and timber. Ahead of them the road ran on for several hundred yards and then crossed a small stream. On the other side the banks sloped up to rolling hills and tree-crowned heights. Concealed in the swales was "Shanks" Evans and the 4th South Carolina and a curious battalion from New Orleans which was to win fame as Rob Wheat's Tigers. On the other side was a house belonging to the Henry family where an elderly woman named Judith Henry lay dying. Before the sun was to set on this day, her soul would have much company at Heaven's gate.

As the sun came up, Sherman's brigade laid down in the fields and waited. Close to the creek there was an occasional spatter of musketry. A battery of regular artillery came up, unlimbered and fired at a small party of men on the other side of the stream at about 8:30. Then another hour passed with no activity. Suddenly at 10 a.m. the strong force of Confederates hidden in the hollows directly across from them stood up in full view of the Unionists and commenced to hurry off in an irregular mass towards the west. The turning movement of McDowell's flankers had been discovered and Evans was going to place his force directly in front of it. If Daniel Tyler had been alive to his chances he would have driven his men across the Stone Bridge and into the center of Beauregard's army. A great opportunity beckoned. Unfortunately for McDowell, Tyler was a cipher. The fuming Sherman had to restrain his ardor for two more hours while Shanks Evans administered a severe check to the Union battle plan.

Not all of Sherman's energy was spent in useless anger. While riding along his line with the dual purpose of acquainting his men with their brigadier and relieving his choler, he noticed a single Confederate horseman cross and recross the run some distance west of the Stone Bridge. He rightly deduced the presence of a ford. When Tyler ordered him to cross his brigade about noon, the swelling sound of battle indicated that the Union Second and Third Divisions had their hands full. During the mid-morning lull, Sherman had shifted the 69th to the extreme right of the brigade so that they were closest to the ford, and so were the first to cross. One of the companies deployed as skirmishers as the men splashed through the cool water. The ground on the other side sloped up to timber and the regiment advanced in a column of companies. Until they were half-way up the hill there was not a living soul in sight. Then, a party of the enemy rose up from a clump of pines and turned to run up the hill. The rifle barrels of the

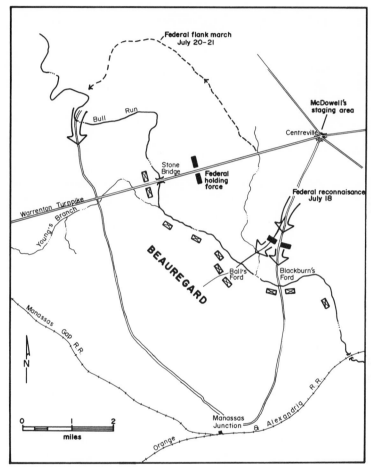

Map by John Heiser

First Manassas: early phase.

45

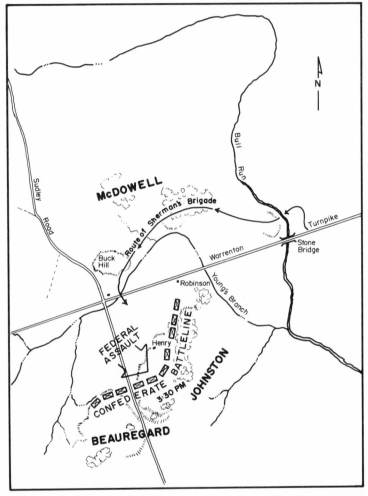

First Manassas: battle on Henry House Hill.

46

skirmishers came down, a mounted figure spurred out in front of the column and uncoiled into a jolting run in the direction of the fleeing Confederates. It was Lt. Col. James Haggerty ("without orders," Sherman reported) and he rapidly closed on the enemy. But just before the last man in the group disappeared into the timber, he turned, leveled his piece and fired. Haggerty's dead body slumped off his horse to the ground and an answering volley from the skirmishers and advance company of the 69th chewed into the trees. The Irish had sustained their first battle casualty.

Hard upon the occurrence came Sherman, afraid that the incident would burst the bond of discipline already frayed by the waiting of the morning, the sound of lowering battle, and the sight of Haggerty's corpse. Sternly he ordered the firing to stop and the march to be resumed. The column veered toward the right and across the slope of a hill with the cannon louder at every step. All at once, the head of the column turned a corner of headland and found the battle before it. A great deal of misinformation was later published as to what Sherman's brigade did immediately after this juncture. In his own report Sherman said:

> . . . we proceeded with caution toward the field, where we plainly saw our forces engaged. Displaying our colors conspicuously at the head of our column, we succeeded in attracting the attention of our friends, and soon formed the brigade in rear of Colonel Porter's. Here I learned . . . that General McDowell was on the field. I sought him out, and received his orders to join the pursuit of the enemy, who was falling back to the left of the road by which the Army had approached from Sudley Springs.[3]

Here Sherman does not sound as though his men were in the preliminary fight, but their time was fast approaching. The Confederates who had struggled so valiantly all the morning were now in position on the Henry House Hill in a concave formation stretching between the Henry House and the Robinson house. Reinforcements had pushed to their aid

3. *OR*, series 1, vol. 2, p. 369.

from the right, among them a brigade commanded by an ex-professor of military science by the name of Jackson.

The regular army batteries commanded by Captains James B. Ricketts and Charles Griffin had contributed greatly to the initial Union successes. Now they were limbered and brought forward to the edge of the Henry House plateau. The Confederates were relieved of their accurate and raking fire for a measurable amount of time, and later some of them said that this cost the Union the battle. Sherman managed to move his four regiments in behind Col. Andrew Porter who had a battalion of regular infantry, a battalion of marines, and some cavalry. McDowell now appeared on that part of the field, and he directed Sherman to attack along the direction taken by the Confederates in their withdrawal. Somehow this attack took a curious turn. Sherman formed a column of regiments with the 13th New York first, then the 2nd Wisconsin, then the 79th New York, and last the 69th. The 13th did very well, mounting the hill and pressing home an attack with vigor and determination. The three other regiments veered to the right in the valley of a creek called Young's Branch which ran into Bull Run, and in so doing completely lost track of the 13th.

Sherman engaged his men with determination. The 2nd Wisconsin came out of the shelter of the Sudley Springs Road, went up the hill and over the crest among the dead and wounded of Ricketts' battery. A hurricane of musketry struck them, but the Westerners halted, returned fire and plunged on into the acrid, enveloping smoke.[4] Later the men marveled at the casualties, the missing friends who had raced up the hill with them and then magically vanished into the ground. The wreckage of the 2nd parted to let the 79th New York into the game.

It is almost regrettable that the apocryphal legend of the 79th wearing its Cameron kilts has been dispelled. That would have been a picture, the skirling pipers out front, a thousand warriors with the Cameron war-cry welling up in their throats; it is almost a shame that it did not happen that way. But they had laid aside skean and sporran for Union

4. *Ibid.*, p. 369.

army blue.[5] They followed the path of the Wisconsin men, charging over the hill into the flat area where the air was full of hissing bullets and flying objects and careening men who shouted unearthly things in the heat and the dust and the smoke. But it was too much for flesh and blood to stand when put into battle so disjointedly. The Scots fought themselves out before reaching the Confederate line.

Now was the time for Corcoran's men, shaken out in line of battle, with the cold hand of fear in their bellies. Even the bravest would mark the shattered remnants of their friends from New York and Wisconsin streaming past them and the blue bodies that covered the hilltop. Corcoran showed some signs of sense by ordering the regiment to shed their overcoats and knapsacks. The colours were dressed very carefully in the center of the line and then the word was given to go forward. Sherman accompanied them part of the way. Perhaps by now he had some premonition that this last assault would do no good, a foreknowledge that it would only add to the list of the fallen. In his report he said:

> This left the field open to the New York Sixty-ninth, Colonel Corcoran, who in his turn led his regiment over the crest, and had in full open view the ground so severely contested. The firing was very severe, and the roar of cannon, muskets, and rifles incessant. It was manifest the enemy was here in great force, far superior to us at that point. The Sixty-ninth held the ground for some time, but finally fell back in disorder.[6]

From what can be gathered from the nebulous reports the Irish penetrated past Ricketts' battery, driving some Confederates before them. Col. Andrew Porter of the 14th U.S. Infantry wrote in his report:

> The marines also, in spite of the exertions of their gallant officers, gave way in disorder; the Fourteenth on the right and the column on the left hesitatingly

5. *Ibid.*
6. *Ibid.*, p. 370.

retired, with the exception of the Sixty-ninth and Thirty-eighth New York, who nobly stood and returned the fire of the enemy for fifteen minutes.[7]

After that, all the Union commands straggled down the slope to Young's Branch and up the opposite ridge to where the Matthews house stood. Corcoran got a good part of the regiment together and formed a hollow square. Sherman saw and noted Corcoran's activity.

> On the ridge to the west we succeeded in partially reforming the regiments, but it was manifest they would not stand, and I directed Colonel Corcoran to move along the ridge to the rear. . . . By the active exertions of Colonel Corcoran we formed an irregular square against the cavalry . . . and we began our retreat towards the ford of Bull Run. . . . There was no positive order to retreat, although for an hour it had been going on by the operation of the men themselves. The ranks were thin and irregular, and we found a stream of people strung from the hospital across Bull Run and far towards Centerville. . . . Colonel Corcoran has been missing since the cavalry charge near the building used as a hospital.[8]

One can almost visualize the twisted lines of tired men turning their faces from the late afternoon sun and heading for safety. It also goes without saying that the sights and sounds of the day would stay with them forever. A numb torpor had settled on the men of the Army of Northeastern Virginia and even the shouts of "Look out! Here comes the Rebel cavalry!" did not always receive their complete attention. But while Corcoran was moving his men off, a considerable body of the 30th Virginia Cavalry swept along the ridge, sabers up and hooves digging great divots out of the ground. There were conflicting stories as to what happened next. Later Corcoran said his men beat off the first attack. But the appearance of the cavalry turned confusion into chaos. Men and the hollow

7. *Ibid.*, p. 385.
8. *Ibid.*, p. 370-71.

square were simply carried along with the tide. Corcoran himself, Captain McIvor, and several others were separated from their comrades and snatched up by the second pass of the Virginians. Col. Richard C. W. Radford of the 30th said that his adjutant, B. H. Burk, captured Corcoran and the national colors of the 69th.[9] Capt. William R. Terry, whose independent company happened to be under Radford's command, inferentially said that he captured Corcoran.[10] About thirty others of the 69th were also captured.

Sherman got his brigade in some kind of order on the east bank and made a circuit to avoid the Cub Run Bridge which was a shambles. Late afternoon darkened into twilight and the exhausted men passed on in the direction of Centerville, and thence to the Potomac and Washington. Sherman observed that the retreat was disorderly in the extreme.

> The men of different regiments mingled together, and some reached the river at Arlington, some at Long Bridge, and the greater part returned to their former camps at or near Fort Corcoran. I reached this point at noon the next day . . .[11]

9. *Ibid.*, p. 552.
10. *Ibid.*, p. 562.
11. *Ibid.*, p. 370.

CHAPTER THREE
THE BRIGADIER

On July 24, 1861, the 69th NYSM broke camp at Fort Corcoran and marched over the Aqueduct Bridge to Washington. That night they bivouacked on the White House grounds, and on the following morning took the train for New York and home. It was a cheerless ride. Michael Corcoran was a prisoner in Richmond, the acting lieutenant colonel, James Haggerty, was dead on the field at Manassas, and Lt. Col. Robert Nugent had been sent home to New York prior to the battle with an injury. That left the regiment under the control of the senior captain, James Kelly, who had just finished writing his report of the battle. It was a curious document in which repressed rage at Sherman was mingled with sadness at the heavy casualties suffered.[1]

On the ride home, which took the better part of two days, it is certain that the surviving company officers got together and pondered their future conduct. Even if the North was stunned and disheartened by the news from Manassas, the war would go on. The three months service by the militia regiments was over. The next enlistment period would be longer. There was much discussion as to what would be the role of the 69th. With the entire roster of field officers gone there was one dominant voice among the surviving captains. Because of his personality and character and celebrity Thomas Francis Meagher must have seemed like a demi-god to the others, and perhaps his ambitions soared as the train neared New York. For he was alive after a real battle where many had been killed or maimed, and he was conscious of the need to celebrate the regiment and its performance before the nation. Perhaps there would be a larger military formation to succeed the 69th NYSM. Perhaps even a brigade, the famous Irish Brigade!

1. *OR*, series 1, vol. 2, p. 371.

Twenty-seven years later when the monument was dedicated at Gettysburg, Robert Nugent declared that the concept
was one in which both he and Meagher shared and placed the
moment of birth on "the morning of the day on which the Sixty-
ninth Militia returned to New York."[2] That was July 27, and the
city turned itself inside out to welcome back the blooded
warriors. They had been expected on the two preceding days
and the Irish element of the city had worked itself up to a fever
pitch. Every maid and serving girl in the city had been
disappointed twice, said the *Times*, and July 27 fell on a
Saturday, usually the day for scrubbing and cleaning. But
when the news spread that the 69th was on the early boat from
Perth Amboy, the entire population flocked into the streets to
behold the heroes.

> If it had been the return of a victorious army there
> could hardly have been more excitement. . . . In
> military matters there is a spirit of rivalry. It is hard
> to get a soldier to acknowledge the efficiency of any
> other regiment save his own. But so conspicuous the
> service performed by the 69th, so unquestionable its
> valor, so complete and heroic its willing self-devo-
> tion that the first word of qualified praise has not
> reached our ear. . . .[3]

The line of march was from the Battery to Union Square,
down Fourth Avenue and the Bowery to Grand Street, and
thence to Essex Market where the armory was located.
Manahan's Band led the way with the brasses belting out
"Garry Owen" and "Saint Patrick's Day." After the first
four companies, there was an interval in which rode Nugent
and Father O'Reilly followed by other prominent Irishmen on
foot, and the wounded Capt. John Breslin in an open
barouche. Then followed the other six companies. Last of all
was the severely wounded Private Sweeney in a carriage
with some of his friends who were determined that he would

2. New York Monuments Commission for the Battlefields of Gettysburg
   and Chattanooga, *Final Report on the Battlefield of Gettysburg*, ed.
   William F. Fox, 3 vols. (Albany, New York: J. B. Lyon Company,
   Printers, 1902), 2:506-507. Hereafter cited as *New York at Gettysburg*.
3. *New York Times*, July 29, 1861.

54

Robert Nugent
Colonel, 69th New York Veteran Volunteer Infantry
Wounded at Fredericksburg

not be left out of the homecoming.[4] Then followed the social, temperance, and marching societies just as though it were the 17th of March.

The private soldiers of the regiment must have had some mixed feelings. Here was a hero's welcome. And yet their national colour was a trophy in Richmond. Their hawk-faced colonel, for all they knew, might be dead. These were undeniable losses and prestige losses too. An organization which lost its colours was disgraced in many an army unless there were mitigating circumstances. Yet as the *Times* said, no one had aught but praise for the Irish except for the esteemed Russell of the London *Times*, now and forever "Bull Run" Russell to the American public. A rather one-sided account of the regimental exploits went out under his by-line. The Irish had allowed their colonel to be dragged away into captivity, he wrote. As for Thomas Francis Meagher personally, Russell cited an unidentified source who had seen Meagher after the battle "running across country and uttering exclamations in the hearing of my informant, which indicated that he at least was perfectly satisfied that the Confederates had established their claim to be considered a belligerent power."[5] If there was any truth in that statement Meagher speedily set out to redeem himself.

On the way north he apparently decided that the cause of the North was now his own, even more so than on the day in April he had so expressed himself to Nugent and Cavanagh. There was no false modesty about Meagher, and he felt that he was the one who could bring his countrymen into the war effort.

The first business at hand was to get the regiment mustered out; this was accomplished on August 3, although they would not be paid off until August 24. Meagher then set about making himself familiar with the New York situation and the prospects for forming not a regiment for the war, but a brigade.

Nugent was quite specific that the project was the joint conception of both Meagher and himself, and there is no reason to doubt his word.[6] But while few of the men who worked as draymen, stevedores, ditchdiggers, or porters would

4. *Ibid.*
5. Russell, *My Diary North and South*, 1:313-14.
6. *New York at Gettysburg*, 2:506.

recognize the name of Nugent, they all knew something of Meagher. "That race did ever love great personages," said an Elizabethan Englishman of the Gaels, and even in the Five Points slum in New York they had not changed.

There were several officers of the regiment who had not accompanied the colours to Virginia and who also were not going to move over and let Meagher run the show. On the day of the return, the following letter had appeared in the *Times*:

> Major Bagley, now the C.O. of the 69th Regiment who has gone to Washington to bring those fellows home in triumph and share the hard-won laurels of Corcoran and Haggerty whose place he should have filled while living has until now been quietly and calmly pursuing his profitable business as Alderman of the Seventh Ward and member of the "ring" in this city unmindful of message after message from Col. Corcoran either to resign or to come on and do his duty. . . . We hope that everywhere this libel upon the Irish name and character and the only one of his regiment who has failed to do his duty may be distinguished from the brave fellows who have been engaged in the war.

An Irishwoman[7]

One would give a good deal to know the identity of "An Irishwoman." Is it possible that Elizabeth Townsend Meagher considered herself so much Irish by marriage that she should so sign herself? Was this the first shot in a campaign to discredit Bagley? Certainly the writer, man or woman, seems to have a familiarity with the affairs of the regiment not usually enjoyed by the casual outsider.

Among the rank-and-file of the 69th, many at once said that they would go off to fight again. The 37th New York was now in Virginia so there was a fine regiment lost to the brigade, but a third Irish regiment from New York had been accepted by the War Department; 800 men were enrolled

7. *New York Times*, July 27, 1861.

57

and Lt. Col. P. D. Kelly was acting as commander. There were also thousands of other Irish in the large cities of the northeast who had been electrified by the good reports of the 69th. Maybe they would like to join also. Meagher and Nugent put their heads together.

The first plan was for New York to furnish two regiments, Boston to furnish one, and Philadelphia one. Obviously the two from New York would be the reconstituted 69th and the 3rd Irish of Lieutenant Colonel Kelly. There is some grounds to think that Meagher was hoping for the 9th Massachusetts, already enrolled and on the scene in Virginia as the Boston representative. In Philadelphia the 24th Pennsylvania was winding up its three-months service, and, presumably, was ready to sign on again. There was also in the City of Brotherly Love the Patterson family, who were rich, distinguished, martial, and Irish. Robert, the patriarch and head of the clan, had not proven to be a military genius during the events preceding Manassas, but he was still influential and he had two fine sons of energy and capacity.

At this point, Meagher returned to Washington, ostensibly to look after some wounded of the 69th who were hospitalized. He was, in fact, shown around the most influential circles and met many famous men. The secretary of war, Simon Cameron, still numbed by the death of his brother at Manassas and the enormity of the task before him, offered Meagher a captaincy in the Regular Army.[8] Very few militia officers were being welcomed into the the tight circles of West Pointers and Indian fighters, so this was a real honor. Yet Meagher's eyes were on a somewhat higher level, and he sidestepped the offer with a graceful request to transfer it to some other officer of the 69th with longer service, say James Kelly, for instance. That would also get rid of the senior captain of the 69th. At the same time he became somewhat of an intimate of Frank Blair of the powerful Blair family. Frank was a congressman from Missouri. His brother, Montgomery, was Lincoln's postmaster general and he was anxious to save the West for the Union. From this connection Meagher was offered the position of aide-de-camp to Maj. Gen. John Fremont out in the Show Me State with the rank

8. Cavanagh, *Memoirs of Thomas Meagher*, p. 409.

James Shields
Major General, United States Volunteers

of colonel.[9] The world was moving fast and furiously for Thomas Francis.

When he returned to New York he found a letter from the 3rd Irish asking a favor.

> The 'Third Irish' have been accepted by the United States Government for the war, and will be ready to enter the field in a very short time. The officers, one and all, respectfully ask if *you* will be the *man* to lead them, they pledging themselves that you will never regret having accepted the command.
>
> P. D. Kelly, Lieutenant-Colonel.[10]

To this Meagher replied on August 5:

> I am too strongly attached to the 69th to be induced . . . to break the ties which bind me to it.

So it may be concluded that Meagher could not be enticed out of New York for either Missouri or Washington. Neither was he to be tempted away from the 69th. Why would he choose to remain a militia captain when other men were being rewarded with oak leaves, eagles, and the stars of command. Did he really feel inadequate to command a regiment? After all, he had witnessed at Manassas the results of inexperienced leadership. Maybe he felt that more training would better qualify him. In the meantime, there was no doubt at all as to who should command the Irish Brigade. Meagher and John Mitchel and James O'Mahony had a special appeal to the Irish in America as Irish patriots, but James Shields had a more transcendent appeal. His origins were Irish, but his accomplishments were indisputably American. He had served in the Mexican War and advanced to the rank of brigadier general. He had been elected to the U.S. Senate from not one, but two states, Illinois and Minnesota. So his choice to command the brigade was only just and right; there was just one large difficulty. He was not in either of his adopted states of Illinois

9. *Ibid.*, p. 408.
10. *Ibid.*, p. 410.

60

or Minnesota. He was not in the United States at all. There was only a residence and a mailing address in San Francisco wherewith to track him.

Shields was, in fact, in the mountains of Sonora, Mexico, checking on the operation of a mine of which he was part owner. Judge Daly had a letter dated June 8 from San Francisco in which Shields had expressed the hope that there would be no civil war, but predicted that if it did come, it would be a matter of years, not months.[11] The fact that Shields was temporarily out of touch did not deter the movers and shakers in New York for a minute. Certain interested parties in Washington evidently got the word to go ahead because Shields was commissioned brigadier general to date from August 19, 1861.[12]

There is evidence that certain parties in New York Irish circles did not like the idea of Meagher as a military man, purely on the ground that he was not qualified. Hence the drive to locate Shields, bring him on board, and move the enterprise forward. The leader of this movement was probably Judge Charles Daly. Daly's wife, the former Maria Lydig, kept a diary and, as shall be seen, the Judge had reservations about Meagher. Meagher also learned that the Irish Brigade would be a more difficult project than he had at first anticipated.

There was a great deal of enthusiasm and no lack of manpower. But a spirit of opposition had developed among a group of officers of the 69th NYSM headed by the ineffable Major Bagley, who was also an alderman. Apparently this was a spirit of opposition to Meagher personally and, by extension, to Nugent who was ostensibly in command of the regiment. A good many officers who had been commissioned by New York had not accompanied the regiment to the field of battle. These stay-at-homes had been formed into a voting bloc by Bagley. When it came to a vote of the officers as to whether the regiment should extend its enlistment to three years, Meagher found that he had been finessed. Many years later at the dedication of the brigade memorial at Gettysburg, Col. James Smith spoke candidly of the situation:

11. Charles P. Daly Letters, New York Public Library.
12. Frederick Phisterer, *Statistical Record of the Armies of the United States* (New York: Charles Scribner's Sons, 1883), p. 269.

The Sixty-ninth Regiment New York Volunteers
. . . was formed by the officers and men of the Sixty-ninth Regiment New York State Militia who were members of that regiment, and who served with it in the three months' campaign, and who, in a spirit of patriotism, desired to serve their country during the war. This action became necessary as the Sixty-ninth Militia at a meeting of its officers had voted against tendering the services of that organization to the government for three years or during the war. The defeat of the motion was mainly owing to the large number of officers present who were commissioned by the State, and who remained at home during the three months' campaign. This was made possible, under the circumstances, by reason of our casualties at First Bull Run, many of our officers being still held as prisoners by the enemy, among whom was our commanding officer, Colonel Corcoran.[13]

So the forces of Alderman Bagley won. It was to be an expensive victory for them. To Meagher, who was riding the crest of a wave of acclaim, the setback was only momentary. If the militia wanted no part of the brigade so much the better. He was well rid of such schemers and poltroons as Bagley. On August 22, the day after the meeting he wrote a note to Judge Daly that gave no hint of a setback but only indicated that he was looking forward.

I want to see you very particularly in relation to General Shields. Some enemies of his are at work to get a revocation of his appointment as Brigadier General. Much depends on his being held in that position. . . .

And later,

This is a serious business with regard to Shields and it is of the utmost consequence I should see you

13. *New York at Gettysburg*, p. 506.

and that without another day's delay. . . . .[14]

On August 28 the *Times* announced,

> The 69th Regiment New York State Militia
> Recruiting offices connected with this popular
> regiment are being opened in various parts of the city.
> Captain Thomas Francis Meagher will take the posi-
> tion of Colonel. Lt-Col. Nugent who has accepted the
> position of Captain in the Regular Army will act as
> Lt-Colonel. The regiment when reorganized will be a
> volunteer regiment, not a militia, but will be known
> as the 69th.[15]

So Meagher was living in the best of two worlds. The sacred
number "69" was still in his possession and he was the new
colonel. This leads one to wonder how Robert Nugent, might
have felt about the situation. The answer would not be clear for
two weeks.

Meanwhile, a group of Irish societies had organized a
large picnic or festival on August 29 at Jones' Wood. (Here
one is struck by the words some time later of Mr. Dooley:
"Bedad if Ireland could be freed by picnics, she'd not only
be free but an empire.") A great deal of money was raised
for the relief of the widows and orphans of the dead of the
69th NYSM. Of course the main orator of the day was
Meagher and he was received enthusiastically by the crowd
which *Harper's Weekly* estimated at 70,000. Never, said
that magazine, was the speaker in better voice.

> The crowd blazed with enthusiasm, the orator
> was never more florid, fiery and felicitous; and of
> all the speeches he has made in this country none is
> so truly direct and sensible as the one he poured into
> the open ears . . . of the great assembly. . . . he said
> that all American citizens who hail from Ireland
> had taken an oath of loyalty not to New York,

---

14. Charles Daly collection.
15. *New York Times*, August 28, 1861.

nor to Alabama. . . . nor to any state, but to all the States. . . ."[16]

Apparently, he had that speech down pat.

There was a letter the next day from Thomas A. Scott, assistant secretary of war, directed to "Colonel" Thomas Francis Meagher and accepting "the regiment of infantry known as the Sixty-ninth infantry . . . for three years or during the war. . . . this Department will revoke the Commissions of all officers who may be found incompetent. . . . you are further authorized to arrange with the colonels commanding four other regiments to be raised to form a brigade, the brigadier general for which will be designated hereafter by the proper authority. . . ."[17] So as the organizer of the brigade he was in business. However, the message was not explicit enough as to the nationality of the organization. On September 7 Meagher sent the following telegram to Washington:

Hon. Simon Cameron,
Authorize positively to organize an Irish brigade of 5,000 men. I can do so forthwith and have it ready in thirty days to march. Please reply at once authoritatively by telegraph, afterward by official letter. Expedition in the matter of vital importance
Yours, sincerely,
Thomas Francis Meagher
Captain, Sixty-ninth Regiment[18]

To which the Secretary replied:

Make application at once to Governor [Edwin D.] Morgan. He will give authority for organization.[19]

In a letter to the *New York Times* the day before, Meagher stated that he was not the colonel of the 69th, had never accepted the position, and would never take it. Ingenuously, he continued

16. *Harper's Weekly*, September 7, 1861.
17. Cavanagh, *Memoirs of Thomas Meagher*, pp. 411-12.
18. *OR*, series 3, vol. 1. p. 491.
19. *Ibid.*

It is true that, a few days ago, I was induced to acquiesce in my name being used in connection with the Colonelcy, with the view of completing the organization as speedily as possible. I did so . . . that the Sixty-ninth Volunteers would be at an early day in the field as a component part of an Irish Brigade, in which I hoped to secure some position in which, though of inferior rank, my services might prove more useful.   . . . I cannot conscientiously promise . . . to accept the command of it on active service. . . . it would be doing the new regiment an injury, instead of a service, for me to deprive it of the control and guidance of an officer who, like my friend, Lieut.-Col. Nugent, for instance, is well qualified to lead it with distinction.[20]

There seems to be great confusion as to just which authority could give the final sanction to the project. It had been initiated by Meagher in a letter to the War Department offering himself and the new 69th; Thomas Scott had accepted on August 30. During the next week there had been a great to-and-froing between New York and Washington. On September 7 Meagher had telegraphed Cameron for positive authority, who had telegraphed back to seek that from the governor of New York. Apparently, no one knew how the new three-year troops were to be marshaled. In the end the difficulty was surmounted. The governor notified Washington on September 10,

Recruiting proceeding with more activity. I have accepted Captain Meagher's proposal to organize the Irish brigade in thirty days. . . . Arms and supplies will soon be in greater demand than soldiers.[21]

In the end it was the state of New York which gave the authority to enlist the Irish Brigade. The recruiting went on apace.

During the months of September and October it is a wonder that Meagher got any sleep at all. There were a million details to see to, and he had little time for the thing he did best

20. *New York Times*, September 6, 1861.
21. *OR*, series 3, vol. 1, p. 497.

which was oration. However, he made two speeches to essentially Irish crowds in New England, one at Bridgeport, Connecticut, and the other in Boston. Even in that day of spread-eagle hyperbole Meagher had an élan, an inner fire that few American speakers could match. The speech was about the same in both places:

> I say this fight is now an Irish fight. If the Irish do not sustain the only government under which they have had a reputation, fortune, and good name, then, any one who speaks to me of Irish liberty is a dreamer and a driveler. This is our home. Thousands and thousands of Irish immigrants have come here. Thousands and thousands of Irish graves have been sunk upon this American soil . . . and what say you? Is this to be a question of party? Is this to be a question of Democrats and Republicans? If so it were better this country had never known its birthday of freedom, bloody and terrible as it was. . . . It is enough for me that the man in power came and took possession of the seat of government under the credentials of the popular will and under the solemn sanction of the Constitution. . . . Look to it, you Irishmen; you have, I know, your grievances to complain of. You have been insulted and aggrieved. What of it? Now you have the hour of vengeance and victory. You can be the saviors of the country and chastisers of sectarianism. Look up from your circumscribed localities. Look up from your parishes, your wards, your counters, your lodging-houses, and your States. Fling away your counselors of Tammany; dash down the Pewter Mug; fling overboard your Mozart philosophers; let the tricksters and intriguers swamp. See the luminous Flag above you broad and splendid as the sky and the earth, bright as the heavens; see the country which it typifies and consecrates and swear with all your heart and soul, with all your strength and with all your mind, with all the fire of the Irish soldier, you will stand by the country![22]

22. *New York Times*, October 16, 1861.

There were now two camps of instruction, the 69th at Fort Schuyler on Throg's Neck and the 3rd Irish on David's Island just off New Rochelle. In addition to the natural and foreseeable obstacles of finding uniforms, arms and even rations, there were the crowds of the humbler Irish people who flocked to both camps. Havoc was created and Meagher was almost driven out of his mind. On November 6 he wrote Secretary Cameron that he was having great difficulty in "reducing the recruits to order and docility in the vicinity of their homes, families and friends having constant access to them and other distractions constantly occurring." He suggested that the organization be moved away from New York. On November 14 there is a note of desperation in his telegram to Cameron:

> Will the Secretary be good enough to direct Governor Morgan to order off the entire Irish Brigade as it stands on Monday next to Harrisburg or elsewhere out of New York?[23]

It was not a complete and glorius triumph for Meagher over everyone. Maria Lydig Daly wrote in her diary for November 10,

> . . . Meagher is evidently double-faced. On Tuesday last, he said nothing would induce him to be a brigadier; on Saturday last he begged Mr. Savage to push the matter with some influential men in Washington. In the carriage, I saw him exchange a very equivocal glance with his wife when the dear, innocent, frank Judge told him his mind upon the subject and dissuaded him absolutely from accepting such a responsibility. "No, Lizzie," said he, "no, I certainly will not. You may look as cross as you please." Then turning to Charles, he said, "You have no objection, I suppose, to my being colonel of the 5th, have you Judge?" I was afraid that Charles, with equal frankness, would have said, "I don't think you have sufficient military knowledge!"[24]

23. Telegrams to War Department, November 14, 1861.
24. Maria Lydig Daly, *Diary of a Union Lady, 1861-1865*, ed. Harold Earl Hammond (New York: Funk and Wagnalls, 1962), p. 75.

In the middle of all this Meagher was commissioned a colonel in the 10th New York Artillery as the artillery contingent of the brigade was known, and everyone referred to him as the acting brigadier. Did the thought occur to him as to what would happen when James Shields appeared on the scene? There is, of course, the standard Fenian view that no friction would be possible between two men of the cause. The sacred objects to be striven for, the unique "Irish" sense of disinterestedness, and the impact of such unselfishness on the American public, would allow only one path for Meagher to take. He must step aside in deference to Shields' earlier commission. But ambitious men are the same the world over. As a result of his exposure in Boston and Bridgeport and the wide acceptances of his speeches as rallying points for the Irish, Meagher found himself in a new position in America. Now the native Anglo stock were joining in the applause for him. No longer was he the revolutionary exile, unwanted in his father-in-law's house. Now, simply because he had led men into battle and offered to do the same again, he was the lamb of the elect. In view of all this does it seem likely that he would produce the Irish Brigade out of thin air and then hand it over to someone he hardly knew? Not likely. So every day that Shields delayed in making an appearance in Washington lessened his chances of ever taking command.

On November 18 there was a flag presentation to the 69th, the artillery, and the 88th in front of Archbishop Hughes' residence on Madison Avenue, and again the turnout was massive. Hughes himself was not there, so the vicar-general of the archdiocese, Father Storrs, filled in for him with a blessing for the troops. Then flags were presented and Judge Charles Daly made a speech. It was the classic Irish military sermon, but part of it was worth remembering:

> . . . you and the organization to which you belong
> have designated yourselves by the proudest name
> in Irish military annals—that of the Irish Brigade.
> That celebrated corps achieved its historical re-
> nown not through the admitted bravery of its mem-
> bers merely, but chiefly by the perfection of its
> discipline; and it will be precisely in the proportion
> that you imitate it in this respect, that you will or will

not be known hereafter. The selection of such a name only renders the contrast more glaring in the event of inefficiency and incompetency; and it were well, therefore, that the officers and men . . . should remember that if any part of the glory which the Irish Brigade achieved . . . is to descend upon them, it will not be by adopting its name, but by proving hereafter, by their discipline and by their deeds, that they are worthy to bear it.[25]

At the end of the ceremony the crowd let out a tremendous shout which followed the soldiers down Broadway to the Battery where they took ship across the bay for the trains that would take them South. They were well received in both Washington and Baltimore. Apparently the Green Flag was a sort of good conduct in the latter place since most of the opposition encountered by Union soldiers passing through was usually attributed to unruly Irish sympathizers with the Confederacy. After parading through the capital the 69th wound up in a place familiar to many of them, Fort Corcoran, where they settled down to garrison life which did not last very long.

Edwin Vose Sumner had been commissioned a lieutenant in the army in 1819. Since then he had fought Indians and Mexicans on the western plains and the southern valleys. If there was one man in America who exemplified the name "soldier" it was certainly this man; to be sure this meant "soldier" in the sense of a fighting man, not in the sense of either strategist or tactician. He knew everything about leading 20 dragoons against the Comanches and very little about how to organize or lead anything above 200 men anywhere. In that he was no different than most other professional U.S. army officers. But now he was fresh from the West Coast and in command of a division under the Young Napoleon, George B. McClellan. Within that division was to be the Irish Brigade. The first thing to be accomplished was to get the 69th out of Fort Corcoran and into a field camp two miles outside Alexandria, called, in honor of Sumner and where he came from, Camp California. Then began a severe and unremitting course of drills, inspections,

25. Conyngham, *The Irish Brigade*, p. 62.

practice marches, and tours of picket duty to harden the soldiers.[26]

Back in New York the 63rd was next to receive the march order. It was a unique organization even for the Irish Brigade. A special group of the officers were recent arrivals in the country, and might prove to be very valuable. Or perhaps not. These men had seen service in Italy as members of the Papal Brigade recruited in Ireland to defend the rights and possessions of His Holiness, Pope Pius XI. At the siege of Spoleto and elsewhere they had met in battle the followers of Garibaldi and Victor Emmanuel. These men could come in very handy so long as they were kept with Irish formations where they could feel at home. Like all Europeans who had seen military service, they were full of little crotchets and affectations. Among their own kind such mannerisms would be forgiven; in the midst of native Americans they would only lead to ridicule.

The 63rd would be glad of their presence for many reasons but chiefly because of the soon-to-be-proven incapacity of its field officers. Col. Richard C. Enright had little military experience even by the standards of 1861, and the case of Lt. Col. Henry Fowler was even stranger. Not only was he forty-two years of age, he was also English! The real heart and soul of the regiment was a most warlike medical man, Dr. Lawrence Reynolds, a graduate of College of Surgeons in Dublin and a genuine man of the world. His wit was renowned and he could whip up a poem to celebrate everything from a battle to a cockfight. He was also an organizer for the Fenian Brotherhood and would become Head-Center of the "Potomac Circle."

The word came for the 63rd on November 27 and they followed the path of the 69th down Broadway on the 28th. The men looked very well until the Battery was reached where a Camden and Amboy boat was waiting for them. At this time the soldiers were, in the words of the *Times*, "apparently sober." What happened next was enough to turn Meagher's hair gray.

> The first three companies passed through the gate
> on to the pier at which the steamer was lying, in good
> military style. Several women desiring to follow

26. *Ibid.*, p. 72.

them, were repulsed by the guard in attendance at the gate. This created considerable excitement among the soldiers, and in order to . . . restore order in the ranks, a halt was ordered, and the gates closed. Several of the soldiers thereupon broke rank, and the example being immediately followed by others, in a very short time a large number of the regiment started for the saloons and drinking shops in Battery-place, West and State streets.[27]

And so the 63rd New York left their home city in an alcoholic haze. When they arrived in Philadelphia that night the officials of the Cooper Shop, a sort of vintage USO, noted that they were still "very drunk." Only 300 men were fed at the Shop. Quite possibly the rest could not abide the sight of food.

The 88th stayed at Fort Schuyler until December 17. Meagher took no chances on a repetition of another brawl, but was on hand himself to superintend the leavetaking. If the scene was not as disgraceful, it was not without its comic element. As the acting brigadier appeared in sight of the usual immense crowd on a towering charger, a tremendous shout went up and many in the crowd made a dash for him. The horse backed up almost into the path of an oncoming horsecar and Meagher nearly met a fate worse than had threatened him at Manassas. In the end he got the last of the 88th and the artillery aboard the ship. He could afford to feel pleased with himself. Even Horace Greeley wrote well of him.

> The persistent labors of Thomas Francis Meagher and his coadjutors have resulted so successfully that within three months three full regiments of gallant Irishmen have been raised in this city, one in Boston and one in Philadelphia. If Meagher's history is ever fairly written his biographer will record this contribution of four thousand men as his most valuable achievement and . . . his account with his adopted country will show a large balance in his favor.[28]

27. *New York Times*, November 30, 1861.
28. New York *Tribune*, December 17, 1861.

This is not entirely true. For there would not be any representatives of Pennsylvania or Massachusetts in the brigade, at least not yet. Gov. Andrew Curtin in Harrisburg protested the assignment of any of the sons of the Keystone State to what he feared might be New York's quota. Governor Andrew in Boston backed him up, and Meagher's cause in those states was lost. Maybe if he had had the time to go to see these earnest, able, cantankerous men personally he could have talked them around. Maybe. But he had his hands full getting his troops down to Washington, and also in preserving his own tenuous status. The rumor was spreading that his days as acting brigadier were numbered. His successor would not be the late arriving James Shields but an American officer whose identity was not known. There was nothing to stir Meagher's heart like this melancholy prospect. With an American in command one could see the day when the brigade would not be the "Irish" but perhaps Jones' brigade or Brown's brigade. Of what avail then the green flags and the serried ranks of fighting men. The fear expressed by Corcoran back in April that the Irish would lose their identity among "strangers" would have come to pass. The impact of their contribution to the American people would be blurred. And, not least, what would become of Acting Brigadier Thomas Francis Meagher? He quickly took some steps to set things right.

The night before the 88th left New York, a meeting was held at Fort Schuyler of the officers of that regiment and the artillery. Col. Henry Baker, a Dublin man, did not beat about the bush as to the reason for the meeting: ". . . for the purpose of giving an expression of opinion as to the appointment of Colonel Meagher to a Brigadier's office." The assembled officers quickly took the hint and passed a resolution to that effect.[29]

When all were assembled with their brothers at Camp California, no time was lost. On December 19, a large delegation of officers of the brigade waited on Abraham Lincoln, introduced by Senator Preston King of New York and Meagher's old friend, Frank Blair. On the next day Lincoln sent

29. Cavanagh, *Memoirs of Thomas Meagher*, p. 428.

Meagher's name to the Senate for confirmation as brigadier general of volunteers.[30]

This would seem to deal the coup-de-grace to the anti-Meagher conspiracy, but Meagher's shadowy foes in New York had one more thing going for them. On January 5 James Shields arrived at long last in the capital. The brigade officers marched in a body to serenade Shields at Willard's Hotel and to present him with an address. He was not a tall man but he was broad shouldered and had the look of having led an outdoor life. He knew that he was being called out this way to declare himself one way or another as to who should command the brigade. He set the matter straight:

> I wish to say a few words relative to myself and the Brigade. I was in the Western States of Mexico, endeavouring to recruit my shattered health, when I received intelligence of my appointment as General of the Irish Brigade. . . . On my arrival in New York I . . . was sorry to find there was a misunderstanding relative to General Meagher and myself.
>
> I know General Meagher well. You did right in selecting him to command your Brigade; he is much better qualified for that position than three-fourths of the men who have been appointed to similar commands. . . . [I] hope to have the "Irish Brigade," with its gallant Brigadier, at some future day in my division of the army.[31]

The key to the performance is in the last sentence. Apparently Lincoln told him more than that Meagher had proposed him for brigadier, and that soon he would be wearing two stars and commanding a division. That made everyone happy.

There was some ground for the creation of an Irish division. Some months earlier the German regiments of New York and Pennsylvania had been formed into a division under the flamboyant Louis Blenker. If the Germans had a division, why not the Irish? In addition to Meagher's three regiments, the following were in close proximity to Washing-

30. *Ibid.*, p. 429.
31. *Ibid.*, p. 430.

73

ton: 37th New York, 9th Massachusetts, 69th Pennsylvania. They all carried the Green Flag. In addition, the 42nd New York was overwhelmingly Irish as was the entire New York Excelsior Brigade raised by the ebullient Dan Sickles. Also in existence was the 9th Connecticut, on the high seas in the campaign for New Orleans, and the 28th Massachusetts. Such a large formation would be an even better illustration of the feelings of the Irish for the Union, an even more effective way to bring them before the American people.

On February 3, 1862 Meagher was confirmed by the Senate. The nomination was passed in some distinguished military company. Winfield Scott Hancock was one of four others confirmed the same day, and the campaign for Shields redoubled. But Irish luck was running out. On February 18, Meagher received a letter from the adjutant general of the army, Lorenzo Thomas:

> General: Your application to have the several regiments composed of Irish citizens now in service consolidated and placed under one command has been considered by the Department and is not approved. The troops referred to in your application are under arms as soldiers of the United States, who have volunteered in defense of the Government of the United States and the maintenance of the Union. The sentiment of the Union that has brought them into rank shoulder to shoulder with the natives of this and other countries is inconsistent with the idea of army organization on the basis of distinct nationalities, and to foster such organization among those who are fighting under the same flag is unwise and inexpedient.[32]

And that was that. There would be no Irish division. James Shields would lead a division fairly successfully, but it would not carry the Green Flag. Why was there the inconsistency that the Germans could have a division and the Irish not? There was a hard fact behind this inconsistancy. The War Department had a new head, and the Irish were to

32. *OR*, series 3, vol. 1, p. 895.

find that he was no friend. To this day Edwin McMasters Stanton remains one of the enigmas of American history. There are those who say that he was a great secretary of war, but he never evolved as simple a scheme as a replacement system for the Northern armies. There are those who say that he wished to see no early end to the war, but wanted it to continue until both North and South would forget their common brotherhood. All of this because he believed passionately that the black man should be free; believed it more than he believed in the Union, the Constitution, and the nation. This mulish, cross-grained, able man was the enemy of the Irish as they found on February 24 when a deputation of brigade officers waited on him to appeal Adjt. Gen. Lorenzo Thomas' decision. Stanton promised to present the matter favorably to the president but nothing ensued.[33] The chroniclers of the Irish put it down to the dark machinations of narrow-minded politicians whose prejudices were stronger than their patriotism or their sense of justice.

Senator Edward Dickinson Baker of Oregon was a close friend of Abraham Lincoln; close enough for Lincoln to name his second son for Baker. Baker had served in the Mexican War and rose to command James Shields' brigade when Shields was wounded. In 1861 Baker was importuned by a number of citizens from the Pacific Coast to form a regiment in the East to the credit of California. Baker decided to take on the project, providing that he could enlist men for three years. At the insistence of the president, the secretary of war wrote Senator Baker: "You are authorized to raise for the service of the United States a regiment of troops (infantry), with yourself as colonel, to be taken as a portion of any troops that may be called from the State of California by the United States."

Baker's law partner was Isaac Wistar of Philadelphia and he began recruiting for the project in that city. When the "First California" paraded in Philadelphia on June 29, 1861, the citizens were dumbfounded to see many of their friends and neighbors marching as Californians.

In October Baker moved his command to the vicinity of Washington and, through his influence with the president,

33. Cavanagh, *Memoirs of Thomas Meagher*, p. 439.

increased his command to a brigade of four regiments, all of which were from Philadelphia. The brigade was composed of Baker's 1st California Regiment (later becoming the 71st Pennsylvania), Col. Joshua T. Owens' 2nd California (later becoming the 69th Pennsylvania), Col. De Witt C. Baxter's 72nd Pennsylvania, and Col. Turner G. Morehead's 106th Pennsylvania.[34]

On October 22, 1861, Baker led his brigade across the Potomac River and into a horrific disaster known as Ball's Bluff. Shanks Evans, the salty Confederate who had been so instrumental in the Union debacle at First Manassas, was again present. The upshot was that Baker was killed, the Union loss was heavy, and the State of Pennsylvania had a sudden rush of acumen. It speedily claimed the Californians as its own and they became known as the Philadelphia Brigade.[35]

It is interesting to know that Baker, in the few short weeks he had in command, spent more time training the 69th than the other three regiments in his brigade combined. He referred to them as an "unpruned field," meaning that they were fairly innocent of any sense of the military. Perhaps, but they were quick to learn.

A sentinel of the regiment stopped the colonel after dark and asked for the countersign. "I haven't it," said the colonel, "but you know me don't you?"

"Faith," said the guard, "I know yer horse, but I don't know you." Calling the corporal of the guard, he passed the commanding officer.[36]

However real and urgent the affairs of Meagher and Shields and the brigade were, to George McClellan they were only one small corner of his huge army. From all parts of the Union had come lumberjacks and shoe salesmen, keelboat sailors and college students to form the shield of the Republic. Now they were in the process of being turned into fighting men, and among the most difficult tasks before McClellan was that of

---

34. Frank H. Taylor, *Philadelphia in the Civil War 1861-1865* (Philadelphia: Published by the City, 1913), pp. 85 ff.
35. *Ibid.*, p. 86.
36. Charles H. Banes, *History of the Philadelphia Brigade: 69th, 71st, 72nd, and 106th Pennsylvania Volunteers* (Philadelphia: J. B. Lippincott and Company, 1876), p. 18.

finding officers to lead them. In many cases the new volunteer regiments had followed the example of the militia in electing their own officers. Or, if a man could persuade enough other men to enlist he might be an officer. If good men were secured in this fashion it could not be attributed to the system. Soon officer qualification boards were set up and these tribunals turned thumbs down on many wearers of shoulder straps. One of the first to feel the cold hand of the pruner was Col. Richard Enright of the 63rd New York.[37] In the 37th New York the ineffable Judge John McCunn was involved in a "Drunk and Disorderly" incident at Willard's Hotel. He was loudly court-martialed and quietly allowed to resign. His successor was the same Regular Army officer who had mustered the regiment into the service, Samuel Hayman, of Chester County, Pennsylvania. Out of this set of circumstances, Meagher was able to get the lieutenant colonel of the 37th, John Burke, to command the 63rd.

It is reasonable to assume that many of the Irish Brigade had prior military experience. Almost one-third of the 88th had seen service in the British army in the Crimean War. One of the most fascinating men in the brigade was a William O'Grady of Company C who had lately been a lieutenant in the Royal Marines Light Infantry Battalion. Just why he should have kept his past a secret is something of a mystery. It may be that ex-privates of British forces were welcome but that an ex-officer might not have been so well thought of by Fenians. In any case O'Grady's past caught up with him and he became a valuable company officer.[38] It is also interesting to point out that a large number of men in the 88th spoke little but Gaelic. The 88th Regiment in the British army was known as the Connacht Rangers and had been first raised in 1793 after the passage of the Hobart Catholic Relief Act. It had been deeply engaged in the Peninsular War against Napoleon. The 88th New York was also called the Connacht Rangers. A young priest from the University of Notre Dame at South Bend, Indiana, joined the 88th soon after it reached Washington. Father William Corby of the Congregation of the Holy Cross, although not a native of

37. Conyngham, *The Irish Brigade*, p. 566.
38. *Ibid.*, p. 558.

Ireland, was deeply esteemed by his flock.[39] A fellow member of the same order, Father James Dillon, also from Notre Dame, became the chaplain of the 63rd. A French-Canadian Jesuit, Father Thomas Ouellette, had joined the 69th at Fort Schuyler in November and was to be associated with that regiment for most of the war.[40]

Something should be said about the troops. If one's only impression of Irishmen in America was gained from the illustrated journals of that period, the physical appearance of the brigade would have been a surprise. *Harper's Weekly* and *Leslie's Illustrated News* had artists who featured an exaggerated upper lip and foreshortened, escalloped nose; sometimes the lower jaw was set off by a straggly, unlovely beard and usually a clay pipe was set in clenched teeth. This was a caricature the Irish came to hate. There seems little justice for it in the photographs that have survived.

The men were physically hardy in a way that the comfort-rich twentieth century would never understand. It is questionable if they were taller and brawnier than the American units from rural districts such as the 1st Minnesota or the Vermont Brigade, but even Bull Run Russell, surveying the 9th Massachusetts as they marched over the Aqueduct Bridge, said that shoulder to shoulder they covered more ground than any other he ever saw. The oddest part is that, although city dwellers for the most part, the Irish proved least susceptible to the waves of sickness which periodically engulfed the army. The men from rural districts habitually suffered badly from pneumonia, "camp-fever," or dysentery, all the things to which men were condemned by an unnatural existence in wet and cold while subsisting on food which for monotony and lack of imagination could hardly have been equalled.

It is amazing that in such a framework an army was being forged that would triumph not only over its great adversary, the Army of Northern Virginia, but also over its own leadership. One can ponder the training-camp process that went on and wonder why the desertion rate was not astronomical. For the most part these were men who were away from home associations for the first time. The rather rigid discipline was

39. *Ibid.*, p. 561.
40. *Ibid.*, p. 550.

a complete anomaly and not a pleasant one. The mid-century American was almost pathological in his resistance to authority. What need of this drill-ground fol-de-rol! Show us the enemy! They will be ours!

Consequently, when boredom and homesickness overtook them, what was the answer? Furloughs were out of the question. It almost took an Act of Congress to get a man past the provost guard in Washington City. Unless he fell desperately sick or was wounded the Civil War soldier did not see home again until the expiration of his enlistment. With all these terrible hazards about him, what kept the soldier from complete mental and moral disintegration? Nothing except his own well-developed stability and his strong motivation. After all, he had volunteered and was in the army of his own free will. If it was not what he expected, no one had forced him to it. Some organism of which he was a part was about to undergo disintegration. He knew nothing of the economic theories on which war was waged, for this was long before the time of Charles Beard. His only term of service was, he thought, the Flag, the Constitution, the Congress, the Presidency. It was a simple and, he thought, an honorable age.

On a somewhat higher plane, consider Secretary of War Stanton's curious attitude toward higher strategy. "Who can organize victory? We owe our recent victories to the spirit of the Lord that moved our soldiers to rush into battle and filled the hearts of our enemies with terror and dismay. . . . the recent victories teach that battles are to be won now, and by us, in the same way that they were ever won by any people, almost since the days of Josue by boldly striking the foe."[41] To Stanton, discipline, organization, and military routine were, apparently, superfluous. All that was required was motivation.

41. Edwin M. Stanton to Horace Greeley, February 19, 1862, New York *Tribune*, Februaury 20, 1862.

CHAPTER FOUR

THE PENINSULA

In his report of the campaign of 1862 which took place on the land between the York and the James Rivers, Gen. George McClellan noted that his army was transported there by three types of ships: schooners, steamers and barges. Apparently he was not aware of the presence in his armada of an ancient ferry-boat named *Champion*. The soldiers of the 69th Pennsylvania who were taken on this grotesque craft no doubt consigned it to many different categories during three of the most terrifying days they ever experienced.

The captain of *Champion* was only too well acquainted with his vessel which had a registered capacity of 500 people. When the entire regiment thronged aboard, somewhere between 800 and 900 soldiers, he objected violently. Anthony McDermott, later the adjutant and historian, disposed of him as follows:

> No attention, however, was paid to his protests, and the men, with their arms and camp equipage, were huddled aboard, and for nearly three days were floundering upon the waters of the Potomac river and Chesapeake bay. The men were obliged to work the pumps night and day to prevent the boat from sinking. On the 30th the regiment disembarked at Fortress Monroe and marched to Hampton, Va., encamping until the 4th of April awaiting the arrival of the balance of the army.[1]

At this pleasant place the 69th Pennsylvania solaced their shattered nerves on oysters and shellfish which were plentiful and there for the taking.

1. McDermott, *69th Pennsylvania*, p. 10.

The other Irish regiments had much happier journeys. The 9th Massachusetts was the first to arrive on the large and comfortable steamer *State of Maine*. Captain Cauldon delighted Cass's men by running their Green Flag to the top of the main mast. The brigade went on *Ocean Queen*, a magnificent steamer, and *Columbia*, smaller but still comfortable. But, once arrived, they were then compelled to stay aboard for a week until the press of men going ashore eased somewhat. Conyngham, the brigade historian, wrote about this period:

> The tossing of the vessels, the nausea caused by the rocking, knocked all the sentimentalism out of the love-sick, and even had reduced the twaddling theology of the chaplains to the dullest possible standard.
>
> The weather cleared up after a few days, and the transports steamed up to Ship Point and dropped anchor. It was an intensely cold evening, with a stiff breeze, which prevented the boats from coming close in. The men had to disembark as best they could; some by getting into the small boats; others by jumping into the water; which was up to their breasts, and wading to shore. . . . No preparations had been made for the Brigade; so, wet, wearied, hungry, and tired as they were, their prospect was to bivouac in the woods as best they could. Noticing fires in the distance, General Meagher sent an officer to inquire . . . the chances of getting any assistance from them. Fortunately it was General Howard's brigade, which had arrived three days previous, and occupied a log-hut encampment left by the rebels. Howard generously ordered his command to share their huts, fires, and rations with the Irish Brigade. This the men did with a willing spirit, and emptied many a canteen to warm their visitors.[2]

Almost all the troops were encamped at or near what had been the picturesque town of Hampton, Virginia. The ashes and chimneys of the houses stood as mute evidence of the torch

2. Conyngham, *The Irish Brigade*, p. 117.

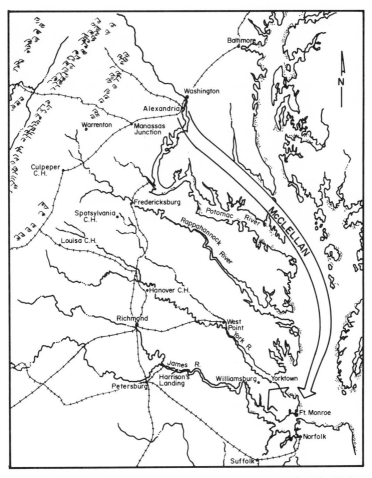

Map by John Heiser

"The Stride of a Giant"
The Army of the Potomac moves on Richmond, spring 1862

83

wielded by Confederate hands in the recent past. Out in Hampton Roads the doughty *Monitor* lay as a shield between the wooden sides of the Union ships and any incursion by the *Virginia*. And so was completed the "Stride of a Giant," a tremendous amphibious operation carried out by a nation that was essentially innocent of either warfare or logistics. In all, more than 100,000 men and mountains of materiel had been shifted in twenty days.[3]

As March moved into April it certainly looked as though McClellan was in business, or was he? His real difficulty did not lay before him and did not wear the Confederate gray. There was more animosity toward him personally, and his ideas for conducting the war in the highest ranks of the administration in Washington. Lincoln had strong reservations about him. In addition, Lincoln did not like the peninsular approach to Richmond, and had only consented to it after considerable wrangling. The new secretary of war, Edwin Stanton, had come out from behind a mask of seeming friendship for McClellan and become almost paranoiac against him. There was also the Radical wing of the Republican Party in Congress. Their formation of the Joint Committee on the Conduct of the War was not a reassuring event for any soldier, and their treatment of luckless Charles Stone over the disaster of Balls Bluff was reminiscent of the French Terror.

On March 11, the War Department's Special Order No. 3 removed McClellan from command of all the armies of the United States, and restricted him to the command of the Army of the Potomac. Nothing wrong with that except that no communication was sent to the general; he learned about it through a newspaper. Not a reassuring message to ponder. On March 15 Stanton offered command of the Army of the Potomac, McClellan's army, to a sixty-three-year-old man in poor health, Ethan Hitchcock, without consulting Lincoln.[4] As of March 12, James Wadsworth, a stalwart of the Republican Party but not a soldier, was placed in command of the Washington garrison. McClellan had already voiced his opposition to this appointment, but Stanton told him that it was necessary

3. Stephen W. Sears, *George B. McClellan: The Young Napoleon* (New York: Ticknor and Fields, 1988), p. 168.
4. *Ibid.*, p. 169.

to placate the "agricultural interests of New York State." Then, on April 3, Stanton closed all the recruiting offices in the nation by General War Order No. 33, an act which has never been explained to this day.[5] While the general was on the peninsula, two midwestern lawyers, Lincoln and Stanton, had in their hands the control of the command apparatus of the armies of the United States.[6]

One of the ablest commentators on the Civil War was Clifford Dowdey of Virginia. In *The Seven Days: The Emergence of Lee*, he quotes Napoleon's maxim that nothing is so important in war as an undivided command. Dowdey then goes on to say that Abraham Lincoln seemed dedicated to the proposition that Napoleon was dead wrong. After agreeing to McClellan's excursion to the peninsula, Lincoln then took a hand in dividing the command and exercising veto power over what should and should not be accomplished.

Lincoln supporters will not see this, of course. First of all, in their view, the proper course for McClellan was simply to go overland at Richmond, right down the pike through Fredericksburg, across the Rappahannock, the North Anna, the Pamunkey, and the Chickahominy to strangle the rebellion. They never look at the costly overland campaigns waged by Pope, Burnside, Hooker, and finally Grant, all of which were unsuccessful. They especially never compare the Peninsular Campaign to the campaign waged by Grant in 1864. Winston Churchill knew something of war and he described it as the negation of generalship.

One wonders how Grant would have fared against the pre-Gettysburg Army of Northern Virginia with Jackson, Stuart, both Hills, Longstreet, and a dozen more of the command structure McClellan faced. Numerically, McClellan was up against more Confederate forces than any other Union commander. And he was not a supreme commander with a suppliant government behind him. Quite the reverse. He could beg for, but not order, reinforcements, as did Grant in 1864 when he dragged the heavy artillery regiments out of the fortifications of Washington and made infantry of them to make up his colossal losses.

5. Ibid., p. 180.
6. Clifford Dowdey, *The Seven Days: The Emergence of Lee* (Boston: Little, Brown and Company, 1964).

In short, in 1862 the administration had a general they did not want in charge of a campaign they did not want. And yet, they lacked the nerve to replace him. Why? The administration always had enough nerve to employ such mountebanks as Fremont, Butler, and Banks in important positions, and to sustain them simply because they were important political figures; they certainly did not do so because of their useful military value, because they had none. Brig. Gen. James S. Wadsworth, for instance, is a case in point. The nation's capital and its defences were so important that a professional of high caliber should have had the job. McClellan had John Dix in mind for it. But in the pressure of mounting the campaign, this fell through, and it might have been the one, small straw that led to the downfall of the campaign.

Of course, the soldiers in the ranks knew little of the background that was deciding the fate of their campaign, and the fate of those of their own number who would fall because of these experiments in policy. The common soldiers never know much about such things. Their struggle for existence on a daily basis against exposure, boredom, hunger, disease, and the terror of combat does not leave much opportunity for musing on higher strategy. The Army of the Potomac apparently trusted McClellan as they did no other leader on the Union side. His numerous detractors, both then and now, cannot fathom and will never accept this. They feel that the American soldier, that cynical and blasé iconoclast, had suddenly gone daft and stayed that way.

As March turned into April, McClellan had 58,000 men ashore confronting the 11,000 of John Magruder. There was a platform of land ahead of McClellan, which, at that time of year, was too thick to drink and too thin to plow. Incessant rains had turned the roads into quagmires and widened the rivers, all of which appeared to run at right angles to the Union axis of advance.

McClellan's opposite number, Joseph Johnston, also arrived in the area with some of the army which had wintered at Manassas and retreated to the Rappahannock in February. Johnston did not think that the Peninsula could be held by the Confederacy, reasoning that a large body of troops committed here would be subject to the danger of envelopment by Union amphibious movements up the York River. If McClellan landed a sizeable force between the Confederates at Yorktown and Richmond, Johnston's whole army might be swept up. Johnston was of the opinion that the Confederate forces, including Magruder's, should be pulled back to the environs of the capital to await McClellan. Johnston felt that a climatic battle could be fought there and the Confederacy would win.

In the end that was something like what happened. But the Southern pullback took place over a protracted period of time, and then only after the evacuation of Yorktown which anchored the defence line of Magruder's forces on the York River. Actually, there seemed to be some confusion on the Confederate side as to whether or not to hang on to the Norfolk area which was bound up with the fate of the ironclad *Virginia*. Although rendered ineffective by the presence of the *Monitor* and its own design, the mere presence of the *Virginia* would keep the Union navy out of the James estuary. So long as the *Virginia* was afloat, the Union amphibious designs had to be married to the York and not the James. And so long as the Confederates held the Warwick River-Yorktown line, the Union navy would not help with any amphibious schemes up the York. The army would have to break the land line, and the heavy rains had turned the land into mucilage. Along the Warwick River, Union patrols eyed equally wet, cold, and miserable Confederates on the other bank. General Magruder had thoughtfully effaced several fords by damming up certain locations.

Brig. Gen. Erasmus Keyes, one of the four corps commanders who had been selected by Lincoln and Stanton, got his Third Corps up to the river and on April 5 reported,

> No part of his line as far as discovered can be taken
> by assault without an enormous waste of life.[7]

Since on that very same day McClellan had received word from Abraham Lincoln that McDowell's First Corps would not be joining him, this news was not welcome. Without the First Corps McClellan felt that he could not carry out an operation against the Confederate batteries at Gloucester Point across the York River from Yorktown. In military lore this has

7. *OR*, series 1, vol. 11, pt. 1, p. 359.

become known as the First Recall of McDowell. Since Gloucester Point could not be neutralized, the navy would not take a chance against the water battery at Yorktown. Since the Warwick River defences looked too strong for assault, Yorktown had to be taken by siege.

Yorktown was a storied name in American history because the British army under Cornwallis surrendered there in 1781, effectually ending the American Revolution, and some of the old British earthworks were still in use in 1862. Of course, the Confederates had improved on them considerably. There was a water battery on the York River to deny passage to Union ships. Across the river at Gloucester Point there were additional guns to form a cross-fire. When Mc-Clellan asked the Union navy to reduce these defences, he was informed that the gunboats could not get enough elevation on their guns to do the job, so the army would have to go it alone. And to McClellan, the man with the engineering mind, that meant a siege as carried out in the days of the great French engineer, Vauban. The soldiers laid down their muskets and reached for pick and shovel.

The weather in the first three weeks of April was mostly wet and cold, but the building of a road network went on full speed. The woods were chopped down, and the tree trunks and branches were used as the base of the arteries toward the invested town. Close-in trenches and zig-zags were carved out and cannon emplaced. The defenders did not suffer this with equanimity and fired at available targets. There was a famous peach orchard around the Moore house where Cornwallis was said to have signed his surrender, and a good deal of infantry skirmishing went on amid the trees. Day by day the Union batteries grew and stretched until the town was enclosed. The opening gun of the bombardment was set for Monday, May 4, and a young artillery officer from New York, Maj. Charles Wainwright, was avidly waiting for it. He anticipated a splendid sight when all the guns and mortars opened fire. One worth half a lifetime to see, and a spectacle he had dreamt of, but never expected to behold.[8]

8. Charles Wainwright, *A Diary of Battle: The Personal Journals of Colonel Charles S. Wainwright, 1861-1865*, ed. Allan Nevins, (New York: Harcourt, Brace, and World, 1962), p. 44.

But the Confederate commander, Joseph Johnston, had a surprise in store, not only for the Unionists, but also for his own side. Without a word to his government, his president, Jefferson Davis, or Davis's military adviser, Robert E. Lee, Johnston evacuated the fortifications of Yorktown on the night of May 3. The Union pickets looked at nothing but empty earthworks on the morning of May 4. The Confederate forces had taken the high road to Richmond via the old college town of Williamsburg. The same New York artillery officer who had longed for the bombardment was dumbstruck. Why had the Rebels departed in such haste? Why did they not stand and fight? But he comforted himself that the evacuation would save many lives for the time, but it would give the enemies of McClellan an argument to use against him. Being a strong proponent of McClellan, Wainwright wanted none of that.[9]

McClellan quickly pushed out a cavalry force under Stoneman to find and intercept the Confederates, encumbered as they were with trains. Sumner was placed in charge of the pursuit and it soon became evident that the old dragoon was out of his depth, especially as the roads were again bad due to a cloudburst. The Union cavalry got close enough to make Johnston turn around a division under Longstreet to buy some time. Longstreet's men went into a line of redoubts four miles east of Williamsburg, and on May 5 waged a sanguinary fight to protect the retreat. The Union infantry divisions of Brigadier Generals Joseph Hooker and Philip Kearny(Third Corps) were engaged along the Williamsburg-Hampton road. About 4:30 p.m. Kearny's Third Brigade under Brig. Gen. Hiram Berry deployed along the axis of this road with the 5th Michigan's right flank on the road and the left flank connecting with the 37th New York (the Irish Rifles). The two regiments were deployed in as loose order as possible, for Berry had some notion of outflanking the Confederates who had been fighting Hooker's men.

But across the way his opposite number conceived the same idea. When Berry's men started forward to clear some brush of the enemy the going was not too bad at first, but soon they came to a cleared space which gave the Confederates a free field of fire. It seemed to Col. Samuel B. Hayman of

9. *Ibid.*

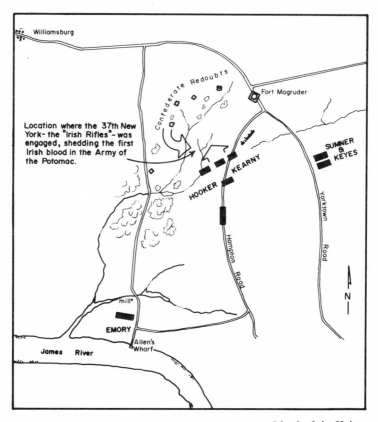

Location where the 37th New York- the "Irish Rifles"- was engaged, shedding the first Irish blood in the Army of the Potomac.

Map by John Heiser

Map by John Heiser

The Battle of Williamsburg

90

the 37th New York that the enemy fire was becoming stronger on his left flank. He put a man forward to scout and held up his forward movement until the situation was developed. The scout excitedly returned with the word that the Confederates were moving off to the left to turn their flank. There was supposed to be a Union cavalry force to the left, but they were nowhere to be found. Hayman had a sudden nightmare of a force of the enemy rolling up his line and the rest of the division, so he quickly started a lateral slide to his left. There was some danger here, for if he lost contact with the 5th Michigan it would open a hole in the brigade line. It was altogether a real test for Hayman's leadership and his regiment's discipline. He bent back his six left companies, extended them at as long an interval as he dared and grimly settled down to slug it out. The Confederates obliged him with almost continuous attacks for an hour. Then, with the light falling, they drew off and the encounter at Williamsburg was over.[10]

In the large sense that the Confederates only fought to cover their trains, they had won a victory. The part taken by the 37th New York was only a small piece of the battle, but they had done well. The brigadier was pleased with them and so was the 5th Michigan which had fought beside them. The colonel of the latter group even said in his report that the 37th had done their duty, understated but high praise. Sgt. Martin Conboy of Company B had been placed in command of Company G when its officers were shot down, and for the rest of the day he had handled it with skill and bravery. Conboy and Pvt. Thomas Fallon of Company K were awarded the Medal of Honor.

Father Tissot and his stretcher-bearers canvassed the woods and fields for wounded men as the night thickened and the shrill sounds of misery echoed. The Irish had shed their first blood in the Army of the Potomac and it had fallen to the 37th New York, as their flag said, "The First Regiment of Irish Volunteers in the Field," to yield it. In the light of what was to come afterwards, Williamsburg was a small battle, but almost twice as many men fell here as went down at First Manassas. The amateurs were showing a capacity for killing each other.

10. *OR*, series 1, vol. 11, pt. 1, pp. 505, 509.

Among the divisions of the army which did not follow the Confederates to Williamsburg was that commanded by Brig. Gen. Israel Richardson in the Second Corps. These troops went aboard ship at Yorktown and sailed up the broad expanse of the York River to where the Mattapony and the Pamunkey Rivers joined to form the lordly York. Here was West Point, only eighteen miles from Richmond. A single track railroad, the Richmond and York River, extended from the city to where the Union troops disembarked. In Richardson's division was Meagher's brigade, and the Irish liked Israel Richardson very much. From his direct manner and general lack of side they recognized a real fighting man.

The brigade's first encounter with the division commander was one which neither party was likely to forget. It had happened back at Camp California at an inspection. As the three regiments stood in tight lines awaiting the great man, one of Meagher's aides, Capt. Jack Gosson, rode up to them and raised his voice in praise of Richardson.

> . . . and what do you think of the brave old fellow, but
> he sent to our camp three barrels of whiskey, a barrel
> to each regiment, to treat the boys of the brigade; we
> ought to give him a thundering cheer when he comes
> along.[11]

To say the least, this was cheering news, and a little later the general was greeted with a thunderous ovation. Richardson, bemused, looked at this demonstration and decided he liked this brigade very much. Interestingly enough the troops did not hold the non-appearance of the whiskey against Richardson, possibly a measure of their complete acceptance of the soldier's lot.

The Union now had a base on the water stretching all the way back to the docks and wharves of Alexandria. As McClellan got even closer to Richmond, he would rebuild the railroad to bring up food, ammunition, medicines, tents, blankets, shoes; everything his army would need. As he stood at White House and looked southwest in the direction of Richmond there was only the Chickahominy River between his army

---

11. Conyngham, *The Irish Brigade*, p. 110.

and Johnston's. In effect, the river was like a moat to the castle of Richmond.

All through the lovely month of May as the weather grew warmer, it also grew damper and the army was struck by the miasmas associated with any low country. A lot of soldiers came down with dysentery and some with malaria. The army also spread out along the north bank of the river. McClellan had reorganized his army into five corps of two divisions each. In this fashion he had gotten two of his own choices to command army corps, Brigadier Generals Fitz John Porter and William B. Franklin, in equal positions with the three Lincoln had saddled him with:

Second Corps	Third Corps	Fourth Corps	Fifth Corps	Sixth Corps
SUMNER	HEINTZELMAN	KEYES	PORTER	FRANKLIN
Richardson	Hooker	Couch	Morell	Slocum
Sedgwick	Kearny	Casey	Sykes	Smith

They were distributed along the Chickahominy from west to east as follows: Fifth Corps closest to Richmond, then Sixth Corps, with Second Corps downstream as far as the repaired railroad bridge. On May 24, Fourth Corps crossed the river and advanced toward Richmond along the Williamsburg Road to Seven Pines. The Third Corps followed in support. McClellan thus had two corps south of the river and three corps north of it. At this point in time the Chickahominy itself takes center stage. Maj. Charles Wainwright of the 1st New York Artillery rode around the country on a personal reconnaissance on May 21 and wrote that Bottom's Bridge where the Post Road crossed the Chickahominy had been almost rebuilt. The river was not all that wide at that point, only fifteen feet across, but the banks on either side were six feet high and the natives said the river rose tempestuously after even a few hours of rain. After a heavy storm the runoff would spread over the banks and became a torrent half a mile wide.[12]

On May 30 Wainwright made another reconnaissance of the Chickahominy bottomland. He noted that the men of Sumner's Second Corps had built a new bridge over the river

12. Wainwright, *Diary of Battle*, p. 69.

about two miles above the Richmond & York River railroad bridge. The new bridge itself was only thirty or forty feet in length, but the approaches on both sides had to be corduroyed to give some sort of stable approach across the swampy ground which would not support the weight of a horse, much less a wagon. Several other similar bridges were under construction so that the army could use them to move closer to Richmond.[13]

In the days ahead the army's fate would hang on the presence of these rude affairs of logs and planks stretching over the murky waters.

Meanwhile, the events out in the Shenandoah Valley had quieted down a bit, and the administration decided to heed McClellan's constant importunities, and permit the First Corps under Irvin McDowell to join in the fight for Richmond. On May 17, Stanton wrote McDowell to proceed there by the line of the Richmond, Fredericksburg, and Potomac Railroad, that is, overland rather than by the water route. The presence of such an overwhelming Union force was the greatest Confederate fear. Lee had been able to forestall such a combination at the start of April by having Jackson impose his deception in the Shenandoah Valley. Now it did not look as though it would work a second time.

McDowell's corps plus Shields' division moved from the north bank of the Rappahannock River on May 27, but the advance elements only got as far as Guiney's Station about forty miles from Richmond. At this point there was a gap of twenty miles between First Corps and the Army of the Potomac. There was a small Confederate force, a brigade of North Carolina troops under Brig. Gen. Lawrence O'Bryan Branch at Hanover Court House in the gap. McClellan ordered Porter's corps to move a division up the RF&P railroad to eliminate Branch's force, and link up with First Corps. The combination that Johnston, President Davis, and Military Adviser Lee most feared seemed about to take place.

The 9th Massachusetts and the rest of the Fifth Corps were closest to Richmond, encamped on Powhite Creek which flowed into the Chickahominy. About a mile above the creek's confluence with the river was a large mill, perhaps

13. *Ibid.*, p. 74.

the largest in the Tidewater, the property of the Gaines family. The 9th was delighted with the locale and set up their shelter tents in company rows. Eight miles away the church steeples and houses of Richmond could be discerned with the naked eye.

Hardly were the tents up when the division was alerted for movement. McClellan had ordered the Fifth Corps to move out to Hanover Court House and attack the Confederate force under Branch. Two days' rations were issued and eighty rounds of ammunition. Then began a long day of waiting. Finally, on May 27, the column moved out on to the road in a fine drizzle.[14] There was a lot of weight in the force of three infantry brigades preceded by a strong force of cavalry. At about noon the horsemen encountered the enemy at the junction of the Ashland and Hanover Court House Roads. The infantry was deployed, the artillery opened up, and the Confederates scampered away. The Union column reformed and continued to the line of the RF&P railroad. There they fell out and devoted themselves to tearing up the steel rails and cutting the telegraph wires. The hot May sun looked down on blue-clad infantry happy in their work. Porter's new Fifth Corps had taken the first step in securing an excellent locale for the link-up with McDowell's First Corps when it came down from Fredericksburg.

Suddenly there was a murmur of musketry from the south, the direction from which they had just marched. Officers started up, clapped binoculars to their eyes and searched the distance. The countryside was too broken up by forests crowning the tips of the gentle ridges to offer much field for observation, but it was undeniable that not all of the Confederates were in front of the Union column, which was facing northwest. Some had made an appearance behind Union forces and were now battling a small force which had been dropped off to defend the line of communication.

Swiftly, the Second Brigade under Col. James McQuade of the 14th New York turned around to retrace their steps. The 9th Massachusetts remembered coming to a wheat field and passing through it. A large wood bordered the field, and on its edge the regiment halted and formed line of battle with

14. MacNamara, *Ninth Massachusetts*, p. 90.

95

the colours placed directly in the center. Up rode James McQuade, to inform Colonel Cass that the enemy had taken two pieces of Martin's battery, and that he wanted the 9th to retake them. The 9th let out a shout and surged forward.

For a while they encountered nothing. There was firing ahead and the spiteful whine of bullets, and then the firing grew heavier. The trees thinned out a bit and the ground became broken by ditches and declivities. Some of their assailants were seen flitting from tree to tree ahead of them, stopping occasionally to load and fire. But the Confederates of General Branch's brigade had been tired by much hard service of late. Soon the 9th found men laying on the ground who could run no more and held up their hands in surrender. It was a confused action for the 9th except that they were going forward and there were reassuring shouts of "Faugh-a-Ballagh" on all sides. They did not know that Branch's men had given up their attack on the Union rear-guard when the stronger Union forces had appeared. The left flank of the regiment came out of the forest and into another wheat field, and saw the right-of-way of the Virginia Central Railroad ahead of them. They crossed it just as the last of the Confederates let loose a volley and vanished down the road to Ashland. Fortunately the fire was high, and Cass halted his men to await the next phase.

Capt. Timothy O'Leary's Company F had captured seventeen prisoners and found many wounded in a farmhouse and its outbuildings. Their antagonists were, they found, mostly North Carolinians. Sgt. Daniel G. MacNamara was surprised to find that many avowed themselves as Union men and said they were glad they had been captured. Both sides fraternized extensively, where a few short minutes before they had been doing their best to kill and maim each other. MacNamara commented on this camaraderie:

> Our men were very friendly and the prisoners appreciated the kindly spirit shown them. During the years that followed in our terrible struggle, this spirit of manly kindness towards prisoners of war continued till the close amongst the *fighting men* of both armies.[15]

15. *Ibid.*, p. 94.

Colonel Cass reported that the Green Flag had been pierced by eight buck-and-ball shots and the lower tie had been shot away. There was only one man mortally wounded with eleven others of various seriousness. The May twilight came down on tired men spread out in the fields.

The next morning they buried their own and the Confederate dead, flushed more exhausted captives out of the woods, and tore up some more of the railroad. Late in the afternoon they started back to their camp at Gaines' Mill, and reached there at 2 a.m. on May 30. Perhaps Cass gave them an easy day; maybe some even got to swim in the pond under the great mill wheel. Many probably reflected on their first encounter with the enemy, and how alike the Southern prisoners were to themselves. On that afternoon there was a terrible electrical storm and rain fell in torrents, continuing throughout the night.[16]

This rain fell on some grateful people. At the Confederate headquarters of General Joseph E. Johnston, the downpour was welcomed with the same thankfulness with which the Israelites received the manna of the desert. As a result of recent heavy rains, the Chickahominy River had achieved its highest level in twenty years. If the present downpour continued long enough to wipe out the bridges which connected the Union army corps south of the the river with those north of it, then the former would be isolated and vulnerable to attack. Even if the bridges were not taken out by the swirling waters, the Union infantry would be faced with a difficult passage, and cavalry and artillery would find the river impassable.

At first Johnston had planned to attack the Fifth Corps north of the river since that body was the possible linkup with McDowell's corps. But late in the day of May 28 he got word that McDowell had halted his march toward Richmond and now appeared to be thinking of other things. It proved to be so. Stonewall Jackson's defeat of a Union force in the Shenandoah Valley had alarmed the administration enough to stop the First Corps movement south and re-direct it to the west in a frantic and useless attempt to trap Jackson. This would be the Second Recall of McDowell. With the blessed rain now falling, Johnston could deal with the Union corps on the south

16. *Ibid.*, p. 98.

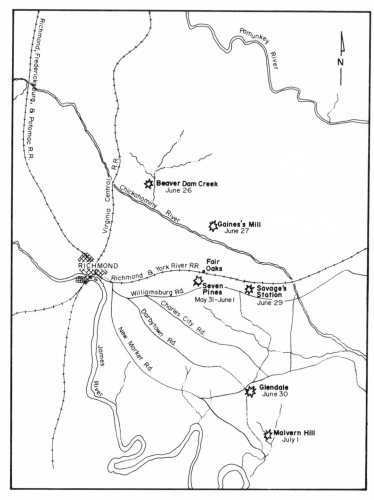

The battles of the Peninsular Campaign

98

side of the Chickahominy.[17] The Confederate divisions of Major Generals Benjamin Huger, D. H. Hill, and Gustavus W. Smith moved out of the Richmond defences and onto the roads that fanned out to the east to hit the Third and Fourth Corps.

Heintzelman was in overall command of the two Union corps and had placed the Fourth Corps closest to Richmond on the Williamsburg Road with Casey's division in front of Seven Pines. His left flank seemed to be well protected by an arm of White Oak Swamp that was thought to be impassable. The other division of the Fourth Corps under Brig. Gen. Darius Couch was on Casey's right flank and stretched along the Nine Mile Road to Fair Oaks Station. The real weakness of the Union position was Couch's right flank which rested on thin air. Sumner's Second Corps on the north bank of the river was the closest Union force, but if the bridges went out in a sudden torrent, this force might not be of any immediate use. A sizeable gap between Couch's men and the river would open, into which the Confederates could advance. Keyes of the Fourth Corps was concerned enough about this space to send a message to McClellan's chief-of-staff on May 31 that the Confederates looked as though they were going to attack. Keyes went on to say that his position was only "tolerably strong," and that his forces were too weak to defend it properly.[18]

The full force of the Confederate attack came from the Williamsburg Road. It was expected. An aide of General Johnston, Lt. J. Barroll Washington, was captured early on the morning of May 31, and it was rightly assumed that his presence in a forward area was significant.[19] Besides, all during the preceding night the Union pickets heard the trains coming out of Richmond with cargoes of infantry aboard. Even though Casey's men knew what to expect, the blow was made in such force and the Union defence was so spotty that the division was driven back to a second line of defence and then to a third. Into the gap between the divisions of Couch and Casey a host of Confederates poured, turning

17. Dowdey, *The Seven Days*, p. 85.
18. *OR*, series 1, vol. 11, pt. 3, pp. 203-4.
19. Ibid., pt. 1, p. 914.

Couch's men in the process so that his division was almost perpendicular to its original position.

Heintzelman first heard the sounds of battle about 1 p.m. at his headquarters near Savage's Station. At 2:00 there was a request for reinforcement from Keyes and it was clear that a full-blown catastrophe was near. Kearny's division of the Third Corps moved up with one brigade going down the railroad track and the other on the Williamsburg Road. The latter was Berry's with the 3rd Michigan in front followed by the 5th Michigan and the 37th New York. The exhausted, dispirited survivors of Casey's division were forced off the road and into the woods by the double-timing ranks of Berry's brigade.

One-armed Philip Kearny sat his horse on the Williamsburg Road directing his brigadiers as to where their commands should go. He had talked to Casey and formed the idea that the Confederate attack was tied to the road. If he could get a force off the road to find the Confederate right flank, the fortunes of the battle might still be recouped. Berry sent the two Michigan regiments off to the south side of the road into the thick timber with the 37th New York right behind them.

The Rifles passed a farmhouse and momentarily lost contact with the Michiganders in front just as a very heavy rifle fire struck them. Hayman had no idea where the Michigan regiments had gone so he did not return fire. The 37th finally broke out of the trees and found themselves in an open space between the 5th Michigan and the Williamsburg Road. By now they had moved far enough forward to overlook the camp and the redoubt from which Casey's division had been driven. Their brigadier finally found them and reported them as "in position and at work." The Confederates were in strength in front of them and attacked fiercely at 4:30. The Rifles fired well-controlled volleys, and the attackers slipped off to their right and seemed to be heading for the Williamsburg Road. They were Alabamans commanded by Brig. Gen. Robert E. Rodes. Hayman had to do something about this flank attack which was typical of the impetuous and headlong charges which had shattered Casey's men. He moved his men by the flank to the right, but halfway there he was dumbfounded to look back and see half of his column moving perpendicularly to him and directly east. Quickly he spurred his horse there only to find

100

that the division commander, Kearny, was conducting this maneuver himself.

The entire center of the Union position had caved in, and Kearny was afraid that the Confederates would interpose between him and the Union position at Savage's Station. He wanted the 37th to face the north and fight off anyone who approached from this direction. He later reported that

> It was on this occasion that, seeing myself cut off, and relying on the high discipline and determined valor of the Thirty-seventh New York Volunteers, I faced them to the rear against the enemy, and held the ground, although so critically placed, and despite the masses that gathered on and had passed us, checked the enemy in his intent of cutting us off against the White Oak Swamp. This enabled the advanced regiments, averted by orders and this contest in their rear, to return from their hitherto victorious career. . . .[20]

Some time after dark most of the 37th made their way back to the position at Seven Pines. Hayman was certainly satisfied with them,

> The officers performed their duty well. . . . Each company of my right wing had an officer disabled, and two of these companies were left entirely without officers, yet the enlisted men acted worthy of their native courage.[21]

Casualties were heavy, totaling eighty-two, but they had fulfilled an important assignment in holding off the Confederate attack. Had they failed it is doubtful if any of the brigade would have survived.

In the meantime an almost separate action was being fought at Fair Oaks Station between Couch's division of the Fourth Corps and various brigades of the enemy. Since Couch's men were the closest to the Chickahominy bridges they were the first to be succored by the Union forces north

20. *Ibid.*, p. 840.
21. *Ibid.*, p. 871.

of the stream. Sumner's Second Corps was there and at 1 p.m. he got orders from McClellan that hell was to pay on the south side of the river and to hold himself ready to move his corps. The old dragoon did better than that, advancing his two divisions to the two bridges which he had built. Walker, the Second Corps historian, wrote,

> Both bridges over the raging and fast-rising torrent were in a terrible condition. The long corduroy approaches through the swamp had been uplifted from the mud, and now floated loosely on the shallow water. The condition of that part of the bridges which crossed the channel of the river it was impossible to ascertain, except by actual trial; but its timbers could be seen rising and falling, and swaying to and fro, under the impulses of the swollen floods. At half past two the order came, and each division tried to pass over its bridge, Richardson below, Sedgwick above, at the so-called Grapevine Bridge, but with different results. Richardson's bridge, which would have been practicable in the morning, had now so nearly given away that when French's brigade only had crossed it became impassable. Sedgwick's division had better luck, though even Sumner's stout heart failed, for the time, as the bridge swayed and tossed in the river. But the solid column of infantry, loading it with a weight with which even the angry Chickahominy could not trifle, soon pressed and held it down among the stumps of the trees, which in turn prevented its lateral motion. And as Sedgwick's rear passed over, the remaining brigades of Richardson's column, coming up from below, entered upon the bridge; and so the Second Corps crossed . . . by a single submerged bridge, which held together just long enough to allow their passage.[22]

Earlier on that same day the Irish Brigade had organized a horse race on a flat space near their camp. The prize was

22. Francis A. Walker, *History of the Second Army Corps in the Army of the Potomac* (New York: Charles Scribner's Sons, 1886), p. 27.

a tiger skin which Meagher had shot in Central America. The entrance fee was $3.00, and twelve horses came to the post. Quartermaster Philip O'Hanlon of the 63rd had entered two horses, one of which he rode himself. Major Cavanagh of the 69th won the trophy on "Katie Darling," a bay mare who showed her heels in the stretch. This was followed by a mule race with the drummer boys of the brigade perched on the backs of some reluctant steeds. A great evening's entertainment was planned as well. But the thunder of artillery on the other side of the river changed all that. The bugles shrilled, and the men headed for the action carrying two days cooked rations and sixty rounds apiece.[23]

Because of the action described at the upper bridge, none of Richardson's division was involved in the first day's action, but Sedgwick's division was deeply committed in the desperate struggle around the Adams and Courtney houses where the indomitable Couch had rallied the wreck of his division. Lt. Edmund Kirby of the Class of 1861 at West Point was in the vanguard of the Second Corps to reach the battlefield. He quickly set up the four artillery pieces of Battery I, 1st U.S. Artillery, which had made it through the mud and swamp, and formed a strong point on which the Second Corps infantry formed. At first their battle was almost directly to the south. But more Confederates came down the Nine Mile Road and compelled their attention to the southwest.

As night fell on the battlefield, the exhausted combatants sank down wherever they could and tried to compose themselves for the morrow. Unknown to most of them, an irreversible force had entered the battle scene. Joseph Johnston had been struck from his horse by a shell fragment and the Confederate army was now under the command of Maj. Gen. Gustavus W. Smith for one day. Then Jefferson Davis placed Robert E. Lee in command of the Army of Northern Virginia.

If the first day's battle was fought in the direction of west-to-east along the Williamsburg Road, the second day's fight was more on a north-to-south direction because the Union reinforcements had come from the north and stabilized the action generally along the line of the railroad. Among the

23. Conyngham, *The Irish Brigade*, pp. 145 ff.

Second Corps commands which had marched over Sedgwick's Bridge was Meagher's brigade, the last to come over. They had reached the field at about 9 p.m. on May 31. Their first impression was the appearance of the field hospitals in the rear areas where the blood-stained surgeons were hard at work. As they came closer they met small groups of exhausted Union infantry. These stragglers informed them with much detail that the Federal arms had met with a severe reverse. Before they rested for the night Meagher ordered that each man should clean his musket.

Fathers Corby and Ouellette, with small parties bearing lanterns, moved out in front of the bivouac to look for dead and wounded. The brigade surgeons had already moved to the field hospitals to make themselves useful. About 11:30 p.m. a courier from headquarters directed Meagher to rouse a regiment and send it back to the Chickahominy River to help with the artillery teams and pieces at Sedgwick's Bridge. With much grumbling, the 63rd New York was roused to do this.[24]

On June 1 the Federals were in an excellent position to stabilize the situation and reverse the terror and panic of the previous day. Sumner moved Brig. Gen. William H. French's brigade down to the line of the railroad, and backed it up with Brig. Gen. Oliver O. Howard in a second line and Meagher in a third line. The Third and Fourth Corps were getting their second wind as well. In light of what had happened, Sumner was not going to attack, but he had a pretty strong defensive line.

Like so many battles, the second day's fight began as an accident. The 5th New Hampshire was put on the south side of the railroad to reconnoitre, and in the dense woods a desultory picket firing broke out as it brushed up against the Confederate brigades of Brigadier Generals Lewis A. Armistead and William Mahone. This escalated to a brisk fire-fight from which the 5th was withdrawn. No one seems to have known who was the attacker and who the defender in what followed. There were three Confederate brigades involved, Brig. Gen. George E. Pickett's, Armistead's, and Mahone's; apparently all were struck by the Union advance. Some of French's men

24. *OR*, series 1, vol. 11, pt. 1, p. 779.

ran out of ammunition and were relieved by Howard's brigade at about 10 a.m. At this point Richardson put in the 69th and 88th New York along with the 5th New Hampshire.

The 69th went directly down the hill inclining to the left of the 5th. On the other side of the railroad tracks was a dense forest of tall trees among which had grown young oaks that made passage difficult. The 88th was directed to the left of the 69th, and they moved through the same kind of underbrush but on the north side of the tracks. Somehow a gap opened between the leading two companies and the rest of the regiment. A staff officer suddenly appeared, and halted the trailing eight companies. He told them not to move as they were needed right there. He faced them south toward the Confederates. Kelly, meanwhile had continued on with the companies of Captain Horgan and Capt. Michael Eagan. It was difficult to keep any formation, but they pressed on as best they could. The officers had been told that they were to relieve the 81st Pennsylvania, reported to be low on ammunition. Suddenly the trees thinned out into a clearing. They stopped for a minute to get organized and were surprised to find themselves alone. They suddenly drew fire from their right and quickly took cover.

After a moment Kelly got them to charge forward down to the track. The Confederates on the south side pulled back somewhat, and the two companies were suddenly heartened by cheering from their eight companies who were floundering to their support. The lines were formed again and the fire-fight continued.

The 69th had also reached the railroad track and found across it Mahone's Alabamans and Virginians who still had plenty of fight left. General French, who was nearby, marked their conduct:

> . . . permit me, however, to mention the admirable coolness and conduct of Colonel [Edward E.] Cross, commanding the Fifth New Hampshire, and Colonel Nugent, commanding the Sixty-ninth New York, and their fine regiments, under a most terrible fire and determined assault of the enemy. . . .[25]

25. *Ibid.*, p. 784.

By 9:30 a.m. the Confederates were beginning to slacken off. Armistead and Mahone had attacked with great spirit and had, in the main, been driven off. No reports of the battle were ever made by anyone connected with these two brigades so their casualties were never tabulated. However, General G.W. Smith who had succeeded to the command after the wounding of Joseph Johnston later went back, and did a great deal of investigating as to just what had happened in those desperate charges in the dense woods east of Fair Oaks Station. He was satisfied that Mahone's brigade lost 339 men, and "from the nature of the Federal counterattack on Armistead, the losses of the latter must have been very heavy."[26]

Pickett, who commanded on Armistead's right, said the latter's men

> had broken and were leaving the field pell-mell. . . .
> I immediately rode to that part of [the] field; found nothing between me and [the] railroad except the gallant Armistead himself, with a regimental color and some 30 persons, mostly officers, with him.[27]

One of Armistead's regiments, the 53rd Virginia, had been in reserve until an hour before. As it moved up into the dense woods, it encountered the 43rd Virginia of Mahone as it withdrew. Each mistook the other for the enemy and there ensued a savage fusillade between them, showing what can happen with green troops under inexperienced officers in difficult terrain. By noontime of June 1, there was no direction on either side; the soldiers simply pulled apart.

Since it was the first engagement for Meagher's men, their performance could be assessed as encouraging. Although they suffered few casualties—only thirty-nine in the whole brigade—they had been willing and eager. Against the poor performance of some of Casey's division on the day before, a Union formation which looked even half-way eager would be reported as "crack" or "seasoned" or "veteran," any of

26. Gustavus W. Smith, "Two Days of Battle at Seven Pines," in *Battles and Leaders*, 2:258.
27. *OR*, series 1, vol. 11, pt. 1, p. 912.

the vague words which are military fictions. Kelly and Nugent wrote reports on the day after the battle that are calm, straightforward accounts of the events as they occurred. Kelly's is a model of brevity. But Meagher's report, dated June 4, is one of the longest reports written on the battle, much longer, for instance, than either Richardson's, the division commander, or Sumner's, the corps commander. There is no evidence that Meagher had control over either of his two regiments when they were committed to battle. Conyngham speaks of him riding up and down, encouraging the soldiers, though no one else does. But he seems determined to see that his men will get their fair share of praise, so there is much hyperbole and elaborate adulation which is completely missing in the reports of Nugent and Kelly.[28] Kelly did single out one of his command as especially distinguished, a drummer boy, George Funk. As Kelly's men were engaged in the woods, Funk had noticed a Confederate sharpshooter firing from the concealment of a tree. Picking up a musket the youngster had worked his way around to the rear of the foe and had stolen up on him. Great was the astonishment of the 88th when George marched out of the woods a tall, husky man twice his age. Kelly says the boy delivered his prisoner to General Sumner in person.[29] It must have warmed the old dragoon's heart.

In the aftermath of the battle the Second Corps stayed on the south side of the river, and the Confederates pulled back closer to Richmond; the lines were about where they had been before the battle. There was no ostensible change except that about 11,000 men had been killed or wounded, constituting a tremendous burden on hospitals behind both camps. But there was one effect of the battle that was to have a tremendous effect on the war. From now on the Union would have to deal with Robert E. Lee.

As we have seen, George Albert Townsend entered the life of the Irish Brigade on June 2, the day after the battle. In addition to what we have already heard, the correspondent for the New York *Herald* had the following to say about the Irish Brigade and its commander:

28. *Ibid.*, p. 775.
29. *Ibid.*, p. 781.

. . . I proceeded, and soon came to the Irish brigade, located on both sides of the way, at Peach Orchard. They occupied the site of the most desperate fighting.

A small farm hollowed in the swampy thicket and wood was here divided by the track, and a little farm-house, with a barn, granary, and a couple of cabins lay on the left side. In a hut to the right General Thomas Francis Meagher made his head-quarters, and a little beyond, in the edges of the swamp timber, lay his four regiments, under arms.

A guard admonished me, in curt, lithe speech, that my horse must come no further; for the brigade held the advance post, and I was even now within easy musket range of the imperceptible enemy. An Irish boy volunteered to hold the rein, while I paid my respects to the Commander. I encountered him on the threshold of the hut, and he welcomed me in the richest and most musical of brogues. Large, corpu-lent, and powerful of body; plump and ruddy—or as some would say, bloated—of face; with resolute mouth and heavy animal jaws; expressive nose, and piercing blue eyes; brown hair, moustache, and eyebrows; a fair forehead, and short sinewy neck, a man of appar-ently thirty years of age, stood in the doorway, smok-ing a cigar, and trotting his sword fretfully in the scabbard. He wore the regulation blue cap, but trimmed plentifully with gold lace, and his sleeves were slashed in the same manner. . . . He was fitfully impulsive, as all his movements attested, and liable to fluctuations of peevishness, melancholy, and en-thusiasm, This was "Meagher of the Sword," . . . the "revolutionist," who had outlived exile to become the darling of the "Young Ireland" populace in his adopted country; . . . He was, to my mind, a realization of the Knight of Gwynne, or any of the rash, impolitic, poetic personages in Lever and Griffin. Ambitious without a name; an adventurer without a definite cause; an orator without policy; a General without caution or experience, he had led the Irish brigade through the hottest battles, and associated them with the most brilliant episodes of the war.

Meagher himself seemed to be less erratic than his subordinates; for he had married a New York lady, and had learned, by observation, the superiority of the pelfish, plodding native before his own fitful, impracticable race. . . . He loved applause, and to obtain it had frittered away his fine abilities upon petty, splendid, momentary triumphs.

A young staff officer took me over the field. We visited first the cottage and barns across the road, and found the house occupied by some thirty wounded Federals. They lay in their blankets upon the floors— pale, helpless, hollow-eyed, making low moans at every breath. . . . By the flatness of the covering at the extremities, I could see that several had only stumps of legs. They had lost the sweet enjoyment of walking afield, and were but fragments of men, to limp forever through a painful life. Such wrecks of power I never beheld. Broad, brawny, buoyant, a few hours ago, the loss of blood, and the nervous shock, attendant upon amputation, had well-nigh drained them to the last drop.

We saw no corpses, however, as fatigue parties had been burying the slain, and the whole wood was dotted with heaps of clay, where the dead slept below in the oozy trenches. . . . At one of the mounds the burying party had just completed their work, and the men were throwing the last clods upon the remains. They had dug pits of not more than two feet depth, and dragged the bodies heedlessly to the edges, whence they were toppled down and scantily covered. Much of the interring had been done by night, and the flare of lanterns upon the discolored faces and dead eyes must have been hideously effective. The grave-diggers, however, were practical personages, and had probably little care for dramatic effects. They leaned upon their spades, when the rites were finished, and a large, dry person, who appeared to be privileged upon all occasions, said, grinningly,—

"Colonel, yer honor, them boys 'ill niver stand forninst the Irish brigade again. If they'd ha' known it was us, sur, begorra! they 'ud ha' brought coffins wid 'em."

"No, niver!" "They got their ticket for soup!" "We kivered them, fait', well inough!" shouted the other grave-diggers.

"Do ye belave, Colonel," said the dry person, again, "that thim ribals'll lave us a chance to catch them. Be my sowl! I'm jist wishin to war-rum me hands wid rifle practice."

The others echoed loudly that they were anxious to be ordered up, and some said that "Little Mac'll give 'em his big whack now." The presence of death seemed to have added no fear of death to these people. Having tasted blood, they now thirsted for it, and I asked myself, forebodingly, if a return to civil life would find them less ferocious.

I dined with Colonel Owen of the 69th Pennsylvania (Irish) volunteers. He had been a Philadelphia lawyer, and was, by all odds, the most consistent and intelligent soldier in the brigade.[30]

So wrote the good Townsend. Although his testimony is not without errors of fact which may call the whole report into question, it is not without value. Beyond doubt it is the honest opinion of a man who is not trying to curry favor with the Irish by praising them, who has no political ambitions involving them, and who is not a militarist bent on making a reputation by using them in battle. Townsend is a white, Anglo-Saxon, Protestant American equipped with the value-judgments and prejudices, congenital and acquired, of a particular age. When he uses the word "Irish" it is a collective noun or adjective not capable of modification or fragmentation. The Irish, for Townsend, had existed in a "fitful, impractical state" since the dawn of time. So were they now, so they would always be. Nothing would ever change them.

But unerring as he was in expressing nativist animus, the *Herald*'s man made a few errors in his piece which should be cleared up. Meagher had not "led the Brigade throughout the hottest battles and associated them with the most brilliant

30. Townsend, *Campaigns of a Non-Combatant*, p. 130 ff.

exploits of the War." Townsend met them on June 2, 1862, the day after the brigade's first battle, and Joshua Owen was not even a member of the brigade. His 69th Pennsylvania while every bit as Irish as any of the New York regiments was in the Philadelphia Brigade, and Owen, himself, was Welsh. Townsend's portrait of Meagher was unflattering, but would, probably, be echoed by many of Meagher's own detractors among the Irish.

It was a wonderful chance for Meagher to capture a newspaperman. Happy was the Union commander who had a newspaper reporter working for him. In that direction lay fame and promotion. Captain Turner of Meagher's staff had been a somewhat irregular correspondent for the New York *Irish-American* writing under the pseudonym of "Gallowglass." But Townsend represented the outside world of nativist respectability, and it was a real coup to contact him at this particular time. One would love to learn the identity of the dry and privileged gravedigger and to learn his fate in the cauldron of battle.

Until now the Irish Brigade had been a tightly-knit family. But though the casualties at Fair Oaks-Seven Pines had been small, losses to the chills and miasmas of the Chickahominy Valley were growing. Richardson decided that an additional regiment should be assigned to the organization. Of course Meagher wanted another Green Flag regiment, the 37th New York, if he could get it, or the 9th Massachusetts. Apparently his brush with Pennsylvania's Governor Curtin kept him from thinking of the 69th Pennsylvania. But the following order removed any possibility of the accession of another Irish regiment,

Headquarters Richardson's Division
Camp at Fair Oaks, Va., June 9, 1862.
[Special Order]
The Twenty-ninth Regiment Massachusetts Volunteers is hereby assigned to the brigade of General Meagher.
By Command of
Brigadier-General Richardson[31]

31. Conyngham, *The Irish Brigade*, p. 172.

Of all the regiments in the Army of the Potomac there was none with more claim to the name, "American," according to their nativist way of thinking. Among the newcomers was a lineal descendant of Miles Standish, and the colonel answered to the name of Ebenezer Pierce. With this kind of addition it was incumbent on Meagher to show the newcomers a traditional welcome, a Cead mille Failthe, and he did. The 29th arrived on June 10, and, not having been issued rations the day before, was dependent on the three old regiments for their daily bread. Apparently a good impression was made on the New Englanders. Years later, their historian remembered seeing

> ... the Major of the Regiment sitting on his horse, wet
> to the skin, asking and receiving a hot dipper of
> coffee from a man of the Irish Brigade.[32]

So a reinforcement had arrived. One which would live in close proximity to the Irish and form several opinions about them as soldiers, companions, and human beings.

32. William H. Osborne, *History of the Twenty-ninth Regiment of Massachusetts Volunteer Infantry, in the Late War of the Rebellion* (Boston: Albert J. Wright, 1877), p. 146.

CHAPTER FIVE
WEEK OF BATTLE

While the mutter and roar of the Seven Pines-Fair Oaks fight swelled on the south bank of the Chickahominy, McClellan's Fifth and Sixth Corps were passive spectators on the north bank. Sergeant MacNamara mentions that Brig. Gen. George W. Morell's brigade was marched down to the river at 7 a.m. on June 1 but could not cross. Not only were the bridges awash, but the entire valley floor was covered and it remained so for some time as the rain fell steadily through the first week of June. Two men of the 9th Massachusetts, Matthew Lyon and John Harron, volunteered to swim the turbulent river with dispatches on June 3 and successfully accomplished their mission.

There was plenty of work on the north bank of the river in moving the wounded from the battle as gently as possible to the rear areas. Heavy details were drawn on the Fifth Corps to work on the bridges and their approaches with the men up to their waists in water a good bit of the time. At noon each day a gill of whiskey was served to each man "to brace him up and ward off the chills."[1]

In the middle of June the Fifth Corps got an excellent reinforcement in Brig. Gen. George McCall's division of twelve Pennsylvania regiments usually known as the "Pennsylvania Reserve Corps." This gave Porter three divisions. On June 19 the Sixth Corps crossed over to the south side leaving Porter's corps the only Union combat force on the north bank. This poses an interesting question. Did George McClellan now begin to despair of ever seeing McDowell's men come overland to join him? For if McDowell did not come via the Fredericksburg road, then the approach to Richmond via the line of York River-West Point-White House was a false one.

1. MacNamara, *Ninth Massachusetts*, p. 104.

It would be better to move over and use the James as the main supply artery, establish another base, and begin anew. The new approach would not have to cross another moat like the Chickahominy. Sergeant MacNamara referred to the river as an "incubus."

On June 16 Robert E. Lee sent a message to Stonewall Jackson in the Shenandoah Valley where he had just concluded a classic campaign. In essence, Lee told him that because of his own fruitful efforts, there was now no longer any possibility of McClellan getting any reinforcement. It was time to bring the Army of the Valley to Richmond where, with the Army of Northern Virginia, a mighty combination would bring about the destruction of the Army of the Potomac. This would be accomplished by striking Porter's corps, still extended in the direction of Fredericksburg like a drowning man's arm. Jackson's men were to be brought in from the Valley on the Virginia Central Railroad to the vicinity of Ashland to aid in the envelopment of the Fifth Corps and the interdiction of the Union supply line to White House. The Fifth Corps would also be struck by the bulk of the Confederate force at Richmond which would cross over to the north side of the Chickahominy. With the supply line of his army severed and the Fifth Corps destroyed, McClellan would be faced with two choices: he could retreat back down the Peninsula from whence he came, or he could launch an all-out attack on the Confederate holding force which would be left on the south bank. Should he choose the latter course he would still have to deal with a victorious army which could descend on his flank and rear. It was a beautiful plan and operable because of the position of the Chickahominy. The Confederate troop concentration began.[2]

It is sometimes forgotten that the first day of the "Seven Days Battle" was on June 25, and that the fight which took place on the south bank was initiated by the Unionists. The Third Corps pushed out its lines to Oak Grove in front of the Seven Pines position, with the main object of gaining a good takeoff point for the Sixth Corps to make an assault on Old Tavern on June 26. This action drew to a close in the late afternoon and the medics on both sides turned their attention to the thousand or so casualties incurred. The commander of

2. *OR*, series 1, vol. 11, pt. 3, p. 602.

114

the Army of the Potomac was suffering from neuralgia, but showed up to see how things were proceeding, climbing a tree to observe the action. When he descended, the orders for the Sixth Corps movement on the morrow stood.

The little town of Mechanicsville on the Telegraph Road north of Richmond held the extreme right flank of the Fifth Corps, the farthest-out element of McClellan's army on June 26. Some companies of the 5th Reserves of McCall's division and some cavalry vedettes were to the west of the Union strongpoint at Beaver Dam Creek, a stream which ran roughly north-and-south to empty into the Chickahominy. The Fifth Corps had made the east bank of the stream virtually impregnable, and it was never in Lee's plan to assault this position. When they arrived, Jackson's men were to move down from Ashland and flank the entire position. However, because Union scouts destroyed some very important bridges over Totopotomoy Creek, the Army of the Valley was slow in getting to the point of attack.

This tardiness on the part of Jackson meant that the Confederates from the Richmond army had to carry the entire load on June 26. Major Generals A. P. Hill and James Longstreet led their divisions across the the Chickahominy and drove the 5th Reserves out of Mechanicsville back on to the Beaver Dam Creek position. Apparently due to mistaken zeal on Hill's part, his men were directed at the strong Union infantry rifle-pits and artillery emplacements, and the result was a tremendous effusion of Confederate blood without any discernible advantage to Lee. McCall's Pennsylvanians, with no threat to their flank from Jackson, simply slaughtered the eager Confederate formations. Lee was faced with a ghastly check to his ambitious plan which now appeared to be disclosed to McClellan. Lee must have had some bad moments as he listened in one direction for Jackson's battle which did not come, and in the other for a Union movement on the south side of the river against the weak holding force under John B. Magruder.

The day of June 26 drew to a close with McClellan and Porter both on the ground at Beaver Dam Creek and both apprehensive as to the whereabouts of Jackson. His advance was expected for some time, and though Hill's division had a bloody repulse, the next move in the chess game was the important one. The chief point is that the Confederate masquerade south of the river had worked. Magruder had repeated his performance at the Warwick River of making 10,000 men seem like ten times that number. So successful was he that the Union corps commanders south of the river thought that they were about to be attacked and told McClellan they could not spare a man for north of the river.

But if McClellan was in the dark about Confederate capabilities, he had clearly divined his enemy's intentions. When the blow fell at Beaver Dam Creek he was able to assess the reports of Union scouts that Jackson was in the Ashland area, and foresee that the strong position occupied by McCall's division at the creek could soon be enveloped from the north. In his projection of the next move McClellan was able to come up with a third alternative. He would not retreat to the lower Peninsula, nor would he assault Magruder's lines. Instead he would abandon the supply line to White House and concentrate his army on the James River where a new supply base would be set up with the help of the Union navy. Only a military commander who has done such a task can properly appreciate its magnitude. It involved moving 100,000 men with their extensive baggage trains and artillery on two narrow roads across a swampy terrain while holding off an aggressive enemy. But what was involved was more than a change of base; it was really a change in philosophy. If he was able to complete his task, then the approach to Richmond from the north and east was finished. If there was to be a second phase of the Peninsular Campaign, it would be tied to the James River and aimed at Petersburg.

It is safe to say that thoughts of future adventures were scarcely in McClellan's head at this point. If he was going to save his army he must get at least one day of supreme battle out of the Fifth Corps. Unaided, Porter must deny the bridges over the river to the Confederates until the army corps south of the river were well started on their trek to the James.

The men of the 9th Massachusetts had been spending their days in the vicinity of Gaines' Mill, taking fatigue and picket duty in their turn with the other regiments of their brigade. There were many Irishmen in the 14th New York and 4th Michigan and the men of the 9th got on well with both of them. But they were particularly friendly with the 62nd Pennsylvania, commanded by Col. Samuel Black, which

116

was raised in Pittsburgh and western Pennsylvania. The brigade had a new commander now, a regular army artillerist with whom they had been associated for some time, Brig. Gen. Charles Griffin, formerly of Battery D, 5th U.S. Artillery. The battery had been attached to Morell's division and Griffin was familiar to all. There is no evidence that the four volunteer colonels felt any loss of face at being superseded by a regular army captain.

McClellan's headquarters was close by Gaines' Mill and the soldiers had the thrill of seeing Thaddeus Lowe's balloon ascend nearly every day. Fitz John Porter, principally, was the one who went up in the basket to survey the Confederate defences. Usually, when the balloon was rising or descending, the Confederates would fire solid shot or shell at the gas bag. Fortunately for Porter, none came close.[3]

The brigade arrived at the Beaver Dam Creek battlefield at 5 p.m., June 26, and the 14th New York and 4th Michigan were immediately committed to spaces in the firing line of the Pennsylvania Reserves division and saw some of the late stages of the battle. The 9th Massachusetts and 62nd Pennsylvania were held in reserve. Under cover of night, most of the Beaver Dam Creek position was evacuated and the 9th moved back to its old camp at the mill. McClellan had decided to move the Fifth Corps back to a position that covered the complex of bridges over the Chickahominy River. There they would stay and fight. The rest of the army would move south and away from Richmond.

The immediate country over which the battle of June 27 was fought covered an area of about nine square miles. The extreme northern and western parts of the field were heavily wooded. In the northwestern section stood the Gaines' mill. The millpond on the upland, back of the mill, empties into Powhite Creek, a small stream that drains the ravines and swamps on the west side of the battlefield as it runs down to the Chickahominy River a distance of two miles to the south. North of the center of the battlefield is Boatswain's Swamp, which is drained by Boatswain's Creek, several branches of which form and run east to west until they meet as a main stream running through a ravine-like valley, lined with brush

---

3. MacNamara, *Ninth Massachusetts*, p. 88.

and trees. After an irregular course it finally turns south and empties into the Chickahominy. Running in a downward course in the direction of the Chickahominy there are, on this field, many small creeks, ravines and gullies which were for the greater part of the year "dry runs," but which in the rainy season became respectably sized feeders to the creeks and river.

Several farms were to be found on the high land and throughout the hills and undulating valleys and tablelands, fenced and ditched. Among the few houses were the McGhee's, Adams', and Watts'. Belts and clumps of woods covered several portions of the field and along the river border which included much swamp land. A few common roads intersected the country from the towns to the mills and the fords on the river.

The 9th Massachusetts tarried long enough in their old camp to eat breakfast and receive three days' cooked rations. The usual eighty rounds per man were also doled out. The six wagons containing the baggage then left the camp and headed south for the river. The men fell in and moved at route step down the road, past the grist mill, gazing for the last time on the old mill building and the deserted millpond. They reached New Cold Harbor, halted, and formed line of battle. The sun came up and shone down on the steel-tipped lines of troops at the soldier's everlasting pastime, waiting.

Sometime in the forenoon General Griffin directed Cass to take the 9th Massachusetts back toward Old Cold Harbor until he arrived where the road crossed the mill creek. "Stop there, hold the bridge, and deny passage of it to the enemy," said Griffin. There would be help from two more regiments of Morell's division. So the 9th went back the mile or so they had gone. Their new position was back a hundred yards from Powhite Creek and perpendicular to the road which went over the creek in front of them and then mounted a hill on which stood Gaines' Mill. That structure and the regiment's presence in this exposed position would name the bloody battle that occupied the afternoon.

Someone made a mistake about their supports because no one else came to strengthen them. The men were quite aware of their mission and had a good idea of what was expected of them. Brig. Gen. Truman Seymour's brigade of McCall's division was the last of the Fifth Corps to leave the Beaver Dam Creek position where they had fought so well the day before. They passed through the 9th Massachusetts at about noon, looking curiously at a section of Capt. John C. Tidball's battery which was throwing shells over the hill at what was presumed to be a rapidly pursuing enemy. As soon as the 9th was in position the artillerymen limbered up and galloped off. The Boston Irish were "for it."

Cass ordered out the two flank companies—Capt. James E. McCafferty's Company I and Capt. Timothy O'Leary's Company F—as skirmishers to advance into the field bordering the stream and take interval. Soon over the brow of the hill came the enemy who knew about cover and concealment and were good marksmen. Rifles flamed and men fell on both sides. Cass could now see the magnitude of the task—he had to hold too much territory with not enough men or cover. If he made his stand on the road he could be flanked easily by Confederates crossing the shallow creek up from the bridge. Very soon the Confederate advance built up enough numbers at the bridge to force their way over. O'Leary's men had worked their way down a little from one side of the bridge and the angle gave them a good enfilade. The first serious attack came to a halt.

Just over the skyline A. P. Hill was forming his division which had taken a mauling from the Pennsylvania Reserves the day before at Beaver Dam Creek. Brig. Gen. Maxcy Gregg's South Carolina Brigade was in front, and shortly after noon Gregg attacked across the bridge with the 1st South Carolina. What happened thereafter is told in two ways, each widely different. MacNamara said that the 9th put up a tremendous fight:

> Again and again did General Gregg's brave South Carolinians seek to advance over that short and narrow defile, in order to drive the Ninth's skirmishers back from their advantageous field, but without avail. Reinforced by two more companies of the Ninth, A and D, with Maj. P. T. Hanley at their head, our gallant band of heroes continued to pour their leaden hail into the daring and devoted ranks of the foe. . . . the enemy now sought to force the passage by large

bodies in column of companies, which were in turn pushed forward by larger bodies in their rear, coming down the incline, until they gained a crossing, over their dead and wounded, and reached the open field in our front. The utter impossibility of holding their ground against the fierce onset of these advancing columns of the enemy forced the Ninth skirmishers to fall back, firing rapidly as they retired to a new line.[4]

The South Carolinians told it differently. General Maxcy Gregg in his report said:

The enemy made some stand at Gaines' Mill, and here our skirmishers, [Capt. John] Cordero's and [Capt. William T.] Haskell's companies of the First [South Carolina] and [Capt. John L.] Miller's of the Twelfth [South Carolina], became sharply engaged. The enemy were sheltered by trees; our riflemen availed themselves of inequalities of the ground, where they could fire and load lying down. This exchange of fire having continued for some short time, while the First and Twelfth were preparing to advance in line, and judging that a rapid charge of the skirmishers would dislodge the enemy with least loss to our troops, I ordered them forward at the double-quick. At the word of command the riflemen sprang to their feet, and advancing impetuously drove the enemy before them. . . . It was now nearly 2 p.m.

The advance across the plain which extends from the valley of the Powhite Creek to that beyond Cold Harbor was made steadily and rapidly under the fire of the enemy's skirmishers. . . . Among the troops driven from the ground the Ninth Massachusetts Regiment was noticed.[5]

It would appear that the 9th put up quite a fight for about two hours against the South Carolinians, and it is interesting that

4. *Ibid.*, p. 117.
5. *OR*, series 1, vol. 11, pt. 2, p. 854.

the descendants of Boston's Columbian Artillery were fighting their Irish cousins of the Charleston Irish Volunteers in Company K of the 1st South Carolina. But there was simply too much weight behind the Confederate attack and Major Hanley prudently pulled back with companies alternately fighting and retreating so as to cover one another.

Lt. Frank O'Dowd of Company I was on the right flank and the last man to retreat. Both Captain McCafferty and Lt. Nugent had been killed, and O'Dowd was in charge of the relic of the company. As he turned to fall back he was struck above the ankle by a piece of shell that broke the bone. His men ran past him, for the Confederates were close, but O'Dowd cried out to his first sergeant, Jim MacNamara, "For God's sake, Jim, don't leave me." MacNamara and O'Dowd had been friends for a long time, and the sergeant came back with two others, Jeremiah Cronin and William Winn. The Confederate fire was thick about them, but O'Dowd was picked up and placed on Winn's back. With Cronin and MacNamara on each side supporting the officer's body they set out for the impossible goal of the Union entrenchments on Boatswain's Hill. Their luck was out. A bullet passed through O'Dowd's back and out through Winn's chest, killing both. MacNamara fell at the same fusillade with a ball in his leg. Cronin turned to his sergeant but MacNamara waved him away and fell back.

In a few minutes the men of Maxcy Gregg reached MacNamara who had sat up to examine his wound. A brawny Southerner "charged bayonets" and yelled, "Get up, Yank!" MacNamara pointed to his leg, said he was wounded, and as the Confederate ran on, called out that he was thirsty. Without breaking stride the other man threw back his canteen. Later, MacNamara reflected that at that time water was worth its weight in gold. The sergeant survived six days without medical treatment and managed to write a short account of each day in his diary.[6]

General Fitz-John Porter wrote glowingly of the stand of Cass' regiment for *Century Magazine* in 1884,

> At Gaines's Mill, Colonel Thomas Cass's gallant
> 9th Massachusetts Volunteers of Griffin's brigade

6. MacNamara, *Ninth Massachusetts*, pp. 118 ff.

obstinately resisted A. P. Hill's crossing, and were
so successful in delaying his advance, after crossing, as to compel him to employ large bodies to force
the regiment back to the main line.[7]

Apparently, in the years since 1862, Porter had learned much about what his men were doing. When the 9th reached the main line of resistance, they were sure that no one else in the Fifth Corps knew or cared anything about their fight with Gregg's men. Everyone else in the Fifth Corps was so busy improvising some kind of a bulwark against enemy fire that the action of the 9th might just as well have been fought in Tibet.

Roughly the front of the Fifth Corps was a ninety-degree arc on the east bank of Boatswain's Creek. The creek ran into a swamp before emptying into the Chickahominy, and the swamp gave Porter's left flank a solid buttress. Rising on the south of the creek was a long hill with steep grades facing the north and west. The hill then sloped down to the river. The Union position was a strong one, and if entrenching tools had been available it might have been made impregnable. There were several excellent batteries as well as the three infantry divi-sions of Morell, Sykes, and McCall to defend the position. The ninety-degree arc of the front was divided between Morell's division on the left and Sykes on the right. Back from the front and up the hill, Porter had placed McCall's men as his reserve. Griffin's brigade was placed on Morell's right flank with the 9th Massachusetts on the right of the brigade, on their left the 14th New York and the 4th Michigan. The 62nd Pennsylvania was held in reserve behind the brigade line. To the right of the 9th was posted Capt. Augustus P. Martin's battery directly in the center of the Union position. As one looks at the maps of the battle it all looks nice and tidy, with solid blobs of black ink to indicate where the troops stood, presumably, throughout the entire afternoon. This is the usual military claptrap and far from the truth. It was on both sides a pulsating affair with the Union defenders surging out of their assumed fixed places to grapple with the Confederates, with reserves on both sides ordered in where they were badly needed to succor men who

7. Fitz John Porter, "Hanover Court House and Gaines's Mill," *Battles and Leaders*, 2:336.

122

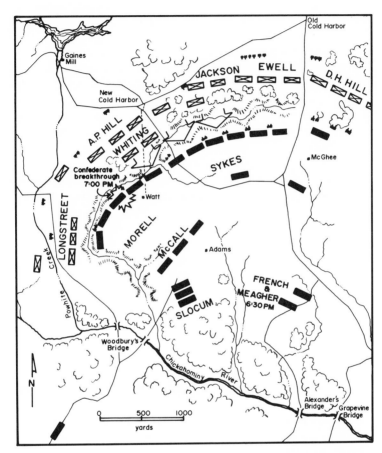

Map by John Heiser

Map by John Heiser

The Battle of Gaines' Mill

123

were exhausted by the physical and mental strain and the heat of the day. There was nothing about the battle on either side that was static or pretty.

Truman Seymour commanded the Third Brigade of the Pennsylvania Reserves at the beginning of the battle and he had as good a view of what happened as anyone:

> The contest here may be described briefly as a struggle for the mastery of a body of woods on our front and left, the possession of which gave control of the open ground in our rear, over which passed the roads to the bridges of the Chickahominy by which we must be supported or retire. Morell's division occupied these woods; Sykes' ground comparatively open to the right. This division was in rear of the woods in reserve. . . .
>
> The engagement commenced fiercely about 3 o'clock, and such overpowering numbers were brought into action by the enemy that it was soon necessary to send forward this division in support of the line already engaged. Regiment after regiment advanced, relieved regiments in front, in turn withstood, checked, repelled, or drove the enemy, and retired, their ammunition being exhausted, to breathe a few moments, to fill their cartridge boxes, again to return to the contested woods. Some of these regiments stood for four hours, scarcely changing position, yielding to no odds, and to no dimunition of their own numbers. At times parts of the line would be driven from its ground, but only to receive aid and drive the enemy in his turn. The woods were strewn with the heroic dead of both sides, and multitudes of wounded and dying painfully sought every hollow affording even momentary shelter from the incessant and pitiless fire.[8]

At 2:30 p.m. the Fifth Corps could look out on the plain in front of them stretching from Powhite Creek to Old Cold Harbor. On it was deployed A. P. Hill's division, and there was

8. *OR*, series 1, vol. 11, pt. 2, p. 400.

no question that Hill was wearing his red battle shirt. Shortly he launched his men forward, and a pattern of attack and defence began that was to last for the afternoon. The Confederate infantry would advance, subjected to the fire of the well-served Union batteries, both those in close support of the infantry line and those on the slope of the hill. When the attackers got within musketry range, the Union footmen would spring up, move in front of their artillery, and deliver their volleys. Since flesh-and-blood could stand only so much, the Confederates would give way and again be subject to the pounding of the Union artillery as they drew off, usually in haste.

It is difficult to tell how many attacks Hill put in here in the center of the Union position where Sykes and Morell's divisions came together. There were, according to MacNamara "many desperate assaults on Martin's battery."[9]

These repeated attacks were met and turned back by the 9th and their friends of the 62nd Pennsylvania, the 14th New York, and some of Col. Hiram Berdan's Sharpshooters. Some of the Union regiments were moved about in the course of the afternoon so that they did not occupy the same ground at the end as they had at the start. Regiments ran out of ammunition and had to be resupplied, and, occasionally, reserves were put in to relieve the exhausted defenders. But by 4 p.m. it was evident that the pugnacious Hill had suffered a costly repulse. Griffin tells of incessant attacks on his men at this time.

Capt. John Edwards of the 3rd U.S. Artillery was in command of Batteries L and M which were distributed in the intervals of Col. Gouverneur K. Warren's brigade of Sykes' division, some distance to the east of where the 9th had started the battle. Perhaps the regiment or part of it had been sent there to stop a particularly threatening attack. In any event Edwards admired their spirit if not their technique:

> After some time a regiment of rebels emerged from the woods waving their flag. The battery plied them with case-shot, and as they approached nearer with double rounds of canister. The Ninth Massachu-

9. MacNamara, *Ninth Massachusetts*, p. 122.

setts Regiment, which was in rear of my battery, then rose up, gave a cheer, and advanced bravely as far as the rear of my limbers, where they crouched down and opened a fire of musketry in spite of all my efforts to stop them, thereby placing my men and horses in great jeopardy. I continued to fire canister, and under its effects the rebel ranks were broken and many men ran to the rear. I then urged this regiment forward. They advanced a short distance beyond my guns. I ordered the latter to be limbered up and to withdraw. The rebels had approached so near one of my guns that Corporal [George] Himmer shot one with his revolver.[10]

By 4 p.m. the first phase of the assault was over, and even the most optimistic Confederate could not regard it as promising. Porter was asking for reinforcements from south of the river, and in the lull before the next assault, Brig. Gen. Henry W. Slocum's division of the Sixth Corps arrived and was directed to fill in the gaps caused by casualties and exhaustion. Even with his early success Porter must have felt apprehensive. The first attack was with only one division—Hill's. If Lee should engage the entire Union line simultaneously, a weak spot could develop and then be exploited. In the end that is something like what happened, but a good deal of time and effort was expended before the final movement took place.

Longstreet made some vague offensive movements on the extreme left of the Union position before deciding that the swampy terrain made an all-out assault impracticable. Jackson was again having a bad day and was late in getting his force to the field. D. H. Hill waged a sanguinary battle against his old West Point roommate, Sykes, without anything decisive resulting.

If McClellan had bolstered the Fifth Corps during this period when the Confederate battle plan was still in a plastic state, then the Peninsula Campaign might have had a happier result for the Union. But he had polled his corps commanders and every one, even the aggressive division commanders, Hooker and Kearny, said they were awaiting attack and could

10. *OR*, series 1, vol. 11, pt. 2, p. 357.

not spare a man for the north bank of the Chickahominy. Slocum's division was committed to battle at 4 p.m., and it was not until 5:00 that French and Meagher of the Second Corps received orders to cross. It is fascinating to conjecture the outcome of the battle had these orders been sent an hour earlier.

When the final Confederate attack went in, the hour was sometime after 6 p.m. Porter said the first phase was repulsed throughout the length of his line, and the thought came to him that the worst was surely over. After dark he could withdraw across the river, having inflicted a severe check to the newly named Army of Northern Virginia.

> The attacks, though coming like a series of apparently irresistible avalanches, had thus far made no inroads upon our firm and disciplined ranks. Even in this last attack we successfully resisted, driving back our assailants with immense loss, or holding them beyond our lines, except in one instance, near the center of Morell's line, where by force of numbers and under cover of the smoke of battle our line was penetrated and broken; this at a point where I least expected it.[11]

That spot was in Brig. Gen. John H. Martindale's brigade in Morell's division. Two of the regiments involved said they were out of ammunition, and there was no alternative except to fall back in the face of a very heavy attack. Once the hole opened, the entire line cracked and the rout was on. Porter had hoped that even though his infantry were worn down, that well-placed batteries would deter the Johnnies. His luck was out, for a Union cavalry force appeared on the scene at the worst possible time. This group of horsemen under the command of Brig. Gen. Philip St. George Cooke attempted an ill-fated charge on the Confederates who were advancing. This movement masked the Union batteries, first, and then, after the charge had been shot to pieces, a stampede of riderless horses bore back through the batteries, running off the Union

---

11. Porter, "Hanover Court House and Gaines's Mill," 2:340.

Patrick Robert Guiney
Colonel, 9th Massachusetts Volunteer Infantry
Wounded at the Wilderness

artillery horses, and promoting general confusion. Porter thought this ill-timed event cost him the battle.

Griffin's brigade was some distance to the east of the break in Morell's line. The 9th Massachusetts had been doing their best with the others of the brigade, and they had a new commander by this time. Cass had been extremely debilitated by a case of Chickahominy fever on top of his flu, and sometime before the last assault he had to be helped to the rear. At first he sat on a stump supported by his staff, some of whom suggested that he should go across the river for safety. At last he assented, and said, "Boys, go back and do your duty like men; God knows I would be with you if I was able."[12] His lieutenant colonel, Patrick Guiney, took over.

Looking to the west, the 9th could suddenly see a mass of fugitives leaving the line they had defended so well during the long day. This was a distinct surprise, for the fire directly in front of them had died down a little. Guiney looked to Griffin for orders, and after a while the regiment fell back by sections keeping their front to the foe, who were now coming through the underbrush in some strength. Slowly, the line backed up the hill. Their friends from the brigade had left a bit before the Irish, so they were the last bluecoats in the vicinity. Even though the sun was now down, the oppressive heat of the day still hung on, and Guiney removed his coat and stood a conspicuous figure in his shirt sleeves. The battery smoke still hung over the hill in patches, and as these began to lift, Guiney was appalled to see that the retreat was turning into a rout. The slope behind them was covered with fugitives making for the bridges. What happened next was described by George A. Townsend of the New York *Herald*, the correspondent who had so much to say about Meagher's brigade after Fair Oaks:

> The Ninth Massachusetts regiment was the rear of the retreating column which had just passed over a hill into a large open plain. . . . To break and run was not for the men who had covered themselves with glory during the day. Col. P. R. Guiney (now in command) decided to form a line of battle on his colors, and resist the approach of the enemy until the

12. MacNamara, *Ninth Massachusetts*, p. 127.

advance of the retreat should have been far enough to leave ground sufficient to enable him to commence his retreat in good order. Colonel Guiney with his standard-bearers, advanced upon the rebels with the words, "Men, follow your colors!" It was enough. Before that small band of jaded heroes waved the Stars and Stripes and the green flag of Erin, and with loud huzzas, they rushed upon the rebels, driving them up the hill. Nine times did the remnant of the Ninth drive, with ball and buckshot, the advance of the rebel army before they could make good their retreat, the rebels being often within sixty yards of them.[13]

MacNamara is quite circumstantial in his account of what happened:

As our lines on the left flank and those on the right flank gave way the centre followed until the Ninth suddenly found itself, as it were, without warning, last in the line of retreat. To them it was an unexpected situation of affairs.

To break and run was not the nature of the men of the Ninth; but to retreat in good order, before the enemy could surround them, was now their only alternative. . . . To halt and rally and fire a volley or two, and then charge the enemy's line with a prolonged Irish yell from time to time until nine successive attacks were repulsed, was the only desperate method of preserving the Ninth from capture or annihilation. As the regiment drew nearer to its own lines in the rear, the atmosphere became somewhat clearer, and support rallied to our assistance from the remnants of survivors of other gallant regiments which like the Ninth had been fighting all day in the hot sun. . . . Twilight had set in as the Ninth, after losing two hundred and forty-nine of their number in killed and wounded, reached the main line in retreat.

13. New York *Herald*, July 4, 1862.

> Loud cheering from our rear in the direction of
> Alexander's bridge on the Chickahominy now broke
> upon the air. Louder and louder it arose as the long-
> looked-for reinforcements came in sight and
> marched upon the field, and into the midst of our
> jaded troops.[14]

Men who passed all through the war would later claim that
never did they hear a more heartwarming sound than the cheers
of the brigades of French and Meagher as they mounted the
river slope of Turkey Hill and descended to the plain of death
below. Meagher said he had received Richardson's order at 5
p.m. to march to Porter's aid. Under the overall command of
General French, the two brigades double-timed to the bridge.
French's men were in the advance at the crossing, and on the
other side of the bridge a huge cloud of smoke welled up into
the air. From the cloud broke terror-stricken teamsters lashing
their horses to a gallop, and careening, stumbling men fought
to the verge of exhaustion. The stragglers constituted a real
threat to the integrity of the relief column.

French halted his brigade and ordered Meagher to take the
lead deploying a company of skirmishers to clear the road for
the column. With fixed bayonets the 69th's Company G under
Felix Duffy moved forward, driving in front of them those who
had retained their arms. The brow of the hill was reached and
there was Porter, still directing his lost battle. Here and there
some semblance of order or organization was maintained by
resolute groups who moved on their colors, and turned at
command to fire into the gray smoke that still hung over the
lower slope of the hill.

The unhappy Philip St. George Cooke had reined up at the
top of the hill and in his report added one more encomium to
the role of the 9th Massachusetts:

> . . . I fell back about 400 paces with the Lancers, and
> found the enemy checked at the brow of the hill by a
> most brave handful of infantry—I was told part of the
> Ninth Massachusetts. . . .[15]

14. MacNamara, *Ninth Massachusetts*, pp. 127-28.
15. *OR*, series 1, vol. 11, pt. 2, p. 42.

As Meagher's men were halfway down the slope, a poignant meeting took place as a shirtsleeved colonel on foot sternly kept his worn command aligned on their colors. But the 9th still had enough breath to give the Irish Brigade a yell. A horseman curvetted away from the fresh troops and rode over. "Hello, Colonel Cass, is that you?" But it was Guiney who stretched up his hand in thanksgiving and gratitude to Meagher, "Thank God, we are saved!" Then the two parted, the 9th to go over the river to the Trent Farm to count their terrible losses, find separated men, and above all to lay down by the river bank and draw in mouthfuls of cool water and lungfuls of fresh air not reeking of gunpowder. When the accounting was finished, the 9th had more men killed and wounded than any other Union regiment on the field. Two other regiments were captured almost in their entirety, but the 9th still led the grisly list.

It was too late in the day for the Confederates to follow up their victory, and their losses were staggering enough to give them pause in any case. Even so, Meagher's men arranged themselves at the base of Turkey Hill and prepared to defend it. Confederate elements were encamped on the south side of Boatswain's Creek, and as the night went on some curious incidents happened. Maj. Thomas O'Neill of the Irish Brigade artillery rode off on a mission and found himself a prisoner. The same happened to two Georgia officers who encountered two pickets of the 88th New York where they were not looked for. But the brigade missed a real prize.

Daniel Harvey Hill was one of the most redoubtable officers of Lee's army. He commanded a division to the eminent satisfaction of everyone except Jefferson Davis which may have accounted for his lack of advancement later on. His men had opposed George Sykes' Regulars during the day and had finally crashed through in the general advance. Between 9 and 10 p.m. Hill and one of his brigadiers, Alexander R. Lawton, walked out alone in advance of their lines

> . . . to examine the line of battle across the road, afterward discovered to be Meagher's Irish brigade. We got within thirty yards of the Federals, and must have been seen, but we were not fired upon, probably because we were mistaken for a party of their own

men sent up to get water at McGehee's well. We met the party going back, and saw them go into their own lines. Not a word was spoken by them or by us. At such times "Silence is golden."[16]

Years later Hill wrote an account of his adventure for the *Century Magazine* and received more exact knowledge of the people he nearly encountered. William Osborne of East Bridgewater, Massachusetts, wrote the journal to say,

> I was especially interested in the circumstances re-lated by you concerning the water party sent out from the Irish Brigade to McGehee's well, and the adventure of yourself and General Lawton. I remember the incident with great vividness, as I was one of the party. I was a member of Company "C," 29th Regiment, Massachusetts Volunteers, which was a part of the brigade referred to, but I have always supposed, till I read your article, that it was later in the night when we started. I have also always supposed that in going for water we went inside the Confederate lines. . . . on one occasion actually seeing your men gathered about a smoldering camp-fire in the woods. I suppose you will not blame me for saying that we should all have esteemed it a great honor if we had made your acquaintance that night.[17]

The private soldier of the Army of the Potomac did not think in terms of lines of communication or supply bases. He dwelt not on the future but on the here and now, and his view of the war was concerned with advancing on the enemy and pushing him back. He knew little of the private war between McClellan and the administration. Years later, when the regimental histories would be written, all these things would come to light, and the writers of the histories would take sides on the basis of personal or political feelings at the time and certain army prejudices that would never die.

16. Daniel H. Hill, "Lee's Attacks North of the Chickahominy," in *Battles and Leaders*, 2:358.
17. *Ibid.*, p. 358-59.

But here and now the army was a mass of worried men and boys, upset because their methodical advance on Richmond had slowed to a crawl ever since the battle of Fair Oaks a month before. The lowlands of the Peninsula did not seem like the healthiest place in the world to fight a campaign, and almost as many men were on the sick list as had been shot in the recent battle. On the morning of June 28 this volunteer army of the Republic looked about and did not like the state of affairs.

However, it was the next twenty-four hours that George McClellan needed to get his huge army underway for a new operating base on the James River. It was a pretty tricky maneuver, 5,000 supply wagons, 2,500 head of cattle, and 85,000 men were to move on two narrow roads a distance of twenty-three miles across a swamp to the safety of high ground at Malvern Hill. This mighty host had a victorious army in its rear and was moving directly across the front of John Magruder's holding force in the Richmond defences. Magruder had gotten a bloody nose on the first of the Seven Days, but he might come boiling out from behind his redoubts and hit the Union flank while it was moving, maybe stop or slow it long enough for Lee and company to arrive on the scene. It was a scary thought.

There were other things that might go wrong. The two narrow bridges across White Oak Swamp would have to be held in strength until the army passed with its long train. Along these approaches could come the loping foot-cavalry of Jackson. Perhaps he was not the Jackson of the Valley these days, but he was still Stonewall. His mission was to pressure the rear guard while the bulk of Lee's army was hurried over to the south side of the Chickahominy River to strike at the vulnerable flank of the long coil of Union troops. If the blue troops faced west to meet Lee, Jackson was on their right flank. If McClellan turned to Jackson's heel-nipping, Lee was on his left flank. The Army of the Potomac could be had.

McClellan's Fourth Corps (Keyes) was the closest to Malvern Hill so they were the first to move off in that direction, followed by the bloodied Fifth Corps of Porter. The Second and Sixth Corps were pulled out of the heavily fortified lines of Fair Oaks-Seven Pines and backed up to a parallel position at Savage's Station. Here had been estab-

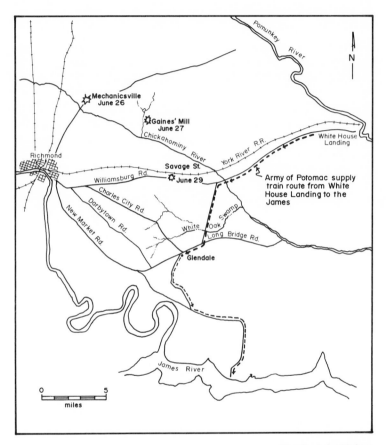

Map by John Heiser

The road network east of Richmond

135

lished the field hospital for the sick and wounded and long rows of tents were alongside the railroad tracks.

When Meagher's brigade drew up on the south bank of the Chickahominy on the morning of June 28, there was little to do but watch the Confederate cavalry which cautiously inched down from the slopes of Turkey Hill on the other side of the water. Then they marched back to their old Fair Oaks position and watched the frantic activity as the great army was shocked into action. Long wagon trains were lined up team-to-tailboard on the roads and long lines of infantry moved along beside them headed south. At first it looked as though they were going on a giant flanking movement around the Confederate position occupied by Magruder. But whatever was to happen, it did not concern the Second Corps. Companies for picket duty moved out to the right and left of the railroad at Fair Oaks. Afternoon and evening were quiet except for the intermittent explosion of Federal ammunition dumps. The soldiers slept peaceably on the night of June 28.

Early on the morning of June 29, Richardson's division got orders to move back to cover the lateral road on which the supply trains were moving. Meagher fouled up the movement completely for some reason and Richardson got angry enough to place him under arrest. The Confederate brigades of Brigadier Generals Paul J. Semmes, Joseph B. Kershaw, and Col. William Barksdale had followed up the retrograde movement of the Second Corps, and at about 4 p.m. appeared at the edge of the woods that bordered the clearing at Savage's Station. Brig. Gen. Edwin V. Sumner drew out the Philadelphia Brigade, which contained the 69th Pennsylvania, to contain the Confederate attack which was delivered with great fury. More of the Second Division of the Second Corps were bled into the battle, but the Union line was thin in the center and the Johnnies caved it in. The commander of the Philadelphia Brigade, Brig. Gen. William W. Burns, was riding all over the field, shouting at his men and sending reinforcements into the maelstrom while the blood ran over his chin from a face wound. He tells of the crucial point of the affair:

A mass of men came up in my rear in full yell. I halted the crowd and asked for their commander. "I am Captain [John] McCartan of the 88th New York, sir," exclaimed an officer. I got them into line (about 250 men), facing up the Williamsburg road, which was raked by the grape and canister of the enemy's batteries. I gave the command, double-quick—charge! They went in with a hurrah, and the enemy's battery fell back.[18]

The 29th Massachusetts was a spectator of the assault of the "Connacht Rangers" although they mistook them for the 69th New York:

> . . . the musketry of the enemy swept their whole line from right to left; they staggered and huddled together . . . and for an instant they nearly paused, dreading to go on. Looking back, they saw the Sixty-ninth New York. . . . Passing their left flank, the Sixty-ninth New York, with fixed bayonets, ran straight toward the gorge, and with an impetuosity so characteristic of them, and such as few troops can withstand, rushed directly on the enemy's soldiers. The Vermont troops . . . followed the brave example of the dauntless Irishmen, and in less than three minutes the railroad was ours.[19]

The Irish had indeed impressed their new comrades of the 29th Massachusetts as the Army of the Potomac beat off Lee's first attempt to interrupt their passage to the James. Sumner was so satisfied with the performance of his men that he did not want to leave the field. Franklin had a hard time talking him into pushing on, but the presence of one of McClellan's aides was enough to convince the old man. So the troops filed into the road and set off, leaving behind 2,500 sick and wounded in the hospitals who could not be moved.

The Irish Brigade fell out at about 10 p.m., exhausted now that the stimulus of battle was behind them, and ravenously hungry. The meat ration carried in the haversacks was spoiling in the damp heat, and the hard crackers were long gone. With the trains far ahead of them there was nothing to

18. *Ibid.*, p. 374.
19. Osborne, *Twenty-ninth Massachusetts*, p. 152.

do but tighten their belts. About 4:00 the next morning they were on the road again, and after a wearying six miles in five hours came to the bridge over White Oak Swamp. As soon as they crossed, the bridge was destroyed, and the last water barrier to the James was behind them. Sumner directed that the crossing be defended and the brigade found a position on the west side of the road with Brig. Gen. Henry M. Naglee's brigade of the Fourth Corps on their right. Artillery positions were dug in the intervals and the Union rear guard prepared for their pursuer, Stonewall Jackson.

The Union movement had reached its most critical stage. In addition to Jackson, who was expected momentarily on the rear, Lee was pushing three separate columns of attack against the right flank of the Federal army. The most dangerous stroke was to fall where the Long Bridge Road crossed the Quaker Road, and both Longstreet and A. P. Hill were forming up to bring the blue-coats to battle. The contest has become known variously as Glendale, Frayser's Farm, Nelson's Farm, and Charles City Cross Roads, and since it spread over all these areas, all of them can be justly applied. Douglas Southall Freeman, the great Virginia historian, has judged that, under any name, what followed was the cardinal battle of the Seven Days; the one supreme chance for Lee to destroy the Army of the Potomac. It was a near miss.

McCall's Pennsylvania Reserve Division had fought well from cover at Beaver Dam Creek on June 27, but Gaines' Mill had been a very bad experience for them, and since then they had been worn down by the continual marching. In addition, one of their best officers, Brig. Gen. John F. Reynolds, was a prisoner in Richmond. So they were placed in line of battle between two divisions of the Third Corps, Hooker to the south and Kearny to the north. In effect, they were "corseted" between two comparatively fresh formations. Longstreet and A. P. Hill assaulted this line with their usual verve, the first attacks falling in the gap between McCall's left and Hooker's right by Kemper's Virginians. The left brigade of the Reserves was driven back.

In the gap were emplaced two Union batteries commanded by Captains Otto Diederichs and John Knieriem. The gunners who were working these pieces did not wait for the Virginians to get too close, but fled through the ranks of

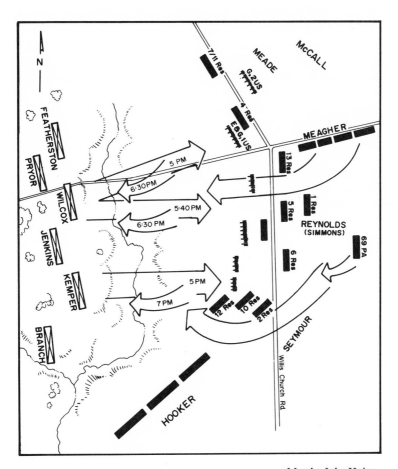

The Battle of Glendale

the infantry backup, which happened to be the 69th Pennsylvania. The Philadelphia Irish were led to their position by Sumner himself. Sumner turned to Hooker and said:

> General , I cannot spare you a brigade, but I have brought you the Sixty-ninth Pennsylvania, one of the best regiments in my corps; place them where you wish, for this is your fight, Hooker.[20]

The 69th formed line and looked up the hill where the abandoned artillery pieces stood quiet and forlorn. As Sumner turned to leave the men, he cautioned them to hold their fire until they could see the whites of their foe's eyes, and to aim low. Then he rode off, waving his cap with his white hair streaming in the battlesmoke.

The Confederates came on in renewed strength and the first waves appeared on the crest of the hill. With no word of command, the 69th stood up and leveled their weapons. A smashing volley stopped the Johnnies and through the billowing smoke came Colonel Owen's men up the slope with the bright steel of their bayonets winking in the sinking rays of the sun. Some of the Confederates stayed to cross bayonets with the Irish, but most turned and ran back across the cleared field, through the swamp, and into the woods from whence they came. Joe Hooker, looking to his right, saw a great, sprawling mass of men disappear over the crest of the hill, and, wondering, rode over to see what was going on. Where the 69th had formed there was not a living soul. Hooker did not forget them when he wrote his report.

> About 3 o'clock the enemy commenced a vigorous attack on McCall, and in such force that General Sumner voluntarily tendered me the services of a regiment, which was posted in an open field on my extreme right and under shelter from the enemy's artillery. This was the Sixty-ninth Regiment Pennsylvania Volunteers, under Colonel Owen.
>
> Meanwhile the enemy's attack had grown in force and violence, and after an ineffectual effort

20. McDermott, *69th Pennsylvania*, p. 14.

to resist it, the whole of McCall's division was completely routed, and many of the fugitives rushed down the road on which my right was resting, while others took to the cleared fields and broke through my lines from one end of them to the other, and actually fired on and killed some of my men as they passed. . . . Following closely upon the footsteps of these demoralized people were the broken masses of the enemy . . . until they were checked by a front fire of the Sixteenth Massachusetts Volunteers and afterward by a diagonal fire on their right and left flanks from the Sixty-ninth Pennsylvania Volunteers. . . .

After great loss the enemy gave way, and were instantly followed with great gallantry by [Brig. Gen. Cuvier] Grover, at the head of the First Massachusetts Regiment, while the Sixty-ninth Pennsylvania Regiment, heroically led by Owen, advanced in the open field on their flank with almost reckless daring.

As Colonel Owen has rendered me no report of the operations of his regiment, I can only express my high appreciation of his services, and my acknowledgments to his chief for having tendered me so gallant a regiment.[21]

All of their days the Philadelphia Irish would remember Glendale and the words of Joe Hooker. In another year almost to the day they would again occupy the very center of attack in a terrible battle when the Army of the Potomac would be fighting for its very life and the nation's existence. Truly, the 69th Pennsylvania could say, "We were there."

But here at Glendale the graycoats came again and again, knocking at this gate to the communication road on which the army was moving. In intensity the fighting reached the same pitch as that of Gaines' Mill. Men locked bayonets and used their fouled rifles as flails. Especially noteworthy was the conduct of the Union artillerists; they were not all like those of the left flank batteries who had fled. When Hill's men surged over the guns of Lt. Alanson Randol, his gunners fought them off with a tremendous élan leading the infantry

21. *OR*, series 1, vol. 11, pt. 2, p. 111.

support in a yelling charge. Now the entire Union front was ablaze, Kearny on the right, McCall in the center, Hooker on the left. In the twilight fresh Confederates came forward, ran into opposition, stayed close-up, dealing and receiving terrible blows. Now the Pennsylvania Reserves were fighting at their last extremity with men stumbling about like sleep-walkers. After beating back a particularly severe attack, the men sank down in a ragged line, completely spent. Josiah R. Sypher, the historian of the Reserves, then described what happened:

> Just then a great noise was heard on the left and rear; all eyes were instantly turned in that direction. Horror seized the hearts of the wearied soldiers, and men stood fixed as statues. A brigade of troops was pouring from the woods, marching under a banner of strange device, which in the dusk of the evening could not be distinguished. "My God," exclaimed Colonel [R. Biddle] Roberts, "what is that?" The next moment the Stars and Stripes emerged from the wood, and the answering shout went up: "It is the Irish brigade!" An officer came dashing forward to Colonel Roberts, and said he had come to relieve his troops. The First and Ninth, and portions of other regiments then retired to the wood and General Meagher moved forward his brigade.
>
> The enemy suddenly opened a most terrific fire of shell, and grape and canister from the woods beyond the field. General Meagher ordered his brigade to charge. . . . The "fighting Irishmen" threw aside their hats and coats, rolled up their sleeves, gave a tremendous cheer, and then following their gallant commander, charged across the field against the murderous fire of artillery, that slew them by hundreds. But, braving death, on went the Irish brigade, over the field and into the woods beyond; so completely routed the enemy, that he did not again renew the conflict on that portion of the field.[22]

22. Josiah R. Sypher, *History of the Pennsylvania Reserve Corps* (Lancaster, Pennsylvania: Elias Barr and Company, 1865), p. 271.

The brigade had come from the banks of White Oak Swamp where they had been awaiting the crossing by Jackson all day, in support of the batteries of Captains Rufus D. Pettit and George W. Hazzard. The Confederate artillery had been active and Col. Ebenezer Pierce of the 29th Massachusetts had lost his right arm when he was struck by a solid shot. Lt. James Turner of Meagher's staff described the relief of the Pennsylvania Reserves already alluded to:

> ... it is only when the black need comes that we press forward to the work. The dead, the wounded, the beaten, the broken and disheartened line our path— but our cheers reanimate—our *élan* gives them hope. I pledge you my word that when the Irish Brigade approaches the turning point of the battles, the hearts of that portion of the army that see them are moved within them, the most grateful and glad cheers greet us all the way, the wounded take heart, and the beaten and broken, reassured, join in our sturdy ranks and go along with renewed courage to the battle front. "That is the Irish Brigade"—"that is General Meagher," uttered in tones of hope, are the words you hear as you march along.[23]

The bone-weary warriors sank down on the trampled earth. Now, with the coming of comparative quiet, the wailing of the wounded men was heard. Stretcher parties and doctors went out to sweep the front of the position. General McCall of the Reserves went out too far in looking for some of his men and found himself the prisoner of the 47th Virginia, an especially valiant Confederate formation. After a short rest the men got to their feet again, and the columns marched back to the Quaker Road and continued through the night. If the soldiers had any feelings at all after the week that lay behind them, few were noted. But a kind of victory was theirs. Not far ahead was the James River and a well-nigh impregnable position. Behind them was the Army of Northern Virginia which had struck them hard blows, and, yet, with all the genius of Lee, had not been able to bring off

23. Conyngham, *The Irish Brigade*, p. 207.

143

the daring strategy that might have ended the war here on Confederate terms.

Many have scoffed at George McClellan as a general, partly because it confirms their devotion to Lincoln by this expected exercise. Yet the conception of the strokes against the Army of the Potomac was pure genius. Perhaps the execution did not measure up to Lee's expectations, but then he had been in command for less than a month. The citizen soldiers, North and South, had shown extraordinary ability and tremendous resolution.

When the Second Corps moved down the Quaker Road in the early hours of July 1, they could barely make out the dim outlines of a wooded hill before them. Almost everyone got the luxury of a couple of hours of sleep, and when the soldiers fell in again the dawn was fast approaching. The hill stood out in more detail. It was not high, but the slope to the top was long and gradual. The flanks fell off in to the marshy environs of the James River. It was, in short, a great place to fight a defensive battle if you had plenty of artillery and determined infantry. The attackers would have to come at you, and, in their coming, could be made to pay a great price. In the near distance the James was a silver ribbon in the morning haze, and there, swinging at anchor, were the gunboats of Commodore John Rodgers's flotilla. It was a welcome addition of firepower.

On the hill already was the Fifth Corps. The divisions of Morell and Sykes and the exhausted soldiers of McCall had preceded the rest of the army and were now resting on the river side of the hill. No trenches had been dug, but even at an early hour there was a great deal of movement of artillery pieces. Sumner's men moved up the slope on the Quaker Road and passed through the Fifth Corps on the right side of the road and the Fourth Corps on the left. Behind them were the Third Corps divisions of Hooker and Kearny, the men stretched out in every conceivable attitude of rest and relaxation.

The worn men of the 9th Massachusetts marveled at the energy of their brigadier, Charles Griffin, who was meticulously placing the guns in front of Morell's division. Griffin had spent all his life in the army in the artillery, and on this day, as on many others, the army would be glad for it. MacNamara wrote about him thus:

144

The troops of the division, while quietly watching his movements, commented freely on "Black Jack's" (a nickname for General Griffin on account of his swarthy complexion) chances of getting hit, momentarily fearing that the danger he courted would surely end in wounding or killing him; but he bore a charmed life it seemed. When asked why he didn't dismount, he said it would not do for him, for his legs shook so that he couldn't stand. No braver man than General Griffin was in the army; notwithstanding his weak legs.[24]

The soldiers were tired and hungry but rations from the train were out of the question. Tobacco was in better supply, and was, said MacNamara, "a great consolation." Canteens had been filled with water, either clear and fresh from the Chickahominy or brackish from White Oak Swamp, and the men sprawled in every direction on the ground. Several hundred yards to the left of the 9th Massachusetts stood the barn of the Chew house and in its cool shade lay the very ill commander, Colonel Cass. Ever since the landing on the Peninsula he had experienced poor health, and the constant movement and the tremendous strain at Gaines' Mill had broken him down completely. Only the intense feeling for the regiment he had raised and led had kept him on his feet. But he absolutely refused to leave, and now he lay in the shade of the Chew barn, coughing up blood and trying to straighten out a command problem. Lt. Col. Patrick Guiney who had shown great promise during the holocaust at Gaines' Mill had been taken violently ill during the march to Malvern Hill. The diagnosis was malarial fever, and he had been removed to a hospital ship. So here was a hole to be filled and Cass, himself, was not up to filling it. The major, Patrick Hanley, had been a cooper back in civilian life. He had done well on June 27, and now he would have to step up and do the job. The 9th was hard put to it for officers, and as for men the companies were down to half the strength they had started with at the Gaines' Mill battle.

But as at Gaines' Mill the soldiers could appreciate a good defensive position. The Confederates must mount the long hill

24. MacNamara, *Ninth Massachusetts*, p. 152.

145

into the teeth of Union cannon. Beside them and behind them and all around them was the gathered might of the Army of the Potomac. It would not be the Fifth Corps standing alone this time.

Like all the battles on the Peninsula, the attack would not start until the afternoon, almost as though there was a rule against bloodletting before midday. It actually was related to the fact that the Confederates had only a sketchy knowledge of the road system here within cannon shot of their capital. The maps furnished to their commanders, said D. H. Hill, were worthless. It was impossible to advance men in the dark on those narrow roads bordered by so many swampy sloughs. The morning hours were used to bring the antagonists together.

There is good reason to think that the last of the Seven Days' battles happened by accident just as had the first day at Mechanicsville. It was not pure accident, of course. Lee had sent his men down the Quaker Road and the Long Bridge Road with the intention of confronting the Union position just as A. P. Hill had crossed the Chickahominy on June 26 to confront McCall. But Lee had never expected to have to assault the fortress of Beaver Dam Creek. He did not then, it appears, expect to assault another strong position, nor did he expect to attack strong men in a strong position. Malvern Hill was strong, he could see, but whether or not the bluecoats upon it remained strong was an uncertainty in his mind. There must also have been some amount of frustration for Lee. As he said later, by all rights the Union army should have been destroyed. It was all because he could not get his orders carried out that it had not been. Glendale should have been the capstone of a Cannae, but it had not happened. Lee could see the opportunity slipping away from him. There was time for one more shot.

There was some Confederate success in the preliminary skirmishing at the foot of the hill, and in the reported retreat of Union troops. There was also some wishful thinking. All of these things may have influenced Lee into making what turned out to be a disaster.

On the top of the hill some distance back from the crest, the Irish Brigade spread on the ground like everyone else in the Second Corps. Apparently, the day Meagher had spent in arrest had been a chastening experience for the brigade commander. Israel Richardson had cut him down as only an old regular could do to a "civilian" political general. But his restoration to command had been swift, and a man like Meagher thrived on success. In the battle at White Oak Swamp he had impressed at least one old army type. Lt. Rufus King had fought Batteries A and C of the 4th U.S. Artillery there. The brigade had been in support, and all hands had expected to see Jackson's corps come splashing across the watercourse. King reported that

> General Meagher stood by one of the pieces, and, exposed to the hottest of the fire, assisted the men in running the gun forward. Upon my telling him how near out of ammunition I was, he kindly volunteered to ride to General Richardson and have ammunition sent to me as soon as possible. . . .[25]

At least he had made himself useful. Not all political generals did. That was at about 2 p.m. on June 30. He had been released from arrest at 8 a.m.

Actually, the brigade had not as yet been deeply engaged except at Savage's Station. Its service at Gaines' Mill and Glendale, while important and noted, had not been counted in heavy losses. But the men of the brigade were winning a reputation in the army. They were distinctive in their speech, in their colors, and in their fighting. That impetuosity, so noted by the historian of the 29th Massachusetts at Savage's Station, was not as present in the Army of the Potomac as in its adversary. Freeman's assertion that the terrible footmen of the Army of Northern Virginia had shown themselves superior cannot be taken without qualification, but there is some truth in it.[26] Already there was a noticeable difference in the way the Unionists and Confederates fought. The measured, "trained" Northern bodies against the elemental, animal-like Southern spirits. The Irish were closer to the Confederates than to their fellows. This also set them apart.

Already the older men were showing the strain. Col. Henry Baker of the 88th New York was forty-two years old,

25. *OR*, series 1, vol. 11, pt. 2, p. 59.
26. Douglas Southall Freeman, *R. E. Lee: A Biography*, 4 vols. (New York: Charles Scribner's Sons, 1934-35), 2:241.

and, apparently, was not showing to advantage. Lt. Col. Patrick Kelly had commanded at Fair Oaks a month before, but, today, the swamp fever had laid him out. Maj. James Quinlan had distinguished himself at Savage's Station and would command the 88th until the return of Kelly. Col. John Burke was still with the 63rd Pennsylvania, and Robert Nugent was doing well with the 69th New York, commanding the brigade while Meagher was in arrest.

The brigade was sheltered in a ravine to the right of Sumner's headquarters and not bothered by the early shelling. Meagher and the other brigade commanders went over to be near the old man in case they were needed. Fortunately, the Confederate artillery was concentrating on the targets they could see, and there were not many "overs." The brigade relaxed.

Relaxation was a luxury Fitz John Porter could not afford on this first day of July. He was going to fight a third battle for his friend George McClellan, and in some respects there was a great deal of similarity to the other two. Both Beaver Dam Creek and Gaines' Mill had been essentially defensive battles in which the Union artillery had played a dominant role. Even with artillery lined up hub-to-hub and with a hillside of infantry, Porter must have had some bad thoughts of his other encounters with the elite of the Confederacy. The artillery battle that raged in the forenoon convinced him that Lee was feeling around for a weak spot where he could launch another of those screaming infantry assaults. There was a constant dribble of men being carried to the aid stations, mostly from the Fifth Corps divisions on his left. He could not know that the well served Union batteries were having an even more devastating effect on the enemy. The Union artillery concentrated on counter-battery fire rather than against infantry, and in this they were eminently successful. There was little Confederate infantry visible for the most part, but the Northern artillery efforts against their counterparts blew away guns, caissons, teams, and gunners. Later, most of the Confederate reports would claim that their artillery support never got off the ground.

At about 3 p.m., the Confederate brigade of Lewis Armistead reacted to a strong body of skirmishers from the Fifth Corps, and charged out of a covering woods where

148

they had been concealed. They covered some of the open ground toward the Union line and suffered heavily from the overpowering artillery before finding a swale close to the Union lines. The artillery could not reach them there, and it looked as though they would have to stay until after dark. Brig. Gen. Ambrose R. Wright's brigades followed the Virginians of Armistead, so a considerable group of Confederate infantry was pinned down, but many returned to their first position in the woods. Wright and Armistead talked it over and decided that there were not enough of them to mount an all-out attack.

At this time General Magruder, who had done such great work of making a few men seem like a large number at Yorktown and on the day of the Gaines' Mill battle, was in some kind of a quandary. He was looking at a message sent from Lee's headquarters at about 1:30 p.m. which for vagueness could hardly be equalled.

July 1, 1862.

General Magruder:

Batteries have been established to rake the enemy's lines. If it is broken, as is probable, Armistead, who can witness the effect of the fire, has been ordered to charge with a yell. Do the same.

By order of General Lee:

R. H. Chilton,
Assistant Adjutant-General.[27]

Since 1:30 the entire picture had changed radically, but Magruder had no way of knowing that. His division had taken the wrong approach road and were late to the battle. Perhaps he thought that he could compensate by a show of spirit and offensive élan. The Confederate brigades started forward at about 4:45. To the men of the attacking regiments, it seemed that they had been sent out alone, with no artillery support, to be killed off en masse.

That is almost what happened. The Union artillery swelled to a roar, and the blue infantry steadied their weapons and took careful aim. Every foot of advance brought heavier casualties.

27. *OR*, series 1, vol. 11, pt. 2, p. 677.

Even as they withered away there was a heavier roll of Union musketry off to their left. D. H. Hill heard the uproar of Magruder's attack going up the hill, he took this to be the signal, and sent his division forward into the mouth of hell. Their enemy had almost a perfect field of fire. At the end of the day Hill framed a thought that he would later use in describing the battle. "It was not war, but murder." MacNamara noted the approach of the Johnnies:

> . . . long lines of gray colored infantry came forth from the woods with a quick, long, swinging stride onto the open plain. Brigade followed brigade and regiment followed regiment into line of battle as they deployed along our front three-quarters of a mile away. As they maneuvered in their thousands they were watched with intense interest by thousands of eyes from our infantry, lying on the ground, and from our batteries of artillery, every gun of which was loaded with double-shotted canister, grape and shrapnel. . . . General Griffin rode up to his brigade, on his spirited bay horse, and, in his clear shrill tones, called on his regimental commanders to "get ready to charge." . . . Again, in a short time, he dashed on to the line of the Ninth and cried out "Colonel Cass! Get ready to charge! They are coming!"
>
> Colonel Cass . . . cried out at once, "Attention, battalion!" whereupon every man of the Ninth sprang from the ground like magic, eager for the fray.
>
> In the meanwhile the enemy's long line of gray had steadily advanced up the slope. So far they had not fired a shot. Their guns were trailed and their long swinging march had increased to a rapid stride. No doubt they expected to be very soon among the guns of our artillery, which so far had waited for orders. The enemy's line was within a hundred and fifty yards of our guns. The heavy tramp of their feet could be heard. The order was then given to our batteries, "Fire!" The lanyards were pulled, and from their muzzles of fifty pieces of artillery death and dire destruction were spread amongst the lines of the gallant foe. Great gaps were instantly seen in the still

150

advancing lines of gray. But they were quickly closed without seeming to check their advance. Again and again our guns poured their death-dealing missiles into the foe as the brave fellows pressed forward with the hope of reaching and capturing our batteries, little heeding that their trail was marked by hundreds of their dead and wounded comrades. The artillery fire was then held back, and the orders rung out along our lines "Charge bayonets!" With a rush like the wind the Ninth went forward, joined by the 4th Michigan on the left and the 62d Pennsylvania on the right. . . . our blue line of glittering steel went over the ground with relentless impetuosity for sixty yards or more, to meet and drive back the now steadily advancing lines of the determined foe.[28]

It took the most determined efforts of the Union infantry to stem the wave that had, incredibly, flowed up the lower slopes of the hill. But so effective had been the artillery that, in many cases, the most advanced Confederates were only individuals and squads where companies and regiments were needed. As the Union infantry launched down the slope in superior numbers there could be only one outcome. Where they could, the Confederates turned and ran for dear life. The Union respite was brief. More Confederate formations thronged out of the woods to face that terrible slope. Again and again the blue infantry came to the support of their gunners, and, as quickly, melted to one side or the other as the gray wreckage slipped downhill. A shocked Lee stood spellbound as an assault he never intended was shot to pieces.

Fitz John Porter, riding restlessly about in the center of the Union position, decided he could use some reinforcement, and an aide was despatched to the Second Corps. When the messenger arrived, Sumner was talking with Heintzelman. The old man read the note and shook his head. He couldn't spare a man, he told the aide, as the Second Corps might be called to some other sector of the field at any minute. But Heintzelman started up to his feet, "By Jove! If Porter asks for help I know he needs it and I will send it!" Sumner

28. MacNamara, *Ninth Massachusetts*, p. 155.

151

reconsidered and finally agreed to send a brigade if the Third Corps would do the same. He turned to the group of brigade commanders, and called, "Meagher!"

Meagher's aides, Jack Gosson (of the whiskey barrel incident) and Temple Emmet, mounted and rode off to bring up the four regiments. An unexpected feast was occupying them. A large herd of cattle was feeding upon the meadows, adjacent to the position; a detail was made from each brigade soon after noon, to slaughter enough to supply the troops; when this was done, the meat, scarcely cold, was served out by regiments. The slaughtered animals lay upon the grass and the men by the scores swarmed around them, each soldier helping himself to a piece of such size and quality as his fancy dictated.[29]

Now they were needed and many of the men placed their unfinished bit of beef on their fixed bayonets. They were old soldiers now and fully expected to eat the meat during one of the long pauses that were always occurring. But this time the pace was double-quick, and the four regiments were soon in the field in front of Sumner's headquarters. Meagher deployed them in four lines of battle, 69th in the front followed by the 88th, 63rd, and the 29th which was this day commanded by Lieutenant Colonel Barnes. The word was given and they started for the edge of the plateau past the West house where the gray-green powder billows hid the blood-letting from sight. Halfway there the 69th started to yell and the others took it up; a terrible echoing that made the hardpressed Union men look back at this new addition in astonishment.

Brig. Gen. Daniel Butterfield's brigade was in the Fifth Corps reserve, and as the Irish passed them, Butterfield rode over to the color-guard of the 69th, took the Green Flag from the bearer, shook its folds out, and waved it in the direction of the fighting. This gesture increased the ardor of the brigade. They were running full-tilt now, past the spent, exhausted men of Morell's division who got up enough energy to cheer them on. A fragment of the 9th Massachusetts was directly in their path. Most recently, they had helped beat off a very strong Confederate sally, and, in doing so, they had lost their colonel at last. Thomas Cass had been hit while riding at the

29. Osborne, *Twenty-ninth Massachusetts*, p. 157.

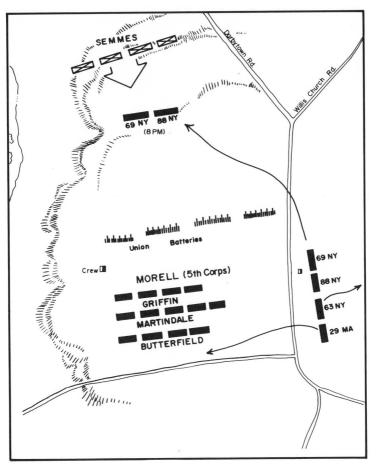

Map by John Heiser

The Battle of Malvern Hill

head of his men. Now he was being carried to the rear while Meagher's men went by.

At the head of the slope a lone mounted figure awaited them. Fitz John Porter had more help both in men and in commanders at Malvern Hill than he had enjoyed on June 27 at Gaines' Mill. Now for the second time he could see the Green Flag coming to his aid in the twilight of another battle-day.

> While riding rapidly forward to meet Meagher, who was approaching at a "double-quick" step, my horse fell, throwing me over his head, much to my discomfort both of body and mind. On rising and remounting I was greeted with hearty cheers, which alleviated my chagrin. . . . I rode rapidly forward, leading Meagher into action. . . . Determined, if possible, satisfactorily to finish the contest, regardless of the risk of being fired upon by our artillery . . . I pushed on beyond our lines into the woods held by the enemy. About fifty yards in front of us, a large force of the enemy suddenly rose and opened with fearful volleys upon our advancing line. I turned to the brigade, which thus far had kept pace with my horse, and found it standing "like a stonewall," and returning a fire more destructive than it received and from which the enemy fled. The brigade was planted. My presence was no longer needed. . . . I had the satisfaction of learning that night that a Confederate detachment, undertaking to turn Meagher's left, was met by a portion of the 69th New York Regiment, which, advancing, repelled the attack and captured many prisoners.[30]

There was a bit more to it than that. The 69th and 88th New York went down the slope under Porter's eye, but Meagher formed the 63rd New York and the 29th Massachusetts in a single line halfway down the hill, figuring to make this force a reserve. Shortly, an officer rode up to Meagher,

30. Fitz John Porter, "The Battle of Malvern Hill," in *Battles and Leaders,* 2:421.

154

identified himself as a member of McClellan's staff, and directed that a regiment be sent to support a battery over on the right. Meagher turned to Lt. Col. Henry Fowler and told him to take the 63rd where the staff officer would show him. Meagher was astonished and infuriated at Fowler's reply:

> This officer, however, undertook to disobey the order I issued to support the battery, alleging that he was under special orders issued by you, general [Sumner], and that mine were consequently without weight. . . . I insisted on Lieutenant-Colonel Fowler immediately executing the order I had given. He refusing to do so, I at once placed him under arrest, and directed Captain O'Neil, the next senior officer of the regiment, to assume command, and to have the disputed order instantly complied with.[31]

Father Corby, the chaplain of the 88th, said that Meagher was wild with rage at Fowler whose conduct was inexplicable. Meagher demanded Fowler's sword and said that he was a disgrace to the brigade. So Fowler retired, and the 63rd New York ran off to the right into the area of the Fourth Corps. The 29th Massachusetts moved off to the left, found themselves with the regulars of Lt. Col. Robert C. Buchanan's brigade, and stayed with them for the rest of the night.

Meanwhile, the 69th and 88th had encountered the enemy at the foot of the hill. Francis A. Walker, the historian of the Second Corps, had no love for Meagher and little for the Irish Brigade. Still, he described their action as follows:

> Anyone who has ever been in action, knows how easy it is to recognize the firing of fresh troops; and the writer has never forgotten the outburst which announced that the Irishmen had opened upon the Confederate column, now half way up the slope. As soon as the Sixty-ninth had exhausted its ammunition, the Eighty-eighth took its place while Nugent's men replenished their boxes. When the Eighty-eighth had in turn exhausted its sixty rounds, the Sixty-

31. *OR*, series 1, vol. 11, pt. 2, p. 73.

ninth was again moved to the front. Scarcely had it relieved its comrade, when Nugent discovered that a daring body of the enemy had mounted the hill and was bearing down on his flank. Changing front with his left companies, and sending back orders which brought Quinlan with the Eighty-eighth up on the left of the Sixty-ninth, Nugent charged with both regiments, and met the enemy in a hand to hand encounter, which speedily resulted in the complete overthrow of the attacking force, and the capture of Lieutenant-Colonel [Eugene] Waggaman, commanding the Tenth Louisiana.[32]

The 10th Louisiana was of Semmes' brigade which had been summoned to the battle at about the same time as the Irish Brigade. In his report, General Semmes spoke of charging up the slope and encountering

> . . . the terrible fire poured by the enemy in our front, caused the line to waver and finally to break, the men seeking partial shelter behind a number of farmhouses. . . . Our line approached that of the enemy diagonally, thereby throwing the Tenth Louisiana, which was on the right, farther in advance. The dead of this regiment were commingled with those of the enemy and very near his guns. It was here that the last was seen of the gallant Lieutenant-Colonel Waggaman, while heading his regiment, who it is supposed was wounded and taken prisoner. Dead bodies of our own men and those of the enemy were found in close proximity at and near those houses.[33]

The darkness was well on when the hatless and spent Nugent found his brigadier. The 69th and 88th could not maintain this position much longer, he said. Their ammunition was exhausted, and the muskets were so fouled from use they were no longer to be serviceable. Meagher should procure some relief until the weapons cooled and their

32. Walker, *History of the Second Army Corps*, p. 83.
33. *OR*, series 1, vol. 11, pt. 2, p. 724.

pouches were refilled. Meagher rode as fast as he could to Sumner's headquarters and got the old man to agree to a withdrawal from the presence of the enemy if all firing had stopped. At about 9 p.m., both regiments withdrew to the top of the hill and sank down exhausted. One sergeant, Francis Haggerty of the 69th, killed in action, was singled out by Meagher; his older brother, Lt. Col. James Haggerty, had been the first casualty of the 69th NYSM at First Manassas.

Meagher's battle reports are rather curious documents. There are two to cover the contests on the Peninsula. The first, written on July 2 is about Malvern Hill alone. The other, dated July 6, deals with the brigade's actions at Gaines' Mill and White Oak Swamp. He mentions being under arrest from 4 p.m. June 29 to 8 a.m. June 30 and refers to a report that Nugent will prepare to cover this period. There is no such report. Meagher also says that he will write another report on the brigade's actions at Glendale, but did not. Throughout, there is no assertion on his part that he exercised tactical control of the brigade in battle. The regiments had all done well, but they had been fought by their colonels or whoever else was in charge. Meagher's function had been to show himself in dangerous places, and encourage his soldiers by his example. In this role he seems to have displayed a high order of courage.

The field at Malvern Hill was a melancholy sight to both Union and Confederate and nightfall did not diminish the horror. Poor, shattered men lay thickly there, screaming and moaning, and little could be done for them. The fighting had continued to darkness and no one knew certainly if it had ended. At last by midnight the soldiers who had spent themselves passed into exhausted sleep. The Peninsula Campaign was over, and Richmond's approaches from the east would not be threatened for another two years.

The casualties for the Seven Days were enormous considering what had gone before. The Confederate casualties totaled around 20,000 men, or about twenty-five percent of the largest effective force Lee was ever to bring to battle. The Union loss was lighter both numerically and percentage-wise, but in the peculiar framework of McClellan's relationship with the administration, anything short of the occupation of Richmond meant failure. In the very midst of the terrible Seven Days the authorities at Washington had created a new army under a general of their own choosing to undertake an approach on Richmond in keeping with their own ideas. A more resounding repudiation of George Mc-Clellan and his strategical concepts would be hard to find. The nucleus of the new army would be the First Corps of Irvin McDowell, the body of troops withheld so long from the Army of the Potomac.

CHAPTER SIX
SUMMER INTERLUDE

The new position selected by McClellan to encamp his troops for rest and refit consisted of a strip of land on the north bank of the James River, five miles long and protected by a swamp on the northeast border. Except for along the river the land was covered by a dense pine forest, and was vulnerable to artillery fire from an inland ridge known as Evelington Heights. The famous Confederate cavalryman, Jeb Stuart, discovered this on the night of July 2, and next morning he moved up a single piece of artillery to shell the Union camp. Had he been content to occupy the ridge until reinforced by infantry, the Federals might have been placed in an uncomfortable position. As it was, a Union infantry force came out and drove the gray horsemen off by 2 p.m. Lee looked the Union position over and concluded that it could not be attacked with advantage. The Peninsular Campaign was over and the Confederates withdrew from the proximity of the Union camp closer to Richmond.

After the growling bellies of the Federal fighting men were filled and some attempt was made to restore order, the Army of the Potomac looked about to see who had survived the preceding week and who had not. The badly wounded were loaded on transports to return to Washington and other hospitals in the North. The lightly wounded were treated in field hospitals. The army had lost a large number of men who were either prisoners or missing; over 6,000 were in this category, about forty percent of the total Union casualties for the period. The marches undertaken, while not long, for the most part had been at night. Men would drop out with fatigue, lose their organization, their bearings, and end up in Libby prison in Richmond. Others were in isolated detachments posted at an obscure ford or roadblock forgotten by harried staff officers. There must have been many adventures among those bypassed by the Confederates while hiding out in the forbidding fastnesses of White Oak Swamp. Some made it back to the Union lines.

Among the many swept up by the Confederate net was Father Thomas Scully, chaplain of the 9th Massachusetts. He was busy tending the wounded at Gaines' Mill, kneeling down beside the dying to hear confessions which came out sometimes around blood-flecked bubbles. When the regiment fell back he was too busy to notice. The next thing he knew some particularly shaggy Confederate soldiers had leveled their weapons at him. MacNamara was amazed at the treatment accorded him.

He declared to his captors who and what he was, and being unarmed and a non-combatant, expected to be allowed to attend to the wounded; but, strange to relate, he was arrested and placed under a guard of soldiers. This unaccountable proceeding of arresting a Catholic chaplain while in the discharge of his office amongst hundreds of wounded men of the same faith, and placing a guard directly over him, can only be accounted for from the fact that it was instigated through narrow-minded Southern prejudice or from a lack of Christian education on the part of his captors.

Finding no mercy at the hands of his enemies, Father Scully resolved to gain his freedom at the first opportunity or perish in the attempt. . . . As the sentinel soon fell asleep the chaplain suggested to a few of the prisoners near him that they quietly crawl away and make their escape. His suggestion was acted upon, and they were not long in reaching the shadows of the woods in the swamps of the Chickahominy. They had barely entered the cover of the woods when they were missed, and the alarm given; at once the sentinels went in pursuit of them.

As Father Scully and his companions broke through the woods they made considerable noise; this brought on the fire of the pursuers, and the bullets whistled quite freely over the heads of the fleeing prisoners. . . . In wading through the river, which was quite low at this time, they lost their boots and shoes in the mud,

160

and of course, were obliged to continue in their stocking feet. They were fortunate in not running up against the enemy, and in coming up with the Union army, where they were soon enabled to join their regiments.

At Savage Station, Father Scully had the misfortune to fall into the enemy's clutches a second time. His capture was somewhat similar to his first experience, that is, he was attending to the wounded, and unaware of his proximity to the foe. He was, if anything, treated more harshly than when first taken. While in their hands he witnessed some brutal treatment of our wounded men by the Southern guard, and at once remonstrated against it in a vigorous manner. A Confederate officer present ordered him away, and in an angry manner told him it was none of his business, but Father Scully insisted that it was his affair, and that he would not stand by and see wounded Union soldiers brutally treated without attempting to prevent it. . . . he was hurried off to Richmond with other prisoners under guard.[1]

At Richmond, however, the chaplain found the kind of forbearance in the provost marshal that was lacking in the rude men who had captured him. He was given the run of the city, being required only to report once a day. But his health failed and he was stricken with fever. A parish priest of the city took him in and nursed him back to health. When fully recovered he was unconditionally released and returned to his home in Boston. Never again was he in good enough health to serve with the regiment.

The chaplain was not the only one the 9th never saw again. Colonel Cass had been badly wounded in the face at Malvern Hill and was placed on ship to be taken to the hospitals in Washington. From there he was passed along to Boston in a greatly weakened condition. He was unable to swallow because of the condition of his mouth and the hot weather on the trip complicated his condition. Death finally released him from his sufferings on July 12. Tom Cass, who

1. MacNamara, *Ninth Massachusetts*, pp. 166-67.

had endured the slings and arrows of the Know-Nothings in 1855 when they disbanded his militia company, gained a victory over his tormentors to which there could be no rebuttal.

Lieutenant Colonel Guiney and Major Hanley were in hospital in Washington, leaving Capt. Timothy O'Leary as the senior officer in command. In all, the 9th Massachusetts had lost 421 men killed and wounded during the eventful week, the heaviest loss in the Fifth Corps. In the Second Corps the Irish Brigade had lost nearly 500 men and the 69th Pennsylvania, which had performed so well at Glendale, lost almost 100 as had the 37th New York in the Third Corps.

On the Fourth of July there was a review of the army for McClellan and national salutes were fired. There was also some slight skirmishing around the perimeter of the position. A notable addition had arrived for the Second Corps, in the brigade commanded by Brig. Gen. Nathan Kimball. Until recently it had seen hard service in the Shenandoah Valley in the division commanded by Brig. Gen. James Shields. One of Kimball's regiments, the 8th Ohio, had an Irish company, the Hibernian Guards of Cleveland. Its second sergeant was a sixteen-year-old warrior by the name of Thomas Galwey. It is important to note his arrival on the scene for he was one of the most indefatigable chroniclers of the Irish in the Army of the Potomac.

The 8th Ohio was one of the unlucky ones sent out to do the skirmishing while the rest of the army took part in the Fourth of July review. They got to see McClellan after the review when he rode out to see how they were doing with the enemy. The general seemed light-hearted, Galwey thought, but earlier his eyes had moistened at the sight of decimated regiments like the 9th Massachusetts as they marched past under the command of a captain with sergeants commanding companies, a command structure resulting from fearfully high casualties among the officers. Before any more adventures could be planned, the army would need some replacements.

Meagher was among the first to ask leave to return to New York to seek more men. On July 16 he was given permission "to proceed on recruiting service for the regiments of his brigade under the special instructions of General Sumner." Further, McClellan said, "The general commanding relies upon General Meagher to use his utmost exertions to hasten the filling up of his regiments and to rejoin his command at the earliest possible moment." So Meagher left the army to return to New York and his wife. This return was much different than his return from First Manassas when he had been under the stigma cast upon him by Russell of the London *Times*. Now Meagher was coming home as the commander of the best-known brigade in the army. The press of the city had become almost lyrical in their descriptions of the actions of the brigade, and it was evident that he would go home to a hero's welcome.

Most of the other senior officers of the brigade stayed on at Harrison's Landing. The 69th New York was in the best shape for leadership with Kelly and Nugent and the worst for manpower, being down to about 250 men. The 63rd New York was in poor shape for leaders, Colonel Burke being in the hospital with a bad wound, and Fowler still with the bad conduct at Malvern Hill hanging over his head. The days of Col. Henry Baker with the 88th New York were numbered also, although he was not dismissed from the service until September. Fortunately, Patrick Kelly was in good health again, and he was as good an officer as there was in the Second Corps. Both the 63rd and 88th had about 500 men apiece. The 29th Massachusetts was the largest regiment in the brigade and feeling more of a kinship with the others all the while. Although the New Englanders had been left behind on the field at Malvern Hill through no one's fault in particular, they had rejoined the brigade the next day at the landing with no untoward result. Meagher and the other officers were glad to see them, said Osborne:

> When the 29th rejoined the Brigade . . . they were highly complimented by General Meagher for their action in remaining, who addressed them in the presence of the whole brigade. The General was an orator of rare ability, and in this speech . . . he took occasion to say some very clever things of the regiment. . . . He told the soldiers of the 29th that they had proved themselves the equals of any others in the Brigade, and had no superiors in the Army . . . as sons of the Pilgrims and Puritans, and natives of the fair land he was glad to call his adopted country, they had shown

163

themselves worthy of their . . . heritage. Although these glowing compliments were duly appreciated, yet they did not cause the soldiers to forget their sufferings. . . . While he was speaking, certain soldiers of the regiment abstracted from his tent nearly all the whiskey he possessed.[2]

Col. Ebenezer Pierce of the 29th, who had lost an arm at the defence of the crossing of White Oak Swamp, heard about Meagher's speech, and from the hospital wrote a letter to Governor John Andrew of Massachusetts, saying,

During this period, five months, the regiment has added to its reputation by the mere fact of its being connected with the Irish Brigade; and it has been our endeavor that the brigade should not by our acts lose any of their already acquired reputation. And, in this connection, I trust I may be excused for alluding to remarks made to the regiment, by the general commanding the brigade, upon its arrival at Harrison's Landing after the terrible seven days preceding. The general said to the whole regiment, "The Twenty-ninth Massachusetts has been tried, and, I am proud to be able to say, has proved itself an honor to the Irish Brigade and to the country." This is nearly his precise language, and it was the proudest moment the regiment had seen. Since that time, the general has not, to my knowledge, revoked his decision.[3]

It will be recalled that the 29th contained men whose antecedents went all the way back to the Bay colony. These were the same men whose fathers had burned down the Charlestown convent in 1834 and who had refused to parade with the Montgomery Guards in 1837. Now in the day of blood and fire the Irish had a brilliant and noble revenge.

After a few days the routine of camp life settled down on the army, but the soldiers found it different than back in the

2. Osborne, *Twenty-ninth Massachusetts*, p. 166.
3. Phineas C. Headley, *Massachusetts in the Rebellion* (Boston: Walker, Fuller, and Company, 1866), p. 326-27.

old days at Camp California. After combat it was hard to endure the make-work of the periods between battles. The army thought long and hard about its past, present, and future. They had not captured the city of Richmond and, for the life of them, they could not figure what had gone wrong. Their artillery had been magnificent. They knew themselves which infantry regiments had fought and which had broken. They had fought five defensive battles and had seen the Confederates pile up their dead like cordwood. There was all this, but still they were twenty miles further from Richmond.

Meagher lost no time in going to New York, and, on his arrival, contacted the prominent citizens who had backed him the year before in the brigade's organization. A large meeting of the New York Irish was scheduled for the night of July 25 at the 7th Regiment Armory with, of course, Meagher as the chief speaker. The hall was the largest in the city, but long before the appearance of the general, every space was filled and hundreds stood in the street outside. The *Times* reporter estimated the crowd to be at about 5,000. Two platforms had been erected, one on each side of the room, on the hottest night of the summer.

When Meagher entered the hall there was the wildest enthusiasm the *Times*' man ever saw. Meagher tried to keep it short. What was needed quickly and spontaneously, he said, was manpower. It was up to the Irish to fill up the ranks of the brigade. After all, it was *their* brigade. The Irish had made a contract with the United States to keep those Green Flag regiments manned.[4] However, Meagher was cognizant that some of his enemies among the Irish of New York had circulated some very damaging rumors about the brigade and its commander. Young and brawny Irishmen were told that "extra risk was to be encountered in this command—it being notorious that the Irish Brigade was assigned more than the average share of hard fighting." According to the rumor, this was due to Meagher's desire for personal aggrandizement which led to the needless exposure of his men.[5]

4. *New York Times*, July 26, 1862.
5. Cavanagh, *Memoirs of Thomas Meagher*, p. 452.

There was only one way to meet that kind of criticism and that was head-on. Of course it was true, said Meagher, that the Irish Brigade did more fighting than most of the others, and in doing so it had won ungrudging admiration from the entire country. He quoted a Confederate general as saying during one of the battles on the Peninsula, "Here comes that damned Green Flag again!" Never had Irish military prowess enjoyed such a flowering as now. To continue the good work more soldiers were necessary. Nugent's 69th was down to less than 300 effectives. "I ask for recruits," said Meagher in conclusion, "I ask for them alone!" "We will, we will," shouted back the crowd, and the green handkerchiefs fluttered. One overenthusiastic man roared in a quiet eddy in the bellowing, "You shall have all you want!" Meagher replied quickly, "Shall I have you? Suppose you come forward and give your name and address!" The voice subsided and the man was quickly lost in the crowd. Then a heckler of a different sort arose. "Why don't the black Republicans go to the war?" The crowd was somewhat discomfited by the first man's action which seemed at variance with the purpose of the meeting. So the second one was hissed and groaned out of countenance, although when they were on the way home, the same thought would occur to many of them.[6]

Meagher wound up the meeting by reading a letter from Capt. John Donovan of the 69th who had been taken prisoner on the Peninsula. Donovan had led his company in the night action at Malvern Hill when Semmes' brigade was encountered and lost an eye, falling behind the fight with what was thought a mortal wound. When Confederate General A. P. Hill had visited the wounded prisoners a few days later, he had remarked on Donovan's missing sword with the observation that the captain would never need it again, his fighting days being over. To this Donovan had retorted, "I have one eye yet to risk for the Union—and when that, too, goes—then—*I'll go it blind.*" This was just the right touch to end the meeting on, and the crowd left in good humor.[7]

But recruitment was slow. The lengthy casualty lists were giving many a good lad pause, and volunteering had fallen off

6. *New York Irish-American*, August 2, 1862.
7. Cavanagh, *Memoirs of Thomas Meagher*, pp. 456-57.

almost to the vanishing point. Now the mistake of Stanton's closing down the recruiting efforts back in the spring was seen for the major blunder that it was. States and cities would have to get together cash money and buy the blood from poor men which those in better circumstances refused to give. In this kind of war Meagher found some willing allies. The members of the New York Corn Exchange by personal subscription got up a fund to pay $10 to the first 300 volunteers for the Irish Brigade. This would be in addition to any federal, state, or city bounty which was offered.

Actually few men were enlisted for the brigade because Meagher was operating at the wrong time and in the wrong place. There had been on July 2 a call for 300,000 recruits for three years, with prominent Republican spokesmen asserting that the Peninsular Campaign was a failure, and that a new tack would be needed. This was a dash of cold water in the face of a nation which had been reading glowing reports of the brilliant successes of the army near Richmond in the newspapers. But most damaging for Meagher was the reconstituting of the 69th New York State Militia, the regiment that Corcoran had led at First Manassas in the ninety-day service. A youthful colonel, twenty-two-year-old Matthew Murphy, was the new commander. He was active in the Fenian Brotherhood, and in a position to sway many men who might have gone to the brigade. In any case this new formation had volunteered their services for three months on May 26. Meagher's biographer, Cavanagh, said these men were "the very element that would have most promptly responded to Meagher's call—had it been first made."

So there was a sad situation from Meagher's viewpoint. In the end it developed that only 120 new recruits would join the brigade to fill up the gaps. The general did not rush right back to the Peninsula as soon as he saw that little would be gained by his staying in New York. There was his future career to be considered. As a result of the indefatigable attention paid to the brigade by the New York press, he was more of a celebrity than ever and was accepted in the best circles. There were interviews to be given, plans for his memoirs to be discussed with his agents, and, finally, his beautiful wife to be attended to and loved. He got back to the job on August 8, back with the hard men of war, the soldiers who could not conceive of clean napery and sparkling silver-ware at Delmonico's restaurant or the bare-shouldered women at the posh receptions. Yet it was on the shoulders and bodies of the privates that he had mounted to such social and political heights.

The 22nd of August was, said the *New York Times*,

> . . . a grand day for the Irish residents of this City, a grander one for Michael Corcoran, and one pregnant with trouble for the gentlemen of the C.S.A. . . . It would be worse than idle, it would be presumptuous, for us to attempt a description of the appearance of the City, the enthusiasm of the people, and the wholeheartedness of the welcome extended to the City's guest. For the benefit of those who were here; and as for those who were not here, we can say to them simply that on no previous occasion has the City of New York tendered to an individual, be he President or Prince, such an apparently heartfelt ovation, such an outpouring of its people, such a rousing, unstinted, undiluted specimen of enthusiastic greeting.[8]

The city's guest was none other than that Michael Corcoran whose conduct had enlivened the last occasion when New York had welcomed a distinguished visitor, the Prince of Wales. Freed from a Confederate prison at last, the colonel of the 69th New York State Militia had gone to Washington first to report to the War Department. The tall, lean colonel was completely surprised by the warmth of his welcome. Everywhere in the nation's capital he was the lion of the day. His old regiment had signed on for another ninety days and was pulling duty in the city's defences at the time. The regiment marched over the Long Bridge to serenade Corcoran at Willard's Hotel, and he was continually inundated by callers and public processions. Congress approved his elevation to brigadier general to date from his capture at First Manassas. In short, everyone turned themselves inside out to make amends for the year that Corcoran spent in captivity, and he deserved it all.

8. *New York Times*, August 23, 1862.

Many American soldiers had to endure captivity. If any were looking for a model for uncompromising behavior, it would be Corcoran. He refused to give any parole in Richmond because he felt it would be a bad example. Many stories circulated about the harsh treatment he was undergoing, and in the North much public opinion was whipped up in the category of "atrocity stories." It was said that Corcoran was festooned with chains and held in solitary confinement. Had he wished he could have reaped a harvest of sympathy simply by remaining silent. But he showed a capacity for integrity by getting out word that the chains story had not a word of truth in it. There were, however, periods of solitary confinement and a particularly harrowing experience in the first autumn of the war.

The Confederate privateer *Enchantress* had been captured by the Federal navy, and the administration had decided to hang the officers and crew as pirates. The government at Richmond replied that if this were done, an equal number of Union officers drawn from the prisoners of war would also dangle on the gallows. Corcoran was one of those selected, and, for a while, it looked as though the matter would go through. Secretary of State Seward looked around frantically for a face-saving way out. He finally found it when Judge Charles Daly published a legal brief which said that there were ample grounds to hold that the privateers were prisoners of war, and so Corcoran did not hang.

It was Corcoran's conduct while in this extremely grave position that gave full credit to all the copy-book maxims ever written. In effect, he said that he was ready to die rather than compromise the Federal government's position. Whatever the wise men in Washington decided to do with the men of the *Enchantress* would be perfectly all right with Michael Corcoran. At least that is what people said of him and it was, apparently, true. Even the Confederates who held Corcoran were impressed. He persevered for fourteen months, some of which were in Charleston, South Carolina. The soldiers who guarded him were drawn from the Irish Volunteers of that city.

Now he was home again in New York, and if anything is needed to show that he was a man of integrity, it is his conduct during the interminable receptions with which he was assaulted on the way from Washington. He had to stay overnight

169

in Baltimore and Philadelphia, and at every whistle-stop the train was halted and Corcoran had to make a speech from the platform of the rear car. Immense throngs were on hand everywhere, and, had elections been in the offing, the new brigadier would have been a strong candidate.

There were men in America at that time who would have no compunction at all in arranging such a scenario, but Corcoran said that he was only interested in raising a new brigade to take the field and do something about ending the rebellion. He had refused a municipal post with the city and also the formal reception which the authorities extended. Over and over he repeated the same story on that 22nd day of August, at Trenton, New Brunswick, Princeton, Rahway, Elizabeth, Newark, and Jersey City.

> The time for speaking is past. I am now going to work. I want to get some soldiers and go at the work and duty of every citizen. I have seen some trouble, but I forget it all—it's nothing. I can, when the war is over, forget all that the rebels ever did to me, but I can never forget the insult offered to our flag until it is wiped out in their blood. I am pleased to see this enthusiasm and these warm manifestations. I know they are not intended to do me honor for anything that I have done. It is intended to prove the devotion of the people to the Constitution and the laws which I have endeavored in part to sustain. I am not going to cater to public opinion or to participate in public ovations, but to do my part in sustaining the Government. . . .[9]

There were some echoes of the Prince of Wales' visit in the homecoming. The *Times* assigned reporters to join the party before it left Washington to report on every scrap of news as it had done for the Prince. Michael Corcoran came back in triumph with the star of a brigadier on his shoulder, and, apparently, a burning passion that he had merited it. His new brigade would have to be recruited by himself, and he was shrewd enough to know that he must capitalize on this new wave of enthusiasm. He went back to Washington the

9. *Ibid.*

next day to bring back the 69th NYSM whose three-months enlistment period had expired. This regiment would be the hard core around which the new brigade would form. There were other promising developments. When he had passed through Philadelphia, a colonel of infantry, Dennis Heenan, had approached Corcoran with the following:

> General, I am Dennis Heenan of the 116th Pennsylvania. You remember that yesterday I told you that my regiment is nearly full, and that if it was consistent with propriety we would like to be one of your new brigade. We have received permission from the Governor to do so, and I formally tender you the services of the 116th.[10]

Corcoran was happy to accept Heenan's offer, and the news that Governor Andrew Curtin of Pennsylvania was willing to approve one of his regiments serving with New Yorkers was a surprise; Curtin had rebuffed Meagher in 1861. But the war had moved on, and higher organizations would no longer be composed of men from the same state.

There were some regiments in New York with which to start the brigade formation. There was certainly the 69th NYSM which Corcoran brought back from Washington with him. It was released earlier than its term of service with the stipulation that it would re-enlist for the Corcoran Legion. But again, as after First Manassas, there was some contention, and again the 69th NYSM did not volunteer completely. Instead, a new volunteer regiment, the 69th New York National Guard Artillery was formed from those willing to go off with Corcoran. Later it would be renumbered the 182nd New York Volunteers.

In western New York three brothers named McMahon, Martin, John, and James were doing about as much for the war effort as anyone could desire. Martin was a captain on McClellan's staff and James was an aide to Maj. Gen. Israel B. Richardson of First Divison, Second Corps. John used his clout as private secretary to Governor Horatio Seymour to garner a colonel's commission to raise a regiment. The Irish of the

10. *Ibid.*

western part of the state had decided that they should have a regiment of their own. Bishop John Timon of Buffalo backed the project, and in three weeks time John McMahon had 400 men enlisted. The new regiment was numbered the 155th, and fit right in with Corcoran's Legion. There was to be some heartbreak for the Buffalo lads.

In October 1862 the Corcoran Legion was forming at Camp Scott on Staten Island. Here were gathered a host of men, companies recruited from all over the Empire State by many earnest fellows who aspired to wear the bars of captain. Once arrived at Camp Scott, however, it developed that the authorities were not going to commission anyone who did not have the requisite number of recruits in tow. The upshot must have been a nightmare for Corcoran. The enthusiasm with which he had been greeted in August led to expectations which could not be realized. He had hoped to enroll eight regiments, two of which would be from out of state. The 116th Pennsylvania was rushed to Washington after Second Manassas in the resulting panic and was lost to the Legion. The 55th Massachusetts had recruiting difficulties. In the early days of September 1862 Camp Scott looked like a shambles as companies were broken up, consolidated, and made over with new and strange officers. There was much animosity, and fights continually broke out. On at least one occasion the 7th NYSM, which had not left its armory for more active service since the previous spring, had to be sent to maintain order.

Under the circumstances, Corcoran had to deal through others and the results were seldom happy. Men deserted in wholesale lots from Staten Island, and in the end Corcoran had to be satisfied with four regiments: the 155th New York, commanded by Col. William McEvily; the 164th New York under Col. John McMahon; the 170th New York under Col. Peter McDermott; and the 69th New York National Guard Artillery (later known as the 182nd) under Col. Matthew Murphy. Three of these colonels were good men. McDermott was a drunk and a troublemaker and a trial for Corcoran who eventually ordered McDermott to resign about four months later.

Corcoran made a trip to Albany to see the governor in September and made a stirring speech in Poughkeepsie.

172

After that he was able to turn his attention to training his new command. The Legion left New York on November 8 for Washington where they spent some time garrisoned at Fort Slocum. By the end of the month they had been sent to Newport News, Virginia. From here Corcoran unburdened himself to his old friend Judge Daly on the trial of having to deal with one's friends in a military way.

> . . . the work of consolidation was a disagreeable duty, inasmuch as some officers were rendered supernumerary, amongst whom are some of my best friends and good and efficient. Yet as they had not recruited the number of men required by law. . . . We celebrated yesterday (Thanksgiving) as best we could. . . . Divine Service at 10 AM and Father Dillon delivered a very eloquent discourse. The health of the command is very good, very few men in hospital.[11]

A month later the inaction of a quiet sector was beginning to get to him.

> . . . I must acknowledge that I am not as full of hope and confidence as to the probable ultimate results of this most unhappy conflict as when I last saw you. Perhaps I may be unnecessarily dispirited by the results of the late battles and the anticipated result of the Proclamation [of Emancipation]. I intend my course to be the same now as at the commencement of the war; using my best endeavors to discharge my duty that hereafter I may have the consolation of having acted to the fullest extent of my ability.
>
> The Irish Legion is now everything its most ardent friends could desire, and I am fully confident that when the great hour of trial arrives they will do honor to their race and their name. The 155th and 164th were absent for three days during last week on reconnaissance. They acted extremely well and returned Saturday night without loss, bringing a few prisoners. I have got Colonel McDermott of the

11. Charles Daly collection.

170th off my hands. There have been four charges against him for drunkenness on duty on four different occasions. He was under arrest and offered his resignation which I recommended for approval. . . . I find Father Dillon a most excellent priest, a good friend, and an agreeable companion. . . .[12]

In the amalgamation, Corcoran had transferred all but two companies of the 155th, plus the two McMahon brothers, Col. John McMahon and Lt. Col. James McMahon, to the 164th. John McMahon was in command. This did not sit well with the Buffalonians who held it against John McMahon. When the legion was sent to Newport News, Col. McMahon contracted the "quick consumption." Sgt. George Tipping wrote to his wife,

You say Col. John McMahon is on his last legs. Well, he could not expect much better luck, the way he used the Buffalo boys. It is a curse for not doing as he represented to do.[13]

John McMahon breathed his last on March 11, 1863, and had the largest funeral seen in Buffalo. His brother James was appointed to succeed him on March 23, 1863.

12. *Ibid.*
13. Sgt. George Tipping to his wife, reprinted in *The Famous Long Ago*, The Buffalo and Erie County Historical Society and the Buffalo Civil War Round Table, n.d.

CHAPTER SEVEN

THE HARVEST IN MARYLAND

The Army of the Potomac did not wax fat along the James River. Most men agreed that it was better than being shot at, but all could think of happier and healthier places for a camp. Diarrhea was prevalent and even scurvy was reported. Also the heat and humidity of the river valley enclosed the locale and flies swarmed in great abundance.

With no present prospects for combat, time hung heavily on the hands of the blooded warriors, and their thoughts turned with increasing frequency to home. There was no organized system for granting furloughs, and the sick and diseased from Harrison's Landing got only as far as Washington City. The more daring might go home from there when they had recovered, but at the risk of stiff jail sentences. In late July a Confederate artillery force moved under cover of night into an area on the south bank of the river and shelled the camp with much noise and little harm. The Union soldiers thought this a particularly reprehensible form of warfare. On the next day an infantry force crossed over and cleared the area.

Actually, the destiny of this army was now removed from the hands of its commander and placed in those of the new Union commander-in-chief, Maj. Gen. Henry W. Halleck. Halleck had come down to the camp on July 25 to discuss the future of the Peninsular approach. McClellan wanted to move on Richmond again, but this time the movement would be tied to the James River instead of the York. He also had ideas of going up the south side of the river to capture Petersburg and shut off the supply lines of the capital. It was not to be. When Halleck returned to Washington, he turned to one of the offensive-minded, Western "fighting" generals who had dealt out mighty blows to the Confederacy in the valley of the Mississippi. Maj. Gen. John Pope assembled three army corps into what was called the Army of Virginia in the region east of the Blue Ridge and directed it at the country around Gordonsville, Virginia.

Pope said that he had been told to threaten this region through which ran the Virginia Central Railroad so as to draw off Confederate troops from Richmond.[1] Then McClellan could resume his offensive operations against the capital. It was a sound scheme and only required some collaboration in timing and execution. Certainly all of McClellan's correspondence in July indicates that he waited only for positive orders and some reinforcements to move along the James. But when he received the orders to move, the direction was not towards Richmond and the Army of Northern Virginia, but to the ships that would take his army away from the Peninsula and bring them to other battlefields in Northern Virginia and Maryland. Not until two more springtimes had passed would the Army of the Potomac again see the eastern approaches to Richmond.

The Second Corps embarked on August 26 and sailed for Aquia Creek, to disembark and march up the Rappahannock River to the support of John Pope and the Army of Virginia who were having their hands full with some very active Confederates. Lee had been freed from the defence of Richmond by the withdrawal of the Army of the Potomac, and now he was making strenuous efforts to "suppress" the mouthy General Pope. Meagher's brigade went ashore at Aquia and marched overland to Falmouth on the north bank of the Rappahannock across from the lovely Georgian town of Fredericksburg. Maj. Gen. Ambrose Burnside, who was in command there, did not know what to do with them and wired Halleck in Washington:

> Meagher's brigade is here, and I have ordered it down to Aquia Creek to re-embark, in compliance with an order from General [Edwin V.] Sumner.

In a second telegraph that day Burnside asked Halleck,

> Shall I re-embark Meagher's brigade for Alexandria or shall it remain at Aquia?

1. John Pope, "The Second Battle of Bull Run," in *Battles and Leaders*, 2:449.

To which Halleck replied,

> . . . send Meagher's brigade [to Alexandria].[2]

There was a good reason for the switch. On that morning Pope's army was in the final phase of the movements which were to end in the Second Battle of Manassas. Here this "fighting" general from the West found out what it was like to be up against the Lee-Jackson command team on a good day. Perhaps Halleck knew even before battle was joined that Pope would be beaten and that the Second Corps would be needed in front of Washington to fend off the victorious Confederates. The Irish wearily climbed back aboard ship and settled themselves for a trip up the Potomac. They disembarked at Alexandria and marched out the ten miles to the old camp site at Camp California. The historian of the 29th Massachusetts evidently thought himself enough of an Irishman by this time to pen the following incident:

> The Irish Brigade, in moving along the road with its tattered flags, the clothing of its men being almost as ragged as its banners, had occasion to pass the camp of a recently-mustered Pennsylvania regiment. The great contrast between the bright, new uniforms of the Pennsylvania troops and the shabby ones of the war-worn Brigade, led to much bantering, and many severe things were said by both sides. Finally, a soldier of the Pennsylvania regiment, with stenatorian [sic] voice and in a triumphant manner, bawled out, "What have you done with your knapsacks; Thrown 'em away, haint you?" . . . Very promptly . . . one of the soldiers of the Twenty-ninth replied, "Thrown 'em away? Yes, —— you, we've thrown away four sets!"[3]

There was a great uproar in the War Department across the river in Washington while the brigade was unloading in Alexandria. The Sixth Corps under Brig. Gen. William B.

2. *OR*, series 1, vol. 12, pt. 3, pp. 714-15.
3. Osborne, *Twenty-ninth Massachusetts*, p. 174.

Franklin had arrived before Sumner, and Halleck had fought a battle within himself as to where he should send these troops into the mystery that was surrounding the whereabouts of John Pope's Army of Virginia. Both corps moved out finally on August 29, and Maj. Gen. John Sedgwick's division of Sumner's corps was engaged at Chantilly on September 1. Then the Army of the Potomac retired into the fortifications about Washington. On the next day the Second Corps crossed the Chain Bridge to Tenallytown and stayed there for three days while the president and cabinet staged a power struggle to see who would command the army in its next trial of strength with Lee. In the end, McClellan was placed in command but under such nebulous orders that almost anything could be drawn from them.

The Confederates crossed the Potomac into Maryland at Cheek's Ford and White's Ford and concentrated around the town of Frederick from which grew the legend of Barbara Frietchie and Stonewall Jackson. Lee's army had a golden opportunity before it. Here, after the successful defence of Richmond against McClellan and the heady outmaneuvering of Pope, the Army of Northern Virginia was riding an incredible tide of success. This was the real high tide of the Confederacy. From Frederick there were several options. They could continue in the western approach to Washington until the Union army commander, whoever he might be, came out from the capital's defences and made his move. There would be a big battle which the Confederates could win, along with the war itself. Or they could move up the Cumberland Valley from Hagerstown to Harrisburg, directly into the Northern heartland. Or, perhaps, by skillful maneuvering, they could make the Union army commander uncover Washington. Then with a quick dash the military and political objectives for which all these tattered, disheveled, gallant Confederates marched and fought could be realized. There seemed to be nothing beyond their grasp.

On the other side, the administration must have felt itself in considerable disarray. A general of their own choosing had just been discomfited after some ringing declarations about seeing the backsides of the enemy, and making empty promises of incipient victory that were found to be arrant nonsense. Lincoln then tried to find another general for the army. In the end, to the president's considerable discomfiture, he had to turn to McClellan.

The controversy as to whether or not McClellan was restored to command is of great interest. Stephen Sears, McClellan's present-day detractor, says that he was never removed from command of the Army of the Potomac, and his later claim that he fought the Maryland campaign without status was sheer theater. Rather than McClellan being removed from the Army of the Potomac, the army was removed from him and passed on to John Pope. So McClellan was still the commander of the army, even though it only numbered a corporal's guard. But orders to the various commands involved had been necessary to convey McClellan's divisions to Pope so that they could take part in the Second Manassas campaign. There never was a reverse mechanism. Instead, there was a clumsy charade where the president and the secretary of war avoided contamination with McClellan by having their names removed from the order.

> War Department, Adjutant-General's Office,
> Washington, September 2, 1862.
> Major-General McClellan will have command of the fortifications of Washington and of all the troops for the defense of the capital.
> By order of Major-General Halleck.[4]

Apparently, the president wanted the command picture to be fuzzy. Perhaps he was hoping that some better solution would appear. There is one thing for certain: Lincoln wanted McClellan to reorganize the army, but not to lead it in the field. There is some indication that Lincoln expected Halleck to lead the field army, and equal indication that Halleck shied away from this. The idea of putting Halleck in a position to engage Robert E. Lee on the field of battle seems almost as ludicrous as another of Lincoln's ideas current at that time, of giving the command to Ambrose Burnside. Fortunately for the Union neither of these schemes went forward.

---

4. George B. McClellan, "From the Peninsula to Antietam," *Battles and Leaders*, 2:551.

Although the Confederates were in the ascendant, Lee was not without problems. His supply line stretched all the way back to the farms and factories of Virginia. This supply line would be a great deal safer if it were transferred to the Shenandoah Valley from the east shoulder of the Blue Ridge where it now rested. Only two things prevented the immediate adoption of this route; the Union garrisons at Harpers Ferry and Martinsburg, West Virginia. These troops had to be neutralized before any of the Confederate projects could take place. So Lee divided his forces, assigning to Jackson's corps the task of reducing both points. Lee is on record as saying at this time that McClellan would take quite a period of time to reorganize the Army of the Potomac before taking the field again.

On September 12 Lee's plans seemed to be in a fair way of maturity. He had his headquarters now at Hagerstown, where his men were finding a warmer welcome than they had received at Frederick. D. H. Hill's division was at Boonsborough, Jackson was dealing with the Union garrison at Harpers Ferry, and the cavalry of Jeb Stuart was to the east picketing the passes of the eastern Blue Ridge. At about noon a report came in from Stuart through Hill that an undetermined Union force was advancing on Frederick. Except that part of Burnside's Ninth Corps was involved, little was reported. Even so, this was quite enough to give Lee pause. Could this be the slow, cautious McClellan of the Peninsula? As D. S. Freeman put it, Little Mac was not running true to form. Harpers Ferry had not yet fallen to Jackson, and only after that was in the bag could Lee reunite his scattered army. Suddenly there was Union pressure where it barely seemed possible for it to exist.

It was all true. McClellan had reorganized and revitalized a beaten army in ten days, and pushed his patrols thirty miles outside the target city he must guard at all costs. He had a lot of help in how to conduct his new campaign from the man who had thought that all was lost on September 1, the major general commanding. Halleck devoted the next week to a gale of messages as to how the army should proceed. Not too fast, not too slow, keep the weight on the left wing so that Lee could not interpose between McClellan and the Potomac, but also remember to cover all the road networks. It was a textbook exercise in how to badger a battlefield general from the rear.

The Second Corps followed the Twelfth Corps on the road to Frederick by slow marches. They were at Rockville on September 5 and Seneca Mills on September 9. Then through lush country they moved, through Middlebrook, Clarksburg, and Hyattstown. On September 13 they arrived at Frederick and received a rousing Union welcome from the civil population. It was here that two privates of the 27th Indiana found a pair of cigars wrapped in a general order signed by Robert E. Lee. It pinpointed the location of each of Lee's divisions and was received, first, with unbelief, and then with wide-eyed rapture at McClellan's headquarters. The game was in the Little Napoleon's hands. He had only to penetrate those hazy blue hills ahead of him and gather in the Army of Northern Virginia bit by bit.

Of course the privates of the army, except for those who had found the cigars, knew nothing of this. They only knew that they had received a fine welcome in Frederick, the countryside was beautiful, and everything was going to be all right, now that McClellan was again in command. Meagher rode a new, white horse at the head of the brigade, but he would gladly have exchanged it for some more replacements. Only 120 men had been the fruit of his recruiting trip to New York City. The three New York regiments numbered only 960 men distributed as follows: 63rd, 341 men; 69th, 317 men; 88th, 302 men. The 29th Massachusetts mustered 450 men, and by now was well integrated. The New Englanders did not care too much for Meagher. He probably made too many speeches to suit them, but they got on pretty well with the rank-and-file.

West from the town of Frederick the Catoctin Mountains thrust a green wall into the sky as a portent of the Blue Ridge barriers a little bit farther west. In the van of the army was Ambrose Burnside's Ninth Corps, not long returned from its amphibious campaign along the outer banks of North Carolina. Now they were on the road to Hagerstown, the old National Road, which passed through a notch in South Mountain called Turner's Gap. A mile south a second east-to-west road, the old Sharpsburg Road, passed through a second notch, Fox's Gap, and bent around to join the National Road at the Bolivar Post Office. As has been said Lee had not expected anything of an

181

offensive nature from the Army of the Potomac for many days. At Hagerstown he had expressed his opinion of McClellan to Brig. Gen. John Walker.

> He is an able general but a very cautious one. His enemies among his own people think him too much so. His army is in a very demoralized and chaotic condition, and will not be prepared for offensive operations—or he will not think it so—for three or four weeks. Before that time I hope to be on the Susquehanna.[5]

Even Stonewall Jackson was puzzled by the word that the Federal forces were in the vicinity of Frederick and getting close to his operation at Harpers Ferry. Lee was exercised enough on the morning of September 14 to order back to the South Mountain gaps D. H. Hill's division of infantry to stiffen Stuart's troopers.

There ensued a bitter and sanguine battle at the gaps where the losses on both sides were heavy. Under cover of this battle and another at the more southerly Crampton's Gap Lee concentrated his troops on the south side of Antietam Creek. This would cover Jackson's throttling of the Unionists at Harper's Ferry. McClellan had sent the Sixth Corps of William Franklin against Crampton's Gap which was then held only by Confederate cavalry. If Franklin was successful, Lee's army would be on the brink of disaster. The debouche from Crampton's Gap would bring Franklin into the rear of Lafayette McLaws' division which was looking down on the Union defenders of Harpers Ferry from Maryland Heights. The only way out for McLaws would be to cross over the Potomac to the Virginia side, thus removing him from Lee's attempt to concentrate his army at Antietam Creek. It was all up to Franklin who is usually spoken of as a competent soldier and a friend of McClellan. The events of the next two days would cast some doubt on both assertions.

The Second Corps received some replacements while waiting at Frederick. In particular a nine-month regiment from the vicinity of Scranton, the 132nd Pennsylvania, joined

5. *Ibid.*, p. 606.

Brig. Gen. Nathan Kimball's brigade. Its adjutant, Frederick Hitchcock, looked about him at the bronzed and hardened soldiers of the other divisions. He noted:

> The celebrated Irish brigade, commanded by Brigadier-General Thomas Francis Meagher, was in Richardson's division. They were a "free and easy" going crowd.[6]

A few days later his opinion was to undergo a change. The brigade was absorbing its new replacements and having some command problems. Robert Nugent was on sick leave in New York, and James Kelly was leading the 69th. Col. John Burke, recovered from his Malvern Hill wound, was back in command of the 63rd. Somewhat inexplicably, Lieutenant Colonel Fowler, who had disobeyed Meagher's direct order at Malvern Hill, was still with the regiment. Apparently, Colonel Baker had left the 88th for good although he was not dismissed from the service for another week. Patrick Kelly had taken over the "Connacht Rangers" and he was one of the best. As far as leadership was concerned the three Irish regiments were in good hands. Lieutenant Colonel Barnes of the 29th Massachusetts was also regarded as reliable. For their greatest battle the brigade was ready.

Richardson's division took no part in the forcing of Turner's Gap, but they were the first ones through on the next day, September 15, and marched to Boonsborough. There they turned off the National Road and headed southwest in the direction of the towns of Keedysville and Sharpsburg. Behind the little country stream, Antietam Creek, spanned by some graceful stone-arched bridges, the battle, known to the North as Antietam and to the South as Sharpsburg, was beginning to take shape. Across the creek Lee was taking a position which was presently manned only by Longstreet's corps. It was a long battleline more or less straight in a north-south direction and tied to the Potomac on Lee's left flank and the Antietam on his right. A slight ridge line paralleled

6. Frederick L. Hitchcock, *War From the Inside: The Story of the 132nd Regiment Pennsylvania Volunteer Infantry in the War for the Suppression of the Rebellion, 1862-1863* (Philadelphia: J. B. Lippincott Company, 1904), pp. 38-39.

the Sharpsburg-Hagerstown turnpike. The Confederate artillery was emplaced on this ridge to cover the bridges previously spoken of. As the vanguard of the Second Corps came into sight on the east bank of the stream, the gray artillerymen fired a few ranging shots over their heads. So dawned September 16.

The sight of those three bridges over Antietam Creek, and the knowledge that Lee was there in great force gave McClellan pause. It was not until late afternoon that he had evolved a plan of battle. As usual, he thought he was outnumbered, and hit upon the scheme of attacking strongly on the right where the creek could be crossed by fords not under Confederate artillery dominance. So Hooker took the three divisions of the First Corps off to the north, made a wide swing and splashed through the water of the stream. The Confederates were alive to this maneuver, a clear prediction of where the initial blow would fall. McClellan said that his plan was to strike the extreme left of the Confederate flank with the First and Twelfth Corps, supported by the Second and Sixth Corps. When this blow made headway, the Ninth Corps on the far Union left was to cross the creek and press along the crest of the ridge. In this fashion the Army of Northern Virginia would undergo a massive squeezing action which would cut it off effectively from ever recrossing the Potomac River. If all went as he planned, McClellan could end the war in a single day.

Richardson's division of the Second Corps lay on the east bank of the creek on the right of the Sharpsburg-Keedysville Road with Sedgwick's division directly behind. The Irish Brigade was closest to Antietam Creek, and directly across the road was the brigade commanded by Nathan Kimball, a new formation to the Second Corps.[7] As nightfall came on, the soldiers on the east bank of the stream could hear the crack of small arms fire as Hooker's men and the enemy came into contact. The darkness became quiet, "terrifically quiet," said some, and the chaplains of the brigade began their battle-eve round of confession hearing. Everyone was a veteran now; there was no vainglorious approach to the morrow. Before another day passed the butcher's bill might be awesome, and

7. John M. Priest, *Antietam: The Soldier's Battle* (Shippensberg, Pennsylvania: White Mane Publishing Company, 1989), p. 180.

a long line of penitents approached the tent of the priests. Then the men turned away and lay down in the golden grass of autumn and slept, utterly spent and exhausted.

Hooker's attack went in the next day at 5:30 a.m. and soon the brigades of Stonewall Jackson were fighting it out with the men of the First Corps. There was a strong Union advance down the Hagerstown Pike and much confused back-and-forth combat as Lee hurried reinforcements from his right to bolster his left wing. Maj. Gen. Joseph K. F. Mansfield's Twelfth Corps was drawn into Hooker's battle and some of the Twelfth Corps men penetrated into the West Wood almost as far as the Dunkard Church. Fresh Confederate infantry rolled them back.

At 7:30 a.m. Sumner got his orders to take the Second Corps across the creek and head into the fight. The old dragoon was about to show the downside of his military personna, an inability to visualize a complicated combat scene. He was not today the canny Indian fighter leading fifty cavalrymen on the plains, but instead a field marshal of old leading Sedgwick's entire division of men as though on a review. Behind him in one line marched the brigade of Brig. Gen. Willis Gorman, four regiments, covering a front of 300 yards, but only two ranks deep. Behind Gorman was the brigade of Brig. Gen. Napoleon Dana with the same formation, same configuration, about fifty yards from Gorman's men. In the third line was Brig. Gen. Oliver O. Howard's Philadelphia Brigade, same formation, same configuration. People remembered that Sumner rode with his hat off, his white locks streaming in the breeze, smiling. The smile did not last long. The division of John Sedgwick was set up for a murderous attack from its left flank which was presented broadside on to the Confederate division of Lafayette McLaws and others. A disaster was at hand.

The West Woods had been fought over several times in the earlier attacks by Hooker and the counterattacks of the Confederates. The bloody debris lay all about as the blue ranks marched along with no flankers out and no skirmish line. Then directly ahead among a limestone outcropping, a sizeable Confederate force rose and fired a volley that stopped Gorman's men in their tracks. As Sumner went forward to encourage his first line, one of his staff suddenly pointed to a tremendous

Confederate force which seemed to appear as if by magic from the West Wood directly on their left flank. A line of battle struck in this way is at its weakest position. The Philadelphia Brigade was hit first and evaporated, followed by the two leading brigades which had a bit more time to change front and put up some resistance.[8] The division of about 4,500 men lost 2,200 in almost the twinkling of an eye. The survivors streamed across the Hagerstown Pike and into the East Wood from which they had marched so jauntily a short while before.

With the collapse of Sedgwick's division, the hard-pressed Confederate lines which had looked to be melting away took a new lease on life. Sumner had led one-third of his corps to utter destruction and now turned to the other two which had splashed across Antietam Creek and then taken a widely different direction than Sedgwick's ill-fated men.

Brig. Gen. William H. French's division, three brigades under Brig. Gen. Max Weber, Col. Dwight Morris, and Kimball, toiled up a slight rise from the creek. After a while French halted the division with Weber's men on the right, Kimball's on the left, and Morris to the rear and waited for orders. To their right was the white-walled Dunkard Church to which some remnants of Twelfth Corps clung tightly. There was a continuous crackle of small-arms at a distance. Now and then there was a spasm of Union artillery fire from across the creek, but here on the downslope of a little swale there was suddenly a curious kind of quiet. Eventually, when French went forward again his men did not move directly at the Dunkard Church but at an angle to it. They found themselves on the farm properties of Roullette and Clipp.

In front of them was the division of D. H. Hill, the brigades of Brigadier Generals Roswell S. Ripley, Robert E. Rodes, and Col. A. H. Colquitt, which had fought so long and well at Turner's Gap on September 14. They had not dug any trenches but had found shelter in land irregularities and behind trees and fences. From the high ground west of the Hagerstown Pike there was artillery to back them up, sited to enfilade any attacking front such as French was now moving forward. Hill's brigades were small and he did not have nearly enough men

8. *Ibid.*, pp. 128-29.

to halt the movement of French's division, but he gave ground grudgingly, making the Unionists pay for every foot. Then, almost imperceptibly, the Northern progress slowed and ground to a halt. The Confederates had found a magnificent firing position.[9]

Until now the Federals had been moving down the axis of a ridgeline which ran roughly north-and-south. Across their front and perpendicular to their line of advance ran a little country road whose surface was depressed three or four feet below the surface of the surrounding ridge. The road did not run straight but zigzagged several times. Hill's men had set up in a defensive position. They stood in the road and laid their rifles on the bank. Because of a fold in the ground they could not be hit by the Union artillery, and their cover from musketry was all that could be desired. It would take some very determined people to drive them away. Behind them the ground rose sharply and was thickly planted with corn. Tom Galwey of the 8th Ohio's Hibernian Guards counted seven Confederate regimental colours and concluded that there were as many regiments there.

If the Union troops thought the gray infantry could be quickly driven from their improvised trench, the Federals were soon disillusioned. Three or four times Kimball's brigade attacked the roadway, and as many times they were completely stopped and driven back by a murderous fire. Even worse, some Confederates appeared on Kimball's left flank which was in the air. Kimball's men defended themselves desperately and looked around for some sign of reinforcements. A Pennsylvania soldier standing on the east bank of Antietam Creek looked across the stream a little before noontime, to see the next attack fall on the Sunken Road. He was amazed by what he saw:

> The enemy's line upon which the advance was to be made was in plain view just outside the edge of a belt of timber. It was flanked by several batteries, whose active work of the morning had much improved their practice. . . . gun and musket belched forth their vengeful volleys with telling accuracy.

9. *Ibid.*, p. 136.

But the gallant Irishmen moved into battle-array with the precision of parade. The sun glistened upon the bright barrels of the rifles and the colors fluttered vauntingly in the breeze. . . . As the advance progressed and the scathing fire cut out its fearful gaps, the line halted with deliberation to readjust itself. The dead and wounded strewed the ground, thickening as the distance from the enemy lessened. Twice and again the green standard   . . . fell, but only to be promptly seized again, still to be borne gallantly onward to its goal. Vast curtains of smoke concealed the enemy, rising at intervals, disclosing him; yet unmoved, holding firmly to his post. But nothing diminished the courage, nothing could stay the onslaught, of these determined men. The deadly moment of impact came, the lines impinged, and the enemy, in irreparable confusion, broke for the friendly cover of the timber. The Irishmen, still maintaining their organization with commendable exactitude, pressed them in their helpless flight, until finally, with shout and cheer, friend and foe were lost to view in the wood the enemy had sought for safety. The unerring fire of Meagher's men had told severely upon his adversary. As he disappeared his abandoned line was distinctly marked by a long array of dead and wounded who had fallen where they stood.[10]

Apparently Cpl. J. L. Smith of the 118th Pennsylvania, usually called the Corn Exchange Regiment, only saw the approach of Meagher's brigade as it came in on the left flank of Kimball's men.

If any sense can be made of the rather involved battle reports, the Irish arrived just in time to meet an attack that D. H. Hill was launching on the left flank of Kimball's brigade. The Irish had fought their way across the fields to the east of the Roulette Farm as was described by Smith of the 118th Pennsylvania. Now they smashed into the flank attack on

10. John L. Smith, *History of the Corn Exchange Regiment 118th Pennsylvanian Volunteers* (Philadelphia: J. L. Smith, 1888), pp. 43-44.

Kimball and stopped it cold. The Confederates broke off and fell back quickly into the Sunken Road.

The Irish Brigade was in line of battle from right to left as follows: 69th New York, 29th Massachusetts, 63rd New York, and 88th New York. As the Confederates drew back into the Sunken Road, the Irish Brigade line came over the crest of a hill and into plain view of the eager men of Hill. There was a tremendous blast of musketry and the Irish stopped as though they had run into a stone wall. Almost half of the 63rd went down with that one volley. The survivors fell to the ground and fired as quickly as they could at the lane full of gray infantry. Meagher had led the charge on his white horse. When the animal was killed, Meagher was thrown and Col. John Burke of the 63rd took over command of the brigade.[11] Grimly he kept them to the work of sending down the hill volleys of musket balls. The adjutant of the 132nd Pennsylvania who had described the Irish as a "free-and-easy crowd" a few days before had also observed the brigade's approach across the fields of the Clipp farm and had an interesting observation to make:

> When we were out of ammunition and about to move back I looked at my watch and found it was 12:30 P.M. We had been under fire since eight o'clock. I couldn't believe my eyes. . . . I would have sworn that we had not been there more than twenty minutes, when we had actually been in that very hell of fire for four and a half hours.
>
> Just as we were moving back, the Irish brigade came up, under command of General Thomas Francis Meagher. They had been ordered to complete our work by a charge, and right gallantly they did it. Many of our men, not understanding the order, joined in that charge. General Meagher rode a beautiful white horse, but made a show of himself by tumbling off just as he reached our line. The boys said he was drunk, and he certainly looked and acted like a drunken man. He regained his feet and floundered about, swearing like a crazy man. The brigade, however,

11. *OR*, series 1, vol. 19, pt. 1, pp. 293.

made a magnificent charge and swept everything before it.[12]

It is well known from the writings of Father Corby that Meagher liked to look on the rye when it was golden, although Corby said Meagher was not a drunkard. There is also the allusion that he may have been drunk at First Manassas. This was suppressed by the newspapers at the time. Not even his worst enemies would impute drunkenness to him unless it could be proved conclusively. But it was a hard-drinking army in the officer corps, and there is some question as to how much of the drinking contributed to battlefield gallantry or, conversely, to stupid mistakes in tactics and maneuvering.

Hardly any of the events that occurred while Richardson's division was nerving itself for the assault on the sunken road were set down with precision and order. There seems not to have been any sudden offensive outburst on the part of the Federals. The Irish simply lay along the crest firing their volleys downhill for a measurable period of time. Later they would say vaguely at their reunions that they "carried the position." But as to whether or not they actually occupied the sunken road after the departure of the Confederates, the answer is probably not. That the Irish beat down the most severe opposition encountered in the center of the battle is not in question. After awhile their fire slackened as the cartridge boxes emptied. Behind them lay Brig. Gen. John C. Caldwell's brigade and Col. John R. Brooke's brigade of their division. Meagher went to Col. Francis Barlow of the 61st and 64th New York and frantically asked him to move Caldwell's men forward in support of the Irish Brigade. Barlow replied that he would not until he was ordered to do so by Caldwell. And where was Caldwell?

At about this time Maj. Gen. Israel Richardson, the division commander, came upon the scene. "Where's General [Caldwell]?" he demanded. Some of Caldwell's men answered, "Behind the haystack!" To which Richardson replied. "God damn the field officers!"[13] Apparently, he took

12. Hitchcock, *War From the Inside*, pp. 64-65.
13. Livermore, *Days and Events*, pp. 137-41.

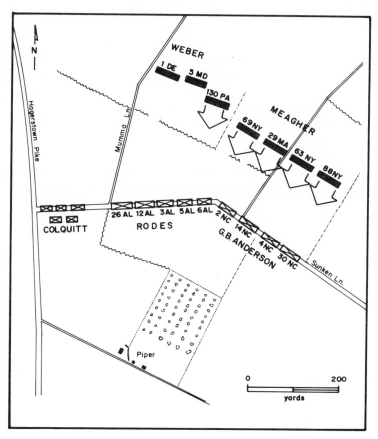

Map by John Heiser

The Battle of Antietam:
The struggle for Bloody Lane

191

over the relief of the Irish Brigade himself and brought forward Caldwell's men with great difficulty. He watched as the Irish Brigade withdrew their shattered ranks. "Bravo, Eighty-eighth," he said to Patrick Kelly, "I shall never forget you!"[14]

The Confederates afterwards said that their evacuation of the Sunken Road was a mistake, that an Alabama regimental commander misunderstood an order from General Rodes. The badly shot-up Alabamans climbed out of their section of the road and took off through the cornfield of the Piper Farm. That left four small North Carolina regiments to face the Federal onslaught. Finally, the men of the Second Corps piled into the road and pushed the Tarheels out. There were colors laying around for the taking, and in their reports the colonels of Caldwell's brigade who did not like to see their men get the worst of it when honor and glory were passed out spoke of "taking colors," giving the impression that the bits of bunting were snatched from a resisting enemy. There was an honest witness to what went on.

Thomas Livermore was a lieutenant that day, became a colonel later on, and was something of an historian and a statistician as well. He wrote that whatever happened in a battle was afterwards very confusing and that he was not exactly sure of how or when certain things happened. He said the 5th New Hampshire fired by file, that is ordered volleys, for a while and when they advanced to the Sunken Road, there was not much opposition. This was due to the Irish regiment which the 5th had relieved. The Irish had done a great deal to use up the Confederate line with which the 5th had to deal.[15] On the basis of their own assertions, the testimony of disinterested spectators, and the terrible number of casualties, the Irish Brigade can certainly claim a lion's share of the fighting at the Sunken Road, soon to have the more appropriate name of Bloody Lane.

Burke halted the brigade back of the lines and still west of Antietam Creek and waited for the ammunition wagons to come forward. Evidently he and all the others who were left expected to be sent back into the furnace as soon as the

14. *OR*, series 1, vol. 19, pt. 1, p. 298.
15. Livermore, *Days and Events*, pp. 137-41.

192

pouches were re-filled. Details were despatched to the creek with canteens for water. Others were sent back the way they had come to gather as many of the wounded as could be found. A head count showed 500 men still able to stand and fight. The pity of it was not only in the number of casualties but also the kind.

Some of the best and bravest had gone down: Captains Felix Duffy and Tim Shanley and three lieutenants killed in the 69th. Lt. Col. James Kelly had been wounded and command of the regiment had devolved on Maj. James Cavanagh. In the 63rd, officers had fallen wholesale: Capt. John Kavanagh and five lieutenants were dead and almost every officer had some kind of wound. The 88th had lost Captains John Joyce and Patrick F. Clooney killed, three lieutenants, and 116 of 302 men, the lightest loss of the three New York regiments. Overall, the 69th had lost 194 out of 317 and the 63rd lost 202 of 341. Curiously, the 29th Massachusetts which had stood between the 63rd and 69th had lost only 7 killed and 21 wounded. In truth the brigade was shattered. Of the 120 replacements who had come down from New York with Meagher, 75 had fallen.[16] This was a case of a surfeit of valor, for, originally, it had been planned to hold the new boys out of the battle and let them serve with the provost guard. But they had clamored for the fighting and in the end it had been granted them.

The survivors found a place of refuge, sat down and tried to collect themselves. A member of the 57th New York remembered passing them on the way to the battle:

As we pass the Sixty-ninth New York, or what is left of them, about a hundred men with colors in tatters, they cheer and we return it.[17]

Now Richardson's battle moved on, getting ever closer to Sharpsburg and the last possible line for the Confederates to stand on. If the Sixth Corps, now coming up, could be put into the gaping hole which the Second Corps had knocked in the center sector, the battle and the war in the Eastern theater

16. *New York at Gettysburg*, 2:466.
17. *Ibid.*, 1:412.

might be about over. But the Union was not saved so easily. As Israel Richardson moved his men forward a Confederate shell fragment struck him down and knocked him out of the fight. Unfortunately the great followup was not made. Although the successor to Richardson, Winfield Scott Hancock, was a paladin of a fighter, he was sent over to the Second Corps from the Sixth Corps in a hurry and did not grasp quickly enough that the Confederates must be pushed. This was unfortunate because the Federal attack going in with the full weight of the the Sixth Corps behind it might well have pushed the Army of Northern Virginia into the river. It was only 1 p.m., there was still plenty of time, and there was no ammunition problem. Some Union formations had suffered extensive damage, but others were standing around, ready to be used. And what was Ambrose Burnside's Ninth Corps doing? Not very much, it developed.

In the end, all of the might-have-beens did not happen, and the war went on for three more years. Antietam had been a soldier's battle right from the start, not a general's battle. Lee had made an almost fatal strategic mistake in standing against a river. McClellan made a larger one by not pushing the issue. Lee had partly redeemed himself by fighting a flawless tactical battle, running his reserves from one point to another all day. Tactically, McClellan had been done in by one old man, Sumner, and two old friends, Burnside and Franklin. If the Ninth Corps had shown any initiative at all, it is very difficult to see how the Confederate line could have held together.

There were many makeshift truces between the combatants during the rest of the day as wounded were looked up and deaths verified. One Confederate veteran in 1896 wrote of fraternizing with six men of the Irish Brigade who were standing in the Bloody Lane. They gave him some of their rations and exchanged some small talk. When a mounted Union field officer and his entourage approached, the suddenly panicky Mississippian realized it was time to go. "I will run; don't shoot me!" he told his whilom friends. "Run, Johnny, we'll not harm ye," they answered.[18] And the sun went down on the bloodiest day in American history.

18. Priest, *Antietam*, p. 312.

The Irish Brigade was in a stupor of numbness and shock. This was the end of the old brigade, whittled down to a corporal's guard. The survivors lay on the Maryland grass and looked at the blue sky over them, afraid to turn to look for comrades lost or broken and bleeding. A military unit has about itself the waxing and waning of a family, but the whole process of birth, maturity, and death is tremendously accelerated. A generation forms, flows, and dies. On that golden September day, the first generation of the Irish Brigade had been dealt a death-blow. All over the field of Antietam other formations and regiments of both sides were looking at the same shocking result. On the Union side the rookie Pennsylvania regiments which had joined just scant weeks before, who had not even been instructed in the barest rudiments of drill, had been thrown into the furnace and decimated. So had the First and Twelfth Corps. On the Confederate side, Jackson's corps had suffered heavily and in Longstreet's corps, Hood's division of peerless fighters was, in Hood's own words, "dead on the field of battle." And so it ran for others on both sides.

Those in the Washington administration simply could not fathom why the conflict was not renewed the next day. Lincoln, who had been sickened by the sight of a few corpses in the Black Hawk War on the frontier of Illinois, was enraged at McClellan as he was to be enraged at Meade after Gettysburg because they did not do a little bit more and end the war. These were the same administration people who were resigned to a Confederate capture and occupation of the capital only two weeks before on the heels of John Pope's fiasco. They had undergone a rapid revival.

When one reads the commentary of the present-day experts on the fallible man who had an earthshaking responsibility but not hindsight for guidance, one is struck dumb. This was, after all, McClellan's first offensive battle. It was not a masterpiece. But then neither had Lee's performances on the Peninsula been tactical masterpieces. The Seven Days had been notable for filling Confederate cemeteries at a staggering rate. And Lee had not been satisfied with himself, his staff, or his army. "The Federal army should have been destroyed," he said in his report of March 1863. And at Malvern Hill he said, "He [McClellan] will get away

195

because I cannot have my orders carried out."[19] No commander has all of his orders carried out perfectly. That is the nature of war and the uncertainty of battle. McClellan could say the very same of Burnside, Sumner, and Franklin in the Antietam Campaign. But there had been nothing wrong with his general plan to initiate the battle on the short flank, draw there the Confederate reserves, attack directly toward the river to segment the field, and then constrict the battle from the left. Maybe Little Mac would have improved, as Lee had, with another turn at bat.

Aside from the intrigues with which he is identified, Stanton is often called a great secretary of war. It was he alone who drove the grafters and thieves from the War Department and put the tools of war in the hands of the Union soldiers. In addition, it is said, he put the good wool uniforms on their backs and filled their stomachs with hardtack, beans, and beef. Each of these tasks was monumental. It is too bad that he did not take on the problem of replacements for battle casualties so the Union armies might confront the enemy with continuity of organization, and with veteran officers and leaders. As it was, every Northern governor was thought to be capable of selecting men to lead other men. So new regiments went to battle, like the rookie Pennsylvania regiments at Antietam, green, unskilled, ignorant, and bound to pay a painful cost which association with veterans could have helped prevent. The only step in the right direction to occur at all was when regiments which were utterly worn down were permitted to return home to recruit. This program, feeble as it was, was marked by favoritism and political advantage. If he was a good quartermaster, Stanton was no recruiting sergeant.

A reinforcement reached the Irish Brigade on October 11 as it was encamped on Bolivar Heights, Harpers Ferry. The 116th Pennsylvania Volunteers under Col. Dennis Heenan arrived and joined. Heenan had offered this regiment to Michael Corcoran for the Corcoran Legion on August 21 when the brigadier had stopped in Philadelphia on his way home from captivity. The regiment was then well organized, said Heenan, and Corcoran had accepted it gladly. How did it happen that the Philadelphians turned up in Meagher's

19. Dowdey, *The Seven Days*, p. 326.

196

St. Clair A. Mulholland
Colonel, 116th Pennsylvania Volunteer Infantry
Wounded at Fredericksburg, the Wilderness, Totopotomoy,
and Cold Harbor.
Awarded the Medal of Honor for actions at Chancellorsville

group? It resulted from the terrible fright into which the administration had been put by the debacle at Second Manassas. Apparently, every regiment then in any condition at all to go to the front was called down to Washington for what might be a last-ditch battle. So, regardless of the offer to Corcoran, the 116th was bundled aboard the cars for the capital.

When they arrived at Washington the regiment was placed in the defences and assigned to the Eleventh Corps. On October 6 it was ordered to Harpers Ferry, joined the brigade and was made very welcome. Meagher and his staff rode over to glad-hand the newcomers, making a good impression on the new boys. Fortunately, Lt. Col. St. Clair A. Mulholland survived the war, during the course of which he acquired four wounds and a Medal of Honor. In later life he became a fairly prominent public figure, practically the only one of the Irish Brigade to do so, serving as police chief of Philadelphia and later as pension agent for the Federal government.

Born in Lisburn, County Antrim, Ireland, in 1839, Mulholland was completely free of any New York connections. He authored the regimental history of the 116th in 1903, and several times in this work he seems to go to great lengths to point out that his regiment was composed of American citizens. This leads to certain insights that are valuable because they are not those usually associated with Irish-American stereotypes. There is no breath of Fenianism, and Meagher, though treated respectfully, is held at arm's length. The brigade is treated reverentially, but the actions of the 116th are always referred to apart from the others in the brigade. Nor did the 116th carry the Green Flag, being like the 29th Massachusetts in this respect. So the question may be properly asked: how Irish was the new group? The answer seems to be that in the beginning it was largely, though not wholly, Hibernian. The chaplain was Father Edward McKee. The colonel, Dennis Heenan, had been active in Irish militia affairs before the war and served in the ninety-day service as lieutenant colonel of the 24th Pennsylvania Volunteers which, as we have seen, became the 69th Pennsylvania in the three-year service. Why, then, does Mulholland imply that the regiment was not Irish? It seems that when he wrote the history in 1903 at the age of 64 years, he was looking backwards selectively. In 1864, after Gettysburg, the regiment had undergone a complete reorganization with a sizeable recruitment in western Pennsylvania that diluted the original Irish contingent measurably. The old veteran placed more emphasis on the development of the regiment than on its origin. Rather surprisingly, his history is laden with Irish dialect stories, indicating a complete "Americanization" of the colonel. Most Irish came to hate the "stage Irishman" caricature. While no Fenian, Mulholland preserved his racial identification by serving as president in later years of the Friendly Sons of St. Patrick of Philadelphia.

There is some question as to how many muskets the 116th brought to the brigade. Mulholland says there were "about seven hundred men" on the rolls when they left Philadelphia, and there was little sickness in the command and only one death while they were encamped at Harpers Ferry. Yet two months later at the battle of Fredericksburg, there were only 247 men present, a discrepancy impossible to explain. In the absence of an epidemic, no regiment could possibly be reduced so sharply in such a short time. Perhaps Mulholland's memory played him false as to the number of men originally enlisted.[20]

The weather took on the gold of autumn and the army was in a beautiful a spot. Soon the president came down to look at the soldiers. He talked to McClellan (affably, said the general) and went back to the capital, ostensibly to write notes designed to get the army onto the back of Robert E. Lee again. But McClellan was not to be pushed. The army was living a hand-to-mouth supply existence which would have to be set right before any more adventures of an offensive nature could be slated. Even Brig. Gen. George Meade, no heel-dragger, thought that the supplies from the Washington bureaus and storehouses were a long time coming. Meanwhile, the soldiers gazed in wonder at the Blue Ridge mountains and the silvery meanderings of the Potomac and Shenandoah rivers, reminding the Irish-born of the lush land they had left behind. Some of the officers'

20. St. Clair A. Mulholland, *The Story of the 116th Regiment Pennsylvania Infantry* (Philadelphia: F. McManus, Jr. and Company, 1903), pp. 10-12.

wives came down to visit, including Elizabeth Townsend Meagher. Fortunately, Robert Nugent returned to the 69th New York. He was badly needed for the loss in officers was proving a crippling loss to the brigade.

On the whole it is incredible that an organization as hard hit as the brigade could have survived Antietam. Normally, the brigade would have been shifted to some easy duty like headquarters guard or train guard and allowed to recuperate gracefully. But it was simply not that kind of a war for the Irish. The wonder is that the survivors were not completely demoralized. Even with the advent of the 116th, a mere increase in numbers would not do. The 63rd had received a severe blow when Col. John Burke was dismissed from the service.[21] Since Lieutenant Colonel Fowler and Major Bentley were both wounded, command devolved on Capt. James O'Neill. There is a curious postscript to the post-Antietam period. On September 19, only two days after the cannon were stilled, Quartermaster Patrick M. Haverty of the 88th wrote a letter to Judge Charles Daly in New York:

> Knowing the interest you have always felt and exhibited for the Irish Brigade, I will take the liberty of soliciting your influence in favor of one of its most meritorious officers. Col. Nugent, who has just re-turned from his sick leave. From the date of his commission until stricken down after the battle of Malvern Hill he was never away from his command for a day. The manner in which he attended to them is best testified by the love and respect his men have for him. He is well deserving of a Brigadier's straps, but if the acquiring of them depends on his own efforts he will never get them. I feel certain that if any friend would bring his name before the War Depart-ment as there are quite a number to be filled from the new levy. Many officers who have not performed half the effective service he has have been appointed. Now, my dear sir, if you would interest yourself in the proper quarter I am sure you would be successful and

21. Walker, *History of the Second Corps*, p. 131.

you would only be carrying out your own axiom, that Irish Brigades should have not only popular officers but ones thoroughly acquainted with their duty. If necessary, a document can be forwarded from all the officers of his own, the 63d and 88th regiments, recommending him for this promotion. General Meagher is not wounded but the fine horse he brought on here from New York was shot from under him.

P. M. Haverty, QM. 88th NY Vols[22]

One can only wonder at this document and speculate what it portends. The Battle of Antietam is not mentioned specifically, nor is the brigade's part in it, and an officer from a different regiment was advancing Nugent's cause. Why is Meagher's name not on the bottom of the letter? Surely his recommendation would carry more weight than a regimental quartermaster. Or does this mean that Nugent was desirous of leaving the brigade? If so, why? Or was Meagher's performance at Antietam so scandalous that a new commander was desired? Most of these questions cannot be answered at all, but there was an indication of a growing antipathy between Meagher and Judge Daly. For this reason, Nugent may have been wise not to have Meagher sign the letter. For, from his wife's diary, it is evident that if Daly had to choose between the two Irish warriors, Meagher and Corcoran, he much preferred the latter. Mrs. Maria Lydig Daly had developed a strong admiration for Corcoran and an equally strong dislike for Meagher.[23] It does look as though there were strong undercurrents of mutual dislike on the command level of the brigade.

Over in the Second Division of the Second Corps, there was a tremendous personality clash between Col. Joshua Owen, the Welsh-born commander of the 69th Pennsylvania, and his lieutenant colonel, Dennis O'Kane. It ended with O'Kane being tried by a court-martial presided over by none other than Winfield Scott Hancock. The case was summarized by Special Order 109:

22. Charles Daly collection.
23. Daly, *Diary of a Union Lady*, p. 180.

Headquarters Second Corps
Oct. 23, 1862

Before a General Courtmartial of which Brig. General W. S. Hancock is president was arraigned and tried Lt-Col. Dennis O'Kane, 69th Pennsylvania Volunteers, on the following charges and specifications:

Charge 1: Violation of the Fiftieth Article of War. In that he remained absent from his regiment while it was on picket duty without sufficient authority at or near Harper's Ferry on or about October 4, 1862.

Charge 2: Prejudicial to Good Order and Military Discipline. In that he was much under the influence of liquor and did enter into a personal altercation with his Colonel, Joshua T. Owen, using violent words and demonstrations at or near Harper's Ferry, Va. on or about October 4, 1862.

To which charges the accused pleaded "Not Guilty."

The Court found: Of the First Charge: "Not Guilty"
Of the Second Charge: "Not Guilty."

And the Court does therefore acquit him. He will resume his sword and duties.[24]

What had happened was a little more complicated. O'Kane's wife and daughter came down to visit him. As they were riding in a carriage near the camp, Owen, who was apparently drunk, rode his horse in a violent manner close to the team of horses drawing the carriage. When he repeated this maneuver O'Kane asked him to desist. Owen persisted in this risky maneuver, frightening both women and calling O'Kane an "Irish son of a bitch," whereupon O'Kane had pulled Owen from his horse, and so the court-martial. Matters probably were a bit strained in the mess of the Philadelphia Irish after that.

24. Court-martial book of 69th Regiment Pennsylvania Volunteers, State Archives, Harrisburg, Pennsylvania.

Chapter Eight

SPRIGS OF BOXWOOD

Probably the thing least desired by the men of the Second Corps in those golden autumn days was more action. But the successor to Israel Richardson in command of the First Division was a driver who hated inactivity. Winfield S. Hancock saw no reason to keep soldiers from their appointed work which was fighting the enemy or seeking him out so that he could be fought. On October 15, four days after the 116th Pennsylvania joined the Irish Brigade, the division was ordered to make a reconnaissance in force to Charlestown. It was done and the new boys from Philadelphia spent a zestful day in the open. The outer line of Confederate pickets was struck and driven in, there was some exchange of artillery fire, and the 116th had all the advantage of being at a battle without being in it. Meagher had honored them by giving them the right of the brigade line, Mulholland noted, greatly setting up the regiment.[1]

There was another week of preparation around Harpers Ferry and then the army began to move. After a telegraphic debate with Washington as to whether Lee should be sought in the Shenandoah Valley or walled into the Valley by a movement down the eastern slope of the Blue Ridge, McClellan chose the latter. It is always significant and instructive to the detractors of "Little Mac," caught in the everlasting Lincoln syndrome, to point out the reasons for the delay between Antietam and the movement of the army. We have spoken of the supply situation, but more important was the geography of the Harpers Ferry debouche at the head of the Valley. If McClellan came down the Valley the Confederates confronting him could suddenly move through the Blue Ridge passes and take up a position between him and Washington, the very

1. Mulholland, *116th Pennsylvania*, p. 16.

last thing the administration desired. His supply line could be interdicted, and the capital would be uncovered. Should McClellan, on the other hand, move down the eastern flank of the Blue Ridge, the Confederates would immediately move across the Potomac into Maryland, again uncovering Washington. The two armies, thus, appeared to be operating a revolving door whose hinge was at that point where the Shenandoah emptied into the Potomac. There was only one out for McClellan, to hold his position until the water in the Potomac rose to its normal level, washing out the fords so well used by the Confederates who owned neither pontoons nor bridging equipment. So for a very clear, logical military reason McClellan endured the slings and arrows of the administration until the rains of autumn put his problem behind him. Though his foes were great marchers, they could not fly. With the river up and no pontoons, the bottle of the Valley was corked.[2]

It is difficult to question the soundness of McClellan's plan of campaign, so most of his detractors simply ignore it. But as the army came to the passes in the Blue Ridge, detachments were dropped off to prevent any surprises in the rear areas. Lee had advantages too. He had a fairly good highway which ran the length of the Valley along his axis of movement. East of the mountains there was no parallel road for the Army of the Potomac to follow, but a rather complex road network whose general direction led to the passes rather than along the base of the mountain wall.

The plan worked better than McClellan could have hoped. The march was almost without incident and Lee reacted in the expected manner, falling back down the Valley with Longstreet's corps and leaving Jackson's corps at Winchester. By November 7 McClellan's army was concentrated in the vicinity of Warrenton while the two Confederate corps were fifty miles apart. Suddenly, when matters looked so favorable for the Union's prospects, a special train from Washington arrived at army headquarters near Rectortown. Aboard was Brig. Gen. Catharinus P. Buckingham with orders relieving

2. William Swinton, *Campaigns of the Army of the Potomac: A Critical History of Operations in Virginia, Maryland, and Pennsylvania, from the Commencement to the Close of the War, 1861-65* (New York: Charles B. Richardson, 1866; reprint, New York: Charles Scribner's Sons, 1882), p. 226.

McClellan of the command of the army. McClellan's successor was Maj. Gen. Ambrose Burnside.[3]

The first snow of the year had fallen on the bivouac area around Warrenton on the day before and it had seemed to bring to the soldiers a sense of foreboding which lasted through the rest of the winter. In the Philadelphia Brigade everyone was angry at and envious of the 69th Pennsylvania which had managed in the midst of a very difficult march to get drunk en masse. Joseph Ward, historian of the 106th Pennsylvania told the story as follows:

> On November 1st, moved to Snickersville and camped. During the march there was considerable trouble with the Sixty-ninth Regiment, "Paddy Owen's Regulars," owing to the profusion of whiskey that in some way or other found its way among the rank and file (I believe mostly received in boxes sent to the men from their homes, that should have reached them while at Bolivar Heights); large numbers of them were tight and enjoyed the Irishman's *privilege* and *pleasure*, "free fight," so that by the time the Regiment arrived at camp it was considerably demoralized in appearance, and its numbers greatly reduced on account of so many being unable to keep up.[4]

There were many poignant scenes on the day that McClellan left the army. Alongside the roadsides the men stood with tear-stained faces. Meagher's brigade was particularly affected, and, as the general approached them, the Green Flags were dipped to the ground for him to ride over—the ultimate salute. But McClellan stopped and motioned them to raise the colors. Then he passed by the bronzed men in their shabby blue uniforms with his hand at the visor of his cap. The soul of the army, said Mulholland, seemed to go with him.

Even when he had passed from sight there were diehards in the officer corps who wished him back even at the cost of a radical change in the structure of American government. Most

3. *Ibid.*, p. 227.
4. Joseph R. C. Ward, *History of the 106th Regiment Pennsylvania Volunteers* (Philadelphia: Grant, Faires, and Rodgers, 1883), p. 139.

of the men realized that national politics entered into the dismissal of McClellan, and that implacable forces in the Congress and the Cabinet were at work to make the army the instrument of a party, rather than a nation. Most men read the papers and were current with affairs. From their experiences of the conduct at the battle of Second Manasssas, the leaders chosen by that party, if full of the offensive spirit, appeared to lack other desirable military virtues. So, in the officer corps, sullen, bitter, mutinous sentiments were freely expressed. Why not? These men were free Americans, and when their government made a mistake in judgment, they realized, above anything else, that it would be paid for with their blood. A free rein was given to their expressions, except in the Irish Brigade.

Meagher put out an order which was a model of copybook maxim propriety; it clearly defined the military's subservience to the civilian government.[5] One of his biographers, Robert G. Athearn, whose picture of the brigadier is deeply etched in acid, sees this as an attempt at boot-licking. Meagher probably had some political advantage in mind, Athearn says. In the light of Meagher's deep attachment to the Democratic Party, this does not seem tenable. The brigadier was a soldier pro tem. His entire career as a civilian had been against the man-on-horseback intrusion into civilian affairs, as exemplified by the British army in Ireland. With all of Meagher's wants, there did not appear to be any political advantage to be gained by his order to the troops; quite the reverse seemed to be true.

There was another incident that took place on the march to the southwest. Some time before, the officers of the Irish Brigade had conceived the idea that a Green Flag should be presented to the 29th Massachusetts as a gesture of respect and admiration. As far as the Irish were concerned, this was the highest honor they could bestow on anyone, the equivalent of the vein-opening and blood-mingling ritual of the Native American act of brotherhood. Unknown to the unsuspecting New Englanders, the flag was procured and a ceremony scheduled. However, with so many in on the secret there was bound to be a leak, and, one day, Lt. Col. Joseph H. Barnes, commander of the 29th Massachusetts, was apprised of the situa-

5. Conyngham, *The Irish Brigade*, p. 324.

Richard Byrnes
Colonel, 28th Massachusetts Veteran Volunteer Infantry
Mortally wounded at Cold Harbor

207

tion. He immediately went to brigade headquarters and asked Meagher if his regiment was expected to carry the Green Flag with their other colors. He then made some statement to the effect that he would not object to having the Green Flag as a possession of the regiment, indicative of good feelings all around, but the 29th should not be compelled to bear it since the men of that regiment were not Irish.

It is not clear that Meagher or anyone else on the staff or associated with the New York regiments had thought deeply into the matter. What had started out as a goodwill gesture with a surprise presentation was now tarnished beyond recognition. No one will ever be entirely sure whether Meagher was piqued more by the failure of his surprise or wounded by Barnes' rebuff. But what followed was certainly definite enough. The 29th Massachusetts was transferred from the brigade and the Second Corps.[6] In its place came a regiment from the Bay State, but one that was indisputably as Irish as any in the world. The 28th Massachusetts, out of Boston and the Ninth Corps, were veterans of amphibious landings and pitched battles at Second Manassas and Antietam. They were blooded and ready. A new colonel by the name of Richard Byrnes had recently been acquired, the regiment having fought at Manassas under a major who was wounded, and at Antietam under a captain.

Richard Byrnes had served as an enlisted man in the Old Army under General Sumner who had recommended Byrnes for a captain's commission in the 5th U.S. Cavalry. Now Sumner was instrumental in bringing Byrnes and his regiment to the Irish Brigade for which they had originally been intended.[7] As for the Green Flag which had precipitated the entire fuss, some time later the threads forming the numeral "2" in "29" were removed, and, very quietly, it was given to the 9th Massachusetts where it was well received by Colonel Guiney.[8]

Perhaps it was this incident that made some officers of the brigade conscious of their own colors which were now in tatters. It was decided to return them to New York for honorable retirement. And, of course, there were great-hearted

6. Osborne, *Twenty-ninth Massachusetts*, p. 175.
7. Conyngham, *The Irish Brigade*, p. 586.
8. MacNamara, *Ninth Massachusetts*, p. 285.

people back in the metropolis, handsomely dressed, financially secure people, who were waiting only for an occasion to which to rise. The New York regiments would have new colors, but these would be the gifts of Americans, not Irish-Americans but the old-line stock, in gratitude and appreciation for valiant services rendered. It made a great human interest story but some events took place before the new colors were delivered.

Ambrose Burnside did not think he should command the Army of the Potomac, but having been tapped for the job twice, evidently felt he could not escape the honor. At least if he was in command, his enemy, Joseph Hooker, would be kept from it. The army, which had been grinding down the eastern slope of the Blue Ridge, came to a halt in the Warrenton area while Burnside prepared a plan of action. McClellan had aimed to attack Longstreet's corps in the vicinity of Culpeper, but Burnside abandoned this plan immediately. He then submitted a new plan to Washington for approval which involved crossing the Rappahannock River at Fredericksburg. Once the Army of the Potomac got a toehold on the south bank of the river, Lee's communication with Richmond would be in danger. No one will ever be entirely sure of Burnside's ideas for engaging Lee's army after that, because too many changes took place in the script. Lincoln thought that the initial plan, the shift to the eastern approach, might work if it were made quickly; "otherwise not."

What Burnside did was to turn his back on the Army of Northern Virginia, one corps of which was in the Culpeper area, and the other in the Shenandoah Valley. He proceeded to march his army away from the combat with the enemy that the administration thirsted for. At least they had been urging McClellan to seek out Lee and fight him ever since Antietam. The new objective made no sense at all in view of what had gone before. William Swinton, the historian of the Army of the Potomac, has an explanation it.

> In point of fact, General Burnside had not matured any definite plan of action, for the reason that he hoped to be able to postpone operations till the spring. He did not favor operating against Richmond by the overland route, but had his mind turned to-

wards a repetition of McClellan's movement to the Peninsula; and in determining to march to Fredericksburg he cherished the hope of being able to winter there upon an easy base of supplies, and in the spring embarking his army for the James River. How he could have counted on being allowed to carry out a plan so adverse to the wishes of the Administration, and involving what the public temper could not be expected to brook, the inaction of the army for the winter, I do not undertake to say. I derive these revelations of General Burnside's motives and purposes from the corps-commander then most intimate in his confidence.[9]

Surely Burnside told no one in the Lincoln administration about this program. The administration had jumped all over McClellan the previous winter when he had done nothing except drill and train. There was no need for that now. The army was blooded and ready. But to even suggest that it would go back to the Peninsula would have alienated every Radical Republican.

The army began its march to the tidewater on November 15 and two days later the Second Corps arrived opposite Fredericksburg. They looked across the Rappahannock at a small Confederate force. The river was fordable in several places, and Sumner was anxious to get a force across and get possession of the heights behind the town. Burnside forbade it, and in the following two days the rest of the Army of the Potomac arrived. Almost at the same time Longstreet's corps showed up on the south bank of the river. A few days after that, Jackson's corps arrived. The two armies surveyed each other across the river.

As usual where the fine, obfuscatory hand of Henry W. Halleck is displayed, there is a plethora of injunctions, cautions, small carping, and large responsibility shifting in the literature of the campaign. The general-in-chief had a labyrinthine mind and most of his activity consisted in mental meanderings in obscure corridors of it, not toward any conscious goal. Fortunately, he stayed in Washington and thus did

9. Swinton, *Campaigns of the Army of the Potomac*, p. 233.

not witness what has been called "an exercise in the murder of Union soldiers." He does, however, deserve to share in the blame along with Lincoln and Stanton for the catastrophe that ensued.

The Second and Ninth Corps had been placed together in what Burnside designated the Right Grand Division under the command of Sumner. Similarly, Franklin commanded the Left Grand Division (First and Sixth Corps) and Hooker had the Center Grand Division (Third and Fifth Corps). Darius Couch who succeeded to the command of the Second Corps said Sumner had orders not to cross the river. Couch was an outspoken critic of Burnside's actions even before the battle, and when the latter held a council of corps commanders on December 9 he singled out Couch and Hancock as being objectors to his plans and may even have implied lukewarmness to them. Both promptly assured him that however much they disagreed with his plan there would be no slackening of effort on the part of either.

On the hills behind Fredericksburg Confederate spades and shovels were busily employed. As many of the town's inhabitants as were able left their homes to invalids, the very old, and a body of Mississippi infantry who found positions along the waterfront to contest the expected Union crossing. The weather turned colder. Normally two footbridges and a railroad bridge spanned the river in the town, but these had been destroyed much earlier in the war. Two blocks down from where the Plank Road bridge had crossed the river and parallel to it, Hanover street ran through the town and on the outskirts became the Telegraph Road which continued on for another fifty miles to Richmond. On the way it went up a long, sloping hill a distance of a quarter of a mile toward a colonnaded house which sat on a bluff that suddenly emerged from the slope. The road turned sharply south at the foot of the bluff and continued in this direction for another quarter mile. The house belonged to a local landowner, Col. E. A. Marye, and it had the most commanding position in the vicinity of the town.

Around such a natural artillery and observation point were ranged the guns of the Washington Artillery of New Orleans. In the road that skirted the bluff was a mixed force of Georgians and South Carolinians who had found an infantryman's dream. On the downslope side of the road was a stone wall to the height of a man's chest, and stretching before the men who would stand there was a magnificent field of fire. They could look down the Telegraph Road leading into the town along which the assaulting troops must come if they were foolishly employed in a frontal attack.

In that bitter winter weather it took great determination for the soldiers on both sides merely to stay alive, let alone to keep warm. On the Falmouth side of the river, the Federals quickly laid out their tent cities in squares and streets, but firewood was scarce. All this while two regiments of engineers were wrestling overland the wagon train containing the pontoons that would get the army over the river. They were too late at that date to realize Burnside's plan of surprising Lee by a sudden movement. Some sort of glacial force seemed to be impelling the Army of the Potomac to continue up a slippery slope of destruction.

When the engineers and pontoniers reported to Burnside, he confided a plan to them for building a bridge downstream from the town at Skinker's Neck. In support of this scheme one of the engineer officers made an after-dark reconnaissance over the river and came back to report that such a plan was entirely feasible. But then Burnside had a change of heart. He decided to cross the river at the town, move out the Telegraph Road and engage the enemy.

The bridges were laid on December 11 under much opposition and the army poured over. By nightfall of December 12, the Right Grand Division was in the town which had been reduced to a shambles by looting. When the Irish Brigade marched up the Stafford County side to cross the bridge, the band of the 9th New York struck up "Garry Owen" in their honor. According to Mulholland there were other greeters as well:

> Not so pleasant was the reception of the professional embalmers who, alive to business, thrust their cards into the hands of the men as they went along, said cards being suggestive of an early trip home, nicely boxed up and delivered to loving friends by express, sweet as a nut and in perfect preservation, etc. The boys did not seem altogether pleased with the cold-blooded allusions to their latter end, and one of them

from the Emerald Isle called out to a particularly zealous undertaker: "D'ye moind them blankets. Well only that we are in a bit of a hurry, we'd be after giving ye the naytest koind av a jig in the air, and be damned to ye."[10]

There was no comfort in the town during the night; so many soldiers had crossed over that there was not enough room for them to lay down even in the streets. The hours passed in bitter cold with the men standing in formation shoulder to shoulder while the wind howled over them. With the morning came a wet fog from the river which enveloped the formations in thick sheets. For some unaccountable reason they were denied fires, perhaps in the mistaken belief that the massive passover had gone unobserved by the Confederates. Officers occupied the homes of the town and there was much singing and shouting, and, possibly, much drinking. Soon there would be a battle where many might die. A dram or two would push the horror away and invest the golden comrades gathered about with the halos of immortality. All had some idea of that height behind the town. A young soldier had asked Father Corby if an attack on the heights was planned, and the chaplain answered that the Union generals would never do that to the men.[11]

Two miles down the river at Hamilton's Crossing the Left Grand Division's commander, William Franklin, was ending a sleepless night. Burnside had visited him in the afternoon, and left him with the impression that the major effort of the day would be made at that end of the line. A strong force of thirty or forty thousand men would be formed there and thrown on the enemy.[12] That had been Burnside's thought at 5 p.m., and, as he rode away, he told Franklin that such an order would issue from army headquarters as soon as his staff worked out the details. Now it was 7 a.m., December 13, and, finally, the word came to the Left Grand Division, a tremendous letdown. Instead of a host of thirty or forty thousand men, Franklin was to direct one division at the Confederates in front of him, "to seize, if possible, the heights near Captain Hamilton's." The

10. Mulholland, *116th Pennsylvania*, pp. 35-36.
11. Corby, *Memoirs of Chaplain Life*, p. 131.
12. Swinton, *Campaigns of the Army of the Potomac*, p. 244.

command echelon of the Left Grand Division was stunned. Instead of an assault they were ordered to mount a probe.

Even worse was the news for the Second Corps. From Burnside to Sumner came the word to move with one division supported by another, "for the purpose of pushing in the direction of the Plank and Telegraph Roads . . . seizing the heights in the rear of the town."[13] It was a sentence of death for the Second Corps. Two of its divisions were to march out of the town and up the Telegraph Road right at the stone wall where stood Brig. Gen. Thomas R. R. Cobb's sturdy brigade of Georgians and the excellent artillery of Louisiana. Howard's Second Division of the Second Corps had been involved in the street fighting that had cleared the town the day before so it was excused, initially, from the attack. French's division, the Third, was to be the first to move out of the streets of the town, and try their luck on the hill.

There was a little drainage ditch for the canal beyond the streets of the town, and the bridge over it had been largely destroyed, three temporary planks being laid over it as stringers. That slowed the movement down considerably and once on the other side, the Unionists found a steep bank behind which they could form a regimental line. By now the Confederate artillery was sending over some ranging shots, and shells were striking the buildings of the town. Kimball's brigade which led French's division, moved over the rise behind which they had formed. The soldiers found that the morning mist still hung in patches on the slopes; a brick house three-fourths of the way up the hill appeared to swim in the fog. About 200 yards to the right of the house was a cluster of other dwellings. All of this the Union soldiers saw in the instant of going over the crest. Then the shells of the Washington Artillery began to hit them, and gory bodies began to go down.

The extent of their task was plain to the men of the Second Corps. They had been ordered to storm hell itself. As they ascended the slope, there was added to the death-dealing artillery bursts the fire of the unshaken Confederate infantry, standing in the road behind the stone wall, almost unbelieving at the idiocy that delivered their targets to them. At about 150 yards from the wall the wreck of Kimball's brigade sank down

13. Walker, *History of the Second Corps*, p. 157.

on the ground, dazed. Dream-like, some of them tried to return fire.[14]

French's other brigades did not reach this advanced line. Three fence lines which ran perpendicular to their axis of advance broke up these formations, and many men, unnerved at the terrible prospect, fell out of ranks and dropped to the ground.[15] Then they joined a swelling tide of stragglers and wounded who were returning from whence they came.[16]

Now it was Hancock's turn. The Irish Brigade stood in column when some of the wounded from French's attack began to stream past. Among the first was a German soldier, probably from Col. Oliver H. Palmer's brigade. He was ensconced on a wheelbarrow pushed by a comrade, with one leg dangling over the side. The foot of his other leg had been shot off, and the blood was flowing from the shattered area.[17] The 116th Pennsylvania had never seen anything like that, and although the German was jauntily puffing on his pipe and directing the man who was pushing the barrow, the scene was too much for Pvt. William DeHaven of Company C who fainted dead away.[18] No one noticed his passing out at the time, for mounted on his horse, Meagher was coming along the street. He stopped before each regiment and gave them a little speech, reminding them to uphold the honor of their native land. The speeches were all the brigade would get from their general for his knee was badly infected and, although he could ride, walking for any distance was out of the question. Hancock had ordered all field and staff officers to go on foot where they would have a better chance.

One more thing before the brigade moved. Only the 28th Massachusetts had a Green Flag today, since the others had been sent home, but there was plenty of Ireland's national color available.

> Green box-wood was culled in a garden near-by
> and Meagher placed a sprig in his Irish cap. Every
> officer and man followed his example, and soon great

14. *Ibid..*
15. *OR*, series 1, vol. 21, p. 227.
16. Walker, *History of the Second Corps*, p. 172.
17. Mulholland, *116th Pennsylvania*, p. 43.
18. *Ibid.*

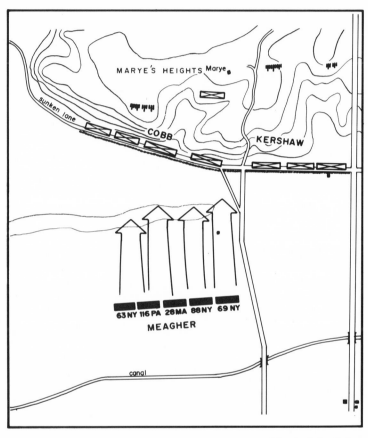

Map by John Heiser

The Battle of Fredericksburg
The Irish Brigade attacks Marye's Heights

bunches of the fragrant shrub adorned the caps of everyone. Wreaths were made and hung upon the tattered flags, and the national color of the Emerald Isle blended in fair harmony with the red, white and blue of the Republic.[19]

Then Meagher gave the order and painfully climbed from the saddle to the ground. He would go as far as his legs could take him. The column turned into Hanover Street and passed him, keeping to the right hand side. Hancock himself was mounted in the middle of the street, commanding, encouraging, shouting, and cursing in his fashion. Capt. Patrick Condon of the 63rd saw Hancock ride behind a house and emerge with a handful of stragglers in tow.[20] At that point a revived Private DeHaven of the 116th rejoined his comrades. "This is what I came for," he said, through gritted teeth. The Irish brigade moved on and left the last of the houses behind; now they were out in the open, going down a gentle slope for about 200 yards.[21] The Confederate fire zeroed in, and a single shell landed within the ranks of the 88th, leveling eighteen men.

The 116th, already shaken by the sights and sounds, was stricken almost motionless as the first shell exploded overhead. Colonel Heenan fell, and the head of Sgt. John Marley was taken clean off. Lieutenant Colonel Mulholland got them moving on as quickly as possible, past the headless body still supported in a kneeling position by his musket.[22] Then there was some delay while the 69th inched over the planks that were all that remained of the bridge. The other four regiments sank down on that exposed plain for what seemed like hours while Nugent's men were passing over.

The last two regiments, 63rd and 116th, plunged through the ice-cold water when it came their turn and found the others forming line of battle. Some slight shelter was available in that slope of the hill which was in defilade from the Confederate fire. Last of all over the bridge came Meagher, supported by two privates who had been slightly wounded. He ordered that

19. *Ibid.*, p. 44.
20. *OR*, series 1, vol. 33, pt. 1, p. 249.
21. Mulholland, *116th Pennsylvania*, p. 43.
22. *Ibid.*, p. 45.

the brigade line should be straightened, and the guides were ordered out. Mulholland was amazed that there was no disorder. The commands were given in normal tones, and the regiments maneuvered without confusion. Now they were spread out and ready for the last push when Meagher made a change in alignment. The new 116th was on the extreme left flank, and the brigadier decided that their inexperience entitled them to a less exposed position; they exchanged places with the 63rd.

Meagher hobbled to the left flank and looked over the top of the slope that was shielding them for the moment. Before them was a plowed field and 150 yards ahead of them was the brigade of Samuel Zook, moving on. Meagher waved his hand and the brigade moved forward as one man. Once into the plowed field they began to double-time, and almost at the same instant the 63rd had to veer to avoid a regiment of French's division laying on the ground.[23] Meagher looked despairingly after them. In his present crippled condition he was of no use to anyone. Another officer might have found a safe spot and stayed there. But Meagher somehow got back across the ditch into the town and looked for his horse.

The brigade moved on. The 63rd encountered an obstruction in the shape of an abandoned earthwork that momentarily divided the command in two just as Maj. Joseph O'Neil was hit and went down. Capt. Patrick Condon of Company G ran over to the left flank which was moving off at a tangent and got it back in contact with the brigade. Men pitched forward and fell, leaped back and fell, ran to the left or right in momentary confusion. Mulholland fell early and had a spectator's view of the later stages of the action.

> The hills rained fire and the men advanced with heads bowed as when walking against a hailstorm. Still through the deadly shower the ever-thinning lines pressed on. The plain over which they had passed was thickly spotted with the men of the Second Corps, dead, in twos and threes and in groups. Regiments and companies had their third and fourth commander, and the colors were borne

23. *OR*, series 1, vol. 21, p. 250.

to the front by the third or fourth gallant soul who had raised them. The gaps in the lines had become so large and so numerous that continued efforts had to be made to close them, and the command "guide centre" was frequently heard.[24]

In the 69th, Nugent went down at one of the three fences which ran across the field of advance, and Major Cavanagh who succeeded Nugent fell a little later. That left Patrick Kelly of the 88th and Richard Byrnes of the 28th Massachusetts to lead the charge, and there is evidence that they tried. Through the smoke Kelly's men saw him out in front of them tugging at the rails of a fence.[25] Some of the 88th knelt down at it and began to fire at the suddenly quiet formation behind the stone wall. More patches of the brigade came out of the battlesmoke and the Green Flag of the 28th loomed up. They were not too far from the wall now, and soldiers from the regiments that preceded them jumped to their feet and went forward. Would this be another Antietam? Would the Irish break the line again? The rifles of the Georgians said no in a tremendous boom of sound that overpowered the artillery roar.

Down went the Irish Brigade. Those who were not casualties were simply blown off their feet by the force of the volley. After a moment, single shots came back from the huddle of bodies mounded up not thirty yards from the wall at one place and sloping back sharply on the left flank of the brigade. The color-bearer of the 116th was down on one knee, waving his flag back and forth although his other leg was shattered. Five balls struck him in succession, a dozen pierced the flag, one broke the staff, and Color Sergeant William Tyrrel pitched forward.

On the left Patrick Condon of the 63rd saw the next brigade coming up the slope, recognized Caldwell's men of their division, and incongruously had the thought that they were keeping a very straight line. His own men were not advanced as far as the men on the right of the brigade but were doing as much as flesh and blood were capable. Caldwell's men came up on the left flank and passed over the 63rd only to meet the

24. Mulholland, *116th Pennsylvania*, p. 50.
25. Walker, *History of the Second Corps*, p. 172.

terrible thunderclap of Georgia musketry. Back they came in less than two minutes over the Irish and rapidly to the rear.

By then even so stout a warrior as Patrick Kelly had had enough. He moved over to the 28th Massachusetts and found Colonel Byrnes.[26] They agreed to go over the field and withdraw whatever could be salvaged. Kelly went to his own men and the 69th where every single officer was a casualty. Byrnes went to the 63rd and the 116th, his color-bearer and about ten men behind him. There seemed to be few of the 116th and even fewer of the 63rd, so Byrnes' party went downhill and soon came on Patrick Condon supporting a wounded private with others of his regiment in tow. Byrnes shook his hand and said that the brigade was indeed gone. They picked a painful and torturous path down the slope and at last reached the comparative safety of the drainage ditch. At that spot were many men, some bleeding, some cowering in terror, some with a hopeless blankness on their faces. The Second Corps had tried; the stone wall and Ambrose Burnside had been too much even for them.

Back in the town, Meagher had finally mounted his horse and again rode up Hanover Street. He had hardly left the shelter of the houses before he met a remnant of the 63rd coming back. Patrick Condon was still carrying the wounded soldier at this point, and was looking for a hospital in which to leave him:

> I recrossed the mill-race, still bearing this wounded man with me, and followed by other men of our regiment, under a fusillading fire from cannon and sharpshooters, and marched up the street on the sidewalk, then the right-hand one of the road we traveled, about 500 yards; and on a cross-road, to the right from the canal, we overtook our colors, in the hands of Sergeant [Patrick] Chambers, of Company I. Captains [John] Sullivan and [John H.] Gleeson and Lieutenants [John] Dwyer, [William] Quirk, [William H.] Higgins, [John] Flynn, and [Lawrence] Daidy were there with 11 men. General Meagher was there on horseback, and said that this should be the rallying

26. *OR*, series 1, vol. 21, p. 252.

point of the brigade. In two or three minutes this place became too hot for us, so we marched down the street toward the position we occupied in the lower part of the city before going into action.[27]

There were few of the 69th with the 63rd, and Meagher must have died a thousand deaths looking at the disheveled, sad remnant of his command. But he directed those fit enough to turn around and take position at the ends of the streets facing the enemy. The wounded were led and carried to hospitals which had been established in the houses of the street where they had formed. There was steady leakage of men back across the ditch and into the town. The long, cold afternoon went on, and more men, bleeding and exhausted, dragged in. The streets of the town became a giant hospital which under the Confederate artillery fire was not much safer than the hillside. Meagher kept a close check on the number of men who came in and by 4 p.m. he had about 300 altogether. So he sent two aides, Capt. William G. Hart and Lt. John J. Blake for Hancock's permission to take this tiny remnant back across the Rappahannock to the camp at Falmouth.[28] He reasoned that the brigade could do little in its condition, either for offensive or defensive purposes. Even as the answer was awaited, artillery salvos exploded over the survivors.

Hart soon came back with what Meagher assumed was conditional authorization, and the battered band made its way over the pontoon bridge to the Stafford County shore.[29] As the afternoon wore on and no more men appeared, Meagher became increasingly distraught. Antietam had been bad enough. This was infinitely worse. At Antietam at least he had personally led in the attack. Here he had only sent it out to die. His mood grew blacker, for here was ruin, both personal and professional. Late in the day, bad knee and all, he began to range through the town, stopping at various headquarters for solace and reassurance. At the Ninth Corps he told Brig. Gen. Orlando Willcox that his own command was gone and asked if he could serve as an aide on Willcox's staff, a sure

27. *Ibid.*, p. 250.
28. *Ibid.*, p. 243.
29. *Ibid.*

indication of Meagher's distraught condition.[30] If ever a man needed help it was Meagher on that afternoon. And from black, bottomless misery, gradually his mood turned to rage, rage at the witless fools who had taken his friends and his men from him. Many a Union commander was going through the same cycle of feeling, for the attacks had been kept up on Marye's Heights all through the afternoon into the evening. Always it had been the same story. The Second Corps' First Division had suffered the most.

Meagher went to the Stafford County side of the river after awhile to see to his men and then rode to see Sumner at his headquarters in the Lacy house. The old dragoon was not there, but, before Meagher left, Burnside himself rode up. He heard the sad story of the assaults on the stone wall with equanimity and even asked after the wounded men with solicitude. Sumner arrived and the story had to be repeated to him. In addition, Meagher asked for rations. His men had thrown away their hardtack before charging the hill, and in their spent condition they badly needed sustenance. Later, at about 10 p.m. Meagher re-crossed the river and went to that part of the town where the brigade hospitals had been established. Many more wounded men had crept in by now, some in great agony. Dr. Francis Powell was summoned and came over the pontoons.

At about 11 p.m., Meagher rode to Hancock's headquarters and reported his actions of the day. He immediately found out that Hancock had never given Meagher permission to withdraw his command over the river. Furthermore, he was ordered to get his men back to where they belonged at once. In telling of this incident Hancock's report is restrained, but everything that is known of his character leads one to believe that Meagher had a bad ten minutes.[31] The weary men on the Stafford County side were got up before daybreak and taken back to Fredericksburg again. There were but 290, Meagher said, who were fit for duty. This gave poetic license to some Irish-American poets intrigued by the age-old Gaelic theme of glorious failure: "Twelve hundred they went, and three hundred came back."

30. *Ibid.*
31. *Ibid.*, p. 228.

In later years it was pointed out, ad infinitum, that the Georgians behind the stone wall, or some of them at any rate, were Irish too, and John Boyle O'Reilly wrote a poem that told of, "But Irish in love, they are enemies still."[32]

In their reports both Zook and Caldwell, who preceded and followed the Irish, claimed that no one got so close to the wall as their men, and almost every regimental commander said the same. Condon of the 63rd says quite frankly that Caldwell's men advanced past him a "little," but Mulholland in his regimental history says that the Irish Brigade got the closest, insisting that Maj. William Horgan and Adjt. John R. Young of the 88th were the bodies found closest to the wall.[33]

The enemy is on record, too, and a gunner who stood by the iron tubes of the Washington Artillery gave the cause of the Irish a great boost:

> . . . our fire was murderous, and no troops on earth could stand the *feu d'enfer* we were giving them. In the foremost line we distinguished the green flag with the golden harp of old Ireland, and we knew it to be Meagher's Irish brigade. The gunners of the two rifle-pieces, Corporals [John N.] Payne and [William T.] Hardie, were directed to turn their guns against this column; but the gallant enemy pushed on beyond all former charges, and fought and left their dead within five and twenty paces of the sunken road.[34]

Although William Miller Owen wrote that piece many years later, it is evident that the sight of the Green Flag stayed with him. By the next day, freezing Confederates had come over the wall and stripped the bodies of the Union dead. In the process, the exact locations of some of the bodies probably changed. Historian Douglas Southall Freeman, says that the bodies closest to the wall wore the badges of the 5th New Hampshire, the 53rd Pennsylvania, and the 69th New York. He gives no

32. J. J. Roche, ed., *Life and Poems of John Boyle O'Reilly* (Boston: n.p., 1888), p. 468.
33. Mulholland, *116th Pennsylvania*, p. 50.
34. William M. Owen, "A Hot Day on Marye's Heights," in *Battles and Leaders*, 3:98.

reference for this statement, but has evidently taken it from the historian of the Second Corps, Francis A. Walker, who says it is the evidence of Col. John Brooke who commanded the 53rd Pennsylvania. On December 17, Burnside asked for a truce to bury the Union dead, and Brooke was the commander of the burial detail for the Second Corps. Brooke said nothing about this in his report of the battle, so Walker was probably quoting an oral statement.[35]

In later years it was not enough for St.Clair Mulholland who was bent on finding out all he could about which brigade got closest to the stone wall. He ran down Brooke, who had continued in the army after the war, in Montana territory where he was in command of Fort Shaw. Brooke wrote back on January 8, 1881:

> In answer to your question as to the dead at Fredericksburg. The dead found nearest the enemy on that field belonged to the 1st Div. 2nd Corps. There was a question about this referred to me early in 1877 and I then settled the matter by the same answer I give you. The particular Regt there belonged to was the 69th NY and it occurred in this way - The Regts on the right of Hancock's three brigades were 53d P.V. 5th N.H. & 69th N.Y.
>
> The three Regts reached the same point in their advance and after the 69th N.Y. came up it was in the same line with the 53d P.V. and 5th N.H. and for a long time they continued to occupy precisely the same line. The Color Sergt. and guard of the 69th N.Y. then moved forward about 20 ft to a low place in the ground, for better protection, I presume, and there I found all or nearly all who went to that point (to be) dead. I do not know if any of the party escaped, it is possible that such is the case but I do not know. These few men were, as nearly as I can remember, about 20 feet in advance of the point which the three Regts, 53d P.V. 5th N.H. & 69th N.Y. reached. . . .[36]

35. Walker, *History of the Second Corps*, p. 187.
36. James R. Brooke to St. Clair Mulholland, January 8, 1881, Mulholland Collection, War Library and Museum, Philadelphia.

A Confederate soldier wrote a letter to the *New York Sun* which appeared in the edition of April 21, 1863. Bismuth Miller said that a dying Union soldier gasped to him that he was in the 69th New York. This man, said Miller, lay "possibly ten feet" from the stonewall.

The piece de resistance of praise for the action of the brigade came from the hereditary enemy. On January 13, 1863, the London *Times* carried the following from its correspondent with the Army of Northern Virginia:

> Never at Fontenoy, Albuera, or Waterloo was more undaunted courage displayed by the sons of Erin than during those six frantic dashes which they directed against the almost impregnable position of their foe. . . . But the bodies which lie in dense masses within 40 yards of the muzzles of Colonel [James B.] Walton's guns are the best evidence of what manner of men they were who pressed on to death with the dauntlessness of a race which has gained glory on a thousand battlefields, and never more richly deserved it than at the foot of Marye's Heights on the 13th day of December, 1862.[37]

Of course there had not been any six frantic dashes made exclusively by the Irish Brigade. It is almost certain that the survivors of the first encounter who stayed on the hill joined in some of the later attempts, but the brigade's actions from the battle reports of the men who knew best, Colonels Patrick Kelly and Richard Byrnes, say nothing of any later concerted efforts.

Probably on one of his several trips back and forth across the river on the night of December 13, Meagher was made aware that a committee of prominent civilians had arrived from New York with new Green Flags, the gifts of American citizens. Accompanying them were several wagons loaded down with the refreshments that went with such a presentation.[38] Perhaps Meagher felt that his days in the army were numbered after his withdrawal of his men without orders. Maybe he was so

---

37. The London *Times*, January 13, 1863, Union defeat at Fredericksburg.
38. Cavanagh, *Memoirs of Thomas Meagher*, p. 471.

disgusted with the leadership that he did not care, or possibly he was in a state of shock after the battle. In any case and for whatever reason, he decided to go through with the flag ceremony, but with a difference. He would have his colonels refuse the colors on the ground that their commands were too weak numerically to carry and guard them properly. This would have two effects. It would dramatize the contributions of the brigade, and it might get them relieved long enough to establish a recruiting mission in New York.[39]

To further dramatize the presentation, he decided to hold it in the streets of Fredericksburg itself. The town contained a little theater building located in one of the upper streets. It would do very nicely for the ceremony and the feast that would go with it. At high noon on December 14, the day after the almost total extermination of the brigade, the chief officers of the army or those who could be spared from duty converged on the small building. On the stage sat twenty-two generals as Meagher's particular guests. In the body of the building were two or three hundred others, mostly of field rank. Directly in the center of the hall were two rows of tables covered with the requisite material for an elaborate banquet. The food had been cooked by some of the same privates who had stormed up Marye's Heights the day before.

Outside, the Confederate artillery intermittently fired at the Union infantry hugging the ground on the rim of the town. Cavanagh, Meagher's biographer, gives the best account of what has become known as the "Death Feast":

> . . . rarely, if ever, was a public banquet held under such discouraging circumstances. No wonder that even some of the most illustrious participants in the festivities at *first* regarded the whole proceeding as inexplicable—save on the theory that the Celtic nature was so constituted, and its temperament so elastic, that, from the lowest depths of depression it could rebound almost instantaneously into the airiest and most exhilarating joyousness of spirit.
>
> But those guests who looked below the surface, soon discovered a deeper and nobler cause for their

39. *Ibid.*, p. 476.

host's action, and that of his comrades of the brigade. For what time could be more opportune for giving public expression to the feelings of bitter indignation against the political partizanship which drenched the neighboring fields with the blood of the nation's best and bravest defenders. . . .

After the presentation of the new Colors to the commanding officers of the several Regiments of the Brigade then present . . . the chairman commenced, in his usual form, to give the toasts of the evening.

In connection with the performance of this portion of General Meagher's duties, a gallant officer of the brigade, then present, related the following thrilling incident:—

"Among the Generals present on the stage, and occupying a seat next to General Meagher, on the left, was Brigadier-General Alfred Sully, who then commanded the First Brigade, Second Division, Second Army Corps. . . . On rising to propose the health of this distinguished soldier, General Meagher said:—

"'Generals, brother officers, and comrades of the Army of the Potomac; fill your glasses to the brim. I have the honor, the pride, and pleasure, to ask you to drink to the health of my esteemed friend on my left,—General Alfred Sully: and I want you to understand, gentlemen, that *he* is not one of your 'Political Generals,' but a brave and accomplished soldier— *who attracted his 'star' from the firmament of glory— by the electricity of his sword!'*"

The effect was startling. A momentary silence was followed by an enthusiastic cheer of delight and admiration. So absorbed were the officers in the beauty and originality of the picture depicted in lightning colors by the inspired soldier-orator, that, for a moment they failed to notice the bold allusion to "Political Generals." It was but a moment, however, when the full significance of the phrase burst upon their mental vision, and a spontaneous shout showed how fully the allusion was comprehended and appreciated. After that there remained no doubt of

Meagher's chief reason for holding the "Death Feast."[40]

Even as the hall rang with the applause engendered by the speech, another development was taking place up on the bluff where the Washington Artillery had fired from on the day before. Some sharp Confederate eyes had noted the concentration of saddled mounts around the theater. Three salvos hurtled into the area and the hardy souls who had served the banquet decided that they had had enough, even if their officers had not. One picked up a roundshot which had recently richocheted off the facade of a building and placed it on a serving platter. He thereupon marched into the hall just as Meagher was at the height of his panegyric to the dead of yesterday. It stopped the show. Perhaps Meagher's guests, having destroyed the provender, were only waiting for a good excuse to decamp. Now they fled in almost reckless haste. That night the Army of the Potomac marched back across the river to the Stafford County shore, numbed by the thoughts of leaving the mounded-up bodies of their friends; numbed by the inconsequentialty of life and the casualness of death.

Maybe Meagher had some second thoughts. Maybe he realized that he had, in the presence of a group of senior officers, thrown down the gauntlet, not particularly to Burnside, but to the administration in Washington. This army had had enough of those hard-fighting abolitionist generals. First there was John Pope, and now Ambrose Burnside. Another such leader and the Confederacy might be an accomplished fact. Many senior officers in the army felt the same way Meagher did, and in the ensuing weeks two of them would bypass the commanding general to approach the civil authorities.[41] All were appalled at the useless sacrifice of life on December 13. But if they cheered Meagher's sentiment in the heat of the moment and the whiskey punch, when they returned to their commands the second thoughts about loyalty to constituted authority would return. Meagher was on very thin ice as a brigadier on the night of December 14.

40. *Ibid.*, p. 472-73.
41. Swinton, *Campaigns of the Army of the Potomac*, p. 263.

Two things probably saved him. First, Burnside was in no humor to punish anyone who took exception to his generalship. The horror and waste of the battle had reduced him to weeping and hand-wringing. Why should others not doubt him? He had always doubted himself. So Meagher's defiance would not even be passed on to the commanding general by sympathetic aides who felt he had enough of a burden. Nor, it turned out, would Hancock press charges for removing his brigade across the river on the night of December 13. It was a small enough thing, and there was evidence that Meagher was misguided. Furthermore, there was evidence that the men had acted as well as anyone else in the battle, and the situation, once known, was speedily rectified. No problem with Hancock.

But there was one thing Meagher would do to bring home to the people of New York the terrible loss his men had suffered. He had Major Horgan's body recovered from in front of the stone wall, embalmed, and sent home for a public funeral. Horgan would stand for all those poor, frozen corpses with the green boxwood sprigs in their caps. In addition, Meagher applied for sick leave because of his knee and accompanied the body of Horgan home. He arrived with his charge on Christmas Day at noon, and Horgan's body was placed in the old headquarters of the Irish Brigade at 596 Broadway with a guard of honor around it. On the following Sunday the corpse was taken to the governor's room in the city hall until 2 p.m. when the largest funeral cortege in the history of New York City accompanied it to its final resting place in Calvary Cemetery.[42] Meagher's knee was going from bad to worse, and after the funeral he took to his bed for ten days under the care of a surgeon. There was time to think about what was to become of the brigade now, as well as what was to become of him.

As for the latter, it must have been apparent that whether the command of the army might be placed in the hands of a Burnside or a Pope, the lower echelons would be filled by men of ability. Even his admirers and men who served under him had no delusions on that score. Although not excellent as a tactician, wrote Lt. William L. D. O'Grady of the 88th,

---

42. Cavanagh, *Memoirs of Thomas Meagher*, p. 472-73.

General Meagher was most solicitous for the welfare of his men.[43] He had been placed under arrest for a day on the Peninsula for misunderstanding an order. His chances for advancing to division command appeared to be slim. If anyone in the administration thought of it at all, which is doubtful, the name of Meagher counted for little. A good bit of mileage had been gotten from it early on in the war in getting the Irish behind the Union cause. But Corcoran was back now and, anyway, the bounty system would bring in the "bould soldier bhoys" of the future. Who needed Meagher?

Actually, although one might feel from some accounts of the battle that only the Irish Brigade of all the Army of the Potomac had been engaged on Marye's Heights, Hancock's division as a whole had been wrecked. Zook's brigade had taken in as many effectives as Meagher's and suffered almost exactly the same number of casualties. Caldwell's brigade had a much higher percentage of loss. Two excellent regiments from Western Pennsylvania, the 140th and the 148th, arrived at Falmouth to join the division a few days after the battle and were appalled at the sights and sounds in evidence on every side:

> As we marched to our place of encampment through the open ranks of a host of spectators from the Irish Brigade and other neighboring commands, with our comparatively new uniforms and equipments and full companies, we were chaffed not a little on the newness of our appearance and the fullness of our ranks. One called out, "Whose brigade is this?" "Aw," chimed in another, who had caught sight of our heavy muskets, "them's the walking artillery." "Luk at them twelve pounders." Further on we hear the greeting, "Glad to see you bys, but ye ought to have been here three or four days ago. Niver mind, bys, ye'll catch it yet," and the like. The men who were thus disposed to criticise our freshness and lack of military experience, were the veterans of the Potomac Army who had just returned from the bloody field of Fredericksburg, and it was pathetic to see the

43. *New York at Gettysburg*, 2:513.

little groups which remained in their company streets, or rallied around their colors, where once had been full companies and regiments like our own. From official sources, as well as from the men themselves, we learned that Hancock's Division had been in the very thick of the fight over the River and that every regiment belonging to it had suffered phenomenally heavy losses in the vain attempts which had been made again and again to take the impregnable defences on Marye's Heights.[44]

So wrote the historian of the 140th who had many occasions to see and observe the Irish Brigade during the next two years. The other new boys, the 148th, set up camp right beside the Irish. They soon found that the commissary of their neighbors could be raided at will, the Irish drawing a great deal more than they needed in the way of rations.[45]

Christmas in camp of 1862 was the low point of the war for the Army of the Potomac. "Winter of our discontent," is a shop-worn line, but there is no more fitting one. The desertions began, the sick lists lengthened. Men who had survived the Dies Irae stole away from the cold, wearying army, leaving their comrades, their hopes, and their country's destiny. In the early part of January, Burnside tried to mount an offensive with a wide, flanking move up the river. The weather was against him and the move disintegrated into a fiasco aptly described as the "Mud March." The Second Corps was not involved in this, fortunately enough, and the remains of the Irish Brigade watched in silence as their cold and miserable comrades straggled back to the camp, too exhausted for anger.

44. Robert Laird Stewart, *History of the 140th Regiment Pennsylvania Volunteers* (Philadelphia: Printed by the Franklin bindery, 1912), pp. 26-27.
45. Joseph W. Muffly, *The Story of Our Regiment: A History of the 148th Pennsylvania Volunteers* (Des Moines: Kenyon Printing and Manufacturing Company, 1904), pp. 167-68.

CHAPTER NINE

CELEBRATIONS AND SUPPLICATIONS

Ambrose Burnside departed the Army of the Potomac at the end of January 1863. The new commander, Maj. Gen. Joseph Hooker, had none of his predecessor's lack of confidence. Hooker had commanded a division on the Peninsula and at Second Manassas, the First Corps at Antietam, and the Center Grand Division at Fredericksburg. There had never been any love lost between him and Burnside.

To men who had known him in the Old Army, Hooker was a curious mixture of strengths and weaknesses. To the enlisted men of the Army of the Potomac, he was a godsend. Rations were improved, the medical service was tightened up, and, best of all, the new leader instituted a system of furloughs whereby a certain number of men from each regiment were given two weeks at home with their families. As it turned out, the system did not work very effectively, and only a small portion of the army ever saw home. It was the idea of the project more than its implementation that brought to the men the thought that someone was looking after them. They had lost a father-image on November 7, and gone through hell on earth on December 13. If Hooker was not a father-image, at least he was a familiar figure from the pre-Burnside era which the army needed.

As the winter softened perceptibly, there was a renewed recourse to the drill field, and if the maneuverings back and forth were no novelty, the routine filled in the hours. On January 26, the 116th Pennsylvania was disbanded as a regiment and reconstituted as a battalion of four companies. Col. Dennis Heenan and Maj. George H. Bardwell were gone from the war, and Lt. Col. St. Clair A. Mulholland, recovered from his wound, took a reduction from his rank to major in order to stay in command.[1]

Meagher came back from New York. In addition to burying Horgan, he had a requiem Mass sung in St. Patrick's Cathedral for the dead of the brigade, and, apparently, gotten no place in his plans for personal advancement. He wrote to the donors of the new colors for his New York regiments, going into a great deal of detail as to their losses and why the colors had been refused. The letter was published in the newspapers, the first shot in a campaign to get the organization sent home for recruiting. Possibly the New York congressmen were asked to put some heat on the War Department along the same lines. But the month of February went by and nothing happened. On February 19 Meagher wrote a letter to Secretary of War Stanton. It seems inconceivable that he would do so without the consent of his superiors up to corps level. It is a restrained letter for Meagher, and the writing of it may indicate that his supporters in New York and Congress had failed. In fact, there is an element of hopelessness in it as though Meagher did not expect a good issue to result, but simply wanted to get his case down on the record.

The letter is only concerned with the three New York regiments which, together, numbered 531 enlisted men. The other two regiments, 28th Massachusetts and 116th Pennsylvania, had a comparable 527 enlisted men. The New Yorkers, however, counted 91 officers against 48 for the other two regiments. Here is the rub. Unless some men were provided soon, there would be a mass exodus of New York officers. Unless a minimum field strength was maintained, the organization itself would pass out of existence. The letter then gave a full and restrained recital of the service of the brigade from its joining the army up to and including the battle of Fredericksburg. The record was long, bloody, and honorable, and Meagher ended it by saying "No brigade in the army of the United States has more assiduously, unremittingly, bravely, nobly done its duty." He then asked that the three New York regiments be furloughed home to recruit, for unless they showed themselves in their home city under their tattered Green Flags, there would be no accession of sturdy Irish lads

1. Mulholland, *116th Pennsylvania*, p. 73.

to succeed them. Then followed the sharp dart thrown. Stanton's attention was directed to the "fact that decimated regiments from Maine, Massachusetts, and Connecticut have been ordered home" to recruit. The unspoken question, of course, asks, "If the black Republicans can take a breather, why, then, cannot the Irish?"

The letter continued by adopting a sort of a "dog in the manger" attitude. Meagher argued that he was exposing himself to all sorts of imputations as to lack of courage, character, and conviction by appearing to dodge his duty to remain with the Army of the Potomac. Nevertheless, he had a greater responsibility to the honor of his men. He was willing to let people say what they wanted to about him.

In the last section of the letter something is veiled:

> I have alluded to considerations of public and national interest in forwarding this application.
>
> These considerations form a part of the application, which I do not conceive it proper or essential for me to submit at large, or in detail to the Secretary of War, and shall, therefore, confine myself, as I do conscientiously, and with the deepest and strongest conviction that the relief of the 1st, 2d and 3d regiments of the Brigade from duty in the field, will result in an important accession to their ranks. . . .[2]

What in heaven's name was Meagher talking about here? Was this a threat to the administration that reprisals would follow from the Irish electorate of the nation if the request was not granted? Meagher should have had a better sense of politics than that. The Lincoln administration, never having had the Irish vote, was in no sense afraid of losing it. If Meagher thought these were sharp teeth he was fooling himself. Stanton would never be frightened by a political specter of this kind. But the letter was written and the general waited for an answer.

Two events came along to fill in the time. Hooker decided that in the interest of better morale each of the infantry corps would wear a distinctive insignia on the flat part of the cap.

2. Cavanagh, *Memoirs of Thomas Meagher*, appendix p. 23.

The First Corps was to wear a solid, circular device, sometimes called a disc. Philip Kearny's old division of the Third Corps had been wearing a red diamond ever since the Peninsula, and that badge was extended to the other divisions of the Third Corps. The Fifth and Sixth Corps wore crosses, the former Maltese, the latter Greek. The Eleventh Corps had a crescent and the Twelfth Corps a star. For the Second Corps there was much speculation as to why a trefoil was picked. The Irish said it was clearly a shamrock, but the Anglos did not agree. It was clearly a club, one of the four suits of a poker hand. But club or shamrock there was no doubt in anyone's mind as to why they were wearing it. The historian of the 140th Pennsylvania, later to become a noted Presbyterian minister, had the following to say about the matter:

> The device assigned to the Second Corps was the trefoil or shamrock. The adoption of this form of badge was probably suggested by General Meagher, or given out of courtesy to the men of the corps who had borne aloft in every battle, with the colors of the Nation, the green flag of Erin's Isle.[3]

Mulholland elaborated:

> The men of the Irish Brigade added to the red clover leaf an emblem of the same form, though of a different color—a small, green shamrock, this denoting the brigade organization as well as the division and corps.[4]

Whatever the device, in each corps the first division of the corps wore it in red, the second division in white, and the third division in blue. But corps badge and all, there was no letter from Stanton.

As St. Patrick's Day approached, Meagher resolved to take a hand in morale-building himself. The day would be celebrated with every single device in the book to call attention to its importance. A committee was formed of officers and

---

3. Stewart, *140th Pennsylvania*, p. 45.
4. Mulholland, *116th Pennsylvania*, p. 75.

collections of money taken up. Men departed on mysterious errands to Washington to buy the makings of a feast. The Death Feast at Fredericksburg was now forgotten. On March 17, 1863, the Day of Patrick would be a day to remember not for the Irish alone but for the entire army.

Throughout the evening of March 16, the musicians of the army kept rattling away at one tune, a spirit-raising, toe-tickling tune for even the most anti-Romanist New Englander, "St. Patrick's Day." When the day broke the morning was sunny and beautiful, the earth gave evidence with its green mantle that the time for renewal was at hand. As soon as the morning formations for fatigue, sick call, and breakfast were over, throngs of soldiers converged on the camp of the brigade. A spacious tent had been erected for Father Corby to say Mass and the service was carried out with as much attention to the fine points of the liturgy as if it were St. Peter's in Rome. Father Joseph B. O'Hagan, chaplain of the Excelsior Brigade (70th, 71st, 72nd, 73rd, 74th New York Volunteers) preached a sermon after the Mass. The outdoor sports were many and varied, but the chief event was a steeplechase race for officers of the brigade riding their own horses. There was as purse of $500, and the race was to be run over a two-and-a-half mile course which had already been marked off.

Just before 11 a.m. up rode Joe Hooker himself, attended by as many of his staff as could be spared from duty. All of the officers of the army had been issued a blanket invitation to the festivities, and large numbers appeared. Some wives of senior commanders were in camp, and they attended also. Hooker at once called for three cheers for "General Meagher and his Irish Brigade. God bless them." Then the horses approached the starting line; oddly enough the two course judges were both Germans, Col. Ernest Von Vegesack, 20th New York, and Col. Paul Frank, 52nd New York. Meagher did not ride but had entered his big gray horse, Jack Hinton, ridden by his aide, Capt. Jack Gosson. It is a wonder that Gosson made the scene, for he had been one of the six officers chosen to mix the whiskey punch the night before. But he rode well enough to win the first two heats and the gray horse was declared the winner.

There were other horse races open to all, and at 1 p.m. an intermission was declared while the guests descended hungrily on the thirty-five hams, a side of roast oxen, pigs stuffed with turkey, chickens, ducks, and game, all washed down with the punch concocted the night before. Ten gallons of rum, twenty-two of whiskey, and eight magnums of champagne had gone into it, and it was dispensed by Captain Gosson from an enormous bowl, thought by Colonel Mulholland to hold not less than thirty gallons.

In the afternoon there were contests for the enlisted men; footraces, weight throwing, Irish dancing, wheelbarrow races, sack races, and finally trying to catch a greased pig. After dinner there was singing, recitations, speeches, and several attempts at theatricals. To end it all was a poem by Dr. Laurence Reynolds of the 63rd. The same sort of program was put on in the Fifth Corps by the 9th Massachusetts who enjoyed a particularly warm relationship with the 62nd Pennsylvania. At 11 o'clock each man of the 9th shared a gill of whisky with a friend of the 62nd. After the races there was an attempt to climb a greased pole to the top of which had been attached a ten day furlough. No one made it to the top because the grease had been applied too thickly to the pole. A note of tragedy was struck in the afternoon when Quartermaster Thomas Mooney was fatally injured in a horse race. The day finished up with a mock dress parade in which enlisted men took the place of the officers. A private of Company F was particularly effective in imitating the voice and mannerisms of Colonel Guiney. The other Irish regiments held smaller celebrations or attended the big affair of Meagher.

The weather turned warmer and the army was back again in the routine of camp life. A Second Corps inspection report had the 88th New York and the 69th Pennsylvania so lacking in discipline and appearance on March 3 that all furloughs for officers in the two regiments were cancelled. By March 14 things had so been straightened out that the furlough possibilities were restored. But there was still no word from the War Department to Meagher as to a furlough for his entire brigade to go back to New York to recruit. It certainly would not have been a numerical loss to the army for the brigade was almost at its lowest ebb. On April 8, President Lincoln visited the army and watched it pass in review. The morning report strength was in the neighborhood of 130,000 men, and Hooker had no hesitation in calling it the "finest army on the planet." He also made some bombastic utterances about not having any mercy on Lee in the coming campaign. He should have be-thought himself of the fate of John Pope.

There was a huge rally in New York City on April 11, held at the Academy of Music to raise funds for Ireland, which was again threatened with famine. The mayor presided and there was the usual contingent of important men, both Irish and American, to whip up enthusiasm for a worthy cause. Arch-bishop Hughes, Gen. George McClellan, Horace Greeley, and Meagher were some of those on the platform. In leaving the army to attend the rally, Meagher lost an opportunity to speak with Lincoln on his visit to Falmouth on April 8. Perhaps Meagher had already received word through private sources that it would do no good. At any rate he had some good words to say of McClellan at the Academy, calling him "the best beloved and foremost of . . . generals." Meagher wound up by saying ". . . I have spoken the sentiments of all that remains of the Irish Brigade."[5] It was not at all the kind of thing the administration wanted anyone to hear, and it is unlikely that it did him or his prospects any good. He was back in Falmouth on April 26, arriving in the midst of Hooker's preparations to carry the fight to Lee in the spring campaign of 1863.[6] The Army of the Potomac was to meet its steadfast opponent again.

Wonder has been evinced that Hooker could conceive so well and move so swiftly as he did in the opening phases of the maneuvering that led to the Battle of Chancellorsville. The courage of the lion and the combativeness of the badger had marked his performances as a division and a corps commander. The cunning of the fox had not been thought of as one of his qualities. But to everyone's surprise, by May 1 his blue columns had breached the watery barrier of the Rappahannock in strength in two widely separated places. Lee might have been in mortal trouble had not another of Hooker's facets manifested itself, the indecisiveness of the doubter. Con-fronted with the entire pot on the table before him, Hooker halted his army when pushing on would have given him a rare opportunity, a double envelopment of the Army of Northern Virginia. Given the man that Hooker was, however, the bubble burst and the golden opportunity was frittered away.

5. Cavanagh, *Memoirs of Thomas Meagher*, pp. 478-80.
6. *Ibid.*, pp. 480-82.

CHAPTER TEN
SPRINGTIME IN A WILDERNESS

In later years, when he had left the 116th Pennsylvania and the war behind, St. Clair Mulholland turned to the arts and there is little wonder. He had an instinctive love and appreciation for beauty, both natural and that fashioned by the hand of man. On April 27, 1863, as he marched his Philadelphians along the north bank of the Rappahannock, his soul was aflame with the wild flowered charm of Northern Virginia. The path of the column led away from the winter camp at Falmouth into the virgin forest laden with the cool, green promise of restoring nature. The 69th New York marched directly ahead, reduced to a two-company battalion of seventy-eight men. Behind at Bank's Ford had been left the 63rd and 88th New York regiments each of which had been similarly reduced to a two-company battalion. Somewhere on a parallel road was the 28th Massachusetts also bound for United States Ford.

Mulholland's march was slow and easy with many halts and rests. On all sides the forest teemed with rabbits, coveys of partridge and quail, and crashing deer in the underbrush. There were imperative orders not to fire, but some men supplemented their diet by knocking over rabbits with thrown cudgels.[1] By sunset they were at United States Ford and Confederate pickets on the other side were exchanging greetings with them. There was no firing, but Mulholland thought that the Johnnies were puzzled and nervous at this appearance of a strong Union force. Patrick Kelly of the 88th was in charge of the detachment, and there was some little doubt, from the reports, as to whether he or Meagher was in charge of the brigade. Meagher had arrived at Falmouth from New York only the day before but had not accompanied

1. Mulholland, *116th Pennsylvania*, pp. 91-92.

the column from the campground.[2] About 5 p.m. he rode up, relieved Patrick Kelly, and sent him back to the 88th at Banks' Ford. The 28th Massachusetts was at Hartwood Church for the night, seven miles away, and would come up the next day. This was important since the Boston Irish were almost as large a group numerically as the others put together. There is some hint of friction between Meagher and Hancock, in the notes passed between them and in Meagher's report. The latter seems quite upset at having to find his way to the ford without a guide.

At 9 a.m. on April 28 the detachment at United States Ford was ordered back to Banks' Ford for a reunion with the rest of the division. They learned that Joe Hooker had proven himself to be a military genius. By stealth and brains the Fifth, Eleventh, and Twelfth Corps had been moved on a wide arc over the Rapidan and the upper fords of the Rappahannock to force the watery barrier. Now they were marching down the south bank of the river to uncover the lower fords. The rest of the army would cross and the great bastion of Fredericksburg would be effectively turned. That terrible slope up Marye's Heights would not again have to be bought with Union blood. Lee was in the bag. Or so everyone thought, not having too good a measure of Joe Hooker as yet.

First Division, Second Corps, crossed on a pontoon bridge which the engineers had erected at United States Ford. The Irish Brigade crossed by moonlight and found evidence that the Confederate pickets had left in a great hurry. Meagher's men were placed across the "River Road" as Maj. Gen. Darius N. Couch called it in his report, facing east in the direction of Banks' Ford. The brigade spent a very uncomfortable night since the road was bordered by a swamp. Water snakes crawled around in frightening numbers, frogs croaked, and hundreds of whippoorwills filled the night with their melancholy calling. When daylight came the men of the brigade became aware of a beautiful dry ridge close by where they could have spent the night in comfort.[3]

Friday, May 1, was a quiet day for the Second Corps, although the distant crash of musketry could be heard to the

2. *Ibid.*, p. 92.
3. *Ibid.*, p. 94.

south and east as the Unionists pushed out the Orange Plank Road and the Orange Turnpike toward Fredericksburg. Then in the afternoon there was a lull. If the men could only have known, this was the time that Hooker lost his nerve. Having outgeneraled Lee, Hooker had come to the moment of crisis, looked within himself and decided that he did not have the moral fiber to outfight Robert E. Lee. In spite of overwhelming force, advantage of position, and the incalculable intangible of momentum, it all came to naught. The Union army fell back to a defensive position and awaited the next step. Lee and his collaborator Jackson were quick to give it to them.

The 88th New York had been detailed to guard the division ammunition train and was separated from the rest of the Irish Brigade. As a result of this the "Connacht Rangers" had a much more active part in the battle than the others. Hancock's division took up a position perpendicular to the Orange Turnpike, and advanced so far in front of French's division of the Second Corps that the latter might be thought of as Hancock's reserve. When the 88th appeared with the ammunition train to supply this force, the men were at once put in the line with two old friends, the 5th New Hampshire and 81st Pennsylvania.[4] On the right Hancock connected with the Twelfth Corps and on his left with the Fifth Corps. The Union line here was quite formidable, and later that day Lee pondered where he could throw his army with effect. After dark he got his answer. Confederate cavalry officer Fitzhugh Lee had found that Hooker had left the right flank of the Union army hanging in the air. If one proceeded westward from the Chancellor House along the Orange Turnpike he found the Union Eleventh Corps facing south. But there were no more Union troops beyond their right flank. If Lee could march some of his small army across the front of the mighty host in blue he could strike the Eleventh Corps a crippling blow. If the right man were to command this operation the entire Union line facing south on the turnpike might be rolled up like a carpet. Fortunately for Lee and the Confederacy, the right man was at hand. At 7 a.m. on May 2 the hard marchers of the Second Corps of the Army of Northern Virginia headed west into the forest of the Wilder-

4. Walker, *History of the Second Corps*, p. 231.

ness under Lt. Gen. Thomas J. Jackson. The greatest coup of the greatest command team in military history was at hand.

At about the same time that Jackson's men were vanishing into the Wilderness, the Irish brigade changed position from watching the River Road to the extreme right of the Union position. Their new station was at Scott's Mills on the Rappahannock. Mulholland said that this was the extreme right of the line and some qualification must be made. Most of the available Union force had advanced past this position on May 1 and then had fallen back late in the day, so that Scott's Mills was the extreme left of the Union line. Next to them in line was Meade's Fifth Corps stretching south to Mineral Run. The entire day of May 2 was spent in listening to the sound of distant musketry as Lee engaged in local frontal attacks to keep Hooker's attention away from Jackson's flanking movement. But even so far from the action the rumors of a Confederate flanking attack were rife and everyone was nervous. Meagher prowled up and down his line, stopping occasionally to encourage the men to make a good fight.[5]

Sometime during the day the line turned around and faced west, exactly 180 degrees from their former position. A strong abatis was cut along the front, but Meagher was justified in feeling uneasy. Both flanks were in the air and there was no connection on either side. Late in the afternoon, as Meagher was addressing the 116th on the extreme right flank, Sgt. George Halpin ran in from the picket line with the word that Confederate skirmishers were very close. Close after him came a deer crashing through the abatis, leaping over the trench, and vanishing into the dense underbrush. The startled men of the brigade then heard a tremendous volley of musketry well over on the left. Jackson's 26,000 men had struck the unlucky Eleventh Corps on their exposed right flank. The sound grew in intensity and the suspense grew unbearable. Then the flood of fugitives from the caved-in Eleventh Corps began to arrive by the dozen, then by the hundred; they were frightened, demoralized, and almost insane in their efforts to escape from that terrible blow.

5. Mulholland, *116th Pennsylvania*, p. 96.

Meagher quickly threw the brigade across the main road to United States Ford to dam up the stream of panic-stricken men. The men of the Eleventh Corps were made to form squads and march to the rear in some kind of order, as the roar of musketry came closer. Mulholland thought that he had never seen such confusion and dismay. He marveled that the men of the brigade could remain so calm; no one seemed to be showing any excitement at all. Fortunately for the Union, Jackson's attack had started too late in the day for the complete knockout of the Union army that he and Lee had envisioned, and the darkness brought a halt to the attack and the wounding of the illustrious Jackson himself. The Irish Brigade stacked arms after a while and lighted cooking fires. They had not fired a shot at the enemy. Things were a little different with the 88th, the detached regiment. They were heavily engaged in repelling the local attacks made by Lee on Hancock's division, among others.

The Army of the Potomac spent a bitter and restless night on May 2. Had they but known it, the game was as good as in their hands in spite of Jackson's thunderbolt, even though Hooker had lost his nerve on the day before. Lee's army was still divided with the larger portion embedded in stronger Union forces. Jackson had left the field wounded and, even more ominous for Lee, the Union Sixth Corps had forced its way over the holding force at Fredericksburg and was advancing on Lee's rear. There was much to be done if only Joe Hooker could pull himself together. His corps commanders almost without exception wanted to fight it out on the present ground. He had only to take an offensive attitude and all his grandiloquent boasting might still come true. The judgment of Francis Walker, historian of the Second Corps, that the Confederate superiority on May 2 was more moral than physical, is a just one.[6]

But when the Irish Brigade woke on the morning of May 3, it was to the sound of battle; loud, prolonged, and growing nearer. The Union army, so far from showing evidence of offensive spirit, was falling back to a defensive line prepared during the night by the engineer corps. Shortly after 10 a.m. Meagher got orders to bring up his men to join the balance of

6. Walker, *History of the Second Corps*, p. 231.

Hancock's division which was then embroiled with the Confederate divisions of McLaws and Anderson. The brigade took the road that ran from United States Ford to the Chancellor House and found along the way a complete catalog of the horrors of war.[7] Streams of wounded men went past to the rear. The sights of that Sunday morning in May stayed with Mulholland a long time.

> Men with torn faces, split heads, smashed arms, wounded men assisting their more badly hurt comrades, stretchers bearing to the rear men whose limbs were crushed and mangled, and others with no limbs at all. Four soldiers carried on two muskets, which they held in form of a litter, the body of their Lieutenant-Colonel who had just been killed. The body hung over the muskets, the head and feet limp and dangling, the blood dripping from a ghastly wound—a terrible sight indeed. Wounded men lay all through the woods; and here and there a dead man rested against a tree, where, in getting back, he had paused to rest and breathed his last. Shells screamed through the trees and, as the Regiment approached the front, the whir of canister and shrapnel was heard and musket balls whistled past, but the men in the ranks passed on quietly and cheerfully, many of them exchanging repartee. During a moment's halt, with the shells falling and exploding around him, Sergeant Bernard McCahey looking back, waved his hand to the earth and air and in the most ludicrous manner exclaimed, "Good boi, wurreld." Another son of Erin said to his companion, "What are we going in here for, Jimmy?" "To be after making history, Barney, to be sure!"[8]

Meagher rode at the head of the column for most of the journey to the scene of the fighting and had a few narrow escapes. A shell passed just over his head and laid out four men in the column behind him. As the firing came ever closer,

7. Mulholland, *116th Pennsylvania*, pp. 96.
8. *Ibid.*, p. 102-4.

246

though, the field officers were ordered to dismount and continue on foot. Mulholland remembered walking along with Maj. John Lynch of the 63rd, a handsome, young man full of life and gaiety. Then the head of the column arrived at the plateau where the Chancellor House stood, and the brigade turned to the right to form line. Mulholland wished Lynch a "Good Morning!" and learned to his horror that a few moments later Lynch had been killed by a shell.[9]

It is a wonder that Mulholland had any time at all to give to the dead for the living were badly in need of his attention. All of the army had fallen back from the position where the Irish now found themselves except Hancock's division of the Second Corps and Geary's division of the Twelfth Corps. Hancock and Geary were there to buy a few more minutes with their blood until the new line in the rear could be firmed up. Along the edge of the woods overlooking the Chancellor House the brigade hugged the ground. On the left of the brigade line Mulholland saw one of the most unequal contests of the war. There was the wreckage of the 5th Maine Battery, six Parrot guns, which had arrived but twenty minutes before the Irish. Now the battery was a shambles. The commander, Capt. George Leppine, had been carried off, dying with a shattered leg. Dead and wounded were everywhere, for the Confederates had concentrated the fire of a number of guns with superior position on that one point. But in the scene of horror a Union corporal and a private were working one of the guns as though their lives depended on it. The Irishmen watched and marveled at the devotion and courage of Cpl. James Lebroke and his fellow. But the concentration of fire on the battery brought with it a certain number of "overs" that fell among the prostrate men of the brigade. It was hell on earth, Mulholland thought, and wondered at the calm of the soldiers under him. Two of his color guard were passing jokes and Capt. Garret Nowlen lighted his pipe from the smoking fuse of a Confederate shell.[10]

They had been there hardly twenty minutes. A mounted orderly had his head taken off by a shell right in front of the brigade, the headless trunk staying on the horse for fifty feet

9. *Ibid.*, p. 97.
10. *Ibid.*, p. 99.

before slumping off. There is some question as to whether or not Meagher took the decisive step of bringing off the guns of the battery by himself. Mulholland says that an aide of General Hancock, Maj. George W. Scott, told him to bring off the guns. Lt. Edward Whiteford, an aide-camp of Meagher, says that the latter ordered it. One hundred men of the 116th were told to drag the pieces away. Whiteford watched the entire performance and marveled at the super-human exertions required to move the cannon from the heavy yellow clay in which they were embedded. Mulholland had ropes attached to the prolonges and the guns were drawn up the road in the direction of United States Ford. Mulholland stayed around until three pieces had been re-moved amid a hurricane of shot. Then he followed his men up the road and there found a fourth piece which had been apparently emplaced some distance from the three he was taking off. More men of the 116th were straining at it under the supervision of Lt. Louis Sacriste of Company D. He had seen something missed by Mulholland and led a party for-ward to secure the fourth gun. A fifth gun was taken off by some men of the 140th Pennsylvania and this led to some controversy later on. The 140th said that they had taken off more than one gun and spoke disparagingly of Mulholland in their regimental history.[11]

Louis Sacriste, born of a French father and an Irish mother, performed several other brilliant exploits during the war and was awarded the Medal of Honor later. Mulholland also received the Medal of Honor for his actions that day. Later, the press of Western Pennsylvania supported the claims of the 140th, hometown boys from the southwest corner of the Commonwealth. It was all set to rest by the corporal who had fought the last serviceable gun so val-iantly. J. H. Lebroke wrote the *Philadelphia Press*:

Camp near White Oak Church, Va.,
May 27th, 1863.

To the Editor of the Press:

Who brought off the guns of the Fifth Maine Battery?

11. *Ibid.*, pp. 100-101.

As this question has caused much discussion, I thought I would let the friends of the battery know through the columns of your paper to whom the honor is due. It has been stated that Lieutenant Whittier deserves great credit for bringing off the guns after the horses were killed. Lieutenant Whittier did not bring off the guns, neither was he there at the time. After the battery had ceased firing, one of the gunners went to General Hancock for a detail to haul off the guns. He sent a detail from the Irish Brigade under the command of Lieutenant-Colonel Mulholland and Lieutenant [William P.] Wilson, of Hancock's staff. The guns were hauled three miles by hand and the same brave men who exposed themselves to a severe fire of shot and shell from the rebel batteries, to save our guns, lost their own muskets, for the enemy held the ground immediately after.

Truly yours,
J. H. Lebroke[12]

This would seem to set the matter at rest. Also at rest permanently were several men of the 116th among whom a shell had burst. Young Sgt. George Halpin of Company A of the 116th had noticed that one of the caissons still stood in the battery position nearly full of ammunition. He ran back and exploded it with a lighted newspaper, miraculously escaping injury.

Mulholland's work was not yet done. With the removal of Lebroke's guns, the Irish Brigade and the rest of the First Division fell back to the new main line of resistance which curved in a great semicircle about United States Ford. Strong entrenchments had been dug and there was plenty of artillery to back up the new Union position. The local probing attacks mounted by the Confederates later in the day were beaten off with ease.

The night of May 3 was clear and cloudless and the Second Corps lay under arms. All were tired, but there were frequent alarms to awaken those who dozed off. One group surveying the heavenly bodies from flat on their backs specu-

12. *Ibid.*, p. 106.

lated on the possibility of war on those far-distant spheres. "Wonder if the people up there go to war?" "Wonder if they have Parrott guns?" "Wonder if the commisary gets up in time when rations is out?" "Wonder if they have sutlers and their government allows them to charge three dollars for a bottle of bad whisky?" And so the long night passed and a clear day came, full of vigilant sharpshooters and a bright May sun. In the afternoon a breeze sprang up, blowing directly at the Union entrenchments, so the Confederates fired the woods to annoy the Federals as much as possible. Some of the abatis was destroyed but the flames were more of a nuisance than a threat. With the night came a heavy rain to cover the Union withdrawal to the north side of the Rappahannock. All night long as the men stole to the rear the rain fell in drenching torrents. The pickets fired random volleys through the retreat to deceive the Confederates into thinking that the lines were still strongly held. Then at dawn the pickets fell back and went for the pontoon bridge on the dead run. After they had crossed, the pontoons were cut away and the Chancellorsville campaign was over.[13]

There was much soul-searching throughout the Union army. The soldiers felt that again they had been confounded by the genius of Lee. Hooker had failed, seeming to labor under a paralysis during the last stages of the battle that was variously attributed to his predilection for the bottle and also to his being rendered insensible by a Confederate near-miss. On the higher level of command there was much recrimination because never had the high command held such high hopes in the early stages. It had seemed at last that a man had come along to cross swords with Lee on something like even terms, and the denouement was depressing. General Couch, commander of the Second Corps and a stout fighter, submitted his resignation because he had lost confidence in Hooker.[14] It seemed perfectly clear that Hooker had lost confidence in himself at the most crucial time in his life.

Meagher was writing a letter of resignation at about the same time. There had never been any reply from Stanton or anyone else at the War Department on his proposal to furlough

13. Ibid., p. 104.
14. Walker, *History of the Second Corps*, p. 254.

the brigade to recruit. Of the 530 men with which he had crossed the Rappahannock, 102 were casualties. Although this was the smallest total in the First Division, Second Corps, it was true, as Meagher wrote: "the Brigade no longer exists." The last two paragraphs are memorable because they sound like the Meagher of old:

> In tendering my resignation, however, as Brigadier-General in command of this poor vestige and relic of the Irish Brigade, I beg sincerely to assure you that my services, in any capacity that can prove useful, are freely at the summons disposition of the Government of the United States. That the Government, and the cause, and the liberty, the noble memories, and the future it represents, are entitled unquestionably and unequivocally to the life of every citizen who has sworn allegiance to it, and partaken of its grand protection.
>
> But while I offer my own life to sustain this good Government, I feel it to be my first duty to do nothing that will wantonly imperil the lives of others, or, what would be still more grievous and irreparable, inflict sorrow and humiliation upon a race who, having lost almost everything else, find in their character for courage and loyalty, an invaluable gift, which I, for one, will not be so vain or selfish to endanger.[15]

The letter of resignation was dated May 8. The letter of acceptance was dated May 14; Lincoln and Stanton did not waste any time. On the evening of May 19 the brigade fell out and formed a hollow square with Meagher and his staff in the center. Also in attendance was General Caldwell who commanded First Brigade, First Division. Hancock was a notable absentee, and so was Couch who did not leave the army until eight days later. The band of the 14th Connecticut was there to furnish appropriate music. Meagher said much but it was all summed up in the following:

---

15. Cavanagh, *Memoirs of Thomas Meagher*, appendix p. 27.

Massachusetts Commandery, MOLLUS
U.S. Army Military History Institute
Patrick Kelly
Colonel, 88th New York Veteran Volunteer Infantry
Killed at Petersburg

Suffice it to say that, the Irish Brigade no longer existing, I felt that it would be perpetuating a great deception were I to retain the authority and rank of brigadier-general nominally commanding the same.[16]

In dead silence with the tears streaming down his face, Meagher passed along the thin single rank of the brigade, shaking hands with every last man. He then returned to his quarters, and the new brigade commander, Patrick Kelly, assumed command and dismissed the formation. The old brigade had truly passed away.

What is one to make of this? Was an injustice done to Meagher and the brigade? One biographer of this century seems to think not. In fact Robert G. Athearn's portrait is as unflattering as it seems hypercritical and even pejorative. There is hardly an instance in Meagher's career where he is not made to appear completely self-seeking and supremely ambitious. Take, for instance, when McClellan was relieved in November 1862, an event widely decried in the officer corps of the Army of the Potomac, Meagher published an order to the brigade in which it was pointed out that each man had taken an oath to the Government of the United States, and that was where true loyalty was engaged no matter how attractive the men found McClellan as a leader. On the face of it this was commendably correct in a democracy, a proof against any "man on horseback" tendency. Yet Athearn assumes that Meagher is currying favor with the administration. Surely Meagher had his faults, but Athearn finds something to criticize in almost every action. Meagher is made to appear ambitious for the two stars of a major general, but so was every brigadier in the army. Meagher was not a complete soldier, it is true, and he did owe his rank to psychological factors that were very real in 1861. Yet so did Carl Schurz, Franz Sigel, Dan Sickles, and many others.

One of the stickiest questions of the Civil War is that of the "political generals." Many are the barbs that have been thrown at them, and many were deserved. But during the war there were only two unrelieved catastrophes, Fredericksburg and Cold Harbor, and both times the army was in the hands of a

16. *Ibid.*, p. 486.

West Point-educated professional soldier, Burnside in the first instance, Ulysses S. Grant in the second. "Political generals" could hardly have done worse. Meagher, in the view of his subordinates, seems to have contributed a father-image to the brigade. He was not, as O'Grady said, "excellent as a tactician." How many excellent tacticians were there in either army? At least he accompanied his men into the fights and acted as a sort of a morale-builder while better soldiers like Patrick Kelly, James Kelly, Robert Nugent, and Richard Byrnes made the moves that would let the men put the best face on their efforts. At the fearsome moment of assault the brigade was as effective as any formation in either army, a summation based on the testimony of unfriendly witnesses.

Under Patrick Kelly there would be no lessening of that effectiveness, even though the men felt sad and depressed. It would be strange if they did not. In the short space of a year they had fought through the Peninsula, Antietam, Fredericksburg, and Chancellorsville with great exertions and heavy losses. Now the man who tied them to their origin, to the new blue uniforms and the unmarked colors, was gone.

Meagher's resignation does not appear in the *Official Records*, nor does the letter of acceptance from the War Department. The Irish press in New York played it up, of course, but the American press has historically been almost completely dumb, even the anti-Lincoln sheets. Since the Tammany organization controlled the city government of New York and had no wish to alienate the "Irish element," the common council was pleased to offer Meagher "the hospitalities of the city, as a token of the esteem in which he was held by the people of the metropolis. . . . the invaluable services rendered by him and the heroic men of the Irish Brigade in defence of the integrity of the union." So the Committee on National Affairs headed by Mayor Opdyke waited on the general at the Astor House on June 16, read him the resolutions, and formally tendered him the hospitality of the city.[17]

In reply, Meagher read them an address which he had probably been preparing for some time. He reviewed his reasons for resigning but declined the gratitude of the city

17. *Ibid.*, p. 488.

until such time as, the war being over, he could participate with the other survivors of the brigade. It was a graceful speech with no partisan sniping, really one of Meagher's best efforts. He was then presented with the Kearny Cross, a decoration instituted in the Army of the Potomac's Third Corps, one of whose divisions had been commanded by Maj. Gen. Philip Kearny, killed at Chantilly. It was a generous gesture on the part of Maj. Gen. David Bell Birney, commanding Kearny's old division.[18]

Two nights later there was a banquet at the Astor House in Meagher's honor, attended by the same dignitaries plus whatever Irish officers were home with wounds. Nugent was there with his Fredericksburg wound healed. There was no room for him with his old regiment, the 69th, now consolidated into a two-company battalion commanded by Capt. Richard Moroney. Also present was the governor of the Nevada Territory, an irascible man by the name of James Warren Nye, originally from the State of New York. The banquet went well, all the proper things being said by the proper people at the proper time. Then some evil genius introduced Nye, who had, very evidently, not been briefed as to the temper and character of the majority of the audience. He started out by scoring off those despicable elements who were of the Democratic persuasion. Such, he said, were no better than rebels and not fit to sit at table with loyal Republican defenders of the right. Several officers who had been a bit closer to the Confederate fire than Nye immediately jumped to their feet and demanded that the speaker retract every single word. More temperate men sprang up and requested order, telling the sensitive ones to hold their peace. For a moment there was all the appearance of an incipient riot. Then Meagher was able to make himself heard and understood. The firebrands were soothed before any blows were struck, and Governor Nye was induced to say some words of an apologetic nature and the affair broke up soon after.[19]

It should be pointed out that Meagher was not the only one present with an animus against the administration. The three New York regiments had each been consolidated into a two-

18. *Ibid.*
19. *New York Times,* June 17, 1863.

company battalion on May 1, and a certain number of officers were mustered out as supernumerary. Only three officers were needed per company which meant many men who could think as well as fight must return to civilian life. The utter futility of this manner of officer procurement shows the bankruptcy of the War Department's thinking. Effective leadership is the single most important element in military operations. The government was now throwing away battlefield experience and placing the new levies in the hands of men drawn directly from civilian life, men with impeccable political credentials, who were good lawyers, butchers, and shoe salesmen, but who had never heard a shot fired in anger. It was enough to make the angels weep.

The Army of the Potomac settled back in their camps around Falmouth that were roomier now in consequence of the 17,000 casualties of Chancellorsville. As mentioned, Couch had resigned his command and Hancock had inherited the Second Corps. No one has ever had a bad word to say about him, an unbending disciplinarian and professional soldier. Mulholland said that Hancock thought well of the Irish and called the brigade his "right arm." It still only numbered 509 men when all possible members had been scraped out of hospitals. There were no new recruits.

In the early days of June, Lee, bereft of his great subordinate Jackson but conscious of the need to carry the battle to the North, began to slip the troops of Ewell's corps westward from the Fredericksburg area into the great, curving arc of the Shenandoah corridor. Longstreet's corps followed, leaving A. P. Hill's men at Fredericksburg across the river from Hooker's host. Hooker had lost much face with the administration but still had strong support in certain blocs of Congress. When it became known that Lee was actively moving to invade the North, Lincoln and Halleck had to make up their minds as to whether or not they wanted Hooker to command the army in another crucial campaign. By June 13 Hooker was enough aware of Lee's movement to order some parallel repositioning of his own forces. The First, Third, Fifth, and Eleventh Corps were to fall back to Manassas Junction. The Second, Sixth, and Twelfth Corps with the reserve artillery would retire by a more easterly route. What would happen in the future would depend on whatever Lee had in mind.

Wherever Lee's army went, there also must go Hooker's army, always in a northwestwardly direction to stay between the graybacks and the capital. Mulholland never forgot the first two days of the movement when hundreds, maybe thousands of men were left by the wayside gasping for water, some dying. When the Occoquan Creek was reached on the night of June 16, the entire Second Corps went for a welcome, refreshing swim and found the stream infested with water snakes.

At Thoroughfare Gap a very significant event took place for the Philadelphia Brigade in the Second Division of the Second Corps. The new division commander, Brig. Gen. John Gibbon, a West Pointer with three brothers in the Confederate forces, had conceived an intense dislike for the commander of his Second Brigade, Brig. Gen. Joshua Owen. The Second Brigade had not been engaged in the fighting at Chancellorsville, having spent its time guarding bridges, so Gibbon had no personal knowledge of Owen's worth in battle. Evidently, what Gibbon saw of the erstwhile Philadelphia lawyer in camp and on the march did not inspire him with confidence.

The commander of the Philadelphia Brigade was placed under arrest and removed from command. George Stewart, in his fine work *Pickett's Charge*, advanced the idea that "Paddy" Owen being Irish, was, no doubt, a great one for the bottle, and this led to his downfall. A sound enough theory, except that Owen was born in Wales and only owed his nickname to the fact that he had been the colonel of the 69th Pennsylvania before being promoted in the fall of 1862.[20]

Owen's replacement was a real, live, West Point graduate, Alexander Stewart Webb, with long and distinguished service on the staff and in the artillery. Recently, he had been made brigadier general of volunteers and arrived at headquarters of the army just as Hancock was casting about for a successor for the hapless Owen. "Because I knew the man" Hancock seized on Webb and hurried him off to the Philadelphia Brigade.[21]

The army pressed north on the Virginia roads and began to cross the Potomac at Edward's Ferry on June 25. Hooker

20. George R. Stewart, *Pickett's Charge: A Microhistory of the Final Attack at Gettysburg, July 3, 1863* (Boston: Houghton Mifflin, 1959), p. 78.
21. New York State Battle Monuments Commission, *Webb and His Brigade at the Angle* (Albany, New York: n.p., 1913), p. 88.

had a pretty good idea that Lee's army was just behind the mountain wall to the west. There were rumors that Ewell's corps had reached Chambersburg, Pennsylvania, and was headed for Harrisburg. The blue columns concentrated at Frederick, Maryland, a favorite place for Union soldiers, and Hooker began a war by telegraph with the administration in Washington. There were several thousand Union troops at Harpers Ferry, and Hooker asked that they be added to his army, an eminently reasonable request. But Halleck refused to order this transfer and Hooker submitted his resignation, apparently to the great happiness of both Abraham Lincoln and Henry Halleck.

Thus it was that Maj. Gen. George Meade, commander of the Fifth Corps became the new army commander. Far back in the past, the Meades of Philadelphia had been Irish. His grandfather, "Honest George Meade" had been one of the founders of the Friendly Sons of St. Patrick in Philadelphia, but the Irish connection was long ago. Now he was known only as a hard professional warrior who knew what he was doing. He had led a brigade of the Pennsylvania Reserves well on the Peninsula, then the Reserve Division, and after that the Fifth Corps. One could say that he was well-seasoned. The army took the road north from Frederick on June 28.

The Philadelphia Brigade was hardly on the road on June 29 when General Webb had an officer's call sounded. He surveyed with distaste the dusty, bearded men who answered. "I presume you are officers since you attend the Call. There are but few of you whom I am able to recognize as officers as you have no insignia of office except your swords." There is little doubt that the officers gazed back at Webb with stupefaction. The Army of the Potomac had learned by hard experience that the Confederate sharpshooters could tell officers easily if they were so foolish as to wear the shoulder straps of their rank. As a result few did. Now here was a spic-and-span bandbox soldier fresh from the staff telling combat veterans how to appear. And there was no doubt that Webb was in earnest. The next time he encountered his officers they had better be suitably accoutred. So Dennis O'Kane, DeWitt Baxter, Penn Smith, Turner Morehead and the rest of the officers had to dig out the signs

258

of rank although they may have done so with some misgiving. Webb was not yet done.

On the next officer's call, Webb told his subordinates that there was too much straggling in the brigade. Stragglers were to be arrested and brought to him; he would shoot them like dogs. Whether or not this was an empty threat, it is a notable fact that there were but twelve stragglers in the brigade after the news was passed around on the following day. On June 29 as the Second Corps moved on to Taneytown, Pennsylvania, the Monocacy River was encountered. Ward, the historian of the 106th, reported the incident:

> . . . at this place there was no bridge, so we were compelled to wade, and, being over knee deep, the men stopped, as they usually did, to take off their shoes and stockings and roll up their pants, but General Webb found that was taking too much time and he was anxious to make up for that lost, so he ordered the men to wade right in, and jumping from his horse stood in the middle of the stream until the whole Brigade had passed, ordering each man that hesitated to move on at once; of course, this met with the disapproval of the men, who were not backward in expressing their feelings in terms not very complimentary to the General, and the remarks might have been heard by him had he chosen to listen. One of the Sixty-Ninth Regiment, more bold than the rest and with his natural Irish bluntness, addresses as he passed: "Sure it's no wonder ye can stand there when ye are leather up to your waist." The General having on a pair of long boots that came up above his knees. This created a good laugh by those who heard it; he paid no attention whatever, but continued to order his men forward and remained there until the last man had crossed.[22]

The brigade and the corps and the army moved on. Hancock had left them early in the afternoon as there was rumor of fighting ahead, at a place called Gettysburg.

22. Ward, *106th Pennsylvania*, p. 178-79.

CHAPTER ELEVEN
GETTYSBURG

The artillery grumble hung over the low hills as the Second Corps moved up from Taneytown on the afternoon of July 1. Contact had been made in the morning between Maj. Gen. Harry Heth's division of the Army of Northern Virginia and the First Corps north and west of the town. The Confederates had been able to concentrate faster than the Federals and had won a decided advantage in the fighting that had spilled back through the streets of Gettysburg. Hancock, sent forward by Meade, arrived on the field in late afternoon, when the remnants of the Union advance had taken position on the green mound of Cemetery Hill. He had looked the scene over and made the fateful decision that the battle would be fought there. Messengers went off to Meade and the other corps commanders, and the army headed for the hills around the little town.[1]

It has been written that Northern regiments cheered wildly on arriving at the Maryland-Pennsylvania border, the line that separated free states from slave-holding territory. This sounds unlikely because that army was long past cheering for anything except food and drink. But spirits generally were on the rise now that the country of stone barns and fat cattle had been reached. And there must have been some feeling that here on Northern ground all that they had experienced so far, the marches, the hardships, the battles, and blood-letting was coming to a focus. One way or another, the climactic moment was at hand.

The shadows of the summer twilight found the First Division of the Second Corps still three miles from the rapidly forming Union lines on Cemetery Hill and on Cemetery Ridge, known locally as Granite Ridge, which led south to the eminences known as the Round Tops. The Third Division was

1. Swinton, *Campaigns of the Army of the Potomac*, pp. 334-37.

closer to the scene of action since it had led the march on July 1, not a terribly exhausting grind that day, nothing like the thirty-four miles they had marched on June 29. The Second Corps was left beyond the outskirts as security for the left flank of the army, and the men sank down on the earth with thankfulness.[2] It was only later, after the cooking-fires were kindled and the fire-walkers appeared on the scene, filled with the news of what had happened to the First Corps on McPherson's Ridge and the collapse of the Eleventh Corps, that it dawned on them that this was the battle that would dwarf the Peninsula and Antietam, Manassas and Chancellorsville. Longstreet's corps was over there, back with Lee after missing the Chancellorsville campaign. Maj. Gen. John Reynolds had been killed, and the First Corps had taken a terrible number of casualties. The unlucky Eleventh Corps had a lot of men taken prisoner.

This was the kind of news calculated to make veterans look to their weapons. And wretched weapons indeed were carried in the Second Corps by some of the best troops. Here, deep in the bowels of the war the Irish Brigade still carried the old pattern Harpers Ferry smoothbore musket, .69 caliber with an accurate range of about fifty yards.[3] It is interesting that over in the First Corps, the Iron Brigade which had sacrificed itself against the overwhelming numbers of Confederates on McPherson's Ridge, also carried inferior Austrian muskets which never should have been issued.[4]

The men of the Second Corps were aroused at 4 a.m. on July 2, and the march began in the half-light. They did not have far to go. The Third Division was still in the lead and they kept on the Taneytown Road past the emerging bulk of the Round Tops. There were other confused stirrings around them, the noises of men coming out of the cool forgetfulness of sleep into the reality of unpleasantness. Along the road were fences with a stone wall on the left hand side. Finally, at the corner of a farmer's stone barn, the advance of the Third Division stopped and the Second Corps came to a halt for a good three-quarters of a mile down the road.

2. Walker, *History of the Second Corps*, p. 268.
3. Mulholland, *116th Pennsylvania*, p. 126.
4. Edwin B. Coddington, *The Gettysburg Campaign: A Study in Command* (New York: Charles Scribner's Sons, 1968), p. 257.

The men stacked arms, fell out, and looked for wood for coffee fires. In the east, the violet of early morning took on orange tints and the soldiers could look about and see where they were. The fight of yesterday had taken place north and west of the town, the center of which was a good mile away. A lovely pastoral scene spread before them, green fields undulating toward the dark hills to the west. The gentle hillside where they had stopped sloped to the east and anyone who walked back to its crest would see the other columns of the army pushing up the Baltimore Pike; infantry, cavalry, caissons, guns, wagons, ambulances—the appurtenances of war were imprinted on a landscape of peace. The Second Corps faced west, connecting on their left with one of the two divisions of the Third Corps. On their right in Ziegler's Grove there was much artillery along with the remnants of the Eleventh Corps.

Apparently, the Union command thought that the first Confederate effort would be against Cemetery Hill, and that bastion bristled with guns dug in to the axle hubs. All of the action of July 1 had been in that direction. There is something in the continuity of thought that leads one to the last point of contact. It is possible that Lee was deceived as to the actual position of the Union defence. Cemetery Ridge, on which perched the Second Corps, is shielded by the bulk of Cemetery Hill. There have been good arguments advanced, especially by the partisans of James Longstreet, that Lee formed his plan of attack for July 2 on the basis of an incorrect assumption, that the Union axis was east-to-west rather than north-to-south. Lee wished Longstreet to to attack "up the Emmitsburg Road" on July 2.[5]

If the Union axis was east-to-west then this attack would be an envelopment of the Union left flank. If the situation was as Lee imagined, Longstreet's movement would be an arrow directed at the heart of the Union position. In order to make the move, however, Longstreet would have to carry out a circuitous march. It is a matter of record that Longstreet did not want to carry out this movement at all. His critics have to this day held that his antipathy caused him to delay his attack. His partisans have just as stoutly maintained that nothing of the

5. *Ibid.*, p. 365.

sort occurred. But the entire plan can only be justified by supposing that the Union forces were on an east-to-west axis. Since their true position was on a north-to-south axis, the envelopment of the Union left was impossible by a thrust up the Emmitsburg Road.

There was comparative quiet during the morning of July 2, aside from small arms skirmishing and some artillery exchanges. As part of the Confederate turning movement by Longstreet, Lee wanted Ewell, whose corps lay in the streets of Gettysburg, to put in an attack on Cemetery Hill simultaneously. Ewell's men got themselves straightened out and waited for the right moment. The right moment was a long time in coming. Longstreet's approach march was long and tedious, and at the end of it he found that Lee's concept of the Union position along an east-to-west axis was fallacious. Instead of being behind the Union left flank, the Confederate First Corps, by moving up the Emmitsburg Road, would present its right flank to a mass of Union infantry on the now disclosed Cemetery Ridge.

In addition, as Longstreet looked up the line of advance ordered by Lee, he saw a sizeable Union force directly in front of him. This was the Third Corps whose commander, Maj. Gen. Dan Sickles, had become very nervous during the day. He thought his position, extending the left of the Second Corps south on Cemetery Ridge, was a poor one. A reconnaisance by Berdan's Sharpshooters about noon made contact with some Alabama troops of A. P. Hill's corps who were settling in on Seminary Ridge. But, more importantly, at 2 p.m. Berdan reported to David Birney, who commanded Sickles' First Division, that three columns of Confederate troops were moving south behind the cover of Seminary Ridge. Birney said he personally saw enemy columns from the left of his position at 2:30. This information was passed on to Sickles, and that was enough for him. He ordered Birney out to the Emmitsburg Road's junction with a farm lane. Here stood a grove of peach trees on the Sherfy farm which would now and forever more be called the Peach Orchard. One brigade was placed along the Emmitsburg Road facing west. The other two brigades were bent around to the left in the direction of Little Round Top. There were not enough troops to reach that far, and the flank which was in a huge jumble of rocks called Devil's Den hung

264

in the air. The Second Division, under Brig. Gen. Andrew A. Humphreys, with the single brigade of Birney's division formed along the Emmitsburg Road extending to the north.

Sickles' movement of the Third Corps has ever since been one of the great controversies of the battle. He seemed completely unconcerned that his forward movement left a wide gap in the Union line on Cemetery Ridge. Hancock, whose Second Corps was just to the north of the gap, was astonished at the spectacle of the entire Third Corps moving out from the established line. John Gibbon, who was standing with Hancock, wondered if the entire line was to move out similarly, and if the Second Corps had not been informed. Hancock replied, "Never mind, you'll soon see them come tumbling back!" He meant that the Third Corps in its new position would undergo a hurricane of attack, and he was right. What he could not have foreseen was the effect on the battle of the untoward maneuver, especially to the Second Corps.

Meade, coming on the scene where one of his corps had changed position without his permission, decided that they would have to be supported in the vulnerable orchard. Very shortly, the hard fighters of Longstreet swept against both sides of this angle. Sickles' men fought long and well, but there were simply too many Confederate troops who could fight just as well and, in addition, had the enfilade fire of well-served artillery going for them. Hancock was directed to put in a division to support the Third Corps. Nearest was his old division, wearing the red trefoil and commanded by Brig. Gen. John C. Caldwell (he who had hid behind the haystack at Antietam).

On the extreme left of the division stood the brigade of Col. Edward Cross. Next to them were the Irish under Patrick Kelly with Samuel Zook's brigade in their rear. On the extreme right was the brigade of Col. John Brooke. Mulholland told of the pause before the march order and the ceremony that filled it.

The brigade stood in column of regiments, closed en masse. As a large majority ot its numbers were Catholics, the Reverend William Corby, the chaplain, proposed to give a general absolution to all the men before going into the fight. While this is customary in the armies of the Catholic countries of Europe, it was,

265

perhaps, the first time it was ever witnessed on this continent, unless, the grim old warrior, Ponce de Leon, as he tramped through the everglades of Florida in search of the Fountain of Youth, or De Soto, on his march to the Mississippi, indulged in the act of devotion.

Father Corby stood on a large rock in front of the Brigade. Addressing the men he explained what he was about to do, saying that each one could receive the benefit of the absolution by making a sincere Act of Contrition and firmly resolving to embrace the first opportunity of confessing their sins, urging them to do their duty well, and reminding them of the high and sacred nature of their trust as soldiers and the noble object for which they fought, ending by saying that the Catholic Church refuses Christian burial to the soldier who turns his back upon the foe or deserts his flag. The Brigade was standing at "order arms," and, as he closed his address, every man fell on his knees with head bowed down. Then, stretching his right hand toward the Brigade, Father Corby pronounced the words of the general absolution, "Dominus noster Jesus Christus vos absolvat, et ego, auctoritate ipsius, vos absolvo ab vinculo excommunicationis et interdicti in quantum possum et vos indigetis; deinde ego vos absolvo a peccatis vestris in nomine Patris, et Filii, et Spiritus Sancti, Amen."

The scene was more than impressive, it was awe-inspiring. Nearby stood Hancock surrounded by a brilliant array of officers who had gathered to witness this very unusual ceremony. . . . the act seemed to be in harmony with all its surroundings. I do not think there was a man in the Brigade who did not offer up a heartfelt prayer. For some it was their last; they knelt there in their grave clothes, in less than half-an-hour many of them were numbered with the dead of July 2. Who can doubt that their prayers were good? What was wanting in the eloquence of the good priest to move them to repentance was supplied in the incidents of the fight. That heart would be incorrigible, indeed, that the scream of a Whitworth bolt, added to Father Corby's touching appeal, would not move to contrition.[6]

Just behind the Irish stood Zook's brigade, and first in Zook's column, was the 140th Pennsylvania from the district around Washington in the southwestern part of the Keystone State. They were Presbyterian almost to a man, and the regimental historian recalled that they were "Scotch-Irish," which meant that their ancestors came from Ulster. A group could hardly be found in the Army of the Potomac more alienated from the Irish in outlook. They had marched in the same division with Kelly's men since immediately after Fredericksburg, and possibly this had a mellowing effect on them. Pvt. Robert Laird Stewart, later to be a learned Presbyterian minister, saw Father Corby's action:

> In a moment every man was in his place. The next command was delayed for a few moments and during that interval we were witnesses of an unusual scene which made a deep impression upon all who witnessed it. The Irish Brigade whose green flag had been unfurled on almost every battlefield from Bull Run until this hour, stood in column of regiments in close order with bared heads while their Chaplain-priest, Father Corby, stood upon a large boulder and seemed to be addressing the men. At a given signal every man of the command fell on his knees and with head bowed low received from him the sacrament of extreme unction. Instinctively every man of our Regiment took off his cap and no doubt many a prayer from men of Protestant faith, who could conscientiously not bow the knee in a service of that nature, went up to God in that impressive and awe-inspiring moment. . . . At the word of command which followed the priest's Amen we moved out quickly by the left flank in the direction of Little Round Top.[7]

6. Mulholland, *116th Pennsylvania*, pp. 407-8.
7. Stewart, *140th Pennsylvania*, p. 101.

267

Later, Father Corby would think back over that public act of devotion and realize that he was not only blessing the brigade but all the soldiers in both armies who were to meet death.[8]

The division headed for the angle at the Peach Orchard, Cross's brigade first, then the Irish, followed by Brooke's and Samuel Zook's brigades. As Edward Cross passed near Hancock, the corps commander said, "Cross, this is the last fight you'll be in without a star!" To which Cross answered, "Too late, General. This is my last fight." The division turned off the Peach Orchard lane and went left into a field of golden grain, forever after known as the Wheatfield. Cross in the lead halted and deployed his men. Kelly moved up on his right and did likewise. Brooke and Zook formed a second line behind them.[9]

There were some Confederates in the wheat who now rose up and delivered their fire at the blue ranks whose pace had quickened. Many of the enemy fell back in the direction of a stone wall at the edge of the grain, but not all of them. The skirmishers of the Irish doubled out into the waving fronds and plucked several score of the men of Brig. Gen. Joseph B. Kershaw's brigade from the smoke just as the ground heaved under them. From behind the stone wall, Kershaw's men let out a blast of musketry that was reminiscent of a colder day at Fredericksburg. Down went the skirmishers and the brigade line slowed and answered with a volley. The Irish then were tearing through the wheat towards the wall. Kershaw's men left hurriedly and Kelly took the time to have his men kneel at the wall and fire once. The ground beyond was a thickly wooded hillside covered with large boulders, and the South Carolinians made a stand here. Mulholland said,

> . . . although the ground was covered with huge boulders, interspersed with forest trees, hilly and rough, the alignment was well preserved and, as it neared the crest, met the enemy and received a volley. But the shots were too high and did but little damage and the men rushed on. Soon the lines were

8. Corby, *Memoirs of Chaplain Life*, p. 184.
9. Mulholland, *116th Pennsylvania*, p. 408.

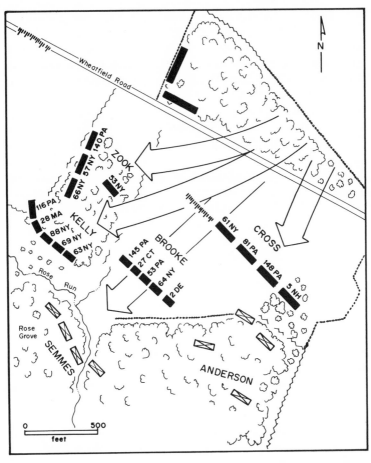

Map by John Heiser

First Division, Second Corps in the Wheatfield at Gettysburg

but a few feet apart, and the men returned the fire with deadly effect. Captain [Garrett] Nowlen drew his revolver and opened fire; nearly all the other officers followed his example. Little Jeff Carl killed a man within six feet of his bayonet. That hero, Sergeant Francis Malin, was conspicuous by his dash and bravery, as his tall form towered above all around him. . . . For a few moments it was hand-to-hand, but the Confederates seemed to have no stomach for the fight; they were tired, weary and glad to call "enough," . . . then the brigade was halted and aligned. . . .[10]

Caldwell's division had gained a little eminence which looked down on the barn and farmhouse of William Rose. In the depression before them other large Confederate formations could be seen through the trees. Directly in front of them was the ground where earlier some of the Third Corps had fought, and dead Union soldiers were all about. Mulholland remembered especially seeing the body of a very young boy on a large rock. The blood was still flowing from a terrible wound in his forehead. The commander of the 116th reflected that he never looked on a dead soldier without feeling that he was gazing at the relics of a saint. From his extreme youth this particular soldier seemed to him more like an angel.

There was not much of a brigade line now, for the Irish had managed to lose one-third of the 530 men they had taken into the Wheatfield and up the wooded hill. On their left Brooke's brigade came up. The 116th held the right flank of the division, and about an eighth of a mile away they could see the Peach Orchard from which all the Union soldiers had now been driven. Mulholland was disquieted because he could see no Union soldiers at all to their right, but they dressed the brigade line and lay down on the ground. They had performed their duty of bolstering a sagging Union position. Now they waited for the next move. When it came, the Irish were lucky to escape complete capture.

After fifteen minutes had gone by, Mulholland noticed what looked like a large body of men passing into the gap between

10. *Ibid.*, p. 125.

his right flank and the Peach Orchard. He immediately went to Patrick Kelly and led him to the vantage point. Quantities of artillery smoke had settled on the ground and reduced visibility, and it was difficult to be sure of what was happening. Kelly was placed in a quandary. He had no orders to abandon the position which had cost so many lives, but a Confederate column on that line of attack would envelop his right flank. Shortly, the Confederate brigade of Brig. Gen. William T. Wofford settled the question for Kelly. The Confederates had penetrated the gap and turned to their right. The Irish had to get out and quickly. Mulholland rolled up his colors and told his men to get out as best they could. At almost the same time, another Confederate formation fell on the left flank of Brooke's brigade. Almost before the story can be told, Caldwell's division was a mass of fugitives streaming from the forested hillside and back across the Wheatfield. Mulholland noted,

> . . . we were in a trap, a line of the enemy was advancing on the Wheatfield from the south, and Wofford's Brigade, the column I had seen marching around the Peach Orchard into our rear, was closing in from the north. We caught it from both sides, the slaughter here being appalling, but we kept on, the men loading and firing as they ran, and by the time we reached the middle of the field, the two lines of the enemy were so close that for a few minutes they ceased firing at us, as they fired into each other. Then I heard voices calling out, "Come here, run this way." A few seconds more and I was over a low stone wall and among [Col. Jacob B.] Sweitzer's Brigade. About ten of my command were with me. I went back to the Taneytown Road. I there found Colonel Brooke, 53d Pennsylvania, reforming the division. He directed me to plant my colors nearby and assist him which I did.[11]

As the weary First Division formed in the gathering dusk, a chill of fear went through them. Another thunder of battle welled up to their right as Confederate assaults went in on

11. *Ibid.*, p. 410.

Cemetery Ridge. This was the most anxious hour of all. To the men who had just been worsted out at the Peach Orchard and the Wheatfield, this premonition of disaster at the other end of the Union line was almost too much.

The assault of Longstreet led to a mass of confused fighting with the Third Corps and spread to the slopes of Little Round Top where the Fifth Corps held off the men of Maj. Gen. John Bell Hood's division. The entire Union left was consumed with shellfire, artillery smoke, and musketry as the bluecoats battled for their lives. Even after Longstreet had caved in the Union positions at the Peach Orchard salient, he was not through. Humphrey's division on the Emmitsburg Road was the next to be struck and hurled back. The triumphant Confederates of Maj. Gen. Richard H. Anderson's division of A.P. Hill's corps continued the thrust across the valley from Seminary Ridge. By now it was almost 7 p.m.

Three Confederate brigades moved across the fields toward Cemetery Ridge. They first struck some of the withdrawing men of Humphreys' division of the Third Corps who had fought savagely but given way under the pressure of numbers. The men of Brig. Gen. Ambrose Wright, all Georgians, headed for the center of the line held by the Second Corps. The dispatch of so many Union troops to the area of the Wheatfield and the Peach Orchard left the defence short of manpower. General Hancock performed prodigies of tactical skill to bring up additional Union troops and direct them where they were most needed. He put in the 1st Minnesota to stop the Mississippians of Brig. Gen. William Barksdale, and he stripped his Third Division of Col. George C. Willard's brigade to help at a crucial moment. There were so many crises happening so swiftly that one could not worry about the consequences of any one act. Catastrophe waited on delay, not on circumstance. Of all the days of his life, on this one Hancock repaid the United States for his education and profession as he waited, like a fire chief with a few precious hosemen to dispatch here, there, and everywhere. As the twilight deepened, one last Confederate assault came over the Emmitsburg Road, the soldiers commanded by Ambrose Wright. Their line of advance would lead them to strike the Second Division of the Second Corps, commanded by John Gibbon.

272

All day long the Philadelphia Brigade lay in the hot sun. The 71st, 72nd, and 106th Pennsylvania regiments were on the crest of Cemetery Ridge looking west. The stone wall that ran along the farm road at the crest of the ridge turned to the west directly in front of the 71st and ran on for a distance of 278 feet. Then it turned south at a right angle and continued south. There lay the 69th Pennsylvania. There is no reason given in his report as to why Alexander Webb chose to place his Irishmen closer to the enemy than his other regiments. In the morning two men were drawn from each company of the brigade and sent out as skirmishers in the direction of the Emmitsburg Road about 150 yards to their front. There was much popping of rifles west of the road out in the swales.

The sun got higher and hotter and many of the 69th turned longing eyes toward the little grove of trees which grew about forty yards behind them. It looked much cooler there but orders were to stay in place. The stone wall which they hunkered down beside was not going to be much protection since it only rose two feet above the ground, but the timbers of the fence that stood in front of it were taken down and piled on top of the stones. This was a little better.

The battle brought on by the Third Corps found them eager spectators and the swaying lines of battle were in full view. After a while the battle was clearly seen to be going against the Federals. Closer and closer came the Confederate musketry. At last it seemed to be coming up the Emmitsburg Road where Gibbon had placed a battery and two small regiments of infantry near the Codori house, the 15th Massachusetts and 82nd New York. Wright's men engulfed them and came on. The pickets of the Philadelphia Brigade were struck. They seemed to have been mostly from the 106th, and they fell back behind the wall. Wright had a clear shot at the geographic center of the Union position. As his men rose to the gentle slope that led to the stone wall, the clouds of powder smoke hung heavily about them. Lt. T. Fred Brown's Rhode Island Battery was overrun and the guns stood behind them forlornly. There were only those Federals before them who were rising to level their muskets. These Georgians had come a long way with death and destruction and they keened the Rebel Yell.

Apparently the fire control of the 69th was perfect. The first volley came with a single crash that paralyzed the Georgians' front rank.[12] The second was a bit more ragged, but the rounds that the Irish poured in were enough to take the starch out of the attack. Wright attempted to rally his men, but the 71st Pennsylvania came up double-quick to add their weight to the fire fight. In a short time the Georgians were heading back across the Emmitsburg Road. The 69th was over the wall in a surge for they had not seen the backs of the Army of Northern Virginia since the Peninsula. For an unexplained reason Brig. Gen. William Harrow, who commanded the First Brigade, Second Division, did not want the Confederates pursued, and he and Webb, being mounted, were able to head off the most ardent spirits and get them back to the wall. Perhaps they feared another attack and did not wish to jeopardize what had already been gained.

They were not as successful in stopping the 106th which had been on the left rear of the 69th. The Blazers, as the 106th was known, kept after Wright's men and brought in 250 prisoners, including Col. William Gibson of the 48th Georgia who was wounded. Back at the stone wall the disgusted Irish watched through the battle smoke their mates bring in the bag of captives. Then they turned to count their own losses. There were eleven killed among whom were Capt. Michael Duffy, Company I, and Lt. Charles Kelly, Company H, and seventeen wounded, among whom was Lt. Col. Martin Tschudy who refused to be evacuated. There were not many casualties considering the importance of holding the position.[13] Had Wright penetrated the position, his boldness might have resulted in a disproportionate gain. The Confederate strike had not been a knockout blow by any means, but coming on the heels of what had happened at the Peach Orchard, the strike could have had a moral effect beyond reckoning. If a large group of Union soldiers had shown weakness in the center of Cemetery Ridge, even a light blow like Wright's could have influenced the council-of-war that Meade held that night.

12. Coddington, *The Gettysburg Campaign*, p. 424.
13. McDermott, *69th Pennsylvania*, p. 29.

The repulse had lifted the morale of the Philadelphia Brigade considerably, and later that night General Webb raised it even higher by announcing that on the morrow McClellan would be operating on Lee's communication line with 40,000 men. Just why Webb thought it necessary to bring out the oldest ploy in the arsenal of the Army of the Potomac is hard to tell, unless it is remembered that the name of Little Mac could bring out the soul of the army. At the same time Wright was being dealt with on Cemetery Ridge, a heavy Confederate attack was taking place on Cemetery Hill not far away. The sounds of this battle were clearly heard, and many an uneasy eye had turned to the area which lay to the right and rear of the Philadelphia Brigade. When it was announced later that Ewell's attacks had been beaten off, the men cheered up. The wounded were succored and the exhausted soldiers sank down to sleep.

At Meade's headquarters the famous council of the corps commanders was held; the opinions reached were written down and passed to the chief of staff, Maj. Gen. Daniel Butterfield. Meade had not slept much since taking command of the army on June 28, and he was in the midst of a tremendous battle. Some of his best formations were wrecked beyond repair and ahead of him was more bloodshed. If ever a man bore the weight of the Republic on his shoulders, George Meade was that man. Now he listened to battle reports, read the written opinions of his chiefs, and thought long and hard. When the conference broke up, Meade spoke to John Gibbon, who had been off-and-on in command of the Second Corps while Hancock was busy stitching the defences on the Union left. According to Gibbon, Meade said,

> "If Lee attacks to-morrow, it will be in *your front*." I asked him why he thought so, and he replied, "Because he has made attacks on both our flanks and failed, and if he concludes to try it again it will be on our center." I expressed the hope that he would, and told General Meade, with confidence, that if he did we would defeat him.[14]

14. John Gibbon, "The Council of War on the Second Day," in *Battles and Leaders*, 3:314.

Although Ewell's attack on Cemetery Hill was not successful, some of the entrenchments on Culp's Hill occupied by the Twelfth Corps were taked by the Confederates. So at daybreak on July 3, the Twelfth Corps counterattacked to regain their position. The artillery roar of this battle awoke the exhausted men on Cemetery Ridge to another day. It continued with varied fortune until 11 a.m. when the Confederates drew off to the bottom of Culp's Hill. Then began an unnatural quiet.

The 69th Pennsylvania lay against their stone wall and watched the picket line out along the Emmitsburg Road. There had been a sharp fire fight at a barn west of the road and the 14th Connecticut had finally burned the barn to keep it from being used by the Confederate skirmishers as a forward position. The hot July sun beat down on the field, making men long for a patch of shade. Over on Seminary Ridge there was considerable battery movement as Col. E. Porter Alexander, the Confederate artillerist, went about placing the cannon which would usher in Lee's last move of the battle. Just as skillful a cannoneer on the Union side, Brig. Gen. Henry Hunt, began to line Cemetery Ridge with all the batteries that the ground could hold along the line held by the Second and Third Divisions of the Second Corps. The infantry watched this with some surprise but much thankfulness. They were experienced enough to know that today they would be supporting artillery and not engaging in any offensive activity of their own.

Two companies of the 106th Pennsylvania were out there on the Emmitsburg Road picket line under a very hard soldier, Capt. James Lynch. The other eight companies of the 106th had not returned from Cemetery Hill where they had bolstered up the the Eleventh Corps in the previous evening's fighting. The Philadelphia Brigade was short one regiment.

Col. Dennis O'Kane was forty-three years old with a luxuriant, black beard. He had been a militia soldier for years before the war, had gone off with the 24th Pennsylvania in the three months service and re-upped, of course, with the 69th. He had seen Glendale, Antietam, and Fredericksburg, marched the roads of Virginia, Maryland, and now Pennsylvania. Once he had a nineteen-day furlough, but aside from that he had been with the army. He was, probably, a man of small education.[15] One of his soldiers wrote of him, ". . . he despised a coward."[16] It is clear that he was not of the "manager class." His men had fought well on July 2. They were fighters well-proven; of his twenty-four officers, eight had been promoted from the ranks in the last month.

The lieutenant colonel, Martin Tschudy, had been hit in the shoulder the day before, but had refused to go to the Second Corps hospital; it might mean he would be kept there. Tschudy had been born in the heart of the Confederacy, Charleston, South Carolina, the son of an Episcopal priest. A career in law had brought him to the Union army and a commission as lieutenant in August 1861. Almost immediately he became adjutant of the 69th and remained in that post until the year 1863 brought him two quick promotions. Now his post was in the rear of the right five companies of the 69th as they stood at the wall.[17]

Behind the left five companies was Maj. James Duffy who had been captain of Company A. All along the line the captains, James O'Reilly, George C. Thompson, William Davis, and Patrick Moran, were experienced men who had seen the face of war. And in Company B was a young Jewish boy, Solomon Aarons, seventeen years old and a fifer.[18] On the day of battle fifers became riflemen, as did company clerks. Among the latter was one Anthony McDermott who had worked for the Pennsylvania Railroad before the war and wrote a good hand. He had picked up a musket on July 2 and joined in the fight. Now he was with the right flank company, Company I, whose commander, Michael Duffy, had been killed.[19] Next was Company A followed by F, D, and B, in that order. Then the color company, C, the tattered banners held against the stone wall. After that was the left wing, commanded by Maj. James Duffy.

15. Samuel Bates, *Martial Deeds of Pennsylvania* (Philadelphia: n.p., 1889), p. 509.
16. Anthony McDermott to John B. Bachelder, June 2, 1886, New Hampshire Historical Society collection, pp. 7-8.
17. Samuel P. Bates, *History of Pennsylvania Volunteers, 1861-5*, 5 vols. (Harrisburg, Pennsylvania: B. Singerly, 1869-1871), 2:707-8.
18. *Ibid.*, pp. 716-18.
19. *Ibid.*, pp. 734-37.

To the right of Company I along the wall there was an open space of about 250 feet. Battery A, 4th U.S. Field Artillery under Lt. Alonzo Cushing was stationed about 200 feet to the rear to fire through this open space. That left only thirty feet of wall before it turned at a sharp right angle to the east and the crest of Cemetery Ridge. In that thirty feet were crammed two companies of the 71st Pennsylvania.Their conduct would later lead to bitter controversy. To the immediate left of Cushing's guns and directly behind the 69th was a clump of trees.[20] No one present on the hot slope in his wildest dreams could ever envision what that group of trees would represent in the popular American mind after the events of this day. Between the 69th and the trees was a good deal of small brush, much trampled after the events of the previous day and that morning.

The artillerists had not dug empaulements for their guns, and the caissons stood almost directly behind each piece. At about noon a stillness reigned that was deathlike and unreal. None of the soldiers were fooled by it. There had been two days of battle without reaching a decision one way of the other. It was inconceivable to leave it this way. Young Anthony McDermott wrote:

> . . . an anxious look could plainly be seen on the faces of the men, and feelings of mingled dread and determination pervaded the minds of all—a harbinger of the coming storm that was to cover the fields with so much blood.[21]

On the other side of the field there was much soul-searching and misgiving. The latter quality seems to have taken complete possession of General Longstreet, who was certain that the next move projected for the Confederates would not meet with success. He had been directed to throw approximately two divisions and part of a third across the valley directly at the Clump of Trees that stood behind the 69th Pennsylvania. This attack would fall where Meade had predicted it would to Gibbon on the previous evening. Of the troops in gray and

20. Stewart, *Pickett's Charge*, pp. 72-73.
21. McDermott, *69th Pennsylvania*, p. 29.

butternut who were to make the push, one division was commanded by Maj. Gen. George Pickett—three brigades of Virginians, who had not taken part in the battle as yet. Heth's division of A. P. Hill's corps, commanded by Brig. Gen. J. Johnston Pettigrew, which had started the battle on July 1 but had not been engaged on July 2, would also be involved, along with two other brigades of A. P. Hill under Maj. Gen. Isaac Trimble. Longstreet had told Lee the task was too much for "any 15,000 men ever mustered" but historians think there were somewhat less than that, around 11,000.

There was no sound of battle at all at noon, as though an Angelus bell had struck both armies mute. There was stirring and movement, of course, as thousands of men got up, sat down, relieved themselves, or worked off nervous energy.[22] In Company E of the 69th Cpl. Joseph McKeever wore a broad-brimmed soft hat, the envy of his fellows who had to make do with the regulation kepi. It kept off a lot more sun. Now in the stillness McKeever lay with his back to the stone wall and the brim sloped protectively over his forehead. Like everyone else in the 69th his stomach was growling. Almost forty-eight hours had passed since they had seen any rations. As McKeever watched the sprawling cannoneers about Cushing's guns, he saw something that brought him instantly to his feet, the sight of food. Bread, or, as the soldiers knew it, crackers, the stone-hard biscuit that was the military staff of life.[23]

Usually artillery ate better than infantry, and suddenly someone arrived in the midst of the battery area with ration boxes. Immediately the corporal was up and running over the slope to share the largesse. Gunners were sometimes generous and might be prevailed on for a handout. As he ran he snatched off his hat which might hold enough for his entire squad. He held up beseeching hands to a redleg sergeant and got a boxful. One box. If he hung around there might be more.[24] But suddenly there was an interruption and the hardtack was forgot-

22. Stewart, *Pickett's Charge*, pp. 72-73.
23. Supreme Court of Pennsylvania, May Term, 1891 #20, 30. Middle District. Appeal of the Gettysburg Battlefield Memorial Association from the Decree of the Court of Common Pleas of Adams County. Paper Book of Appellants. Testimony of Joseph McKeever. Hereafter cited as Trial.
24. *Ibid.*

ten. Over on Seminary Ridge a grayback gun crew was running a cooling wad down the throat of their cannon. Through the valley was echoing the sound of the first round of the Third Day's fight. McKeever seized his box of crackers and ran back to Company A. As he ran there was an echoing gun to the first and then the earth began to shake. It was between 1:00 and 1:15 p.m., July 3, 1863.

Henry Hunt had an artillerist's appreciation of the work of good, well-served ordnance. Moreover he was on Little Round Top and out of the target area for the Confederate artillery.

> All their batteries were soon covered with smoke, through which the flashes were incessant, whilst the air seemed filled with shells, whose sharp explosions, with the hurtling of their fragments, formed a running accompaniment to the deep roar of the guns.[25]

In Company I of the 69th Anthony McDermott crouched as close to the stones of the wall as he could get. He and his fellows had not the same appreciation of the shelling as Hunt. Fervently they wished it over, for never had the Confederates mounted so many guns to bear on one position.

> The air is filling with the whirring, shrieking, hissing sounds of the solid shot and the bursting shell; all throw themselves flat upon the ground, behind the low stone wall; nearly one hundred and fifty guns belch forth messengers of destruction, sometimes in volleys, again in irregular but continuous sounds, traveling through the air, high above us, or striking the ground in front and ricochetting over us, . . . others strike the wall, scattering the stones around.[26]

The Confederate fire was especially noticeable on the batteries of Cushing and Brown positioned just to the rear and on the flanks of the 69th. Guns were dismounted, horses disemboweled, and finally, worst of all, two caissons exploded

---

25. Henry J. Hunt, "The Third Day at Gettysburg," in *Battles and Leaders*, 3:372-73.
26. McDermott, *69th Pennsylvania*, p. 30.

in Cushing's battery completely destroying the artillerists. In time the Union gunners pulled themselves together and fired back on Hancock's express order. He had a fixed idea that infantry undergoing shelling stood it better if they could see and hear answering fire from their own side. Artillery commanders hated this "firing for effect," for it lowered their ammunition supplies. In later years, Hunt and Hancock would have a lively controversy about the subject.[27]

After the battle it was strange and wonderful to ask men who had undergone the Confederate fire how long it had lasted. An hour, said some. An hour and a half, said others. There were no impartial referees standing about with watches in their hands, only terrified men, tensed against the earth's breast, awaiting the unwelcome metallic fragment, resentful of the travail, and knowing that when the cannonading stopped, there would be worse. Sometime the horrible noises would slow down and stop, and the air would clear of death at long distance. Then it would be man to man, bluecoat against butternut, infantry action that would decide the fortune of the day. Now the soldiers simply endured, some praying, some cursing this abomination to the eardrums, some in a gray fog where all appearance of rationality had fled. A half hour, an hour, still the roar went on.

Brown's battery had spent some time in the hands of the enemy yesterday, before the 106th had recaptured its guns, and had no better luck now. A shellburst right at the muzzle on one of the pieces had inflicted terrible death and wounds among the gunners. It was evident that the battery would have to be replaced.[28] A battery from the Sixth Corps, 1st New York Independent, was dispatched to the scene. Its commander, Capt. Andrew Cowan, lived to a fine old age and made many pilgrimages to the field in later years. Never did he forget the scene as his men came in at a gallop. One of his guns went past the Clump of Trees and the battery went into action with five guns south of the trees and one to the north, near the wreckage of Cushing's battery. Cowan rode over to this one gun to repeat the range and fuse settings and dismounted as Lt. Cushing limped up with a shrapnel wound in his leg. Cowan explained

27. Coddington, *The Gettysburg Campaign*, pp. 497-98.
28. Stewart, *Pickett's Charge*, p. 146.

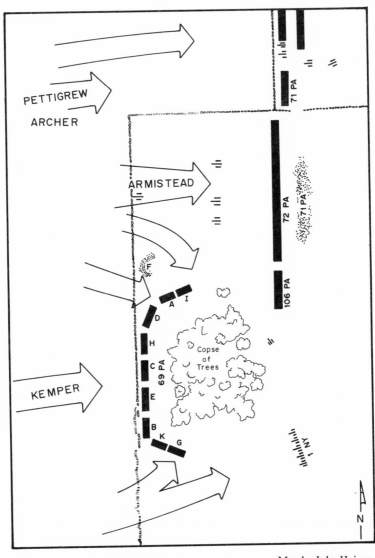

Map by John Heiser

The 69th Pennsylvnia fights in The Angle at Gettysburg.

282

why his one gun was out of position, and in the midst of the hurricane of shot Cushing made "some pleasant reply" and turned away to his own problems.[29] Only two of his guns were firing now, most of his other crews having been killed or wounded. So Cushing ordered that one gun be dragged forward to the stone wall just to the right of the 69th's Company I. As he did so the Confederate fire began to diminish in volume, and then seemed to come to a sudden halt.

The Union infantrymen knew that their time had come. All along the stone wall men raised their heads, looked at each other, and then, reluctantly, as though dreading what they would see, turned to gaze across the swales toward Seminary Ridge. Over in Spangler's Wood and along the slope that led up from Pitzer's Run to Seminary Ridge there was a stirring among the Virginians of Pickett's division, and among the Tennesseeans, North Carolinians, Georgians, Virginians, of A. P. Hill's corps. Lee's last throw was in his hand.

The first sight of the Confederate infantry was a relief to Anthony McDermott,

> . . . from the dread of being plowed into shreds or torn to fragments by the solid shot or bursting shell that had so thickly filled the air a few moments before.
>
> While the enemy was advancing across the plain towards us, Col. O'Kane, commanding the regiment, ordered the men to reserve their fire until they could plainly distinguish the whites of their eyes; he also reminded the command of their being upon the soil of their own State, concluding his remarks with the words, "And let your work this day be for victory or to the death."[30]

There is something almost pathetic in Dennis O'Kane's words. The men he was talking to had lived in the city named for Brotherly Love. Many times while marching through the streets of that city during their militia days they had heard the scathing words of the nativists; stones and brickbats had fallen on their backs and shoulders. Not even New England had a

29. *Ibid.*, p. 166.
30. McDermott, *69th Pennsylvania*, pp. 30-31.

Dennis O'Kane
Colonel, 69th Pennsylvania Veteran Volunteer Infantry
Killed at Gettysburg

worse name for anti-Irish pogroms than Pennsylvania's "Greene Countrie Towne." If there was one state in the Union that was not their own, it was that beautiful, green Pennsylvania where they now stood, looking up at their bearded colonel on the stones of the wall. Yet in the name of Pennsylvania they had gone to Virginia to kill and be killed. On one side of their flag was the coat-of-arms of Pennsylvania. From Glendale to Fredericksburg they had left dead comrades by the score. Their attachment to the Keystone State was legal, if one-sided. Today they would fight for both sides of their flag. They stacked their ammunition on top of the wall. Alexander Webb walked up and down the line of the companies, "If you do as well today as you did yesterday," he told them over and over, "I will be satisfied."[31]

The ground before them was still covered with the dead of Wright's Georgians from the previous day's fight. Enterprising Union soldiers had gone over the wall and picked up every rifle and musket in sight. Now, loaded and capped, these pieces made the 69th armed and thrice-armed. They could let loose a lot of firepower.[32]

When the Confederates started across the valley, the conformation of the ground and the standing timber contributed to the rather mixed first impression of the Union infantry. Pettigrew's division came into sight first, directly across from the Second Corps, a panorama of butternut forms turning and turning out of the woods. Here and there was the red Confederate battle flag and a few mounted horsemen. It seemed to the watchers that the woods were becoming men, men who formed into block-hard units, got their intervals and moved at the Union line with long, swinging strides. "Here they come! Here comes the infantry!" The mutter ran along the Union line and the bluecoats stood with mouths agape to marvel at these others who were coming to kill them; to break the Union and finish the war. The Confederate movement flowed along the face of the woods, completely covering the Second Corps front and stretching down toward the Peach Orchard. Down there were the Virginians of Pickett who would this day become immortal.

31. Trial, testimony of Joseph McKeever.
32. Trial, testimony of Robert Whittick.

But as impressive as the grayback deployment was, there were still Union artillerymen who remembered their lessons. They had not much long-range ammunition left, a good bit of it having been spent in answering the afternoon barrage. What was left was packed into the iron tubes and sent across the valley to smash into those formations, to knock men down, and leave bloody forms in the corn and wheat and grass.[33]

Heavy skirmish lines preceded the Confederate divisions and the Union skirmishers engaged them with sharp duels while slowly giving ground. Capt. James Lynch of the 106th was in charge of the skirmish detail drawn from the Philadelphia Brigade and he kept his men at their work until the last possible moment. Then they broke for the stone wall, covering each other when possible.[34] To the 69th the fully developed battle line filled their entire field of vision. To their front and slightly to their left there was a slight gap in the Confederate line, but the division of Pickett was moving in on this gap at an oblique to fill it. When they reached the Emmitsburg Road there was a humping up of the ranks as the men climbed over the fences lining both sides of the road. Then the Southerners felt the full blast of the Union batteries ranked on the lower part of Cemetery Ridge and Little Round Top. Seemingly oblivious of it, they hurried on, inclining to their left.

To the 69th it seemed as though they were following in the footsteps of Wright's Georgians of the day before. They were coming in at an angle from the left. At the wall the men were calm, watching with rapt attention. Alonzo Cushing stood on the right of Company I, directing the fire of the gun which had been run down to the wall. He had been hit terribly in the crotch and held his hands over the wound. The Irish could hear his voice telling the gunners to lower the elevation as the range closed rapidly.[35] On the right another gun of his battery nearly up against the Angle in the wall, and manned partly by artillerymen and partly by men of the 71st Pennsylvania, was banging away. They were down to their last two or three rounds, and the soldiers were loading everything they could lay their hands on into the barrel, even a bayonet. Then the gun

33. Coddington, *The Gettysburg Campaign*, p. 505.
34. *Pennsylvania at Gettysburg*, 1:553.
35. McDermott to Bachelder, June 2, 1886, p. 4.

fell silent and the gunners left for the rear. From here on the fight belonged to the footmen.

All along Cemetery Ridge the soldiers thumbed back the hammers of their muskets. Webb had a final word for the 69th as the Confederate line got straightened out and came up the slope. "Do as well as you did yesterday, and I will be satisfied!" Now the brigades of Brigadier Generals James L. Kemper and Richard B. Garnett were directly in front of the Irish. The Confederates had some pressure on their right flank from Brig. Gen. George J. Stannard's Vermonters which pushed the Rebels square on to the Irish. The 69th was standing now with pieces leveled and the word to fire was given. A solid sheet of flame blazed out and the Virginians were halted in their tracks. Ordinarily an infantry regiment volley fired by alternate platoons or by front rank and rear rank.[36] But with fewer than 250 effectives to hold 300 yards of front, the 69th had put every man in line. They then reached for the extra loaded muskets of yesterday's fight and used them with effect to fight an all-out duel with Kemper's men at a distance of about fifty yards.[37]

There were some good Irishmen among the Virginians. Capt. John Dooley of the Richmond Emmet Guards had gone down with a wound west of the Emmitsburg Road, but would live to return to Georgetown and study for the priesthood.[38] Willie Mitchell, son of the most irreconcilable of the Fenian leaders, had marched beside the flag of the 1st Virginia right up to where the volleys of the 69th were striking into Southern bodies. Grimly did the fight go on, the Irish kneeling down to reload, spring up and fire into the acrid, billowing clouds of smoke. In those clouds the Virginians stood just as stoutly, similarly employed, biting cartridge, ramming it home, and firing as though in a dream.[39] Here in the center of battle the temperature was hottest. Irish and Virginians looked each

36. D. Scott Hartwig, "It Struck Horror To Us All," *Gettysburg Magazine*, no. 4 (January 1991): 89.
37. *Ibid.*, p. 98; McDermott, *69th Pennsylvania*, pp. 28-29.
38. John Dooley, *John Dooley, Confederate Soldier, His War Journal*, ed. Joseph T. Durkin (Washington, D.C.: Georgetown University Press, 1945).
39. Coddington, *The Gettysburg Campaign*, p. 516.

other in the eye and stood fast. But suddenly pressure built up on the right flank of the 69th. The 71st had skeedaddled.

About this time Lt. Frank Haskell, Gibbon's aide, was spurring his horse over the reverse slope of Cemetery Ridge behind the Philadelphia Brigade. A terrible shock awaited him.

> . . . great heavens! were my senses mad? The larger portion of Webb's brigade—my God, it was true— there by the group of trees and the angles of the wall, was breaking from the cover of their works, and, without orders or reason, with no hand lifted to check them, was falling back, a fear-stricken flock of confusion![40]

No one knew how many companies of the 71st were right in the angle of the wall, either two or six, but they were being hit from the front and the right at the same time. They ran back up the slope of Cemetery Ridge and over the crest. This is attested to by several of the men who stayed and were taken prisoner by the Virginians. The fire was so hot at this point that these prisoners asked permission of their captors to pass over to the Confederate side of the wall to get out of the storm.[41] McDermott disposed of the action of the 71st with a sentence:

> For some reason or another the troops on the right of this regiment, and between it and the Angle, abandoned their position.[42]

Brig. Gen. Lewis A. Armistead's brigade, Pickett's second line, had now joined with the men of Kemper and Garnett. The entire division was now massed in front of the stone wall position. Through the smoke billows the Irish could see a senior Confederate officer running along the line of the graybacks, shouting and gesticulating with his sword.[43] He had

40. Frank A. Haskell, *The Battle of Gettysburg*, Harvard Classics (New York: P. F. Collier and Company, 1910), p. 406.
41. Trial, testimony of William Stockton.
42. McDermott, *69th Pennsylvania*, p. 31.
43. McDermott to Bachelder, June 2, 1886, p. 5.

seen the open space vacated by the 71st. A torrent of soldiers rose up with unearthly screams to follow him as he ran for the hole in the Union dike. Just at the corner of the Angle a large boulder lay against the wall and the Confederates used it as a gangplank. They came over the wall in full cry. Down in the middle of the 69th, Corporal McKeever heard the keening of the Rebel Yell and turned to look to where the Confederates were appearing. Years later, he remembered "We thought that we were all gone."[44]

But O'Kane, Tschudy, and Webb thought something could be done about it. Webb had been trying to get the reserve regiment, the 72nd Pennsylvania, to fill the gap caused by the departure of the 71st. When the 72nd would not move forward, he decided to go to the Irish who were still fighting savagely at the wall. From time to time the Confederates had rushed the position but had not gotten over except as prisoners. Robert Whittick, one of the color guard of Company C, described one of the happenings of the day:

> . . . a fellow was taken in with me and I knocked him over and took him prisoner, and took him in over the stone wall.
>
> We were fighting both sides on the front and rear of us at that time.[45]

Apparently, the first Confederates behind Armistead went into the Angle shortly after Webb reached the 69th. Thinking quickly, Webb decided that, at all costs, the Confederates must be denied the protection of the clump of trees. Once firmly ensconced in the grove, a sizeable enemy force would be a cancer in the center of the Union position. He decided that the right flank companies of the 69th must be pulled back to cover the front of the woods and seal it off. Companies I, A, and F were told to change front to the right by the simple expedient of grasping men by the shoulder and shoving them in the right direction. The din was fearful, but Anthony McDermott and Joseph Garnett and their comrades of Company I moved back, firing as they did so. McDermott remembered that the

---

44. Trial, testimony of Joseph McKeever.
45. Trial, testimony of Robert Whittick.

movement was not made in very good order, but "in some kind of order." This movement brought them to bear on the Virginians who were following Armistead up the slope, and they fired hastily at this group. Webb had seen the change of front maneuver of the 69th get under way, and he then raced up the slope to where the 72nd still lay along the crest. If he could get them to move down, the day might still be saved.[46]

The Virginians who had followed Armistead up the slope had now encountered the fire of Companies I and A of the 69th and turned to deal with them. George Thompson, captain of Company F, was killed before he received the order to change front, and his men remained at the wall firing at the men of Kemper and Garnett still a scant twenty paces away. Companies I and A were not numerous enough to cover the ground from the crest of the ridge to the stone wall and serious consequences resulted. A sizeable hole developed between Company A and the men of the 69th at the wall. Into this hole a large group of Confederates fought their way. The men of Company F were attacked from behind, clubbed and bayoneted. Disaster for the 69th was at hand.[47] Indeed the Virginians, drunk with combat, called for the surrender of the whole line. The blue Virginia flags were waving all along the open gap in the stone wall where the 71st had stood not ten minutes before. The very crux of the battle was reached. The 69th was battling furiously for life, its right swung back and a goodly number of the enemy between the swung-back companies and the rest of the regiment.

There was a huge corporal in Company D, Hugh Bradley, and he led his comrades into the breach with clubbed musket and hoarse shouts. A terrible hand-to-hand epic took place between the Irish and the Virginians. Before the gap was sealed off, some of the Confederates penetrated into the clump of trees and made their way past the 69th toward the crest of the ridge. Then Bradley and Company D closed off the hole, battling furiously with clubbed muskets and fists, howling and shouting.[48]

46. Coddington, *The Gettysburg Campaign*, p. 518.
47. McDermott to Bachelder, June 2, 1886, p. 5.
48. *Ibid.*, p. 6.

Some of the Confederates battling Companies A and I on the slope had leaped over the north side of the connecting wall and used it as a barricade. All alone a senior Confederate officer was making his way across that terrible web of fire on foot. In his right hand was the sword with which he had led his men. Originally, his hat had been placed on the point for his men to guide on; now the sharp point had pierced the felt and it had slipped down to the hand guard. He trotted up the slope toward the three silent guns of Cushing's battery which stood there. As he approached, he was struck and pressed his hand on his stomach, dropping his sword and hat. He made two or three more steps and, reaching out for the muzzle of a cannon, fell to the ground.[49]

Anthony McDermott was fifteen paces away. Later he thought that it may have been his shot that brought down Armistead. Not far away was Webb with his hat swinging, trying to motion the 72nd forward again. McDermott ran to him and pointed out the recumbent figure of Armistead. Webb turned from the 72nd and returned to the scattered men of the right flank companies of the 69th. They were still firing and the Confederates began to slacken off. Not many had come over the wall after Armistead and many of those who did had been struck down. In the clump of trees directly behind the Irish, the Virginians who had penetrated there were still fighting against the 19th Massachusetts and the 42nd New York, two small veteran regiments of First Brigade, Second Division. In the slashing and underbrush they had a hand-to-hand struggle, but it did not last long. There were now too many Union troops on hand for the comparatively few Confederates who had made it over the wall and into the Angle.[50] When the 19th Massachusetts fought their way out of the trees into the open space where stood Companies A and I of the 69th, the fight was as good as over.

The New Englanders were amazed at the performance of the Irish. Capt. William Hill of the 19th Massachusetts said,

> The fighting, of course, ceased, as soon as those
> men threw down their arms and came in. Then there

---

49. *Ibid.*
50. Hartwig, "It Struck Horror To Us All," p. 99.

appeared to be a lull in the battle and our men went down to about the angle where the Sixty-ninth were, at all events, only, I suppose, to see the Sixty-ninth. . . . There was no fighting at this point after the enemy came in. The few who retired to get back across the field were not followed up and there was no fire, except an occasional shot. There was no organized fire I mean. The men who went down there immediately after seemed to be prompted more by a sense of curiosity than through any need of their presence there.

The Sixty-ninth appeared to be fighting on their own hook. They did not yield one inch and the enemy swarmed right over them. . . .

The Sixty-ninth, as I saw it, simply got up and faced about, and as the rebels came in they put in a shot wherever they got a chance, and they were doing some pretty good fighting.[51]

It is strange, even in the biggest battles, how the mechanics of the decisive action may be in the hands of a comparatively small number of soldiers. Here was one small regiment reinforced by two others of about the same size disputing the key point with what remained of a division. There was always some question as to what happened here at the Angle until George Stewart's *Pickett's Charge* was written in 1959. Haskell's famous letter to his brother was published in the early years of the century, and many took his carelessly written words about the 71st to mean that the entire Philadelphia Brigade had fallen back in disorder. Many Confederate writers have wished to crown the unbelievable feats of Pickett's division, and Pettrigrew's and Trimble's men with the oft-repeated asssertion that they had broken the Union line beyond repair. In this controversy it is well to call on a participant from Garnett's brigade. Maj. Charles Peyton of the 19th Virginia was in command of the brigade after the battle. On July 9 he wrote his official report; some extracts from it are the best evidence as to how the 69th kept the wall:

51. Trial, testimony of Capt. William Hall, 19th Massachusetts.

Our line, much shattered, still kept up the advance until within about 20 paces of the wall, when, for a moment, it recoiled under the terrific fire that poured into our ranks both from their batteries and from their sheltered infantry. At this moment, General Kemper came up on the right and General Armistead in [the] rear, when the three lines, joined in concert, rushed forward with unyielding determination and an apparent spirit of laudable rivalry to plant the Southern banner on the walls of the enemy. His strongest and last line was instantly gained; the Confederate battle-flag waved over his defenses, and the fighting over the wall became hand to hand, and of the most desperate character; but more than half having already fallen, our line was found too weak to rout the enemy. We hoped for a support on the left (which had started simultaneously with ourselves), but hoped in vain. Yet a small remnant remained in desperate struggle. . . .[52]

If anyone can tell a true tale of the events in front of the stone wall it was Major Peyton, for he was there, and it is clear that the Virginians did not drive the 69th from the position that had been entrusted to them. There was fighting over the wall, tremendous fighting, attested to by both sides, but a handful of tough Irishmen did not relent in the face of a foe as valiant as themselves.

On the right the fall of Armistead had brought a sudden check to the men of his brigade. For a few minutes they kept up the fire but the light of the assault was going out, not in the sudden bolt of sound or silence but rather in the realization dawning on the Virginians that they had been sent too far. In a thousand single backward steps, in a thousand separate head turnings, the relics of the most famous charge in American history disengaged from the Angle, from the silent cannons where Alonzo Cushing lay dead, from the hard-breathing Union footmen who had finally proven the mettle of their pasture.

52. *OR*, series 1, vol. 27, pt. 2, p. 385-87.

As Captain Hill said, few shots pursued the survivors back to Seminary Ridge. The men who had held the stone wall, the clump of trees, the Angle, and the crest of the ridge had also had enough. Slack-jawed and empty-eyed, the survivors looked about them with incomprehension. The ground was paved with broken bodies stretched out in the finality of death or twisted in agony. Around the guns of Cushing's battery were piled the gunners who had held on with their young commander. Stunned with success, not realizing the unusual taste of it, the bluecoats stood in silence. As the poet said, it was a famous victory. Farther down Cemetery Ridge where there had been no fighting, some Union soldiers shouted one word at those tortured graybacks making their way home, "Fredericksburg!"

Anthony McDermott wandered along the wall looking for his tent mate, only to find him dead.[53] Someone told Hugh McKeever that his cousin, Neal McCafferty, was gone. So were many others: Colonel O'Kane, Lieutenant Colonel Tschudy, the captains of Companies F and I, George Thompson and Michael Duffy, Lieutenants Michael Mullin and Charles Kelly. Six other officers were wounded including Major Duffy. The two lieutenants of Company F, John Ryan and John Eagan, were in the hands of the enemy. Of the enlisted men forty were killed and eighty wounded. In all, the casualties totalled just over fifty percent of the complement with which they had started the day. The 69th had indeed fought for both sides of its flag.

A number of reinforcing infantry regiments had been rushed to the clump of trees, but with the exception of the 19th Massachusetts and the 42nd New York they were not needed, in spite of what many brigade and regimental commanders wrote in their reports. The number of Confederates who advanced over the wall was never estimated with anything like precision, but it could not have been large. Three hundred men would probably be a generous estimate.

A word should be said for the color-bearers of Pickett's division who were quite conspicuous in the final phase of the action. These individuals had to be a breed apart, for the flags always attracted fire and casualties among the bearers were

53. Trial, testimony of Anthony McDermott.

heavy. Only extremely dedicated and pertinacious men took the banners into the fighting or snatched them from the failing hands of others. The converging of Pickett's three brigades at the stone wall had the effect of concentrating the colors of the division together. Just before Armistead made his final thrust that went over the wall, apparently there had been some kind of halt during which the color-bearers came to the fore. When the Confederates went over the wall, the color-bearers headed the torrent. There was no return for most of those fragile pieces of cloth for which brave men gave the last full measure of devotion. All but two were left on the field.

Some of the colors were picked up in front of the wall. Some were found in the Angle beside the bodies of their guardians. Col. Arthur Devereux of the 19th Massachusetts said that his men captured three by plucking them from the hands of their bearers, but McDermott thinks this is only hyperbole. He was much upset over the "captures." The flags were laying all about, he said, there for the taking. When a group of soldiers from the 42nd New York picked one up and ran off with it, he jeered at them, saying there was no honor in that. On the 69th's monument the inscription merely says "eight flags were picked up on the front of the regiment," which is certainly honest enough.

Perhaps later, when medals were passed out to those who made off with the downed colors, the men of the 69th may have been sorry they had not been more perceptive. McDermott reserved his harshest diatribes for those Union regiments which claimed, in the post-battle bragging, to have fought at the wall.

It may be proper to here state that other organizations have claimed to have fought at the stone wall, mingling with the men of the Sixty-ninth. This claim is based on the fact of individuals from other regiments picking up rebel flags thrown down or abandoned by the enemy at the close of the fight, and for which service medals have been awarded by Congress. We here state emphatically that no regiment, company, or part thereof, approached that part of the stone wall held by the Sixty-ninth Pennsylvania during the period of the fighting. The Seventy-second Pennsylvania advanced to the crest of the ridge, and perhaps a little below it; also Hall's Brigade, and, we have been informed, other regiments approached our rear and fired upon the enemy.[54]

Some years later General Webb was questioned about the positions of the monuments of the Philadelphia Brigade which had been erected at the stonewall.

Q. Have you seen the position of the Sixty-ninth's monument?
A. I recognize the position from the map, but I have not seen it.
Q. That would be the correct position, would it not?
A. They have the right to be there; they were there.[55]

In this curiously understated opinion the Philadelphia Irish were granted the supreme accolade. Other men might come to Gettysburg and speak with rolling thunder and golden words of death and heroism. The 69th needed none of it. So long as the stones of the wall remain beside the granite shaft with the harp and shamrocks on it, so long shall the memory remain of the men who always stayed where they were put.

Two weeks later Webb wrote to his father in which he said,

... all my command knew that we were never to leave that hill or mound. The 69th lost all its field officers. It obeyed orders. After the Rebs were inside the fence I went to them and told them to fire to front and rear and to a man they replied that I could count on them.[56]

The next few weeks after the battle Webb got to know more about the 69th Pennsylvania, even in its reduced complement. It was his first experience with Irish soldiers and he found that there was much about them that was different. On August 11 he wrote a letter to Governor Curtin of Pennsylvania:

54. McDermott, *69th Pennsylvania*, pp. 32-33.
55. Trial, testimony of General Alexander S. Webb.
56. Alexander S. Webb to his father, July 17, 1863, Webb collection, Yale University.

I have the honor to inform you that discovering that Murdoch Campbell holding a commission as Lieutenant in the 69th Regt. P.V., but not yet mustered into the United States Service, has been guilty of challenging an enlisted man, a private in his Regiment, to fight him with his fists. I have forwarded an application to the Mustering Officer of this Corps, requesting that he be not mustered into the United States Service.

I would especially call the attention of your Excellency to the fact, that it is impossible to govern "Irish Regiments," when the Officers do not belong to a more intelligent class than that of which Murdoch Campbell, Lieut. [Charles] McAnally, and Lieut. [Charles] Fitzpatrick 69th Regt. P.V., are typical. I shall do all in my power to get rid of these disorganizing stumbling blocks.

Lieut. Fitzpatrick has tendered his resignation.

Your obdt servt

Alex. S. Webb[57]

Obviously, Webb had spent a sheltered life doing staff work, and encounter with the great unwashed men of the infantry was a rather frightening experience. Four days after writing the letter to Curtin he left command of the Philadelphia Brigade. Two of the three men he castigated had rather exciting lives later on. The record shows that Murdoch Campbell was promoted to second lieutenant of Company B from sergeant major on November 5, 1863, and was wounded at Spotsylvania on May 12, 1864. Charles McAnally was promoted from first sergeant, Company D, to second lieutenant on September 18, 1862, to first lieutenant on May 1, 1863, was wounded at Spotsylvania on May 12, 1864, wounded at Cold Harbor on June 3, 1864, awarded the Medal of Honor for capture of a Confederate flag at Spottsylvania, and promoted to captain of Company G on October 4, 1864.

57. Alexander S. Webb to Governor Andrew Curtin, August 11, 1863, 69th Pennsylvania file, Pennsylvania Archives, Harrisburg, Pennsylvania.

Chapter Twelve

ENTR' ACTE

Mr. Lincoln wrote an impatient letter to George Meade after the Army of Northern Virginia made good its passage of the Potomac River. Why, he asked, did you let them get away? Here was the second lost opportunity to liquidate Lee's army north of the river. It was so easy, Lincoln said. One more push and then the killing would be over once and for all. The president had this to say to the only Northern general ever to defeat Lee in open battle, a man who had been pitchforked into command on June 28, began the great contest two days later, and had gone through as much trial in the next three days as any mortal could stand. Fortunately the letter was not sent. Meade had a crusty temper of his own, and, at the end of the epic, he was in no frame of mind to take criticism from someone who had not seen that terrible field.[1]

He had slept little since the weight of command had fallen on him. For three days it had been in his power to lose the war disastrously. His army had been the wall between the Confederates and the government. He had seen the price exacted for the famous victory. His close friend John Reynolds was dead, and so were many others, old West Point comrades and men who had been with the army since First Manassas. Some of the best formations were irrevocably wrecked. The First and Eleventh Corps which had initiated the battle would never be potent forces in the field again. The Second, Third, and Fifth Corps had carried the load on July 2. The Twelfth Corps had stubbornly defended Culp's Hill. Only the Sixth Corps, hurried up so precipitously by Maj. Gen. John Sedgwick, was relatively unscathed. It was all very well for civilians a hundred miles away from the blood-letting to carp and moan

1. Carl Sandburg, *Abraham Lincoln: The War Years* (New York: Harcourt, Brace, and Company, 1939; reprint, 1954), p. 415.

and second-guess. The general on the field had to regroup the dispersed men, replace the downed leaders, and, most important, find untapped physical and spiritual reservoirs in men exhausted by blood, excitement, and effort.

Actually, this is a further development in the Lincoln-McClellan syndrome in which a school of historians is forever locked. The Lincoln-McClellan syndrome spreads into an East-West syndrome, and in this exchange the Army of the Potomac is the bloody shuttlecock. The "Westerners" sneer that the army had never been fought all-out, that if a simple, direct, informal, fighting general from the west was in command of that army, the war would be over in a jiffy. They seem to forget John Pope. The bloody shuttlecock would have to wait almost a year for the rebuttal. A simple, direct, all-conquering soldier did come out of the West to cross swords with the Grey Captain. The army was fought all out, as no other army in American history was ever fought, and there was no victory.

After the Confederates retreated down the Shenandoah Valley from Williamsport, the Federals moved to the familiar confines of Harpers Ferry. On July 18 the Second Corps crossed the river and moved down the east side of the Blue Ridge. There was a sharp fight at Manassas Gap two days later, after which the Confederates withdrew. The Federals moved on to Warrenton Junction and reached Morrisville in the beautiful Loudoun Valley on July 31. About this place Mulholland wrote:

> Never were the men in such health and spirits. Food was plentiful and even luxuries abundant. The country was overrun with blackberry bushes, and the fruit, juicy, luscious and ripe, was perhaps the greatest blessing that ever the men came across. The whole army literally feasted on blackberries. The result, health. Every case of diarrhea disappeared and blackberries saved the lives of hundreds. Blackberries were of more value to the army of the Potomac than all the medical department.[2]

2. Mulholland, *116th Pennsylvania,* p. 157.

The Second Corps spent the entire month of August and the early part of September in the same place. Gradually the rest restored the army to its former condition. When Lee detached Longstreet's corps to the western theater in September, Meade decided to strike a blow of some sort, and the Federals were put in motion. The Second Corps crossed the Rappahannock on September 13 and two days later pushed to Raccoon Ford on the Rapidan. As the Irish Brigade reached the bank of the river, Confederate pickets opened fire. This made no sense at all to the Irish.

> The Confederates seemed mad and full of fight and blazed away vigorously. The useless firing across a river indulged in by most of the army was never relished by the men of the Irish Brigade, who thought it sheer nonsense to blaze away and keep everyone from enjoying rest and comfort without accomplishing the slightest result. An effort was made at once to have the firing cease and cook supper. Captain [Charles M.] Granger, of the Eighty-eighth New York, jumped from cover, waved his sword and stuck it in the ground. The Southern boys understood the signal and, inquiring "what troops," found it was the Irish Brigade. A picket truce followed immediately and all hands settled down to boil their coffee in peace, while for miles to the left and right the useless fusillade continued far into the night. During the 16th and 17th not a man was hit in the battalion, and the picket truce was honorably observed in front of the brigade. . . . A number of sheep were captured by the men of the brigade, and to show their good feeling for the men on the other side of the river, three or four were sent over—the result, mutton stew on both sides of the stream.[3]

The Second Corps was pulled back to Culpeper during the first week of October. Once it had been a pleasant, country town, but the historian of the 9th Massachusetts noted that it

3. *Ibid.*, p. 162.

was now war-stricken and deserted by its owners and inhabitants except in a few cases.[4]

The 9th was in good spirits. They had not been heavily engaged at Gettysburg, and their colonel, Patrick Guiney, had exchanged their old-fashioned smooth-bore .69 calibre muskets for the .58 calibre rifled Springfields. In addition, they had acquired a new chaplain, a Dominican by the name of Costney Egan, who had come down from his parish in Washington to attend a deserter who was to be shot. Guiney had earnestly implored the priest to stay with the army. The regiment had not had a chaplain in over a year, he said, and it needed one badly. After some negotiation with the superior of the Dominican order in America, Father Egan stayed on and became a fixture with the Fifth Corps and the army.

Capt. William Davis was the surviving senior captain of the 69th Pennsylvania after Gettysburg, but he was not the most popular with his regiment. When he was detached to Philadelphia for duty, the idol of the men, Capt. Thomas Kelly, took command. It is a measure of Kelly's ability that he was able to bring the Philadelphians to a peak of efficiency while in camp at Morrisville. They counted only 164 men now, but in drill, obedience, and cleanliness they had no superior in the Second Corps, and a special order from division and corps headquarters recognized the fact.[5]

The Union defeat at Chickamauga in the west on September 19-20, 1863, had some repercussions for the Army of the Potomac in that the Eleventh and Twelfth Corps were shifted to the Army of the Cumberland in Tennessee, never to return. Lee was aware of this and on October 9, he began a series of maneuvers calculated to pass his army around the right flank of the Army of the Potomac and interpose between it and Washington. Meade moved back, and there followed a race for the capital, with the two armies marching on parallel lines. The marches were hard and tiring and the Irish Brigade formed the rear guard for the army at one critical period. The most spectacular accomplishment was the covering of seventy-six miles in fifty-six hours by the brigade. Mulholland was lost in admiration for them:

4. MacNamara, *Ninth Massachusetts*, p. 343.
5. McDermott, *69th Pennsylvania*, p. 41.

> . . . no fatigue could daunt the spirit of the men of the
> Irish Brigade and, as they were filing on to the road,
> they saluted the Corps Commander by going through
> the manual of arms as they marched. Warren was
> delighted with the exhibition of pluck and endur-
> ance.[6]

The morning of October 14 found Meade at Centreville and the race for the capital won. Lee fell back behind the Rappahannock and the 116th found that one of their officers had so distinguished himself at the action at Auburn Station that he was recommended for the Medal of Honor. At least Lt. Louis Sacriste had an Irish mother.

The Union army also returned to the Rappahannock area and effected a concentration by November 7 so that Meade entertained offensive ideas of his own. This led to the Mine Run campaign, an excellent strategic concept which came to nothing because of the incapacity of Maj. Gen. William French who was now in command of the Third Corps. The army crossed the Rapidan and attempted to interpose between Ewell's corps and A. P. Hill's corps, Longstreet's corps still being in Tennessee. On November 27 the 69th Pennsylvania found itself on a straggly farm belonging to a man by the name of Robertson. There were Confederates about, and as the Union line advanced, there was sharp skirmishing and some loss among the Philadelphians. Capt. Thomas Kelly, now in command and handling the regiment very well, went down with an early wound. Throughout a cold and cheerless day the Unionists moved forward. It was an equally cold and cheerless night without fires, and on the next day they made a long and tiring march to the south while Meade tried to find the Confederate right flank. McDermott remembered,

> On this march the utmost quietness was requested,
> and the men were obliged to muffle the utensils
> dangling from their haversacks. Arriving at the de-
> sired point, we were concealed in woods . . . and,
> amid the darkness of the hour, we were moved to a
> ravine within a few hundred yards of formidable

6. Mulholland, *116th Pennsylvania*, p. 166.

looking works of the enemy, and here rested. Shortly after daylight Gen. Webb addressed the brigade, informing us that we were selected to charge the works in our front. The men being anxious, peeped over the brow of the hill and saw that the ground across which we were to charge was a very level, open field, of at least 500 yards in width, swept by the guns of several forts connected by breastworks, and which could be brought to bear on any portion of the field. The men were intelligent enough to take in the situation; they knew that when the next roll would be called, there would be few to answer. Each one, however, with a grim cheerfulness, determined to make this charge a success or surrender his life. Few there were in the brigade line that morning who felt that they had even a chance of returning in safety from the attack. Watches and trinkets, to be sent to the loved ones at home, were given to the chaplains, surgeons and the other non-combatants always attached to regiments. Most of the officers and men wrote their names on paper and pinned them to their coat collars or vests, that they could be identified in the event of their death.[7]

Fortunately, there was a reprieve. Maj. Gen. Gouverneur K. Warren, who now commanded the Second Corps in the absence of the wounded Hancock, came over to have a look for himself. Not far from the 69th was a grove of trees. Before giving the word to go in, Warren carefully surveyed the Confederate position with binoculars, even climbing one of the trees to get a better view. Confederate sharpshooters fired at him, but the man who had saved Little Round Top for the Union paid little mind to the whistling bullets. Finally, he came down from the tree, put away his binoculars, and called off the assault. The infantry of the Second Corps let out a sigh of relief. They would die on other fields. Meade was tempted to be harsh with Warren, but when he had ridden over and had a look at the opposition, he seconded his subordinate. The army drew back across the river to the familiar camps.

7. McDermott, *69th Pennsylvania*, p. 36.

Among those who recrossed the river was Brig. Gen. Thomas Francis Meagher, who had arrived on a visit to the army on the evening of the movement and gone along as a supernumerary. He was loudly cheered by some of the Second Corps units even though he wore civilian dress. He must have been gratified at the way the brigade operated on November 29 against a Confederate skirmish line. Back at the winter camp at Stevensburg there was a "first-class jollification" for a few days. Then the ex-brigadier traveled back to Fairfax Court House where Brig. Gen. Michael Corcoran was encamped with his Irish Legion along the line of the Orange & Alexandria railroad. For several weeks the two were constant companions, and there is little doubt that one of the subjects under serious discussion was the Fenian Brotherhood of which Meagher had become a member soon after his return to civilian life. The Brotherhood had held a convention in Chicago in November which Meagher had been expected to attend as the representative of the Army of the Potomac.[8]

Heaven only knows the state of Corcoran's mind at this juncture. His first wife had died and he had quietly remarried. It is evident that he was completely disgusted with the quiet role to which his legion had been relegated since leaving New York. He had been back in service for over a year and, except for some skirmishing around Suffolk, Virginia, his men had smelled very little powder. Corcoran had pulled every string he knew in Washington to get his men attached to the Army of the Potomac, or even sent out West. Anywhere, just so the men would not be forced to spend their days guarding empty stretches of railroad track, a job not fit for an Irish soldier.

Meagher left Corcoran on December 22, intending to entrain from Fairfax to Washington City to meet his wife and Corcoran's mother-in-law. The plan was for the entire party to return to spend the holidays at Corcoran's headquarters. Corcoran ordered out a cavalry escort and with some of the other senior officers of the legion accompanied Meagher from the Courthouse to Fairfax Station. They shook hands and Meagher boarded the train, the cavalcade turning to ride back to headquarters. Not far from there, Corcoran's horse reared

8. Cavanagh, *Memoirs of Thomas Meagher*, pp. 357, 491.

305

and threw him. His body was carried to shelter, apparently unconscious. In a short time he was dead.

The officers and soldiers of the Irish Legion were desolate. On the following day they viewed the embalmed corpse. Meagher had, of course, returned from Washington, and at once took charge of the funeral. With Corcoran gone, Meagher would again be the First Irish Soldier. Or would he? Judge Daly's wife wrote a very interesting passage on this:

> Meagher sent the Judge a telegraph, most eloquently worded, expressing his own distress and appreciation of Corcoran. The telegraph containing no information, however, that had not been in the papers the day before. Meagher supposed the Judge would send the information to the newspaper, of course, and Meagher would have the benefit of it.
>
> Meagher's telegraph ran thus: "Dear Judge: You have by this time heard of the lamentable and sudden death of our gentle, gallant friend, General Corcoran, the Colonel of the valiant 69th, the leader of the Irish Legion, the brave and consistent Union prisoner. We hoped to have had him long with us to have shared with him the festivities of Christmas, but it is a black Christmas for us. Yours, Thomas Francis Meagher." Of course, the telegraph was not paid for, and it cost Judge five dollars and thirty-eight cents. At my instigation, however, it did not go to the paper.
>
> Meagher was first pallbearer, and in the paper of yesterday, I saw a paragraph from Fairfax saying it is already talked of that the command will be given to General Meagher, but that Meagher has too high a sense of the merits of the deceased, too delicate a regard for his memory for him, to listen to such a proposal (for the present). When I remember how useless he thought it in Mr. Savage and the Judge to do so much to release this brave Union prisoner two years ago . . . I cannot but marvel. . . . Meagher is cautiously frank, prudently *reckless*, and brave enough to risk his life when reputation actually requires it. He wears a swashing and martial outside with an appearance of whole-soulness. His generosity and

306

liberality are very taking, but he pays no one. He is the fox all over, as anyone might see by watching his small bright eye. I confess I do not want him to come near us. In his neighborhood, there can be no good luck for others. He ruined General [James] Shields, covered him with flattery . . . and swallowed him whole. Now that Corcoran is gone, he is the representative of the Irish brave—what he has all the time been aiming at![9]

Meagher had never fooled Maria Daly. He had not fooled other people as well, for he was not restored to command. Corcoran had a magnificent funeral and was buried in Calvary Cemetery on December 27, 1863.

On January 14, 1864, the following appeared in the *New York Times*:

The 88th Regiment commanded by Col. Murphy arrived in this city yesterday morning from the Army of the Potomac. It belongs to the Irish Brigade and has participated in nearly every battle in Virginia. The 88th numbers about 150 men, all of whom have re-enlisted for the war. Immediately on arrival the men were granted furloughs.[10]

Re-enlistment. It was a magic word. The backbone of the Union armies were the three-year enlistees who had signed up in the late summer or early autumn of 1861. These were the soldiers who had fought the battles, endured the marches, baked or froze according to the season and had lived on hard-tack and beans. Now their contract with the U.S. Government would draw to a close in the summer or fall of 1864. They could take an honorable discharge and go home. There were, of course, terms of enlistment other than three years. New York had signed up a number of regiments for two years in the early summer of 1861. When they had exited the army just before Gettysburg, the army command had gotten a chill foreboding of what would happen in 1864 when the three-

9. Daly, *Diary of A Union Lady*, p. 418.
10. *New York Times*, January 14, 1864.

year men would leave. There had been some regiments who had signed for nine-months such as the Vermont Brigade which had done so well on the third day at Gettysburg. With their task completed the Vermonters promptly went home. What were needed were veteran soldiers who would sign up for the rest of the war. The War Department began figuring an alternative plan to keep the veterans around and fighting.

In the end, the scheme appealed to patriotism, unit pride, and the need of men to see their homes and families even if only for a little while. There was also money involved. At least the men who had placed their bodies on the line would get a small amount back, around $700. If they re-enlisted they could go home on a month's furlough, and if enough men in a regiment re-upped, they could keep the same regimental number and would be known as a Veteran Volunteer Regiment. $700 was about two years wages for a laborer, almost four years for a soldier. And it would be nice to keep the regiment going as it was. But the best thing of all was the month furlough at home, to see the well- or poorly-remembered faces, the children they had fathered and never held, the wives and sweethearts who had filled their dreams. Even so, many men held back. Whatever they did, the war would go on. There were plenty of men in the North who had not served, would never serve, because of the hole in the Conscription Act that allowed a man with $300 to get out of it. "The rich man's war and the poor man's fight." The administration seemed bent on proving that patriotism was for fools and idiots and the poor.

In the end the administration was proven right. More than 26,000 men in the Army of the Potomac re-upped. That meant that however many of the scrapings of the country came in as conscripts, there would be a solid nucleus there to make soldiers out of them, to inflict the Old Army discipline on them, to take them to the fields of blood and death and make them fight. It was the flaring of the flame of idealism against the background of profiteering and civilian greed. As is true in all wars, there were hard-faced men who made out well during the killing. In this one, the alliance of the new Republican Party with the new industrialism was forged.

The 150 men of the 88th New York who came home on January 14, 1864, were the first large group from the Irish

Brigade, but smaller parties had preceded them. On January 15 there was a grand banquet and reception for all the re-enlistees. A group of officers from each of the regiments had formed a committee and solicited the original financial backers of the brigade. The economy was booming and the return was lavish.

At noon over 250 non-commissioned officers and enlisted men were received at city hall. They then marched up Broadway behind Dodsworth's Band to 14th Street and from there to Irving Hall. Present at the head table were Meagher, Robert Nugent, Capt. James McGee and Richard Moroney of the 69th, and prominent civilians. The hall was festooned with regimental colors and red-white-and-blue bunting. At the command of Sergeant Major O'Driscoll, the repast began at 2 p.m. There were ten toasts drunk during the affair:

1. Abraham Lincoln
2. Our Dead Comrades
3. No Negotiation
4. The Emmets of the Irish Brigade
5. Irish Soldiers in the National Armies
6. The Memory of General Michael Corcoran
7. Private Miles O'Reilly
8. The American Press
9. Mr. Spaulding and the Merchants of New York
10. Our Friend, L. F. Harrison

Meagher read letters of regret from General Sickles, Judge Brady, and A. F. Spaulding. He then launched into a fiery speech against "copperheads" and any suggestion of slackness in the war effort. Nugent, in replying to the toast "No Negotiation" hit the same vein. There should be no peace until the forces of the rebellion were swept from the land. The former colonel of the 69th was now the acting provost marshal of New York City. At the same time he had retained his Regular Army commission as a captain in the 13th U.S. Infantry. Perhaps he often wished himself back with the brigade. During the draft riots in the terrible summer of 1863 he had looked on scenes every bit as terrifying as any on a battlefield.[11]

11. *Ibid.*, January 15, 1864.

To the shame of Meagher, Nugent, Judge Daly, and every other respectable Irishman in New York, the surging, lawless mob had been largely composed of fellow Hibernians. During the hot July nights when the flames of burning houses illuminated scenes of riot and plunder, the "good image" manufactured on the battlefields of Virginia by the brigade was obscured by the old, unlovely face of the wild man. What mattered a Malvern Hill, a Fredericksburg, a Gettysburg now? The name of the Gael had been tarnished in the early reports of the rioting apparently beyond recognition. It was only later that there was a softening of the denunciations and admissions that poor men were placed at a serious disadvantage by the provisions of the Draft Act.

For a period of time the New York Irish were execrated and justly so. Irish warriors like Nugent were placed in a terrible cul-de-sac. They could not give aid and comfort to their own kind who were, in a word, aiding the Confederacy. Still, there was sympathy for anyone of Irish blood who was imprisoned in the Five Points slum with a family to feed and clothe and possibly a thirst to slake on a stevedore's pittance. Why should such a man be taken off to Virginia because $300 was an astronomical sum to him, possibly a year's wages? Other Americans, rich and comfortable, could ante up the money and escape the terrible forced marches, the humdrum food, the chilling summons to fight and possibly die. Only one who had gone through the terrible cauldron had the right to point the finger. With this choice before them, men like Nugent almost unanimously hedged. Instead of denouncing their own kind, they reaffirmed their committment to the war, hoping that such a declaration would get them off the hook. Perhaps, they reasoned that such a "correct attitude" would be extended to the entire Irish body. Winfield Scott Hancock himself came to Nugent's aid by placing all the recruiting for the Second Corps under his charge during the winter of 1864. Even so, Robert Nugent must have wished himself back with the unwashed men of the army many times, especially when one of his "American" friends dwelt on the draft riots.

The 69th Pennsylvania did not return to Philadelphia on reenlistment furlough until March 7. Perhaps the performance of the regiment at Gettysburg had been noised around

310

the City of Brotherly Love. Perhaps the citizens remembered the hero's funeral given to Dennis O'Kane. Six generals had carried his body to Mass at St. James's Church and on to rest at Cathedral Cemetery. There were no nativist cat-calls now or references to drunken Paddies. Instead the tattered green flag was taken from the color guard and placed behind the statue of Washington in Independence Hall.[12]

On St. Patrick's Day the 69th paraded for Mass and marched through the city at the head of a large group of their fellow countrymen. It was hoped that the demonstration would help the recruitment effort, but not many prospective soldiers came in. When they returned to Virginia on April 14, only 324 were present for duty. Unfortunately, among the missing was Maj. James Duffy who had commanded the left wing of the regiment at Gettysburg. The severe wound he had taken there had not healed and he resigned. No other field officer had survived and William Davis, captain of Company E, was promoted to the command of the regiment. McDermott records that this selection was not an unqualified triumph:

> While he was in every way worthy of promotion, yet his appointment gave a great deal of dissatisfaction. Not because of any ill will, but they felt that this promotion should have gone to Capt. Thomas Kelly, the senior captain of the regiment, who was a most thorough disciplinarian and tactician, twice wounded and unfortunately absent by reason of his wounds received at Robertson's Farm. Accordingly a protest was signed by nearly every commissioned and noncommissioned officer of the regiment, and sent to Governor Curtin, who, to his credit be it said and in spite of all opposing influences, promised to rectify the matter by promoting Capt. Kelly to the position of Lieut.-Colonel when the regiment's numbers were sufficient to entitle it to an officer of that rank.[13]

12. Banes, *History of the Philadelphia Brigade*, pp. 214-15.
13. McDermott, *69th Pennsylvania*, p. 38.

One wonders how Capt. William Davis felt about that vote of "no confidence."

Actually, the first regiment of the Army of the Potomac to re-enlist "for the war" was the 1st Delaware Volunteer Infantry, commanded by Col. Thomas Smyth who had first seen the light of day in Ballyhooly, County Cork, Ireland. The regiment arrived home in time for a New Year's celebration. Smyth had commanded a company of the 24th Pennsylvania back in the three month service before it became the 69th Pennsylvania. However, at the end of the three month service he was snatched away from the Philadelphia Irish and offered the majority of the 1st Delaware. The Diamond Staters had missed the Peninsula, but they came the rest of the way with the Second Corps. Tom Smyth commanded the regiment at Fredericksburg, got his colonel's eagle in February 1863, and commanded a brigade in the Third Division at Gettysburg. There his men had been stationed just north of the Angle and had helped repulse Pettigrew's division. In the winter of 1863-64, Tom Smyth was as seasoned a warrior as there was in the Second Corps. He operated to the eminent satisfaction of Hancock.

On February 12 Smyth had returned from Wilmington to the camp of his brigade at Stony Mountain. Aside from visits to the picket line on the Rapidan River there was little to do for the rest of the month. Occasionally Smyth had those of his officers who were being visited by their wives in for a night of dancing and festivity at his headquarters. The weather was very cold. On February 17 Colonel Smyth wrote in his diary, "I very near froze last night."[14]

The Second Corps celebrated Washington's birthday with a magnificent ball which Smyth attended, reaching his quarters at 6 o'clock the next morning. There were brigade drills from time to time, and in the zone closest to the enemy along the Rapidan, vigilance was close and searching. In early March, for instance, there was a great alarm that the enemy was crossing at Germanna Ford, which was false, and on the same day Smyth received a commission from the Fenian Brotherhood. Two days later his wife's picture came through the mail. He was a strong Fenian and, had he survived the

14. Thomas A. Smyth diaries, February 17, 1864.

Massachusetts Commandery, MOLLUS
U.S. Army Military History Institute

Thomas A. Smyth
Colonel, 1st Delaware Veteran Volunteer Infantry
Brigadier General, United States Volunteers
Commanded Irish Brigade March 25 - May 17, 1864
Mortally wounded at Farmville, Virginia

war, it is possible he would have been a leader in the invasions of Canada the Brotherhood mounted.

The weather warmed up a little in March. Tom Smyth had routine drills, visited officer friends in other commands, and on the 19th saw, with a pang, the last of the lady visitors leave the camp. It was a foreboding sight, a reminder that grim-visaged war was coming closer day by day. St. Patrick's Day was fittingly celebrated with all manner of toasts to the dead of the brigade. On March 25 Smyth was called to Second Corps headquarters and was shown an order which brought about much hard feeling. The five infantry corps were to be consolidated into three corps. The First and Third Corps would disappear and their men would be assigned to the Second, Fifth, and Sixth Corps. Two divisions of the Third Corps would become part of the Second Corps, and the Second Corps would also have some internal restructuring. Until now, Smyth had commanded a brigade in the Third Division. Now the Third Division brigades would be consolidated and attached to Second Division. Smyth was assigned to command the Irish Brigade pending the return of Col. Richard Byrnes of the 28th Massachusetts who was scouring Irish communities in the North for recruits. Tom Smyth became commander of the Irish Brigade where he was, of course, favorably known. He was much distressed at leaving the "brigade I commanded with pride and pleasure."[15]

There were not many warm bodies on the duty list for the Irish Brigade. Many of the re-enlistees had not returned from furlough, there were few officers on hand, and a general air of disinterest hung over the entire army. A winter camp was never a very happy locale. The camp of a year ago following the debacle at Fredericksburg had been the low point of the war for the army. It was much happier in 1864. There was Gettysburg and Rappahannock Station to dwell on and a steady succession of good news from the Western theater. The relaxed atmosphere had also communicated to an unmilitary posture. For the Irish Brigade Tom Smyth was going to provide an antidote. On March 27 he took over and was appalled at what he saw.

15. *Ibid.*, March 25-26, 1864.

I assumed command of the Irish Brigade and issued my first order. This headquarters is a d____ gloomy looking place. I feel lonely and miserable but trust in Providence.[16]

The camp was inspected the next day and for many days thereafter. In April, Smyth bore down harder:

Policing camps all day. Gave the Devil to some of the officers. The 63d sutler sold out. Had the Inspector General changed.[17]

By then the weather had changed for the better, and the men of the brigade made the acquaintance of the drill field again under the eye of a real disciplinarian:

I had the three New York regiments out this afternoon for drill. I drilled them as one battalion. Several of the officers arrived this evening.[18]

The drills and inspections followed thereafter in close succession, and real progress was made. It was a good thing too. Brig. Gen. Francis Barlow was the new division commander, and one would have to say that he was a warrior, even if an unlucky one. He had been wounded at Antietam where he had refused to come to the support of the Irish Brigade at the Bloody Lane. He had commanded a division of the Eleventh Corps at Gettysburg, was wounded again and taken prisoner. Now exchanged, he was placed in command on March 25. He was no friend of the Irish.

The brigade continued to improve. On April 17, Hancock sent Smyth a note saying that "never had the Irish Brigade looked as well as it did at the review." Possibly due to the fact that he had come from the outside, Smyth had been able to proceed on a new foundation. On April 26 there was another drill for the First Division under the eye of Barlow. That night Smyth wrote in his diary:

16. *Ibid.*, March 27, 1864.
17. *Ibid.*, April 11, 1864.
18. *Ibid.*, April 13, 1864.

. . . the drill passed off very nicely. The other three
brigades made several mistakes, but the Irish Brigade made none. . . .[19]

Even with these apparent effects the new commander
leaned on the rod day after day. In the evenings there were
serenades by the division band and courtesy calls on the
officers. The Fenian Brotherhood was particularly active in
the spring of 1864.[20] The Potomac Circle met regularly in the
quarters of Doctor Lawrence Reynolds of the 63rd and the
good doctor took an immediate liking to Tom Smyth. Richard
Byrnes still had not returned to the army, and it looked as
though Smyth would go into the spring campaign as commander of the brigade.

While all this was taking place in Virginia, Mulholland was
recruiting all over Pennsylvania for the 116th, and he had the
most luck in the western part of the state. The 116th still
retained Companies A, B, C, and D from the original organization. The new companies F and G were from Schuylkill
County, H and I from Pittsburgh. K was from Uniontown and
E from Philadelphia. Among the new officers was Lt. Charles
Cosslett, brother-in-law of Mulholland, and the new adjutant
was Louis Sacriste, who had been recommended for the Medal
of Honor. The 116th was in pretty good shape except for
surgeons. Father McKee had made only one campaign as
chaplain, but the faithful Father Corby, sometimes helped by
Father Ouellette, was sufficient to minister to the needs of the
Catholics. The new companies were mostly Protestant and not
especially Irish. For their spiritual consolation, one of the new
company commanders, Capt. Samuel Taggart, was an or-
dained minister.

All during April the new recruits for the other regiments
came in by dribs and drabs. Big John Gleeson brought down a
complete company of new men for the 63rd. They had started
life as the Kings County Volunteers but were glad to join the
brigade. Smyth welcomed them with plenty of close-order
drill and target practice, it having been realized, belatedly,
that it might be handy for the recent civilians to know some-

19. *Ibid.*, April 26, 1864.
20. *Ibid.*, April 30, 1864.

316

thing of a musket. The brigade was still poorly armed; only the 28th Massachusetts carrying rifles. On April 30 the army was paid and Barlow came again to inspect the brigade. Smyth said that he was highly pleased with things in general, especially with the Irishmen for saluting so promptly. Two days later the winter huts which had sheltered the army since November were ordered torn down. Shelter tents were issued and everyone spent the night of May 2 under canvas. Not many slept soundly. A tornado passed through the Second Corps area and ripped things apart. Trees were uprooted, tents blown away, and several score men were injured. That was the natural storm; ahead lay the man-made storm. The campaign would begin on the morrow, and leading the Union forces would be that simple, direct soldier from the West, Lt. Gen. Ulysses S. Grant.

CHAPTER THIRTEEN

THE MONTH OF BLOOD

Civil War historians refer to the progress of the Army of the Potomac toward Richmond in the spring of 1864 as the Overland Campaign. This is to differentiate it from McClellan's 1862 approach which was well and unfavorably known to every administration apologist as the Peninsular Campaign. When Grant came east to accept the rank of lieutenant general, he had not intended to stay in the environs of the capital for very long. He regarded the West as the crucial region and expected to accompany the western armies in the forthcoming campaign against Atlanta. Even Grant's warmest admirers regarded him essentially as a dogged military machine, the bulldog who wore out the seat of the Confederacy's breeches. But, a perceptive man dwelt behind the cigar and beard. In just a few days he changed his mind and decided to stay in the East.

A short exposure to the Washington bureaucracy apparently convinced him that the commander of all the armies should be in the East. If he were to return to the West, the lines of communication with the Army of the Potomac must pass through the government apparatus; willful and capricious men of strong passions and prejudices. God alone knew what could happen to the simplest telegram under such conditions. So he came east to stay.

At first he seriously considered retracing McClellan's footsteps of 1862 on the Peninsula with flanks anchored on the York and James Rivers and with secure supply lines. But Lincoln and Stanton would not hear of it. This army, said they, must be kept between Lee and Washington. That had been their philosophy ever since they had brought McClellan's army back in August 1862. In the end Grant went over land, over river, and over everything, and it was not easy.

When the Army of the Potomac had completed its campaign and settled down to the siege of Petersburg on or about

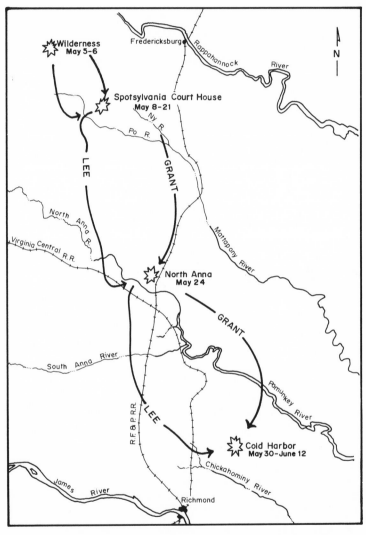

Map by John Heiser

Battles of the Overland Campaign, May 3 - June 12, 1864

June 20, the casualties suffered amounted to about 60,000 men. Sergeants led companies and lieutenants commanded what were left of regiments. For the first month, there was alternately assault and movement, movement and assault. When it could be done the men buried their dead comrades. The first order of events, however, was battle, tremendous bear-hugs of battle, terrible cauldrons of battle, crisping the slender threads that held men's souls to their bodies. There was little time for eating and sleeping. There was no time for report writing. When the shadow of the Army of the Potomac's former self groggily settled itself to the siege of Petersburg, orders went out to the commanders to write reports of what had happened.

The quality of the resulting work is quite uneven. Men who had started the campaign as lieutenants commanding platoons were now field officers who had seen the inexorable finger of death pass through the roster of field and staff and along the seniority route of line captains. Periods of command were measured in hours and minutes, seldom in days, even less seldom in weeks. It was a month of blood, a month when horror-struck Nature held up her hands at such wanton giving and taking of human life.

To provide guidelines for the numbed memories of the writers of reports, army command by Special Order No. 209 decreed certain arbitrary time periods in which to sort out events. Very fittingly these periods were designated as "epochs." In the dictionary an epoch is defined as "a period of time characterized by a . . . memorable series of events." None of the soldiers who survived the days that fell between May 3 and June 3, 1864, would ever forget the horror. Not the Peninsula, not Gettysburg, Antietam, or Chancellorsville ever had the ultimate inhumanity of the month of blood. It was as remorseless as a glacier, as terrible as a fiery Moloch, gorged on the flesh of man.

The first epoch began with the passage of the Rapidan River on the night of May 3 and ended with the sidewise lurch of the contending armies after the Battle of the Wilderness on May 8.

At dusk on Tuesday, May 3, the shelter tents of the Second Corps were struck and the columns formed in the road. Each man carried fifty rounds of ammunition, three days full rations in haversacks, three days bread and small rations in knapsacks.

The corps moved at 11 p.m., and, keeping to familiar roads through the night, the head of the column reached the Rapidan at Ely's Ford at daylight. Some cavalry were laying a canvas pontoon bridge downstream from the ford, but the infantry plunged through the water to reach the Spotsylvania County side of the stream and continued on. Sometime after the noon hour they reached the clearing where the ruins of the Chancellor House stood. The surroundings were certainly familiar to the veterans who had fought on that very ground a year before. Colonel Smyth wrote in his diary, "Well do I remember one year ago on this spot."[1]

The Second Corps had now been on the march for fourteen hours, and Hancock ordered a halt. Pickets were thrown out, the roll was called in each company (not a man was missing), and a general order from Meade was read by the regimental adjutants. The order started out, "Soldiers: Again you are called upon to advance on the enemies of your country." and ended, ". . . victory, under God's blessing, must and will attend our efforts."[2] The veterans had heard many such orders. It was to the new men, the four out of five in the Irish Brigade, who would realize the chilling finality. They had been put out on this thickly-wooded spot to fight, to kill, and probably to die.

Mulholland noted that Hancock and his staff were resting on the very spot where Leppine's Maine Battery had been destroyed, its guns saved by the 116th a year ago. He and his new lieutenant colonel, Richard Dale, wandered over the terrain. In spite of the debris of battle, spring's renewing hand was everywhere.

> The apple trees and lilies bloomed again. Pink and white roses struggled to life in the trampled garden of the old homestead. . . . The shallow graves of the men of the brigade were . . . found overgrown with wild flowers and forget-me-nots.[3]

The new lieutenant colonel was deeply affected at the profusion of little blue flowers on the shallow ground. For a long time he stood wrapped in thought. Then, said Mulholland,

1. Smyth diaries, May 3, 1864.
2. *OR*, series 1, vol. 36, pt. 2, p. 370
3. Mulholland, *116th Pennsylvania*, pp. 183-85.

. . . he spoke in a strangely poetic strain of the goodness of the Creator in covering with beauty and perfume the last resting places of those brave men.

It was little wonder that Dale was moved so strongly. Around the army for the second straight year was the flush of Virginia spring even in the Wilderness. From the impenetrable thickets on every side, the fragrance of the blossoms drifted on the balmy air and sweetened the May night. There has been much written of the locale of the great battles of May 5-6, but words cannot do full justice to the region. The roads over which the army advanced consisted of narrow lanes cut through the forest, covered in some cases with planks or hewn logs. It was, however, no place to fight a battle. Advances into the woods from the roads in any kind of military formation were impossible; the growth was so dense that one end of a company was not visible from the other end. If Grant had searched all over North America, he would have been hard-put to find a place where his great advantage in men, artillery, and conventional military organization would be so easily thrown away.

In the dark defiles, a platoon in the right location was equal to a regiment in the wrong one. Grant partisans hold that their man thought he would not have to fight there, that the battle would take place to the east or the west of the Wilderness. An army commander cannot afford the luxury of such thinking, especially when he is confronting someone of the subtlety and character of Robert E. Lee. In this campaign Grant appears to be determined to overcome what he perceived to be the inferiority complex of the Army of the Potomac by ignoring the presence of the Confederates. At the conclusion of one of the early stages of the Wilderness Battle, Grant heard one of the "Potomac" officers (as compared to one of Grant's "Western" officers) wonder aloud as to what Lee would be up to next. He rounded on this individual and berated him and said that he was "heartily tired of hearing about what Lee is going to do"; that it was time for the Federals to think about what they were going to do and get on with it.[4]

---

4. Bruce Catton, *Grant Takes Command* (Boston: Little, Brown and Company, 1968), p. 200

Overcoming a feeling of inferiority on the part of the Army of the Potomac could best be accomplished by Grant's showing great military genius in his strategy and tactics. There is no evidence that he consulted closely with men who had fought in the Wilderness region during Hooker's Chancellorsville Campaign or Meade's Mine Run Campaign of November 1863. Grant is supposed to have said, "I never maneuver." And Meade is supposed to have answered something like, "General, you will be up against a man with whom you will have to maneuver." Certain writers of history adulate the lieutenant general because he was fond of putting his head down and driving ahead with his legs pumping and his arms swinging. There is an echo of this in Stephen Vincent Benét's epic poem, "John Brown's Body," where the poet likens the Army of the Potomac to an unlucky stallion ridden by too many inferior riders until the coming of Grant, who simply wore down the hurdle instead of jumping over it. All of these views come from the standpoint of the successful conclusion of the war. In August 1864 there was no such atmosphere of triumph.

The Irish Brigade slept on the year-old graves of its comrades on the night of May 4, and shortly after reveille on May 5, the Second Corps started along the road to Shady Grove Church on the Catharpin Road. Barlow's division was in the lead, followed by Gibbon, Birney and Brig. Gen. Gershom Mott. The latter two divisions were formerly in the Third Corps until the great reorganization. When Todd's Tavern was passed by the head of the column, a sudden halt was ordered and the column about-faced. Lee had not waited for Grant's blow, but had ordered Ewell's corps to attack the Fifth Corps under Warren on the Orange Turnpike. The Second Corps was being recalled for support. Now Mott's division led the corps as it went north on the Brock Road. Just north of the intersection of the Orange Plank Road and the Brock Road Hancock found a division of the Sixth Corps under Brig. Gen. George W. Getty standing in the Brock Road and facing west. Getty had been ordered to move west into the underbrush as soon as the Second Corps was lined up next to him. At 4:15 p.m. Meade ordered the westward movement and as fast as the Second Corps came up they were shaken into line of battle and sent into the thickets. They did not have far to go. Confederate troops of A. P. Hill's corps were coming up the Orange Plank

Road just as Ewell had attacked the Fifth Corps on the Orange Turnpike. About 300 yards west of the Brock Road a tremendous blast of musketry announced the collision of the two forces. Mott's and Birney's division of the Second Corps were quickly engaged and two brigades of Gibbon's division were quickly fed in.

The terrain was impossible. Men were unable to see their enemies and fired mostly by smoke and sound. Solid sheets of minié balls cut off the underbrush and smashed huge chunks of wood out of trees. Lines of soldiers moved forward, backwards, sideways, changed direction, lost direction, and milled about helplessly. Pockets of the enemy were found, engaged, and bypassed. Heth, who commanded the Confederates on the spot, had constructed some light earthworks, and these proved a tough nut for the Unionists to crack. The smoke from the continuous musketry was trapped and held in the heavy underbrush, further obscuring the scene.

After the entire Second Corps got turned around facing west, Barlow's division was the extreme left flank of the corps. At this point, they lapped over Hill's flank and forced it back. For awhile there was a tremendous exchange of fire. The 28th Massachusetts was still the only regiment in the Irish Brigade to be armed with rifles and consequently they formed the skirmish line covering the entire front of the brigade. They came in contact with the Confederate brigade of Brig. Gen. W. W. Kirkland, composed of North Carolinians. These graybacks fought about as well as men could, but between Col. Nelson A. Miles' brigade and the Irish, they were bent back until their line was facing south. As night fell, the Irish pushed on with men dropping left and right. Maj. Tom Touhy, commanding the 63rd New York, went down with a mortal wound. Mulholland was down with a severe wound, and Lt. Col. Richard Dale, the handsome, sensitive ex-teacher, took charge of the 116th. Strangely enough, not an officer was a casualty in the 69th. Even with the preponderance of new men in the ranks the brigade showed its old élan. There was no chance for any of the offensive surges they had made in the past, but there was dogged determination as the men made their way into the deepest thickets. Success attended their efforts as well. One of the most balanced Union writers on the campaign, A. A. Humphreys, was of the opinion that, given another hour of

325

daylight, Hill's corps would have been wrecked by the flanking action of the brigades of Miles and Smyth. The 28th Massachusetts and 63rd New York spoke of heavy casualties. The 69th and 88th had the same number of men down, fifty-two, and the 116th had been hurt the least.

Tom Smyth filed no report, but made an entry in his diary,

> . . . engaged the enemy three hours. Fought there until dark. My loss heavy. After dark fell back to the ridge where I erected a rifle pit. . . . At 4 o'clock I changed front forward with three regiments of my brigade and charged the enemy. But finding them again on my left I had to change front to the rear on my right company.[5]

Hancock had some warm words for the Irish in his battle report:

> The Irish Brigade was heavily engaged, and although four-fifths of its numbers were recruits, it behaved with great steadiness and gallantry, losing largely in killed and wounded.[6]

Mulholland was most pleased with the spirit with which his beardless boys from Western Pennsylvania had stood the difficulties of the day.

> . . . a broad smile passed along the line when Sergeant John Cassidy, of Company E, finding fault because when shot through the lungs, he had to walk off without assistance, some one said to him: "Why, Cassidy, there's a man with all of his head blown off and he is not making half as much fuss as you are!"[7]

There were the usual narrow escapes during the battle. A ball had grazed Lieutenant Colonel Dale's side, cutting the undershirt without breaking the skin. Lt. Charles Cosslett,

5. Smyth Diaries, May 4, 1864.
6. *OR*, series 1, vol. 36, pt. 1, p. 320.
7. Mulholland, *116th Pennsylvania*, p. 186.

Mulholland's step-brother, had his scalp creased. Pvt. Daniel Chisholm's cap had been shot away entirely without harm to him, and so on. It was better to talk about the miracles that had preserved the living than to speculate on the fate of those who no longer formed up to touch elbows.

Capt. John Gleason, the "Big John" Gleason who had ended the day at Antietam with the colours of the 63rd wrapped around his waist, succeeded to command of the regiment with the death of Maj. Thomas Tuohey. Mulholland's wound, his second, was not thought to be too serious, and he was expected to return. The entire brigade had acquired a tremendous respect and affection for Tom Smyth. Now the harsh martinet was gone, swallowed up in the charismatic leader who pointed the path to battle. He was a renowned and convinced Fenian, one of the leading lights who met in the tent of Surgeon Reynolds, and coming from outside the brigade he did not have to rely on any formed relationships or show any favoritism.

In the Fifth Corps the fighting had been of the same close and fierce nature. Ewell had brought his Confederates against Warren's men along the axis of the Orange Turnpike. Brig. Gen. Charles Griffin's division of the Fifth Corps was pushed out on the turnpike to oppose him. The skirmishers of both sides clashed in the thick underbrush, and the Union infantry, following closely, shattered the leading Confederate brigade. Ewell quickly got a flanking column in action south of the pike which restored the situation. A two-gun section of Battery D, 1st New York Light Artillery got too far forward in support of the Union infantry and was overrun and captured.

Among the Union forces sent to recapture the guns was the 9th Massachusetts under Patrick Guiney. This was the first battle since the Peninsula in which the Boston Irish were heavily involved. Antietam had seen the Fifth Corps in reserve, as had Fredericksburg and Chancellorsville. At Gettysburg they had again been fortunate to have been held out, but now their time had come. Griffin, their first brigade commander, had long since gone up to division command. Jacob Sweitzer, originally of the 62nd Pennsylvania, was now the brigadier. There had always been a close bond between the 9th and the 62nd from the start of their service together, but Sweitzer's actions during the Wilderness indicate that he had no love for the 9th, or perhaps that he was not a very good brigadier. Fortunately, Griffin kept them in mind.

About 2 p.m. on May 5, Sweitzer moved his brigade up to the point where Ayres' brigade of their division had experienced momentary success in the morning. The men threw up some light earthworks and then moved forward. They were spectacularly unsuccessful:

> Coming under fire of the enemy's skirmishers our line drove them through the dense woods across the pike and suddenly broke into a valley-like clearing of several acres. The bullets were flying thick and fast from the unseen enemy in the woods beyond. Under this unexpected heavy fire the officers and men of the Ninth were quickly dropping. Our gallant Colonel Guiney fell, terribly wounded in the head, losing an eye, and was carried from the field. The command of the regiment was then taken by Lieutenant-Colonel [Patrick T.] Hanley. . . . As the regiment went forward they received a terrific fire from a large body of infantry concealed in the woods on the front and flank, under which, if repeated, not a man would have been left. Colonel Hanley perceiving no supports on either flank, nor in his rear, quickly fell back with his regiment to the shelter of the woods in his immediate rear where his men opened fire on the still unseen enemy in the dense woods beyond the guns in the clearing, and gradually fell back to the original line.[8]

It had been a costly mistake. In hardly the time it takes to tell it, the 9th had lost 12 officers and 138 men killed or wounded. That was bad enough, but when they had reached the brigade line and stood there ready to repel a counter blow, there was worse to come.

> . . . Colonel Sweitzer, commanding, rushed up shortly afterwards from the rear and demanded of Colonel Hanley in a loud and insolent tone of voice, "Why don't you take your regiment in?" Colonel Hanley

8. MacNamara, *Ninth Massachusetts*, p. 372.

replied, "We have been in, and just come out!" "Well," said Sweitzer, "take 'em in again." Colonel Hanley, without a murmur, gave the order to the men of the regiment, who were then resting on the ground talking about the trap they had been caught in, "Fall in, Ninth." The regiment promptly formed line of battle, and as Colonel Hanley was about to give the order "Forward!" a staff officer came galloping down towards the regiment, and on nearing it, cried out, "General Griffin's orders are not to take the Ninth in again." Colonel Sweitzer heard the order and moved off to headquarters in the rear, without a word. The Ninth resumed its place of rest. It afterwards proved that when the brigade went forward to the attack that its commander, Colonel Sweitzer, remained in the rear, and was, therefore, ignorant of what his regiments did, or where they went. General Griffin, however, knew all about them, as that gallant officer did of every regiment in his division.[9]

The night of May 5 found both Federals and Confederates exhausted, and both sides slept on their arms. As has been previously stated, Grant had not expected to fight in the Wilderness, and his battle was disjointed, with his three infantry corps fighting separate actions out of supporting distance of each other. The most efficient arm of the Federal service, the artillery, had been rendered totally ineffective by the terrain. Even so, the fact that Lee did not have Longstreet's corps on May 5 had almost rendered the position untenable. Although Ewell had administered a severe setback to the Fifth Corps, on his right A. P. Hill was in dire straits by nightfall. The Second Corps had driven forward and enveloped Hill's right flank, and, given a few more hours of daylight, the Union corps commanders, fighting the battle on their own, might have found the gap that existed between Hill and Ewell. It could have happened on any battlefield but the Wilderness.

When darkness came, the two lines drew apart and tried frantically to reorganize. Some Confederates wandered into Union lines and vice versa, and stretcher parties stumbled

9. *Ibid.*

through the pitch-black thickets searching for poor wounded men who lay like animals in their misery. The harried staff officers sorted out commands and tried to improvise an attack order for the morrow, for Grant had decided that the offensive would be pushed at first light. Longstreet was approaching, and the job on Hill and Ewell had to be finished as quickly as possible. Hancock was reinforced with an additional division from the Sixth Corps and told to assault at 5 a.m. All through the night, shadowy bodies of men were moved about to bring them into approximations of selected positions. The Union maps were about as bad as those of the Confederates, but the latter had the advantage of some personal knowledge of the area.

On May 6 the early Union attacks on Hill were successful and the Johnnies were forced back, although there is some controversy as to just how far. The 69th Pennsylvania was in this action. William Davis had been promoted to lieutenant colonel and he wrote a complete report. It was a morning of steady success and then near-disaster. A strong counter-attack by Longstreet was made against the Union left flank and to all intents and purposes ended the Union offensive for the day. The Second Corps fell back to the entrenchments that had been built the previous day and held off the Confederate surges. It was a terrible day, much worse than the first one. In several places the brush was set afire and the screams of badly wounded men who were trapped in the flames stayed with many of the participants all their lives. Mulholland said,

> This was the saddest part of the battle. How many
> poor, wounded souls perished in the flames none but
> the angels who were there to receive their brave
> spirits will ever know; but the very awfulness of the
> situation seemed to call forth renewed evidence of
> courage and, when volunteers were called for to
> rescue the wounded, Lt. Cosslett and a score of noble
> men rushed into the smoke and fire to save them.[10]

In many respects the days in the Wilderness were a repeat of the Chancellorsville experience. Again an overwhelmingly

10. Mulholland, *116th Pennsylvania*, p. 189-90.

superior Union force had crossed the river, fresh and full of ardor. It had encountered its old nemesis with spirit, and in the early going had gained some success. But in 1863 the genius of Lee had triumphed over Hooker who was not so much Lee's inferior in military art as he was in character. Now another Union commander, the most successful of the war, had crossed swords with the Virginian and come off, not with a complete rebuff but with the kind of riposte which tended to throw the entire campaign out of step. The first epoch came to an end on May 7.

Grant decided to move southeast to the important crossroads of Spotsylvania Court House early on the morning of May 7 and Warren's Fifth Corps started for there sometime in the afternoon. The Fifth Corps had been roughly handled on both days of the Wilderness and did not carry out this movement with the celerity necessary. Lee had already foreseen the move and a Confederate welcoming party was on hand when the exhausted Fifth Corps division commanded by Brig. Gen. John C. Robinson appeared. Again Grant was aware that he was up against the first team. In the campaign that followed, the gray captain read his adversary's mind perfectly. Only the simply overwhelming odds in manpower and the steady erosion of his top echelon of command tied the Virginian to a defensive role.

How many times must Lee have longed for his pre-Gettysburg capabilities. Ulysses Grant was made for that duality of command that Lee and Jackson could muster. Fortunately for the Union, the business about Vicksburg had lasted long enough to keep him in the West until the Confederate deterioration was evident. At that, only the extreme bad judgment of Richard Ewell had prevented a potential Cannae on the late afternoon of May 6. He had restrained his division commander, John Gordon, from putting in an attack on the Union right flank until it was too late for it to be decisive. It, however, had shaken the Sixth Corps just as the Second Corps was shaken by Longstreet's assault. Grant's headlong movement and injudicious dispositions had presented Lee with a real opportunity. The only thing to criticize on Lee's part is the dispersal of his army in the face of the Union advance. Had Longstreet's corps been available on May 5 or earlier on May 6, the possibilities are frightening to contemplate.

Early on the morning of May 8, the Second Corps withdrew from the slender line of fortifications it had held on the Brock Road and moved in the direction of Todd's Tavern. The day was hot and the clouds of dust suffocating. There was no water and the men felt its need excessively. During a halt General Grant rode along the column. Mulholland remembered it well:

> It was the first time that the men of the Regiment had seen the great commander and they had not yet learned to know him. The general rode slowly by, pausing a moment to look at the command while the men gazed with curiosity but without the slightest show of enthusiasm or feeling at the serious sphynx-like face.[11]

Upon reaching Todd's Tavern, the Irish Brigade halted in a pleasant wood overlooking open fields. Apparently army command was feeling a little more sensitive about the flank exposed to Lee's army than it had on May 5. Miles' brigade and some artillery were advanced west of Todd's Tavern and ran into Mahone's Confederate brigade of A. P. Hill's corps. A sharp fire fight ensued and the Irish were ordered out on the double to back up Miles. As the order was issued, the lieutenant colonel of the 116th was holding a prayer meeting for those of the regiment who wanted to attend, most of the new boys from Western Pennsylvania. The "Amen" was quickly said, and in less than five minutes they were going on the run. Tom Smyth recorded what happened as follows:

> At 5:30 PM the enemy made a brisk attack on Miles. I went forward at the double quick to his support and by a gallant charge of 88th and the 69th drove the enemy across the river. A large body of the enemy was coming down on the right of the Corps. We were ordered back to our earthworks under a shellfire of the enemy. . . .[12]

11. *Ibid.*, p. 192.
12. Smyth diaries, May 8, 1864.

The 116th, now led by Dale, had in some manner become detached from the rest of the brigade by a staff officer and was pinned down by the shelling Smyth mentioned. The situation became serious when some Confederate infantry moved into the area vacated by the retreating Second Corps. Dale's men could not move because of the shelling which, fortunately, was case instead of canister. After a while the 116th moved back into a wood and started in the general direction of the Union position. There ensued an extremely anxious period of wandering through the forest. One wonders how 500 men are led by an uninformed commander through a wilderness maze without some of the bewilderment and worry being communicated to the humble privates. However, Dale was able to bring off the trick. At about dark the Union position was found and the camp of the Irish Brigade reached. The 116th was received with gladness and surprise:

> The command had been reported lost and not a soul in the division but fully believed that the One Hundred and Sixteenth Pennsylvania Volunteers—colors and all—was at that moment in the hands of the enemy.[13]

In looking back at the incident Mulholland seemed most impressed that his men were summoned to battle from the midst of a prayer meeting:

> At the time it did not occur to one, but now, when years have passed and we look back we must feel astonished at the high moral standard of the army that fought the War of the Rebellion, and the Regiment was second to none in that respect. . . . Meetings for prayer were of almost daily occurrence, and the groups of men sitting on the ground or gathered on the hill side listening to the Gospel were strong reminders of the mounds of Galilee. . . . Ofttimes in the Regiment the dawn witnessed the smoke of incense ascend to heaven amid the templed trees where serious groups knelt on the green sod and listened to the

13. Mulholland, *116th Pennsylvania*, p. 194.

murmur of the Mass. In the evening Lieutenant-Colonel Dale or Captain Samuel Taggart would hold a meeting for prayer where the larger number of the men would gather in reverence and devotion, while others would kneel around the Chaplain's tent to count their beads and repeat the Rosary.[14]

This is the best evidence of the different structure of the 116th, that "the larger number of men" would be found at the prayer meeting. All the survivors from 1862 had been consolidated in Companies A, B, C, and D, the relic of the "old regiment."

On May 9 the Second Corps, having secured the right flank of the move to Spotsylvania, continued down the Brock Road to the developing situation there. A mile past Todd's Tavern the corps turned to the right on to what was little more than a cowpath and took a noon break overlooking the valley of the Po River. At this point a small occurrence happened which affected the future of the Second Corps for the next few days.

As the men cooked a meal at noontime on the north bank of the Po River, a Confederate wagon train appeared on the opposite bank on a parallel road. Someone got a battery in action and the pandemonium was something to behold. Some wagoners simply jumped down from the seats and ran away, and the scene was one of utter confusion. At this auspicious moment, Grant and Meade rode up to have a word with Hancock, and, apparently, on the spur of the moment, told him to put a division over the Po to capture the wagon train.[15] With much difficulty Barlow's division led by Brooke's brigade crossed the stream and found that in some unaccountable fashion the teamsters had returned and removed most of the wagons. But the presence of the bluecoats on the south side of the Po had put another bee in Grant's bonnet.

Already reports were coming in to army headquarters of the strong position Lee was taking at Spotsylvania. It appeared that this position would be anchored on the Po some distance downstream from where Barlow had crossed. If the Second Corps could move down the right bank of the stream beyond

14. *Ibid.*, p. 197.
15. Swinton, *Army of the Potomac*, p. 447.

where Lee's anchor point touched it, then recross the river, it would be in the rear of Lee's position. Great advantage to the Union cause might follow. Whether or not Grant had this in mind is doubtful, since his knowledge of the Confederate position was probably not developed as yet. Perhaps he was only going to block off the Shady Grove Road to any enemy troops still on the way down from the Wilderness. In either event, Barlow's division was followed across by Gibbon's and Birney's men so that the Second Corps had about 15,000 effectives on the south bank at nightfall on May 9. Hancock had his engineers put three bridges over the Po to guarantee a return passsage in case there were any surprises in store.

The immediate objective was to get troops on to the Shady Grove Road and move east on it. The road crossed the Po over the Blockhouse Bridge and did lead into the rear of Lee's position. It was imperative to seize the bridge and gain a foothold on the other side. Owing to the lateness of the crossing and the density of the underbrush, Hancock was only able to get his skirmishers up to the bridge by dark, and here the troops rested for the night of May 9-10. Under cover of darkness patrols moved up and down the stream looking for fords and enemy infantry. The 116th was directly involved here:

> No sooner had the line halted for the night in the pitch dark forest, than the Regiment was detailed for picket along with several hundred members of a German regiment. The picket force moved very cautiously and were as noiseless as could be until the head of the column reached the bank of the stream at the Block House Bridge. The Regiment in perfect silence filed to the right and was deployed along the bank, the officers issuing their orders in whispers and the men groping their way and finding their posts as best they could in the intense darkness. . . . Every man seemed to instinctively feel the necessity of getting into position without the enemy, who was supposed to be on the other side of the river, being aware of his presence, and the success up to a certain point was remarkable.

But when the German detail filed to the left of the bridge and began deploying in the darkness matters were very different. Tin cups rattled now and then, and the officers gave their orders in tones loud enough to be heard on the further bank of the stream. Then a man fired his musket. Some one else promptly followed, and the whole detail began blazing away in the darkness. . . . the man who fired the shot on the Union side, and so brought on the trouble, was the direct cause of the failure of all the plans for turning the flank of the enemy's line, for the volleys of musketry echoing through the still woods notified Hill of the presence of the Union Army, and, when morning broke, his men were discovered hard at work intrenching and getting artillery in position to cover the passage of the bridge.[16]

In the morning, Grant had changed his mind about a penetration behind Lee's left flank. Gibbon's and Birney's divisions were withdrawn to confront the formidable field works that the Confederates were erecting at Spotsylvania. Barlow's division was left alone to hold the south side of the Po, and was withdrawn also later in the day.

May 11 was a quiet day for the Second Corps and the rest of the army. Grant had decided that a breakthrough of the Confederate position could be made if an overwhelming weight could be placed at one point. So, while the generals cogitated, the men rested. Many wrote letters home, among whom was Lieutenant Colonel Dale of the 116th who wrote to a Pittsburgh newspaper:

> I suppose all who have friends in the army are now anxious to get some tidings of them, knowing that active operations have commenced in earnest. As there are three companies from western Pennsylvania in our Regiment, I thought I might relieve the anxiety of some of your readers by sending you for publication, a list of our killed and wounded up to this time. It is possible, however, the list may be lengthened

16. Mulholland, *116th Pennsylvania*, pp. 197-98.

before you receive this, as the fighting is apparently not yet over. I write this upon my knee behind breast-works upon which our men are still at work, while in plain view the "rebs" are also intrenching. We left camp at about eleven o'clock on the night of Tuesday, May 3d, crossing the Rapidan the next morning about seven o'clock, and about noon reached the memorable field of Chancellorsville, where we rested until the next morning. Some of us who had been present at the battle there little thought at the time that we would have returned to the field just one year to the day from our retreat in 1863. . . . the battlefield is covered with wild flowers, nearly all of a purple color, as though the blood of our brave soldiers had so drenched the soil as to darken the very flowers that grew upon it. Perhaps some who have lost friends at Chancellorsville may take pleasure in thinking that though their dead heroes may sleep in unmarked graves, yet the flowers bloom over them as profusely as if interred in any of our beautiful cemeteries at home. . . . We have had more or less fighting daily, culminating yesterday in a great battle. Our Regiment has lost up to yesterday, forty-two in killed and wounded. In addition to these there are a number of missing. . . .[17]

Rain started to fall halfway through the afternoon, a blessed relief to the men, especially the hard-working Confederates who were continually elaborating the extensive field-works which had appeared almost as if by magic. In their completed form, these trenches rested on the banks of the Po River. They ran in a northeasterly direction for a mile and a quarter. On the property of a farmer named McColl, the works then bent around at more than a right angle and went on for a mile and a half in a southwesterly direction. Where the two lines joined, the juncture was not a sharp angle but rather like a rounded point. Sometime on the afternoon of May 11 Grant decided to assault this point and the Second Corps would do the job.

17. *Ibid.*, p. 203-4.

The Fifth and Sixth Corps were nearer the point of attack, but both had been used in the attacks of the last two days. In addition, the Sixth Corps had a new commander, Brig. Gen. Horatio Wright, after John Sedgwick was killed in the Wilderness. There is probably something to the theory that Grant was becoming frustrated with the Confederate entrenchments which stood squarely in his way. There is much mention in his messages back to Washington that the enemy would not oppose him in the open field, and he implies that it was very unfair for Lee to fight from behind cover. So this assault must be unstoppable. He picked his best corps commander and his most dependable soldiers for the job.

The rain which was so refreshing at 4 p.m. was a miserable nuisance two hours later. Cooking fires could not be kept going for the evening meal, and after a few attempts the sodden soldiers tried to shelter themselves in their dripping blankets. At 9 p.m. they got the word to move:

> It did not take long to obey the order; each one had only to rise from the earth, shake himself in a vain effort to get rid of the chills that were ever coursing up and down the spine on nights like this, wring the water out of his shoes, lift the cold, heavy musket from the stack, and all was ready.[18]

At 10 p.m. the troops were put in motion. The night was pitch dark and the road was bad. There were a few incidents, such as the accidental discharge of a musket and the escape of a pack mule, but the men were not nervous. Perhaps they would have been had they known of the sketchy reconnaissance which had preceded the movement. The officers who had been told to lay out the lines of attack on the formidable position had gotten lost and had only arrived at the take-off point as darkness fell. Mott's division was nearest to the salient and the field officer of the day was the only source of what lay before the Second Corps. He knew very little, it turned out, because the enemy skirmishers had kept the Union observers a good distance from the attack point.

18. *Ibid.*, pp. 211-12.

At midnight the troops arrived where it was thought they should be, just to the west of the Brown house. Almost the only open ground on which to form was a clearing about 400 yards wide, curving south and then southwest toward the enemy lines. Across this open space, Barlow's division was formed in two lines of masses. Brooke's and Miles' brigades were the first line, Brown's and the Irish in the second. The men were crowded elbow to elbow except for the 66th New York which was to act as the skirmish line for the entire division. They were aligned in the heaviest skirmish line of the war, each man being at an interval of one pace from his comrades on either side.[19]

It was nearly daylight before the preparations were finished. Grant's attack order had placed the start time at 4 a.m., but at that hour it was still too dark and a heavy fog spread over the ground, obscuring the landscape. Hancock delayed the start until 4:30, and then the Union mass started forward, one huge, crawling advance. There was a slight ascent to the route, and in the half-light a forest of tall pines loomed on the left flank. Suddenly, the enemy skirmishers, yawning and chilled, were engulfed by the 66th New York and captured to a man. Only one managed to fire his piece and there was no reply from the Union muskets, unloaded as they were. The head of the column topped a small rise. Down a gentle slope before them and up another ascent stood their goal, fifty yards away. The face of the last ascent was covered with an abatis. A tremendous cheer welled up from the rear of the division as the men left the bond of discipline behind and started to run forward.

There were firewinks on the parapet as those Confederates who were awake responded to this fearsome blow. In a twinkling the Unionists were over the parapet and down among the startled enemy. Many were still asleep in their blanket rolls. A few tents were scattered about, and the inmates crawled out to find themselves prisoners. However, enough Confederates were on their feet to give the Second Corps a fight. Lt. Peter H. Frailey of the 116th had a hand-to-hand struggle with a color-bearer, Frailey running him through with his sword. A private of the 28th Massachusetts captured Brig. Gen. George Steuart who had commanded a

19. *OR*, series 1, vol. 36, pt. 1, p. 409.

brigade of Virginians with great skill. A Confederate shot one of the 116th at almost point-blank range and then threw down his piece, calling out, "I surrender!" The 116th's Pvt. Daniel C. Crawford killed him instantly. Little knots of men struggled in the shadow of the entrenchment, but the greatest feat of arms of the war was in the grasp of the Second Corps. A division commander, a brigade commander, thousands of men, colors and guns were in their hands; they had only to press on into the sundered position. The Army of Northern Virginia was open to its death stroke. Never since the terrible day at Antietam had Lee been closer to extremis.

The soldiers who had accomplished so much milled about in the Confederate encampment and the belt of woods behind it. Regiments were intermingled irreparably; officers called out to their commands, waved their swords, set color staffs on the ground, and attempted to rally their victory-crazed men about them. It was no use. Victory had stunned the Unionists as badly as it had hurt the Johnnies. There were some graybacks, however, who were showing the razor-sharp reflex that had preserved Lee's army through two terrible years. At the base of the salient, John Gordon, the impetuous brigadier who had wanted to envelop the Union right flank on the second day of the Wilderness, gathered a line of last-ditch fighters from the brigades of Col. Clement A. Evans and Brig. Gen. John Pegram. They came running to battle out of the same, foggy, dark background that Hancock had exploited to capture the works.

The Unionists stopped as the high-pitched yell came throbbing out of the dense woods before them. A sheet of fire announced that Lee's army was not yet ready to quit. The Second Corps was as disorganized as Jackson's corps had been after the flank attack at Chancellorsville. In the end, a surfeit of victory achieved too easily was the reason why a complete knockout was impossible. Perhaps there was no help for it. The only kind of mass attack that had a chance of penetrating Lee's defences led to the poorest kind of exploitation that could be imagined. When Gordon's attack went at the victorious Union men, some regiments, rallied by officers of exceptional merit, refused to give way and stubbornly traded volleys with the Johnnies. Mulholland described the fate of his lieutenant colonel, Richard Dale:

. . . Colonel Dale, sword in hand, was ever at the front; and when the retreat began, he lingered behind with his face to the foe, waving his sword and calling to the men to stand firm. Those of the Regiment who saw his heroic efforts, pressed forward to gather around him. Suddenly his sword was seen to drop, his voice ceased and he sank to the earth. . . . Some men of Company K, who saw him fall, tried to reach him, but were pushed back by the surging mass of fighting, struggling men; the Confederate line swept over his body, and none of his friends or comrades ever saw him again.[20]

So went down a man who was not Irish by birth or connection, only in the deep sensitivity of his ardent nature. He had lasted in combat seven days.

Fortunately he went down with something of the aura of victory about him. The Union attack was blunted at that time; soon it was bent backward by the overpowering assaults of the Johnnies. Other Confederate brigades were fed in because Lee was keenly aware that the Unionists must be thrust outside of his perimeter. With much expenditure of blood it was done by those incredible footmen of the South. Slowly, step by step, the Second Corps, by now reinforced by elements of the Sixth Corps, was pressed back until the entrenchments over which they had poured in the gray dawn were directly behind them. As the battle furor mounted higher and higher, the line of contention was clearly drawn at the peak of that entrenchment, Confederates on one side, Unionists on the other. For the rest of that foul, rainy day the two hosts recreated a picture out of hell itself. Anthony McDermott wrote of it:

There was, perhaps, no more desperate struggle for a position during the War than was the efforts of the enemy to retake his lost works. He made five or six attempts to drive us out, and, in his desperation, some of their men actually succeeded in planting the colors of their regiments on their lost ramparts, but they were in the end forced to give up. In one of

20. Mulholland, *116th Pennsylvania*, pp. 211-12.

these charges Capt. Charles McAnally, of Company E, of this regiment, fought a hand-to-hand struggle with a rebel color-bearer; while so struggling, the rebel color-guard rushed to the assistance of their standard bearer, and would have undoubtedly killed McAnally and saved their colors but for the heroic action of Sergeant Hugh McKeever, who quickly dispatched one of the guard about to fire on his captain, thus saving his life and enabling the lieutenant to strike down the standard bearer and capture the flag, which he threw to the rear and continued his efforts to repel the enemy until the struggle was over.[21]

The color was inscribed "Anderson's Division" and in 1895 McAnally was awarded the Medal of Honor for his action.

All day long the close-in struggle went on. Crazed by the horror, men would leap up to the top of the entrenchment and fire down on their enemies with loaded muskets tossed up to them by others until enemy bullets sought them out. Some genius on the Union side actually got up a battery of artillery whose snouts were pushed through the barricade and spread destruction in the Confederate ranks. In that welter all organization was inevitably lost, and no man could see more than a handful of comrades about him.

Even the hard fighters were shaken by the killing. Tom Smyth withdrew the Irish Brigade sometime in the late afternoon; as usual they had suffered, and so had the entire division. Francis Barlow had never been beloved by the Irish and they held him responsible for the frightful casualties. Since crossing the Rapidan the division had suffered a total of 3,200 in killed, wounded, or missing in but eight days. Even with the terrible day behind him Smyth could write only of the glory of the morning:

> . . . at daybreak we stormed the enemy's works in mass column, capturing three thousand prisoners, 40 guns, one major general and three brigade commanders. In the afternoon the enemy made a most

21. McDermott, *69th Pennsylvania*, p. 40.

vigorous attack to break our lines but signally failed. All through the night the enemy kept up a very sharp fire with the skirmishers. . . .[22]

The next morning found the salient known as the Mule Shoe to the Confederates and the Bloody Angle to the Unionists evacuated by all elements of the Army of Northern Virginia. During the hours of darkness Lee had built a new line of entrenchments across the base of the salient. Except for the dead, the maimed, and the prisoners, the great charge of May 12 might never have happened, for the two armies were in the same relative positions. May 13 passed with both sides feeling deep depression, the Confederates because of the fact it had happened at all, and the Federals because there had been no lasting result. So much had been anticipated after the initial breakthrough that even the possession of trophies and prisoners did not recompense for the escape of Lee's army from destruction.

For the next few days the Second Corps was not called on for any heavy lifting or hauling as the army command carried out certain schemes with the Fifth and Sixth Corps. These schemes did not work because heavy rains turned the terrain into a quagmire and slowed everything down to a walk. Grant had a few days to look about and make some decisions. He had already called for reinforcements and, indeed, they were needed. Since May 3 the army had suffered 36,872 casualties. The Second Corps had suffered the most, and as a result, Mott's division, which had come over from the Third Corps when it was discontinued, was consolidated into a brigade and attached to Birney's division. And wonder of wonders, the first contingent from the "Washington Garrison" joined the army on May 17.

These regiments, known as "Heavy Artillery Regiments," had been living in the embrasures and barracks of the forts that ringed the capital. They were double the size of an infantry regiment, and the Army of the Potomac had heard of their happy existence: growing flowers and vegetables, eating regular meals, and getting paid on a regular basis. They were indeed glad to hear that these brawny fellows

22. Smyth diaries, May 12, 1864.

Matthew Murphy
Colonel, 182nd New York Volunteer Infantry
Mortally wounded at Hatcher's Run, Virginia

would emerge from the cocoon of civilization and join them, living in the open air, and, not least, standing fire. For these lads would leave their heavy guns behind and become infantrymen. It should be noted that Grant himself ordered them out of their safe homes. He did not have to beg for reinforcement as McClellan did in 1862. As general of the armies he did not have to go hat in hand to the administration. However, he still had to put up with Ben Butler whose foray toward Richmond had come to a halt. And Maj. Gen. Franz Sigel in the Shenandoah had come a cropper on May 15 at New Market. So two of the four prongs of the Great Plan had been blunted and turned. Sherman was doing his part in the Georgia mountains, but here in Virginia it was a different story.

There was an additional reinforcement in the Corcoran Legion which had been employed most recently in guarding the Orange & Alexandria Railroad. Now its commander was Col. Matthew Murphy of the 182nd New York. The emissary of Secretary Stanton, Charles Dana, sent back this report of Murphy's brigade:

> Colonel Murphy, with the Irish Legion, reported last evening 1,600 muskets; the remainder, according to Colonel Murphy, being drunk on the road. They are assigned to the Sixth Corps.[23]

It did not turn out that way, as Matthew Murphy later reported:

> . . . on the 17th day of May, the Irish Legion, under my command, joined this army, and was assigned to the Second Division, Second Army Corps, as Fourth Brigade.[24]

So the Second Corps fell heir to another Irish unit. If their numbers were few because of intoxication, they would, in the next few weeks, make these numbers count. Actually, it is difficult to see these four regiments at much more than an average strength of 400 apiece, which would leave not many

23. *OR*, series 1, vol. 36, pt. 1, p. 72.
24. *Ibid.*, p. 459.

on the road. They had marched from Belle Plain to Fredericksburg to Spotsylvania in two days. Little time was lost in putting them into the grinder. The heavy artillery contingent was kept as a brigade apart, but the legion was assigned to Gibbon's division where it became the Fourth Brigade, and, for the moment, Murphy was left in command.

The operation of May 18 did not require much acumen on the part of the leader, only immense resolution on the part of the soldiers. The Second Corps was trying to repeat the assault of May 12. As before, 4 a.m. was the time for the attack, and the assembly point was the Landrum House which during the previous week had been enclosed by the Confederate defences of the salient. Now the entire area was in Union hands and would be a good takeoff point for the center of the Confederate position, exactly as had happened six days before.

Barlow's and Gibbon's divisions were to make the assault on a four-brigade front, each providing two brigades. One of the front line brigades contributed by Gibbon was Murphy's since it was reasoned that the new men would put more vigor into the assault. Also in the front line of Barlow was the Irish Brigade, now led by Col. Richard Byrnes of the 28th Massachusetts. Tom Smyth had shifted back to his old command in the Second Division because Byrnes was senior in rank. The front line of assault was composed of Irish troops and their attempt was to be a desperate one indeed. Lee might be fooled once by such an attack; it was unlikey the trick would work again. Further, the Confederate position did not now jut out into a salient. The ground over which the men would have to advance was rough and broken, but most deterring of all was the heavy slashing which covered the front of the enemy. In addition, the dead bodies of those killed on May 12 still lay unburied. The sight was hideous and the stench was overpowering.

Most of the Union reports emanating from the Second Corps say that the attack was made as directed. These are contradicted by the Confederates who say that Hancock's men did not come into contact until 8 a.m. There was plenty of daylight for the Confederate artillery and infantry; the attack did not penetrate the abatis.

There was the usual mixup for new troops at the start of the Irish Legion action. Colonel Murphy said that a staff officer

346

had detached his two right regiments, the 155th and 164th New York, and led them off at an angle to the main body without, of course, informing the commander. The two remaining, the 170th and 182nd New York, made their way through a dense forest, encountering and driving in some enemy pickets. Some enemy rifle-pits were then overrun and, the country opening up a bit, Murphy found that he was leading two and not four regiments. With the main Confederate work directly in front and appearing formidable, Murphy halted his attack and went off to find his missing soldiers. He rode to the rear initially, to find division headquarters, and there he was told that his missing men were off to the right, and had been engaged for more than an hour with some determined Confederates. Murphy quickly returned to the 170th and 182nd and led them in the proper direction.

Here he found Col. James P. McMahon falling back with the 155th and 164th, almost completely out of ammunition. Murphy moved his two regiments into position and awaited a counterattack. It was not forthcoming. The enemy could see no advantage in leaving a strong position merely to kill more Unionists. The Irish Legion hunkered down and found that they had been in quite a scrap. In their first action they had managed to lose 209 men just in approaching the main line of resistance. The corps and division command apparently found their efforts encouraging. Hancock wrote,

> The Corcoran Legion, of Gibbon's division, was particularly marked for is good conduct on this occasion, its losses being heavy.[25]

And Walker, the Second Corps historian and no friend of Irish soldiers,

> The Corcoran Legion showed itself every way worthy of the company it had come to keep.[26]

To the left of Gibbon's division the Irish Brigade had about the same luck with the heavy slashing. Mulholland wrote,

25. *Ibid.*, p. 338.
26. Walker, *History of the Second Corps*, p. 485.

. . . the men were confronted by a deep and heavy abatis that completely covered the Confederate line, the slashing being so dense that all efforts to penetrate were impossible. The Irish Brigade undoubtedly came nearer to getting through than any other, many of the men throwing themselves forward into the tangled wood and branches in their efforts to reach the works. One sergeant of the Regiment penetrated the mass for eight or ten feet beyond any of his comrades, and stood there, waist-deep in the abatis, while he loaded and fired three or four times. . . . To hold the men in front of the abatis to be shot down would be a useless waste of life. They fell back in excellent order, and, under the circumstances behaved with wonderful steadiness.[27]

As had been the pattern so far in the period since May 3, the 28th Massachusetts had suffered most severely, especially in officers. Maj. Andrew Lawlor and Captains James Magner and William Cochrane had gone down with mortal wounds. Mulholland suggests that a spirit of fatalism had enveloped the entire army. A corporal in the 116th had gripped the arm of his companion and said,

"Do you see the Reb works?" said Crawford, "well, I will be killed just as I reach there" And he was. He fell shot through the head as he came to the abatis. McClean lost his arm a moment later at the same spot.[28]

Both armies were nearing total exhaustion. That night men slept standing at their posts. Lt. Charles Cosslett of the 116th Pennsylvania and a sergeant making the rounds of the pickets lost their way and found themselves among the enemy; but all were fast asleep, and they returned safely to the brigade. In the withdrawal of the Second Corps picket line the next day, two officers of the brigade, Capt. Frank R. Lieb, 116th Pennsylvania, and Lt. David Lynch, 69th New York, distinguished

27. Mulholland, *116th Pennsylvania*, p. 222.
28. *Ibid.*, p. 222.

348

themselves enough to warrant a commendation from Barlow, who hated the brigade. The commendation was also endorsed by Hancock and Grant.

After the failure of the assaault of May 18, the Second Corps was placed in reserve until 10 p.m. on May 20. Grant had decided to slide around Lee's right flank and Hancock was to lead the way. By this time the thought of any more assaults on fortified positions was enough to give the entire army a fright. So the Second Corps marched all through the night of May 20-21, and at daybreak reached Guiney's Station on the Richmond & Fredericksburg Railroad. There was a difference in the character of the country. The roads were wide and good and the fields were cultivated. The column passed through Bowling Green, a town of frame houses, and in the afternoon forded the river Ny. Colonel Mulholland, who had been hit on May 5 in the Wilderness and again on May 10, rejoined the 116th here. He was badly needed because the casualties of the brigade had been top-heavy in officers.

Although the wide end run of the Second Corps was probably the only alternative left for Grant in his effort to get between Lee and Richmond, the result was a failure. Moving on interior lines Lee took up a strong position on the North Anna River where the Richmond & Fredericksburg Railroad crossed on a trestle bridge. Of all the defensive positions where Lee ever placed his army, this was the most ingenious and admirable. When Grant moved against it he divided his army and placed the Second Corps in a very uncomfortable position. Fortunately for the Union cause, Lee was not a physical superman; at the time he was much debilitated in health, and he had no strong subordinate to whom he could turn for the needed executive ability. A most critical period for the Army of the Potomac had passed. May 21 marked the end of the second epoch.

On May 26 the sidling movement toward Richmond continued. There is evidence that four or five days without battle had a tonic effect on the troops. Mulholland wrote that the troops,

> May 27th, marched at ten a.m. A long and trying
> day, dusty roads, heat oppressive and water scarce,
> but men cheerful and all filled with hope that soon

a great victory would reward the labor and suffering.[29]

They crossed the Pamunkey River the next day about four miles above Hanovertown and heard the sounds of battle from the direction of a place with the charming name of Haw's Shop where the cavalry screens were in contact. On May 29 the march was resumed and the wreckage of the cavalry fight encountered; dead men and horses lay about in the road and the fields. The trees were torn by shellfire and every house and barn was filled with wounded. East of Haw's Shop at the intersection of two country roads the Second Corps encountered some Confederate cavalry which slowly fell back. They were close to Totopotomoy Creek, and, as usual, the enemy was entrenched on the other bank.

There was some skirmishing and some success the next day, but the entrenchments looked too strong to Hancock. He did not press an assault until the following day when another partial success was gained. The army then disengaged and sidled off to the south to run yet another race for still another crossroads. This one was called Cold Harbor, and men who had soldiered on the Peninsula two years ago remembered something about it. It was a sleepy little place, not far from Gaines' Mill where Fitz John Porter had fought a tremendous battle in the Seven Days. To the southwest by ten miles lay their target city, Richmond. May 27 marked the end of the third epoch.

Now it was June again with its ever-lengthening days and full of hours of daylight into which could be packed endless fighting. The Army of the Potomac came upon Cold Harbor in sequential fashion, first the Sixth Corps, and the new Eighteenth Corps drawn from Ben Butler's stagnant Army of the James at Bermuda Hundred. When these troops arrived at the Cold Harbor position, they were, as usual, welcomed by the Confederates, but managed to secure a position of sorts. The Second and Fifth Corps moved into line next, although the latter had much difficulty in withdrawing from the position at Bethesda Church.

When the Federal supply depot was relocated to White House at the head of the York River, the Union army as-

29. *Ibid.*, pp. 230-31.

sumed almost the same position it had held under McClellan before he pushed soldiers over the Chickahominy River. The Federal line now reflected more the army's course from the North Anna and was slightly more to the north and east of the positions of 1862. Some authorities are of the opinion that Grant wished to extend his army, now augmented by detachments from Butler's forces and the Washington garrison, so the Army of Northern Virginia would be stretched too thin to defend the position. This school of thought then sees a Union concentration on the Cold Harbor flank and a breakthrough of the thin gray line.

Apparently, Grant had grown tense and irritable as the terrible days had gone by. In all the bloody journey there had been only the one small success of Hancock's on May 12 at Spotsylvania. Lee's army had simply refused to be beaten. Always across the Federal's path had stood stout earthworks, manned by the alert, hard soldiers who had taken such a tremendous toll of the bluecoats. Lee had attacked at the Wilderness, and then let the Unionists beat their heads against his entrenchments for the rest of the month of May. Now it was June; perhaps Grant really thought that he had hurt his enemy as badly as he had been hurt. Perhaps he thought he needed only one more strong push to settle the issue decisively.

On June 2 the Army of the Potomac was in a line six miles long running roughly northwest-southeast. On the left flank was the Second Corps, close to the Chickahominy and extending inland. Next came the Sixth Corps, but the nature of the ground prevented a straight extension of Hancock's line. Instead the Sixth Corps was at an oblique angle to the Second Corps. If the lines advanced directly ahead, each corps would diverge from the other so that neither would cover the flank of the other. On the right flank of the Sixth Corps was the Eighteenth Corps and a similar situation. Should the army advance as planned, instead of a single battle line smiting the Confederates as one, there would be three separate engagements.

The Second Corps was in position at 7:30 a.m. on June 2, and there was light skirmish contact during the morning. At about noon Lt. Col. Charles H. Morgan, the Second Corps chief-of-staff, and Lt. Col. Francis A. Walker, the Second Corps assistant adjutant general, rode along the front and almost into a Confederate prison camp. The enemy picket line was masked in a thick wood, and they blundered into it. By luck and hard riding the two got away safely. If they were not shaken too much by their close call, they might have noticed that the countryside before them was thickly wooded, and in the vicinity of the two rivers between which the armies stood, very swampy. On their return to corps headquarters, they found that the attack for June 2 had been called off. At 2:30 p.m. Walker put out a circular letter to all division commanders telling them of a new order. The time was to be used for resting the men since, in his words,

> It is very probable that an assault will be ordered at the earliest hour to-morrow.[30]

In the late afternoon a steady rain began to fall, a blessed relief to both armies from the overpowering heat. The Federals lay on the ground and tried to wish away the terrible, numbing fatigue that had enveloped the army for the past week. The steadfast foe in their entrenchments were employed in like fashion. In addition, the Confederates were about as close to starvation as they were ever to come. In light of the subsistence level to which his men were reduced, the feats of Lee in the month of blood become even more admirable. Bereft of able lieutenants and with some of his best formations decimated, the great Virginian had led an unbeatable army from the thickets of the Wilderness to the vicinity of Richmond. Now, on the last of the terrible thirty days, he and his men awaited the expected assault with equanimity.

At 8:30 p.m., Colonel Morgan sent a second circular to the division commanders:

> The divisions of Generals Barlow and Gibbon will attack the enemy, at such points on the front of the respective divisions as the commanders may select, at 4:30 to-morrow morning.[31]

The order was the death knell of the Second Corps. The wearers of the trefoil had been the keen edge of the Union

---

30. *OR*, series 1, vol. 36, pt. 3, p. 483.
31. *Ibid.*, p. 484.

attacks since the crossing of the Rapidan. Now the edge was very thin.

As the cooling draughts of rain fell on them, the men of the Irish Brigade found a few trees laden with green apples which were speedily devoured. When darkness fell, the divisions of Barlow on the left and Gibbon on the right were assembled so that there would be no need for shuffling around on the morrow. Each had a two brigade front, Barlow's being arranged with Miles and Brooke in front, and the Irish and Col. Clinton D. McDougall in the second line. Gibbon had Tom Smyth and the Irish Legion in front and Brig. Gen. Joshua T. Owen and Col. H. Boyd McKeen behind them. It is interesting to note that Joshua Owen, whom Gibbon had replaced with Webb just before Gettysburg, was back in command of the Philadelphia Brigade.

One of Grant's aid-de-camps, Horace Porter, was transmitting some final orders on the eve of the battle and wrote as follows:

> As I came near one of the regiments which was making preparations for the next morning's assault, I noticed that many of the soldiers had taken off their coats, and seemed to be engaged in sewing up rents in them. This exhibition of tailoring seemed rather peculiar at the moment, but upon closer examination it was found that the men were calmly writing their names and home addresses on slips of paper, and pinning them on the backs of their coats, so that their dead bodies might be recognized upon the field, and their fate made known to their families at home. They were veterans who knew well from terrible experience the danger which awaited them, but their minds were occupied not with thoughts of shirking their duty, but with preparation for the desperate work of the coming morning. Such courage is more than heroic—it is sublime.[32]

32. Horace E. Porter, *Campaigning with Grant* (New York: The Century Company, 1897), p. 174.

There was little talk about this act of fatalism and no banter. It was apparent that even if army headquarters had high hopes for the attack, the troops felt otherwise. And even high command level types were beginning to have doubts about head-on attacks on entrenchments. Walker, the Second Corps assistant adjutant general, was always astonished the assault was made where it was and when it was. The whole purpose of the sliding movements in which the army had been engaged since the Wilderness was to place a numerically superior Union force at a point on the Richmond arc before a comparable Confederate force could interpose. If the element of prior arrival was lost, then the movement must be extended.

No probing of the defence was attempted like Brig. Gen. Emory Upton's attack of May 10, which had set up the momentary triumph of May 12. The army would attack all along the line and in fairly complete ignorance of what would be encountered. Why, lamented Walker in later years, could the assault not have been postponed even for a day? One answer was that the Republican National Convention would open on June 7, and a smashing victory would help Lincoln's renomination. The government had concealed the terrible casualty lists from the public, and kept up a drum-fire of optimism about the campaign.

At least the troops would not have to be moved around during the night of June 2. They were going to attack directly ahead from the positions they now occupied. Brig. Gen. Robert O. Tyler had brought a division of heavy artillery regiments down from Washington two weeks before. In the last days of May it had been broken up and the individual "heavy" regiments had been assigned to various brigades. The Corcoran Legion got the 8th New York Heavy Artillery and General Tyler, a West Pointer who had only dealt with artillery commands, as its new commander. The 8th was, apparently, as numerous as the entire Irish contingent together. The 170th New York had been handled roughly at the crossing of the North Anna River and was to be kept in reserve. On the left, where Gibbon's division connected with Barlow's division, Tyler placed the 164th under its fine colonel, James McMahon, who had succeeded his brother upon his death in March 1863. To the right of the 164th was the 182nd New York, under Lt.

354

Col. Thomas Reid, the 155th New York, under Capt. Richard Doran, and the 8th New York Heavy, under Col. Peter Porter.

In Barlow's division, Col. Richard Byrnes was forming the Irish Brigade in the second line behind the brigade of Nelson Miles. Colonel Mulholland had been wounded on May 31 for the third time since the campaign opened, seriously enough to get him sent back to Washington. Capt. Richard Moroney of the 69th New York commanded the 116th Pennsylvania on the brigade's right flank. Major Garrett still led the 69th New York, Capt. "Big John" Gleason led the 63rd New York, and Capt. Dennis Burke led the 88th New York. The spectacle of regiments under the command of captains is indicative of the difficulties of the campaign. Capt. James Fleming of the 28th Massachusetts wrote that on the way down from the North Anna the 28th was much affected by straggling; they were only able to put about 130 men in the line of battle.

Over in the Philadelphia Brigade, the 69th Pennsylvania was about to be placed in an embarassing position through no fault of their own. Their old brigade commander, Joshua Owen, who had been superseded just before Gettysburg by Alexander S. Webb, had been restored to command before the start of the campaign. For some reason or other, John Gibbon, the division commander, had been able to get along with him up until now. Owen was, however, to perform badly enough on this occasion to get relieved once and for all.

Usually the men were awakened at 3 a.m. for dawn attacks. Now there was nothing to do except deploy and go forward. Old veteran, new bounty man, bearded sergeant, and callow recruit all took their places in the ranks and waited. There was no breakfast, for army command was hoping for a surprise which might be given away by cooking fires. Some men chewed hardtack and washed it down with water from the rivulets which ran down to Powhite Creek and Boatswain's Swamp. Ahead of them the ground sloped up to a low hilltop and then fell away to a fairly thick wood.

There was open ground and then the Confederate works, manned here in front of the Second Corps by A. P. Hill's corps which included some new replacements. A division led by Maj. Gen. John C. Breckinridge of Kentucky, who had opposed Lincoln in the 1860 election for the presidency, had come in from a successful campaign in the Shenandoah Valley.

Massachusetts Commandery, MOLLUS
U.S. Army Military History Institute

James McMahon
Colonel, 164th New York Volunteer Infantry
Killed at Cold Harbor

Also a scratch formation of Floridians under Brig. Gen. Joseph Finegan made its first appearance and was put in the line. Good entrenchments with excellent artillery positions led Lee to feel reasonably secure.

The Union line moved forward at 4:30 a.m. and filtered through the wood. On the far side the ground fell gently down, marshy in spots; after the night's heavy rain it was very soft. This was especially so in front of Gibbon's men on the right of the Second Corps where a heavy slough loomed in front of the Corcoran Legion. McMahon, leading the 164th New York with the Green Flag in his hand, moved his regiment to the left around this obstacle. Next to him the 182nd New York moved to the right, opening up a sizeable but unavoidable hole in the brigade line. By this time, both Barlow's and Gibbon's divisions were halfway between the edge of the woods and the Confederate works, now seen to consist of stout looking entrenchments. Confederate rifles spoke from the advance rifle pits and men began to fall. The artillery then opened and hideous gaps appeared. The tolling of the guns became a death knell for the Second Corps. The Confederates had sighted their guns to deliver a cross-fire, and whole ranks fell under the familiar iron rain.

A sunken road at the foot of the Confederate position sheltered the enemy's first line in front of Barlow. His men stormed over it, taking a color and some prisoners. The Confederates later explained that some troops had been allowed to leave the sunken road position for breakfast, and, consequently, it was not strongly held. The wearers of the red trefoil mounted the bank and plunged into the Confederate position, and for an incredible moment it looked as though as improbable an event as Spotsylvania's Bloody Angle would be repeated. Barlow's second line thronged up to join the first. It was an illusion. They occupied a salient where Lee's line jutted forward of the main position. The enemy reinforcements arrived, and the deadly artillery cross-fire began. Such a hurricane of fire fell that nothing could have lived through it. In that blast Colonel Byrnes of the Irish Brigade went down, mortally wounded. His soldiers bore him back in the direction from which they had come; anything to get out of that hellish storm. Those caught in the open dug feverishly into the damp soil with their hands, their mess kits, their bayonets. The blue bundles of their dead comrades lay all about them, carpeting the ground.

To the right of Barlow, James McMahon led in the 164th with his sword uplifted and the Green Flag clutched in his left hand. His men encountered heavy musketry fire from the first, and it was only a handful who followed the valiant colonel up the face of the entrenchment. There was a terrible climactic scene with McMahon on top of the works, waving the flag and shouting for his men to come on. For an instant he was there outlined, against the sky of the summer morning, the beau ideal of the Irish warrior. Then he was down and gone and the Green Flag fallen across his body. It had been lost as honorably as any color could be, as honorably as those of Pickett's division at Gettysburg.

On the north side of the swamp, the rest of Gibbon's men did not get so close, the fields of fire stopping them cold. As Barlow's men had done, the wearers of the white shamrocks fell back some distance, as far as they could get, and dug for their lives. In less than twenty minutes the Second Corps had lost 3,000 men. To their right the Fifth and Eighteenth Corps and the Ninth Corps had been as equally unsuccessful. In the mounting sunshine lay fields of moaning men. Never on any field of the war had so many fallen so quickly. Never since Fredericksburg had troops been thrown into an engagement with less preparation or less plan. It had been a straight-ahead smash and the worst disaster since Burnside's at Marye's Heights. Considering what had gone on since they had crossed the Rapidan, this last straw was worse than Fredericksburg.

There followed a desperately uncomfortable day for Union soldiers, of both high and low rank. Those who had fallen back from whence they had advanced were mostly in the open and without protection except for the little mounds of earth they had scooped up in front of them. The enemy marksmen were vigilant and kept them pinned down for the long, terrible daylight hours. It was impossible to stand, sit, or move in any way, even to obey the calls of nature. After the assaults at Fredericksburg, there had been a day of fierce cold; now the sun was a red ball in the Virginia sky shining down on the writhing wounded, the cries for water, and the frenzied screaming for home and friends. Hancock gazed over a holocaust again. In twenty-two minutes six colonels had been killed in

358

taking the men of the Second Corps as far forward as it was possible to go.

Twice later that day army command ordered a resumption of the attacks. Winfield Scott Hancock, the most combative officer in the Army of the Potomac, refused to take the responsibility for renewals. Sick at heart, he looked over the wreckage of the two best divisions in the army. In the 28th Massachusetts 3 lieutenants and 66 men were all that was left of the 505 who had crossed the Rapidan on May 3. As Capt. James Fleming observed bitterly,

> . . . the Twentiy-eighth Massachusetts Regiment suffered much in the loss of officers and men without having the satisfaction of punishing the enemy in return. We formed in line and charged the enemy over the earth-works, and our men fell in heaps.[33]

There was an affecting scene at a rear echelon when the mortally wounded Richard Byrnes learned that Capt. Frank Lieb of the 116th was there with a smashed foot. There had been an altercation between the two some days before. Byrnes had himself carried to where Lieb was lying. Here the dying commander of the Irish Brigade

> . . . apologized in the most courteous manner for anything rude that he might have said.[34]

In the Corcoran Legion the three regiments in the first line, the 155th, 164th, and 182nd New York, had suffered heavy losses, although only one regimental commander, James McMahon, had been killed. Reports of him speak in the most flattering terms. Gibbon wrote,

> On the left, and separated from his brigade by the swamp, the heroic Colonel McMahon, with a portion of his regiment, One hundred and sixty-fourth New York, gained the breastwork, and, while alongside

33. *OR*, series 1, vol. 36, pt. 1, p. 390.
34. Mulholland, *116th Pennsylvania*, p. 238.

of his colors cheering on his men, fell covered with wounds, and expired in the enemy's hands. . . .[35]

Francis Walker, the Second Corps historian, also penned an encomium:

> Colonel James P. McMahon, of New York, had been but a brief three weeks with the Army of the Potomac; but he brought to it a lofty courage and chivalrous sense of duty which did honor even to the old corps of Sumner.[36]

There is a sequel to the horror of Cold Harbor which reflects little credit on Ulysses Grant. In front of the Army of the Potomac were many men who were seriously wounded or slightly wounded who could not move because of the Confederate fire. All that was required to help them was for the Union commander to ask for a truce to remove these poor broken ones from the field. This was a standard tactic, and there is no doubt that Lee would have given permission for he was notably humane. However, it entailed a loss of face on the part of the commander requesting the truce and Grant was not willing to do this. It would be an admission to the public that he had lost the battle. After four days had gone by and most of the poor unfortunates were beyond the help of medical or any other attention save that of a gravedigger, Grant grudgingly asked for a suspension of hostilities. Even more shameful was the attempt by Grant partisans in after years to throw the responsibility for the matter on Robert E. Lee. Morgan, the Second Corps chief-of-staff, said that at 5 p.m. on June 5, sixty hours after the assault, Grant proposed a truce of mutual accomodation, as though there were Confederate wounded to be attended to as well as Union. On June 6 Grant sent two notes to Lee inferring that men of both sides lay between the lines and proposing both sides labor under truce flags. In restrained language, Lee parried this rude attempt to escape responsibility. He had severely repulsed the Unionists, he had no men out between the lines,

---

35. *OR*, series 1, vol. 36, pt. 1, p. 433.
36. Walker, *History of the Second Corps*, p. 513.

and he had no need to take the initiative in the matter. By refusing to admit the defeat that was signal and apparent, Grant sacrificed a number of poor men to needless death as he had sacrificed countless others in the straight-ahead assaults on entrenchments.[37]

After the truce was official, Capt. Martin McMahon came over from the Sixth Corps where he was Horatio Wright's chief-of-staff to find and identify the body of his brother, James. Unfortunately, a number of bullets had found the valiant colonel's body, and only the buttons on his sleeves were conclusive identification.

Grant's modern day partisans refuse to admit that this is a callous attitude. If one reads Catton's works, either *A Stillness At Appomattox* or *Grant Takes Command*, one is struck at the attempts at explanation. In the first, Catton is carried away by Grant's single-minded offensive nature. He says: "Before he even bothered to seek a truce so that dead men might be buried and wounded men brought back within the lines—they lay there, untended, for several days, bullets flying low above them—he set things in motion for a new move."[38] This is patently untrue. In the period after the misshapen assault of June 3, the Army of the Potomac hunkered down and entrenched. Nine days elapsed before the march to the James began.

In *Grant Takes Command* Catton puts the assault of June 3 on a lower scale. Only 7,000 men were casualties, many less than the Wilderness or Spotsylvania. He does imply that Grant did not know what was going on, hence his message to Halleck of 2:30 p.m., June 3:

Our loss was not severe, nor do I suppose the enemy to have lost heavily.[39]

Catton then says the battle "has been hard to interpret since. It gave final proof that good trenches properly manned cannot be stormed and that an offensive against an entrenched foe is

37. *Ibid.*, p. 518.
38. Bruce Catton, *A Stillness at Appomattox* (Garden City, New York: Doubleday and Company, 1953), p. 177.
39. *OR*, series 1, vol. 36, pt. 3, p. 524.

hard to manage . . . but beyond these points the battle meant less than it seemed to mean."[40] This is a very interesting approach. After all, the Confederates could only shoot as many Union soldiers as Grant sent against them. If the survivors of the early attack had not gotten back to their lines as quickly as they did, perhaps the casualty list for either of those earlier Grant battles could have been surpassed. Catton then quotes several sources who say that morale in the army was still high. However, Morgan, chief-of-staff of the Second Corps, wrote of Cold Harbor,

> The Second Corps here received a mortal blow, and never again was the same body of men.[41]

This was the corps that had been the heart of the army. Smash 'em-up tactics had finished them off. Actually those tactics had finished off the Army of the Potomac as an offensive force as will be seen in the next misshapen effort, the dash to Petersburg. Grant had set out to destroy an army, and he had succeeded. Unfortunately, it was his own.

For ten more days the armies confronted each other. By night the Federals raised up works every bit as strong and impervious to assault as the Confederates were. In some places the trenches were as close as fifty yards, and sharpshooters plied their grisly trade all the day long. Covered ways had to be constructed from the rear to the front lines so the troops could be supplied. At night, furious fusillades kept both sides awake expecting instant assaults. But there were none. Even so, there was excitement. On June 7, Col. Tom Smyth wrote in his diary,

> I was aroused from a doze by the crack of a sharpshooter's bullet going through my tent. My HQ is not a pleasant place this morning for nervous men. I don't think I will be troubled much from visits from the division staff or friendly callers.[42]

40. Catton, *Grant Takes Command*, p. 268.
41. Walker, *History of the Second Corps*, p. 522.
42. Smyth diaries, June 7, 1864.

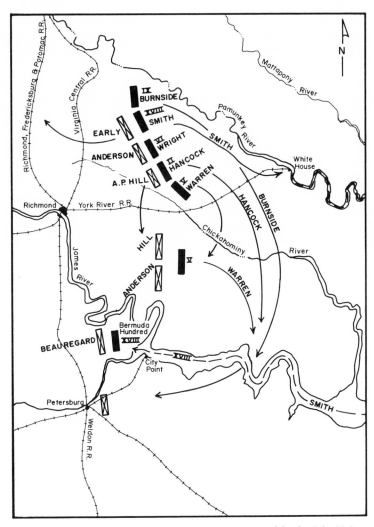

Map by John Heiser

Grant moves to the James River, June 12 - 16, 1864

Even more illuminating is his entry for June 8, describing the truce of two hours to bury the dead:

> Plenty of Richmond papers in camp this morning exchanged by the men. The best of feeling exists now between the two armies.[43]

So a week passed and a great scheme took shape in the mind of Grant. It was not an easy one for him to adopt, and it went directly contrary to the administration's idea of always keeping the army between Lee and Washington. After Cold Harbor, Grant was at the end of the line. He could invest Richmond from the north which was what the War Department seemed to want, or he could move his army south over two rivers and seize the city of Petersburg, twenty miles south of Richmond. With Petersburg in his hands the Confederate capital must fall, for through it passed the Weldon Railroad, Richmond's lifeline stretching to the south.

In 1862 McClellan had notions of operating on the south side of the James River at the end of his Peninsular Campaign. Just before being corked up at Bermuda Hundred a month before, Butler's Army of the James had tried to sweep into Petersburg and had failed. If Grant could hold Lee's army north of the James for an appreciable length of time while transferring his army to the new area, he might be able to make the plan work. Much depended upon the engineers who would have to construct a bridge 2,100 feet long across a swift tidal river thirteen fathoms deep. Much would also depend on the men; some heavy marching would be required of them.

All of the soldiers would be glad to leave the lines at Cold Harbor. Replacements came up and the old organizations which had suffered so much were now almost completely unrecognizable. The Irish Brigade was again commanded by Patrick Kelly who had led it at Gettysburg, but there was little left to command. The same held true in the Irish Legion. Until the hospitals returned their patched-up wounded, neither would ever count for much in the line of battle. The brigade's great days were behind it. Ahead lay the grim, boring days of siege

43. *Ibid.*, June 8, 1864.

364

warfare, the most repugnant kind to the Celtic nature. As the column pulled out of the Cold Harbor position, ahead of them was more hardship and death. There would be no more days like Antietam where they had gone into the attack with the eyes of the army on the Green Flags, no more nights like Malvern Hill where the 69th and 88th demonstrated their soldierly ability for all the world and Fitz John Porter, in particular, to see. The fourth epoch of the Overland Campaign ended on June 12, 1864.

The Second Corps did not make use of the great bridge which the engineers had constructed over the James. Hancock had four river steamers acting as ferries and by 4 a.m. of June 15 his entire command was at Windmill Point on the south side of the river. A great opportunity was before the Federal forces. The city of Petersburg was but fifteen miles away, and already on the road to attack the lightly-held defences was the Eighteenth Corps under Maj. Gen. William F. Smith. For the moment Lee was held north of the river.

All that stood between the Army of the Potomac and total victory was a flamboyant Confederate general named Beauregard and a patched-up force. That force had been corking up Butler's Army of the James at Bermuda Hundred. The difficulty was that while this brilliant prospect was opening up, there had been a complete breakdown in communications. Grant had neglected to tell Meade that the Eighteenth Corps was going to Petersburg and should be backed up. As far as Meade knew, Hancock and the Second Corps were merely moving toward Petersburg with no orders to attack the place or to support the Eighteenth Corps. Hancock's orders were to move toward Petersburg and take up a position "where the City Point Railroad crosses Harrison's Creek." When the Second Corps arrived on the south side of the James, rations were issued to the men. This took time, and their movement away from the river did not start until 10:30 a.m. On top of all these blunders Hancock was furnished with an erroneous map and so took the long way to Petersburg.

The day was hot, and as the march continued into the afternoon the men could hear artillery firing to their front and left. At 5:30 p.m. Hancock received a message from Smith asking for reinforcement. Almost simultaneously he received word from Grant to support Smith, and for the first time he realized what the objective was and that haste was needed. The two divisions closest to the action, Birney's and Gibbon's, were speeded up; Barlow's was on another road and was not able to get into the attack that night. For some reason Hancock held this against Barlow, and they had a long correspondence on the subject. On the next day the Second Corps assaulted and captured some of the redans in the outer line of fortifications. Barlow felt he had to demonstrate his manhood after the contretemps with Hancock, and he led his division, cap in hand. The attack did not have the weight to continue into the main line, and, in addition, enough of Lee's army had now arrived to stiffen the defenders. Grant's last and best effort to crack the nut without a siege had failed. It had failed for a number of reasons, but most importantly because of the breakdown of communications on June 15, for which the lieutenant general had no one to blame but himself.

The Irish Brigade was at low ebb in this latest phase of the operation to deliver the knockout blow to Lee. Since Cold Harbor and the death of Richard Byrnes, Patrick Kelly had been in command and he was a tower of strength. But the members of the five regiments were too few and those who were left were too worn to be a factor in battle. The marching, the hot weather, and the strain of the last six weeks had simply taken the fibre out of them. Although the attack on the outer line of Petersburg went in with élan, the 116th especially deserving of praise, it was not up to any of their past performances. In the last stages of the assault Patrick Kelly was shot through the head and killed. The brigade was again orphaned with not a field officer left. It had entered on the campaign with ten field officers; six had been killed and the other four were severely wounded. As an organization, the brigade was finished for the time being.

There were a few more days of half-hearted assaults on Petersburg, but by June 22 Grant had decided that it was no go. The gateway to Richmond was put under formal siege, the railroads into the city were to be closed off, and the defenders harassed until starvation and exhaustion brought down the citadel. The Army of the Potomac started to dig trenches.

CHAPTER FOURTEEN

THE WAR BECOMES A SIEGE

By the beginning of July the Confederate defences had become so formidable that assault was considered impracticable. The line consisted of a chain of redans connected by infantry parapets. In front of these fortifications the approaches were completely obstructed by abatis, stakes, and entanglements. Beginning at the south bank of the Appomattox River, this line covered Petersburg on the east and south, stretching westward beyond the left flank of the Union army. The city is twenty-two miles from Richmond with which it is connected by the Petersburg & Richmond Railroad. Feeding into Petersburg were three railroads from the south: the Lynchburg, running to the southwest; the Weldon, running directly south to North Carolina; and the Norfolk, running to the southeast. As it stood, Petersburg was the key to the lock of Richmond. An army in possession of the city could force the evacuation of Richmond by shutting off the routes which supplied its vital needs. Behind the entrenchments of the two cities, Lee and his army stood vigilant, ready to take advantage of any openings which the Federals might present to them.

Although overwhelming infantry assaults would not break the Confederate line, it could be threatened by shifting Federal forces to various points on the defensive perimeter. Should the Confederates be slow in reacting, the Unionists might get possession of an undermanned redan and thus gain local success. If enough local successes could be gained in this manner, the evacuation of a part of the defence system might be forced. A pontoon bridge over the Appomattox River enabled Union forces to be swiftly moved from Petersburg to Richmond and vice versa. Grant thus had some degree of initiative. The Confederates were condemned to eternal vigilance by this constant threat.

First, however, the Federals set to work building a parallel system of forts and trenches with which to confront the enemy. Picks and shovels were wielded under the hot July sun and Union batteries emplaced. After the first frenzied digging established the system, the entrenching became a settled part of the routine. Men who had lived through the Month of Blood were now able to look about them and see what had happened to the Army of the Potomac. For one thing, some regiments which had served out their enlistment period were no more, gone home to glory. That is, the survivors of the three-year enlistments had gone home; men with unexpired enlistments were placed in other outfits which were going to stay.

Among the departures was the 9th Massachusetts, the only Green Flag regiment which had not re-enlisted in a body. The Boston Irish were not heavily engaged in the later parts of the Overland Campaign. Their last day in contact with the enemy was on May 19 in the Spotsylvania position. On June 9 they "stood fire" for the last time, and shipped out on June 10, three years to the day since they had been mustered in. As a parting gift to the regiment, Brig. Gen. Charles Griffin, their old brigadier, now commanding First Division, Fifth Corps, sent over a nicely crated Confederate shell which had landed near his headquarters without exploding. The 9th said good-bye to their friends of the 62nd Pennsylvania and 4th Michigan, with whom they had served since November 20, 1861. A steamer took them up the Potomac to Washington, and railway cars took them the rest of the way to Boston. On June 15, the Boston citizenry met the men at the station and cheered them. There was no "cold-roast Boston" today. Brahmin and Puritan stood with the misty-eyed Irish as the relic of the regiment marched to Faneuil Hall. In all, 1,691 men had served in the regiment. Of these, 211 were killed or mortally wounded and 387 discharged for wounds of disability. Three hundred men had transferred to other commands by reason of re-enlistment. Only 461 were left to hear the speech of Massachusetts adjutant general William Schouler. Many relatives learned for the first time that the loved ones they were seeking were recently killed or wounded. Of course Patrick Guiney was there. His Wilderness wound had necessitated the removal of an eye.[1]

1. MacNamera, *Ninth Massachusetts*, pp. 406-8.

There were other losses to the Army of the Potomac, and, in late June, a wholesale shuffling of organizations. In the Second Corps the Irish Brigade was disbanded. In Barlow's division a Consolidated Brigade was formed consisting of the remainder of ten New York regiments. To it was assigned the 63rd, 69th, and 88th, and Col. Clinton McDougall of the 111th New York was placed in command. The 28th Massachusetts was placed in the First Brigade under Nelson Miles and the 116th Pennsylvania went to the Fourth Brigade under John Brooke. Although he was not present because of his wounds, Mulholland wrote of the melancholy event:

> The members of the Regiment left the Irish Brigade with regret. They had participated in all the glories and triumphs of that famous brigade for two years, and although the One Hundred and Sixteenth was composed almost entirely of American-born citizens, the men had learned to love and esteem the men of the Emerald Isle.[2]

There may have been those among the surviving officers of the Irish Brigade who protested in their hearts this loss of identity. But after the campaign they had just come through, it is unlikely that many of the men, mesmerized by battle and hardship, would get upset over the action. Numerically, they were a corporal's guard; they would, therefore, be treated like one.

With the muster out of the 71st Pennsylvania, the Philadelphia Brigade was also broken up and the 69th Pennsylvania found itself serving in the Third Brigade, Second Division. They were glad to be commanded by Tom Smyth, and he was glad to have them. The Corcoran Legion and the 8th New York Heavy remained as the Second Brigade in this division.

Late in July, in order to give the explosion of the Petersburg Mine the greatest effect, Grant attempted to draw off a good portion of Lee's strength to the north of the James River. The Second Corps was selected for this maneuver and marched from the siege lines on the afternoon of July 26. They crossed the pontoon bridge over the Appomattox River and moved to

2. Mulholland, *116th Pennsylvania*, p. 279.

the east of Butler's entrenchments at Bermuda Hundred. Dawn found them north of the James at a place called Deep Bottom, one of the great loops in the river where several small watercourses empty into it. One of the streams is known as Bailey's Creek. Butler's men had laid two bridges over the James at this point. One bridge was laid from the south side to the north side west of the mouth of Bailey's Creek. The other was laid to the east side of the creek.

When the Unionists crossed by the bridge to the east, it was to find Kershaw's division ready behind earthworks and full of fight. More Confederate troops came up during the day which, of course, was exactly what Grant wanted, and Hancock carried out a demonstration all day. Lee had only one division in place in the Petersburg lines when the Mine blew. It should have been a walkover for Burnside, but the unlucky star that pursued that poor man for four years was again to prove his undoing. The worst fiasco of the war took place. The Confederates recovered with their usual resiliency and sealed off the hole in the ground as well as in their lines. The Second Corps marched back to the Petersburg lines just in time to see the vast mass of earth rise into the sky. So ended their first excursion to Deep Bottom.

There was not much action for the next two weeks. A Court of Inquiry was held on the Mine fiasco and Hancock was its president. The troops appreciated the inactivity. On August 12 the Second Corps got orders to undertake another movement north of the James. There was a good bit of subtlety in this maneuver. Lee had released Lt. Gen. Jubal Early for the celebrated raid on Washington, the Second Coming of Stonewall Jackson. Naturally there was a great hue and cry in the capital that apparently worried Ulysses Grant not at all. He did send some of the Sixth Corps up the Potomac to reassure the panicky administration. At the same time he got the idea of putting the Second Corps on ships at City Point, ostensibly directing them also down the James and up the Potomac. This time, however, some slick maneuvering would go on. The troops would load on the ships and head down the James, but, under cover of night, the ships would run up the James to Deep Bottom again. This time there was to be no demonstration but all-out assault.

Hancock had plenty of doubts about the scheme, as Walker wrote,

> It is hard to believe that such a scheme could have been seriously considered before adoption. It is only to be explained by supposing that those who conceived it were familiar with the operation of landing men, cattle, and goods, from light-draft steamers, on western rivers. Large coastwise steamers, on a tidal river, however, were certain to offer a very different problem. Sixteen vessels, ocean-going or large river steamers, some of them drawing as much as thirteen feet, were provided for the expedition.[3]

Before the troops arrived at the spot of debarkation, Hancock scouted out the landing place. He found the nature of the banks and the state of the water would prevent most of the vessels from landing men over a gangplank. He did, however, find the remains of three piers and, securing a load of lumber at City Point, directed one of his staff to put the wharves in as good a condition as he could.

When the troops boarded the steamers, there was an incredible moment when the rumor passed around that they were going back to Washington, presumably to be garrison troops for the rest of the war. Everyone cheered up and began singing while the ships filled up with men and pulled out into the Appomattox River. Then at 10 p.m. the bubble burst as the steamers headed upstream in the James River for Deep Bottom. Mulholland wrote:

> No one thought of sleep. There was no time to even doze while the boys were having such a good time. Were they not on their way to the North! With the tolling of the midnight hour came a sad ending to the Washington dream. The steamer, on which the Regiment was rejoicing and having such a jolly time, slowed up and a tug came alongside with the orders. In five minutes every man knew that it was Deep Bottom and a fight in the morning, instead of Wash-

3. Walker, *History of the Second Corps*, p. 569.

371

ington and a trip to the north. The singing quickly
died away. The river did not seem half so beautiful
nor the stars half so bright. Quickly everyone lost
interest in the passing shores. The silence of disappointed hope settled over the men.[4]

The ships reached Deep Bottom at 2:30 a.m. on August 14,
and the trouble began. Mott's division was not on shore until
7:30, four hours after it should have been there to effect
surprise. Finally, however, everyone was ashore and heading
in the proper direction. It was a hot day and during the forced
march that followed the landing, many men passed out due to
sunstroke. Hancock had the Tenth Corps from Butler's army
under his command as well as plenty of cavalry, so he gave
Barlow command over both First and Second Divisions of the
Second Corps. Apparently, he was moved to do this because a
successful operation might bring Barlow the promotion he
longed for—major general of volunteers.

After an all-day march the troops had to assault the same
field works they had seen on their first excursion to Deep
Bottom, and they were completely unsuccessful. Barlow reported that the troops showed little spirit; he had intended to
attack with two brigades, but one of them showed such signs
of demoralization that he decided to use only one. Walker
wrote of this:

> Concerning the reported ill-behavior of the troops
> on this occasion, it is enough to say that the two
> brigades referred to had been among the chief glories
> of the Second Corps. General Morgan justly remarks:
> "Nothing could so clearly show the disorganization
> brought about by the terrible losses of this campaign
> as that such language could be truthfully used about
> these troops. The Irish brigade had left its dead,
> with their sprigs of green in their caps, close under
> the stone wall at Fredericksburg; and had shown on
> every field the most determined bravery. Brooke's
> brigade had fought its way to the front as far as our
> flag was ever carried, at Gettysburg . . . had led

4. Mulholland, *116th Pennsylvania*, p. 286.

Barlow's charge, side by side with Miles' brigade, at Spotsylvania . . . had penetrated the enemy's line in the desperate charge at Cold Harbor; and now with its fourth or fifth commander, was, according to General Barlow, loath to look at the enemy. It is evident," concludes Morgan, "that assaults 'all along the line' had left very little of the old material there."[5]

Barlow, Walker, and Morgan all seem to have forgotten that the Irish Brigade had been organized out of existence on June 30, and that the three New York regiments were now part of the Consolidated Brigade of eleven New York regiments under a brigadier who was a complete stranger to them. Perhaps this was a way for Barlow to vent his spleen on the Irish for his lost promotion. After that day, it was back to the Petersburg trenches and more sun-baked days with only the sharpshooter's bullet to pass the time.

The first course of action open to Grant, the massing of superior forces at one weak point of the Confederate defences, had not been successful. He then set in motion the second part of the program open to him, the closing of the supply lines into Petersburg and the interdiction of the Virginia Central Railroad, Richmond's lifeline to the Shenandoah Valley. The three railroads feeding into Petersburg from the south could be acted upon by a gradual extension of the Union left flank or by cutting loose a column which would be strong enough to meet any force which Lee could detach to protect his communications. The Fifth Corps had extended across the Weldon Railroad on August 18, cutting its use directly to Petersburg. However, the Confederates continued to use it below the break. Trains were run from North Carolina to a point about one day's wagon haul below the break. Supplies were then placed in wagons which passed around the west end of the Union lines and into the city. To destroy this practice the Second Corps was sent to take up as much of the railroad track as possible in the direction of Rowanty's Creek.

Sometime in the middle of August, Lt. Col. John Byron of the 88th New York had taken over command of the Consolidated Brigade, only to lead it on one of the worst days the

5. Walker, *History of the Second Corps*, pp. 573-74.

Second Corps was ever to know—a day on which even the sanguine Hancock said he hoped he would not leave the field alive. The place was Ream's Station, a whistle-stop on the Weldon and Petersburg Railroad, about eight miles southeast of the besieged city. Only two divisions were employed in the tiring and unmartial labor of railroad track destruction, but two brigades of cavalry under Brig. Gen. David M. Gregg were attached. By August 24, Gibbon's division had reached Ream's Station and learned from the cavalry that some Confederates were in the vicinity. There were some old entrenchments around the station, the relics of an older action. The Federals were later to curse these fortifications which seem to have been designed by an amateur. Of course it is questionable why Gibbon, who was a professional, did nothing to modify them himself.

On August 25, a strong Confederate force began to probe the Union outposts, and the working parties which had been tearing up the track were told to fall back into the entrenchments. At about 2 p.m. a strong attack was mounted on them and was beaten off. It fell at a point on the Union perimeter where the works made a sharp angle, and the men behind the position were the men of the Consolidated Brigade under Byron. As the afternoon wore on, there were other "brisk dashes" by the enemy skirmishers which were also beaten off. Unknown to the Federals, a very strong enemy force was being positioned in the thick underbrush which surrounded the position.

Before the next assault, A. P. Hill, who was in command, ordered that an effective artillery preparation be made. Because of the faulty position of the entrenchments, the Confederates were able to get an enfilade on the western side of the enclosure. When the shells began to fall on the men of Miles' division from behind, a complete demoralization took place. The bombardment was followed by a strong infantry assault which succeeded in breaking into the Union perimeter where stood the Consolidated Brigade. The only reserve present refused to advance to repair the break. Three batteries of Union artillery fell into the hands of Heth's division and the makings of a real disaster was at hand. When Hancock ordered Gibbon's division to restore the situation, the response was very feeble. Upon meeting resistance Gibbon's men retreated, exposing the entire Union position.

Except for the superhuman efforts of Hancock and Miles it is doubtful if the Second Corps would ever have left the field as an organized body. Miles got together a handful of men from his old regiment, the 61st New York, and finally managed to halt the Confederates. One of the Union batteries was retaken as well as some entrenchments. Very fortunately for Hancock, some Union cavalry took a hand at this time, saving the situation from complete disaster. The cavalry maintained a close and effective fire and thwarted the efforts of Heth to penetrate the Union position. Hancock was riding all over the field, appealing to his men to stand and fight. He helped Miles to get an attack going that won back some more of the lost ground, but it was impossible to get Gibbon's men into the fight at all. Even Tom Smyth said that he could not get his men to advance.

By this time it was getting close to nightfall and Hancock decided to withdraw from the battlefield. A division from the Sixth Corps was said to be advancing to his aid. Morgan noted:

> It is not surprising that General Hancock was deeply stirred by the situation, for it was the first time he had felt the bitterness of defeat during the war. He had seen his troops fail in their attempts to carry the intrenched positions of the enemy; but he had never before had the mortification of seeing them driven, and his lines and guns taken, as on this occasion. . . . Never before had he seen his men fail to respond to the utmost. . . .[6]

In the 116th Pennsylvania, Capt. Garret Nowlen had been in command and was killed in the first heavy Confederate attack which had caved in the Union line. Capt. Samuel Taggart, who had left the United Presbyterian Theological Seminary in Allegheny, Pennsylvania, in the winter of 1863 to organize a company for the 116th, took over but not for long; he was killed a few minutes later. The men of the regiment recovered both bodies and carried them back to the

6. *Ibid.*, p. 598.

Petersburg lines on stretchers that night. Both would be sorely missed. When Nowlen had been home on furlough the preceding winter, he had told a fellow officer, Lt. Eugene Brady, "we will say farewell to our friends, for we will both be killed in the coming campaign."[7]

As a result of the outcome at Ream's Station, Gibbon published an order on August 30 depriving three regiments of his division from carrying colors. They had lost their flags at Ream's Station, and this order forbade replacement. Meade endorsed the order, the grounds being that unworthy conduct would thus be recognized. One of the three regiments singled out was the 164th New York of the Corcoran Legion, the others being the 36th Wisconsin and the 8th New York Heavy Artillery. There was no doubt that no one had looked good at Ream's Station. With the weight of the past six weeks on their backs, the men of the Second Corps were showing signs of coming unstitched. Maybe Gibbon thought a severe example would be salutary for all concerned. However, there was one dissenter. No one felt worse about the sorry day of August 25 than Hancock. But he did not feel like making an example of three regiments where others could be cited as well.

So Hancock wrote Grant a letter explaining the situation and advancing the idea that Gibbon had been too severe. Very calmly he told of the unparalleled success of the Second Corps, enumerating the trophies they had captured from Lee's army, the great days they had seen, and the casualties they had suffered. In the midst of all this he was able to inject a small dart at the lieutenant general:

> . . . it is, perhaps, known to you that this corps has never lost a color or a gun previous to this campaign, though oftener and more desperately engaged than any other corps in this army or, perhaps, in any other in the country.

Hancock had reminded his chief of the unparalleled sacrifices he had exacted from the Army of the Potomac. Then he turned directly to the three affected regiments:

7. Mulholland, *116th Pennsylvania*, p. 336.

I may say, however, that these regiments first appeared at the battle of Spotsylvania. At Cold Harbor the colonel of the Thirty-sixth Wisconsin—as gallant a soldier as ever lived—fell dead on the field, as did the colonel of the Eighth New York Heavy Artillery. The colonel of the One Hundred and Sixty-fourth fell mortally wounded beside his flag on the breastwork of the enemy. These regiments have since that action suffered severely, one of them, at least, having lost two commanding officers.

I respectfully request that these colors may be returned to them.[8]

A month later army command was able to get itself out of the corner in which it had been painted by Gibbon's action. There was a sizeable fight at a place called Hatcher's Run southwest of Petersburg. All three of the cited regiments did well here, or so it was said, and the colors were restored by Meade.

Even though they were now without identity, the Irish celebrated the third anniversary of the founding of the brigade on September 4. Col. Tom Smyth was present and so were as many of the other Irish officers of the Second Corps as possible.

There had been much indignation among the Irish and also among the "Americans" that Smyth was still a colonel although he had commanded brigades in action as far back as Gettysburg. Several times he had commanded Second Division, Second Corps, during the summer when Gibbon had been incapacitated. The ubiquitous Surgeon Lawrence Reynolds of the 63rd New York had even composed an acid poem about the curious indifference of the War Department to Smyth's merits. It went,

Though stars are falling very thick on many a curious spot,
And warriors rising very quick who never heard a shot
Still though you perilled limb and life
And many a fight went through
And laurels won in every strife

8. *Ibid.*, p. 305-6.

There's not a star for you, Tom Smyth
There's not a star for you.[9]

There were four more like verses, and though it is certain
that Stanton would never be moved by anything from the Irish
Brigade, Smyth had some other things in his favor as well. For
one thing, his home state of Delaware was properly angered;
for another he was well-regarded in the army. So on October
1 the news came that he had been promoted to brigadier
general. On October 17 he wrote in his diary:

> . . . In the evening the 63d New York Volunteers,
> "Irish Brigade" paid their respects and presented me
> with a horse. We had some pleasant speeches and
> songs. . . .[10]

In addition, there was an address, probably also crafted by
Reynolds:

> General, We come this day to express our delight at
> your well-earned promotion and to bear with us our
> offering of affection. We have purchased for you a
> powerful war-horse, and with our warmest wishes for
> your welfare and prosperity, we give him to his new
> master. Ours is indeed the widow's gift—the non-
> commissioned officers and privates of the 63d Regi-
> ment—Irish Brigade; we have not rank or wealth, and
> you, knowing it, will prize our offering as much as the
> most costly.
>
> We have no connection with you, as our Brigade
> is not now under your command, but the ties of
> affection still remain and will forever. We found in
> you a strict disciplinarian, but you had the singular
> felicity of combining mildness of manner with firm-
> ness of purpose, and we endured with pleasure every
> labor you commanded, for we knew your lofty mo-
> tives and your love for us.

9. David W. Maull, *The Life and Military Services of the Late Brigadier
   General Thomas A. Smyth* (Wilmington, Delaware: H. & E. F. James,
   printers, 1870), p. 22.
10. Smyth diary, October 17, 1864.

Brave, courteous and humane, you bring before our eyes a living portrait of the Irish hero of yore, and may the day come, when, after preserving the glorious Union of this land, you will lead us across the ocean to raise to independence and happiness our own dear, unforgotten Ireland. . . .[11]

Grant continued operations against the railroad arteries of Petersburg with what the Second Corps called the Boydton Plank Road expedition. By now, only the Southside Railroad from Lynchburg carried traffic into the city. With the advent of colder weather, all Union operations were slowing up. The strike was made with two divisions of the Second Corps under Hancock. The operation was unsuccessful because the Confederates were vigilant as usual and were able to take advantage of the local topography. The Second Corps fought well on this occasion and inflicted heavier losses than they received. However, ammunition supplies were exhausted in the action, and Hancock was forced to withdraw. For all practical purposes both armies went into winter quarters.

On October 30 the acting assistant provost marshal of New York City, Robert Nugent, was recommissioned a colonel of New York Volunteers and assigned to the 69th New York Volunteers.[12] Like the Phoenix, the Irish Brigade was about to rise again. Apparently, it was felt that only a well-known figure from the past like Nugent could restore the organization's former pride. The 63rd, 69th, and 88th were, of course, the heart of the reconstituted brigade. The 28th Massachusetts came back from the First Brigade, First Division, where it had served since June. The 116th Pennsylvania did not return. It had probably undergone such a change from colonel to drummer boy that all sense of the old association was lost. The 7th New York Heavy Artillery was added to give enough numbers to the brigade.[13]

In late November Tom Smyth wrote in his diary of taking dinner with Col. Matthew Murphy of the Corcoran Legion and Surgeon Reynolds. Two days later he had a visit from Colonel

11. Maull, *Life of Thomas A. Smyth*, p. 36.
12. *OR*, series 1, vol. 46, p. 450.
13. *Ibid.*, p. 524.

Cartwright of the 28th, and this must have been concerned with the affairs of the Fenian Brotherhood. Cartwright was soon to be mustered out at the expiration of his term of service. Perhaps he was to represent the Fenians of the Potomac Circle at the Fenian National Convention in Chicago. On November 27 Smyth visited the Irish Brigade and about a week later received another delegation of officers from the brigade.

By now the rains of winter were falling and the war came to a standstill. The first snow fell on December 10 and all hands were trying to make their huts as comfortable as possible. Christmas 1864 was observed in the usual fashion. Father Corby was gone from the brigade, but Father Ouellette was back to say Mass, assisted by Father Costney Egan who had remained with the Fifth Corps as division chaplain with the muster out of the 9th Massachusetts.

It is interesting to note that even during the hiatus of the brigade, their existence was recognized in some odd ways. Mulholland, who was temporarily in command of the Fourth Brigade, First Division, was one day directed to mount a diversionary assault against the Petersburg defences which fronted his sector. He selected a party from the excellent 148th Pennsylvania. Just as they were about to move out, Capt. Henry Price of the 116th Pennsylvania galloped up. He had heard of the planned assault at division headquarters and had ridden like a madman to take part in the affair. Mulholland did not want him to go, but, on Price's repeated insistence, he allowed himself to be persuaded. The young captain was killed on the Confederate entrenchment. Mulholland was deeply affected for he looked on Price as a son. The sequel was affecting also.

> After a few days a flag of truce went out, and the body of Captain Price recovered. We learned that on the morning after the assault, an Irishman of a Georgia regiment had seen the body and recognized by the number of the Regiment as a former member of the Irish Brigade. He had tenderly wrapped him in a blanket and carefully buried him.[14]

14. Mulholland, *116th Pennsylvania*, p. 328.

The experience of the 69th Pennsylvania was indicative of the manner in which the veteran organizations endured the winter:

> . . . the strength of the regiment was much increased by the return of of a number of convalescents and the receiving of a number of recruits. The strength of the regiment was raised to an aggregate of 173.[15]

In the brigade "Big John" Gleason, now a lieutenant colonel, commanded a 63rd New York consolidated into six companies. The 88th mustered only five under Lt. Col. Dennis Burke. Richard Moroney, now a major, led the 69th. Matthew Murphy, who had brought the Corcoran Legion down to the army back in May at the height of the Spotsylvania battles, was still in command and still a colonel. He was wounded on the first day the Legion was committed to battle, May 18, but returned to command from July 14 on. The most important change in the Second Corps was the retirement of Hancock from active duty on November 26. His Gettysburg wound had never completely healed, and the continuous strain of the siege had lowered his vitality. He was to go north and organize a corps composed entirely of veterans. His replacement was Maj. Gen. Andrew A. Humphreys.

In early February Union cavalry, supported by elements of the Second and Fifth Corps, moved out to strike at the Confederate supply route which passed up the Boydton Plank Road through Dinwiddie Court House. While Gregg's horsemen were out looking for enemy wagon trains, the Second Division, Second Corps under Tom Smyth dug in on the north side of Hatcher's Run. The Confederates attacked strongly, hitting the Corcoran Legion on Smyth's right. Wounded for the second time was Col. Matthew Murphy, replaced by James McIvor of the 170th New York. The assaults were beaten off and the Federals gained an excellent takeoff spot for operations against the Southside Railroad. In his report Tom Smyth spoke especially well of the 69th Pennsylvania which fought under the command of young Charles McAnally who had so earned the animus of Alexander Webb after Gettysburg. He

15. McDermott, *69th Pennsylvania*, p. 50.

was now a captain and led both the 69th and the men of the 106th who had re-enlisted.

There was little activity for the rest of February and the early part of March. On March 25 Lee made a tremendous assault on Fort Stedman, one of the key-points in the Union siege line. The Confederates had an initial success, and, for a time, a great disaster threatened. There was a Union rally and the attackers were driven out. It was realized that other parts of the Confederate defences must have been denuded to form so strong an attacking party, so the Union forces were promptly sent against the works that had defied them for so long. The front line of outposts were overrun and then defended against heavy counter attacks. Brig. Gen. Nelson Miles watched the forward progress of First Division, Second Corps, and wrote of their action,

> The fighting on the part of the troops of this command was marked by an unusual spirit of determination and enthusiasm; they fought in line of battle, without works, in as perfect order as if upon drill. . . . Colonel Nugent particularly distinguished himself by the gallant manner in which he fought his brigade, resisting and repulsing the several attacks of the enemy in the most stubborn manner. His conduct is worthy the highest praise.[16]

The beginning of the end was at hand. On March 29 the movements which culminated in the Battle of Five Forks began. As planned this was to be confined to the Fifth Corps and Sheridan's Cavalry Corps. They were to move against the Southside Railroad from the takeoff position that the Second Corps had gained in February. Lee reacted with his usual promptness, although his capabilities were greatly curtailed. A column of infantry and cavalry under George Pickett moved against the Union forces and a sanguinary battle was fought on March 31 that lasted until nightfall. At first the Confederates were successful, but in this success was laid the foundation for their later defeat. In following the rebuffed Union force, Pickett advanced too far. The Fifth Corps was rallied and two

16. *OR*, series 1, vol. 46, p. 197.

divisions were directed on the flanks of the enemy. After a hard fight, the Confederates suddenly caved in, and, for all practical purposes, Pickett's command ceased to exist. Almost five thousand prisoners were taken and the way to the Southside Railroad lay open. Now Petersburg must fall.

On April 2 the Army of the Potomac sprang at the iron lines which had defied its best efforts for so long. With the loss of one of its strongest formations, the Army of Northern Virginia was stretched too far. All around the perimeter Union infantry cracked through abatis and captured trenches and artillery positions. That night Lee pulled his weary army over to the north bank of the Appomattox river, and the war turned from a siege to a pursuit. Lee had to march his army westward along the north bank of the river to protect it from the Federals on the south bank. If he could strike the Richmond and Danville Railroad and move down it before the Federal command could collect itself, he might be able to withdraw into North Carolina for a junction with the army of Joseph E. Johnston. This all depended on his keeping the railroad open until his columns cleared the areas where the Union forces might be encountered. Somewhere to the west of Five Forks, Lee crossed the river, and on the night of April 5 he bivouacked at Amelia Court House on the railroad. Here the great Virginian received bad news.

Only five miles away to the south was trouble in the shape of the Second and Fifth Corps across the line of march of the Army of Northern Virginia. The route to North Carolina and Joe Johnston was closed. Many other commanders with so many pressing problems would have thrown in the towel, but Robert E. Lee was different. He turned his weary men westward, and the pursuit that could have but one result continued. The events of April 6 are best seen through the eyes of Walker:

> The day thus opened was one of the most memorable in the history of warfare. For many hours portions of the Union troops were marching in lines parallel to those taken by the Confederates, never at a great distance, often in plain sight, each column so intent upon reaching its goal as to be unwilling to lose the briefest time in collisions which could not affect the grand result. While thus portions of the Union

James P. McIvor
Colonel, 170th New York Volunteers
Brevetted brigadier and major general

army were stretched out in this great race, neck and neck with the hostile column, other corps, fastening upon the rear of the Confederates, maintained a running fight from morning until nearly night. To bring Lee's army to a stand was now the supreme object of every officer, high or low, and of every soldier in the ranks. So intense was the pursuit that men forgot fatigue; and wherever an opportunity to strike a blow was offered, either by change of direction or by some check to the movement of the Confederate columns, attacks were made upon the instant, without preparation, and without regard to opposing numbers. Doubtless a broken and demoralized army has more than once been thus pursued by victorious forces hanging upon its flanks and rear. That which makes the 6th of April altogether unique in war is that the Confederate army was not demoralized. Its valiant regiments and brigades were still full of the spirit which had animated them on a score of battle-fields; its seemingly wild and unregarding rush westward was no *sauve qui peut* of terror-stricken men, but was ordered throughout by the same sagacious, resolute commanders who had so often led that army to victory, and who, amid the appalling exertions and privations of this bitter retreat, still kept their hold unbroken on their faithful soldiery.[17]

Even in its death throes, Lee's army was going out with grace and courage attested to by its enemy.

On April 7 the Second Division, Second Corps encountered a strong body of the enemy at Farmville. Francis Barlow had recently returned to the Second Corps from a lingering sickness, and he had been placed in command of Second Division. He attacked with the reckless impetuosity for which he was noted and got a bloody nose. Tom Smyth was told to straighten matters out and rode out to the skirmish line, part of which had been captured. A Confederate sharpshooter put a bullet into his head from which the gallant Corkonian never recovered. He was removed to a rear area, conscious but partially para-

17. Walker, *History of the Second Corps*, p. 677.

385

lyzed from pressure on the spinal cord. Everything possible was done for him at the Second Corps Hospital. On April 8 he was placed in an ambulance and started for Burkesville Station. Twelve miles had to be negotiated over fairly rough terrain. About two miles from the destination, Smyth began to sink rapidly. Even now he was conscious of his condition and asked that the party stop, "that it was all up with him, and there was no use in his going any further." He was taken into the house of a Colonel Burke where he was shown every attention. His biographer gives a touching account of the end:

> At 4 o'clock on the morning of 9 April he died as he had lived—a hero; he was perfectly resigned to his fate. Conscious within a very short period before his decease, he talked calmly. Not a groan or complaint had escaped him. He showed no emotion but as a stoic endured the reflection that his once powerful, vigorous frame was but a complete wreck of humanity liable at any time to be engulfed. . . . He added, "Now Doctor, you know that I am no coward, and that I am not afraid to die," and throughout he spoke calmly about passing away.[18]

There is something particularly significant in Smyth's passing. He was the last general to be killed in the war, and he fell in the aura of victory, for on the day he died, Lee met with Grant in the McLean House to surrender.

Another of Doctor Reynolds' poems would serve as Smyth's epitaph:

> Though few were the days you were here,
> Your memory never shall fade;
> No man on earth is more dear,
> Than Tom Smyth of the Irish Brigade.[19]

Smyth had the same rank as Meagher and Corcoran, brigadier general of volunteers. However, he commanded a division in those periods in the summer of 1864 when Gibbon was on

18. Maull, *Life of Thomas A. Smyth*, p. 44.
19. *Ibid.*, p. 19.

leave or in command of the Second Corps. It may be said that he attained the highest rank of any of the combat officers connected with the Green Flag regiments. He was, indeed, the beau ideal of an Irish soldier.

On the last day, April 9, the Second Corps made contact with Longstreet's corps at 11 a.m. and prepared to attack. Fortunately, a local truce had been arranged. Confederate officers gave positive assurance the conditions of surrender were being worked out. All hands waited in an agony of suspense throughout the early afternoon. At 4 p.m. the glad news was announced that the fighting was over. At first there was a vast silence. George Meade himself announced the surrender to some of the the Second Corps regiments. McDermott of the 69th Pennsylvania said that the Second Division went mad with joy:

> It would be impossible to attempt to give a description of the scenes following the announcement of the surrender, but that scene will live forever in the hearts of the men who participated in that event. Our work was done; the Union was saved. . . .[20]

Robert Nugent wrote a more restrained report of those final days, but he could not hold back from summing up at the end a final word for the Irish Brigade:

> . . . it gives me sincere pleasure to add that the officers and men of my command behaved, under the most trying circumstances, with courage and fidelity, carrying out all orders to my complete satisfaction, they having now the proud satisfaction of seeing a stubborn enemy, whom they have combatted against for nearly four years, humbled, thereby adding their feeble mite to promote the life, prosperity, and independence of our nation.[21]

The armies which had fought all over Virginia, in Maryland, and in Pennsylvania vanished from the land as though swept by

20. McDermott, *69th Pennsylvania*, p. 51.
21. *OR*, series 1, vol. 46, p. 726.

the hand of a giant genie. There was a final review in Washington for the Army of the Potomac on May 23. For the Irish, it was farewell to the capital and they bedecked their caps with sprigs of boxwood as they had on a much colder day at Fredericksburg. It was then home to New York for the brigade and the legion where there was another parade on the Fourth of July. In the crowd there were many who had seen the troops march away in 1861 and 1862. Now they counted less than 700 men altogether, a thin reminder to the people of the Five Points slum of the cost of their citizenship.

Epilogue

What did it all mean in the end? There were immediate results of course. On the surface the Union was restored and State's Rights in the unvarnished sense vanished from the scene. The slaves were freed. The killing stopped. The cemeteries were filled and the hospitals were running over, but gradually, the smell of gunpowder went away. The veterans, North and South, turned to rebuilding their lives.

In Shakespeare's *Henry V*, the greatest of all military pageants, on the night before the Battle of Agincourt, the young King Henry, disguised, goes among his men to observe their feelings about the battle on the morrow. He has a conversation with three of his soldiers, and, since they do not know they are talking to their King, they are quite frank with their opinions. One of them speaks of the heavy burden of those who start wars and are thus responsible for the deaths and maimings of others. The thought of all pacifists is in his speech:

> . . . how can they charitably dispose of anything when
> blood is their argument?

Here Shakespeare is asking, "What good is war? Where is its positive value?" The manner in which some of the chief actors in the Civil War answered this is certainly uncompromising enough. "War," said Sherman, "is hell." "There was never a good war or a bad peace," spoke Grant. These opinions seem to rule out any positive results, since good does not flow from evil. But the war had its effects. Specifically, what were its effects on the Irish in America?

John Higham, a distinguished sociologist at the University of Michigan, says that the war was a watershed event for the Irish. Their sterling performance on the battlefield was rewarded by the disappearance of the ideas of nativism from public life. The slaughter of the Irish Brigade was related,

389

says Higham, to the end of the nativist persecution. This view confers nobility both on the men who walked through the fire and on the American public who rewarded the performance. Some of this is true. The burning of Catholic churches stopped after Appomattox and would never regain its former appeal. The next phase of the relationship was a wary and watchful stomaching of each other by both sides.

There were many small positive gestures in the veteran organizations that sprang up. There were some reprehensible events as well. As might be expected, one of the most reprehensible took place in the Massachusetts of the Elect. Patrick Guiney, colonel of the 9th Massachusetts and brigadier general by brevet, died on March 21, 1877, from complications of the dreadful wound he suffered in the Wilderness. He left a daughter, Louise, a minor poet and scholar. In later years she was almost destitute and had to petition the government for a position to support herself and her mother. A postmistress job was found for her at Auburndale near Boston. This charitable act so affronted the local goodfolk that they carried on an active campaign to buy stamps elsewhere so that the "papist" would not reap the advantage of the tiny commission.

Consider the Irish as the first "out-group" to encounter the solid white, Anglo-Saxon, Protestant citadel of America. Dr. William Burton, the author of *Melting Pot Soldiers* does not agree with this proposition, pointing to the Germans as more likely candidates for this confrontation. But the Irish arrived here speaking a form of English and were more culturally unlike the WASPs than the Germans because of their political and religious background. The Irish came into direct cultural conflict with the WASPs, and the Germans did not. The results of the WASP-Irish relationship set the pattern for all the other groups who arrived in the following decades from Italy, Poland, Greece, the Balkans, Hungary, and everywhere else.

The most important thing that the Irish gained was a degree of self-confidence and self-respect for themselves that would carry them on. The NO IRISH NEED APPLY signs did not come down overnight. No matter what the future held, they knew deep within themselves that the blood of the O'Kanes and Kellys, the Haggertys and Horgans had not been wasted. They were losers no longer. A new world opened, and they entered it.

Appendix A

Battle Honors of the Irish Regiments of the
Army of the Potomac
Enrollment and Casualties

9th Massachusetts
June 11, 1861 - June 21, 1864
Battle Honors: Hanover Court House, Mechanicsville, Gaines'
Mill, Malvern Hill, Fredericksburg, Chancellorsville,
Gettysburg, Mine Run, Wilderness, Spotsylvania,
Bethesda Church. Also present at Second Manassas,
Antietam, Totopotomoy, Cold Harbor.
Total Enrollment - 1,691
Killed or Mortally Wounded - 211
Wounded - 503
Died of Disease, Accident, or as Prisoners - 69
Missing - 24

28th Massachusetts
October 10, 1861 - July 15, 1865
Battle Honors: James Island, Second Manassas, Chantilly,
South Mountain, Antietam, Fredericksburg, Gettys-
burg, Wilderness, Spotsylvania, Totopotomoy, Cold
Harbor, Petersburg, Strawberry Plains, Deep Bottom,
Reams' Station, Hatcher's Run.
Total Enrollment - 1,778
Killed or Mortally Wounded - 250
Wounded - 597
Died of Disease, Accident, or in Prison - 51

37th New York
May 24, 1861 - June 22, 1863
Battle Honors: Williamsburg, Fair Oaks-Seven Pines, Glendale,
Second Manassas, Fredericksburg, Chancellorsville.

Total Enrollment - 795
Killed or Mortally Wounded - 74
Wounded - 186
Died of Disease, Accident, or in Prison - 38

63rd New York
August 15, 1861 - July 15, 1865

Battle Honors: Fair Oaks-Seven Pines, Gaines' Mill, Glendale, Malvern Hill, Antietam, Fredericksburg, Chancellorsville, Gettysburg, Bristoe Station, Wilderness, Spotsylvania, North Anna, Totopotomoy, Cold Harbor, Petersburg, Deep Bottom, Reams' Station, Sailor's Creek, Farmville.

Total Enrollment - 1,411
Killed or Mortally Wounded - 156
Wounded - 365
Died of Disease or Accident - 63
Died in Confederate Prisons - 30

69th New York
August 15, 1861 - July 15, 1865

Battle Honors: Same battle honors as the 63rd New York. The 69th lost the most men in action, killed or wounded, of any infantry regiment from the State of New York.

Total Enrollment - 1,513
Killed or Mortally Wounded - 259
Wounded - 535
Missing - 148
Died of Disease or Accident - 86
Died in Confederate Prisons - 56

88th New York
August 15, 1861 - July 15, 1865

Battle Honors: Same battle honors as the 63rd and 69th New York.

Total Enrollment - 1,352
Killed or Mortally Wounded - 151
Wounded - 381
Died of Disease or Accident - 54
Died in Confederate Prisons - 18

155th New York
November 19, 1862 - July 15, 1865

Battle Honors: Deserted House, Suffolk, Spotsylvania, Cold Harbor, Petersburg, Deep Bottom, Reams' Station, Boydton Plank Road, Hatcher's Run.

Total Enrollment - 830
Killed or Mortally Wounded - 114
Wounded - 325
Died of Disease or Accident -73

164th New York
November 19, 1862 - July 15, 1865

Battle Honors: Same battle honors as the 155th New York.

Total Enrollment - 928
Killed or Mortally Wounded - 116
Wounded - 321
Died of Disease or Accident - 69
Died in Confederate Prisons - 60

170th New York
November 19, 1862 - July 15, 1865

Battle Honors: Same battle honors as the 155th and 164th New York.

Total Enrollment - 1,002
Killed or Mortally Wounded - 129
Wounded - 352
Died of Disease or Accident - 50
Died in Confederate Prisons - 48

182nd New York
November 19, 1862 - July 15, 1865

Battle Honors: Same battle honors as the 155th, 164th, and 170th New York.

Total Enrollment - 712
Killed or Mortally Wounded - 73
Wounded - 260
Died of Disease or Accident - 53

69th Pennsylvania

September 17, 1861 - July 1, 1865

Battle Honors: Yorktown, Fair Oaks-Seven Pines, Savage
Station, Glendale, Chantilly, Antietam, Fredericks-
burg, Gettysburg, Mine Run, Wilderness, Spotsylvania,
Cold Harbor, Petersburg, Weldon Railroad, Deep
Bottom, Reams' Station, Boydton Plank Road,
Dabney's Mills, Hatcher's Run.

Total Enrollment - 1,715
Killed or Mortally Wounded - 178
Wounded - 460
Died of Disease or Accident - 81
Died In Confederate Prisons - 29

116th Pennsylvania

August 15, 1862 - July 1, 1865

Battle Honors: Fredericksburg, Chancellorsville, Gettysburg,
Bristoe Station, Wilderness, Po River, Spotsylvania,
Totopotomoy, Cold Harbor, Petersburg, William's
Farm, Deep Bottom, Reams' Station, White Oak Road,
Sutherland Station.

Total Enrollment - 1,661
Killed or Mortally Wounded - 145
Wounded - 383
Died of Disease or Accident - 61
Died in Confederate Prisons - 28

APPENDIX B

General Officers Associated with the Irish Regiments

Michael Corcoran, born in 1827 at Carrowkeel, County Sligo, Ireland, emigrated to the United States in 1849. He enlisted as a private in the 69th New York State Militia in 1851, and was promoted to colonel in 1859. He was commissioned colonel in Federal service April 29, 1861. Captured at First Manassas on July 21, 1861, Corcoran was exchanged August 15, 1862, and promoted to brigadier general, U.S. Volunteers, retroactive to July 21, 1861. He recruited the Corcoran Legion: 155th, 164th, 170th, and 182nd New York Volunteers. Corcoran died on December 22, 1863, of injuries sustained from a fall from his horse, and is buried in Calvary Cemetery, New York.

Thomas Francis Meagher, born August 23, 1833, at Waterford, Ireland, emigrated to the United States in 1852. He married Elizabeth Townsend of New York in 1856. Meagher served as acting captain, 69th New York State Militia at First Manassas. He organized the Irish Brigade in New York City in the autumn of 1861. Commissioned brigadier general, U.S. Volunteers on February 3, 1862, he resigned May 14, 1863, when his brigade was decimated and ineffective, but his resignation was canceled December 23, 1863. He resigned May 15, 1865. Appointed secretary of the Territory of Montana by President Andrew Johnson, Meagher was lost overboard on July 1, 1867, from a steamboat sailing up the Missouri River and his body was never recovered.

Thomas A. Smyth, born December 25, 1832, in Ballyhooly, County Cork, Ireland, emigrated to the United States in August 1854. He moved to Wilmington, Delaware, in 1858, in which year he married Miss Amanda Pounder of that city. At the outbreak of the war he raised a company for three-months service which was accepted as Company H of the 24th Pennsylvania Volunteers. After muster out in early August 1861, he

395

was chosen major of the 1st Delaware on October 2, 1861, became lieutenant colonel of this regiment on December 18, 1862, and colonel on February 7, 1863. He commanded Second Brigade, Third Division, Second Corps at Gettysburg. After re-enlistment of his regiment in early 1864, he became commander of the Irish Brigade on March 27, 1864, and held the command until May 17, 1864, on the return of Col. Richard Byrnes who held a prior commission. Smyth returned to command of Third Brigade, Second Division, Second Corps. On October 1, 1864, Smyth was commissioned brigadier general, U.S. Volunteers. Mortally wounded on April 7, 1865, at Farmville, Virginia, Smyth died on April 9, 1865. He was brevetted major general U.S. Volunteers for his service at Farmville. Smyth is buried in Brandywine Cemetery, Wilmington, Delaware.

Robert Nugent, born July 27, 1824, at Kilkeel, County Down, was lieutenant colonel of the 69th New York State Militia. He was not present at First Manassas, having fallen from his horse, and having been sent back to New York. He became colonel of the 69th New York Volunteers and was present on the Peninsula, at Antietam, and at Fredericksburg where he received a serious wound in the groin. He was acting assistant provost marshal of New York City for eighteen months and returned to the command of the 69th New York Volunteers and the Irish Brigade in October 1864, continuing to the end of the war. He held a permanent commission of captain in the Regular Army dating from August 5, 1861, and retired from the Regular Army in 1879. He was brevetted brigadier general of U.S. Volunteers on March 13, 1865, and died June 20, 1901. He is buried in Cypress Hills Cemetery, Brooklyn, New York.

Appendix C

Colonels of the Irish Regiments

9th Massachusetts

Thomas Cass: Age 39 at muster-in on June 11, 1861. Wounded at Battle of Malvern Hill, July 1, 1862. Died of wounds July 12, 1862.

Patrick Robert Guiney: Age 26 at muster-in on June 11, 1861. Promoted to major October 26, 1861, lieutenant colonel January 28, 1862, colonel July 26, 1862. Wounded and lost an eye at the Wilderness, May 5, 1864. Brevetted brigadier general. Mustered out June 21, 1864. Died March 21, 1877, and buried in Holyhood Cemetery, Brookline, Massachusetts.

28th Massachusetts

William Monteith: Mustered in as colonel on December 13, 1861. Placed under arrest on May 20, 1862, and discharged from service on August 12, 1862.

Richard Byrnes: Age 28, commissioned colonel on September 20, 1862. Commanded Irish Brigade from May 17, 1862, until June 3, 1862. Mortally wounded at Cold Harbor June 3, 1864. Died at Washington June 12, 1864.

37th New York

John McCunn: Mustered in as colonel on June 5, 1861. Dismissed from service on August 14, 1861.

Samuel Hayman: United States Military Academy Class of 1842. Mustered in as colonel on September 28, 1861. Mustered out with regiment on June 22, 1863. Commissioned major, U.S. Army on June 21, 1863. Brevet brigadier general, U.S. Volunteers for Chancellorsville, Wilderness, and Fair Oaks.

63rd New York

John Burke: Mustered in as colonel on February 6, 1862. Wounded at Malvern Hill. Dismissed October 1862.

69th New York

Robert Nugent: Mustered in as colonel on November 1, 1861. Mustered out of U.S. Volunteer service November 28, 1863. Mustered in as colonel of the 69th New York October 30, 1864. Wounded at Fredericksburg. Brevetted brigadier general U.S. Volunteers for war service. Continued in Regular Army after the war until 1879. Died 1901.

88th New York

Patrick Kelly: Mustered in as colonel October 20, 1862. Commanded Irish Brigade at Gettysburg and Petersburg. Killed at Petersburg June 16, 1864.

155th New York

William McEvily: Age 24, commissioned colonel on December 5, 1862, discharged November 3, 1863.

164th New York

John E. McMahon: Age 28, commissioned colonel November 17, 1862. Died of consumption March 11, 1863. Buried in St. Agnes Cemetery, Utica, New York.
James P. McMahon: Age 27, commissioned colonel March 23, 1863. Killed at Cold Harbor June 3, 1864. Buried in St. Agnes Cemetery, Utica, New York.

170th New York

James P. McIvor: Age 27, mustered in as colonel on January 5, 1863. Brevetted brigadier general and major general for Appomattox Campaign. Mustered out with regiment on July 15, 1865.

182nd New York

Matthew Murphy: Age 22, mustered in as colonel November 17, 1862. Wounded at Spotsylvania May 18, 1864. Wounded at Hatcher's Run February 5, 1865. Died at Field Hospital, City Point, Virginia, April 16, 1865.

69th Pennsylvania

Joshua Owen: Age 40, mustered in as colonel on August 18, 1861. Promoted to brigadier general November 29, 1862. Mustered out July 18, 1864. Died 1887.

Dennis O'Kane: Age 41, mustered in as colonel on December 1, 1862. Killed in action July 3, 1863, at Gettysburg. Buried in Cathedral Cemetery, Philadelphia, Pennsylvania.

116th Pennsylvania

Dennis Heenan: Age 45, mustered in as colonel about August 15, 1862. Wounded at Fredericksburg, December 13, 1862, and discharged on January 26, 1863. Died July 4, 1872, and buried in Cathedral Cemetery, Philadelphia, Pennsylvania.

St. Clair Mulholland: Age 25, mustered in as colonel on May 3, 1864. Wounded at Fredericksburg, Wilderness, Po River, and Totopotomoy Creek. Brevetted major general for Chancellorsville. Mustered out July 15, 1865. Awarded Medal of Honor for Chancellorsville. Died February 17, 1910, and buried in Cathedral Cemetery, Philadelphia.

Appendix D

The Relics of the Irish Regiments

On the Army List of the United States of America, there are still two organizations which trace their lineage back to the Irish regiments in the Army of the Potomac. One is the 1st Battalion, 182nd Infantry Regiment, Massachusetts National Guard, headquartered in Boston, which descends from the 9th Massachusetts. The 9th kept its name and number until the Federalization of the National Guard in 1917. At that time it became the 101st Infantry Regiment, an element in the 26th (Yankee) Division which fought bravely and well in both World Wars in the European Theater of Operations. The 101st was amalgamated with other elements of the Massachusetts National Guard. Presently, its descendant is the 1st Battalion, 182nd Infantry Regiment.

The other regiment is the descendant of the Fighting 69th. In 1994 it was switched from infantry to artillery and became the 69th Air Defence Regiment. It may return to being an infantry or mechanized infantry regiment when the Defence budget is straightened out. The 69th was a regiment of the New York State Militia until 1917, when it became the 165th Infantry and served in the 42nd (Rainbow) Division in World War I in Europe. It stayed with that designation through World War II, serving in the 27th Division in the South Pacific Theater. When the Army adopted the Combat Arms Regimental System of classifying organizations in 1957, the 165th again became the 69th. It is still a New York City based organization and maintains a regimental museum at its armory on Lexington Avenue. For many years it led the St. Patrick's Day Parade on Fifth Avenue.

Appendix E

"The Irish Division"

If Secretary of War Stanton had permitted the formation of an Irish Division in 1862, it would have embraced the twelve regiments below which endured as follows:

Regiment	Enrollment	Killed and Mortally Wounded	Wounded	Died from Disease
9th MA	1,691	211	503	69
28th MA	1,778	250	597	51
37th NY	795	74	186	38
63rd NY	1,411	156	365	63
69th NY	1,513	259	535	86
88th NY	1,352	151	381	54
155th NY	830	114	325	73
164th NY	928	116	329	69
170th NY	1,002	129	352	50
182nd NY	712	73	260	53
69th PA	1,715	178	460	81
116th PA	1,661	145	383	61
Total	15,388	1,856	4,668	748

One will note that this table does not contain a column labelled "Missing." The War Department continued the unjust system of denying that most of those listed as missing were really dead. Although disagreeing with this dictum, it is followed.

APPENDIX F

Letters Home

My friend Ben Maryniak of the Buffalo Civil War Round Table has told me of the letters home of Sgt. George Tipping who started out in the 155th New York, and then found himself, to his discomfiture, in the 164th, commanded, first, by Col. John E. McMahon, and, after that worthy's death through consumption, by his brother, Col. James P. McMahon, who was killed at Cold Harbor. Sergeant Tipping was a blacksmith before enlisting in the army. He was married and the father of three girls and a boy. He was mustered into the 155th New York on November 19, 1862. His youngest daughter, Margaret, was born on April 11, 1863. Some excerpts from his letters follow:

December 23, 1863:
. . . Well, Catherine, it is drawing nigh Christmas. I only wish to God I was home with you this Christmas, but I hope in God before another one is past that I will be home, but I have got to weather it out now and I hope I will. Catherine, keep up courage. Everything will be all right yet. The time is coming fast but not too fast for me. . . . I will conclude this time by sending my love to Mary, Margaret, Ann, Mary Ann, Edward George.

October 10, 1864:
. . . Well, Catherine, we have a great time out on picket, and that is every day now since the troops have been drawn away from here. We make a bargain in the morning before daylight not to fire at one another all day. We agree to it and after breakfast we may walk any place inside our lines and chat with them all day long. They sing out the first thing in the morning to

stop firing until we get breakfast. "Say, Yank, stop firing." "Very well. Johnnie." "All day?" "Yes, all day, Yank." Then there is a white rag hung out on a pole with the rebs and us, and, after sundown they will sing out, "Get into your holes, Yanks, we are going to fire," and the firing is kept up all night until morning again. So much for the rebs.

I see in your letter there are some exciting times in Buffalo and elsewhere. I am very glad you got your wood. I am also glad that they continue giving you your just reward from the City. I thought it was discontinued on account of your not saying anything about it for some time past. I am in good health, thank God, as ever in my life. Plenty of exercise every day and also plenty to eat, which I very much appreciate. . . . I will be on picket tonight and we will have another chat with the rebs for six hours more. . . . Hoping to see you once more, I remain your affectionate husband. George.

Tipping was killed in action at Hatcher's Run seventeen days after he wrote the above letter.

Appendix G

The Brave Colonel James P. McMahon
at Cold Harbor

Would you like to have me tell you of how the Young Colonel
    died?
God grant my memory may not fail nor that my tongue be tied.
Twas the second weary night of that hot and bloody June,
We marched along the pickets, we camped beneath the moon.
Behind us sixty miles of death, Virginia thickets lay,
Before us was Cold Harbor, the hell to come next day.
Sitting in the tent door in the silvery dew,
We talked of old Buffalo and of the girls we knew.
Spread o'er the silent fields below, the mist lay like a pond.
We seemed to see the long dark streets, and the white lake
    beyond.
We charged at noon. The Colonel led green Erin's old Brigade.
While Longstreet's blazing cannon from behind their breast-
    works played.
The Colonel led through fire and smoke. His sword did wave
    and shine.
And still the brave sound of his voice drew on our struggling
    line.
As o'er the surf at Wicklow I've heard the seagull cry.
His voice did rise above the storm and sounded clear and high.
Then all at once our colors sank, I saw them reel and nod
And the colonel sprang and caught them before they touched
    the sod.
Another leap and with a shout, the Rebs do mind it well
He stood alone upon their works, waved the old Flag, and fell!
We left him at Cold Harbor. The spot was bleak and bare,
I hate to think that I'm at home and he's still lying there.
I know his sleep will not be sweet nor his gallant spirit still,
Till we lay him alone in the friendly dust of yonder slanting
    hill.

Where from the town he loved so well will come the daily hum,
And the lake's loud roar upon the beach when quiet nights shall
  come.
Well might his city rear his tomb in marble words to tell
How the bravest of her blood was shed when young McMahon
  fell!

The poem above is a fragment of that written by a member of the 8th New York Heavy Artillery, and was provided to the Buffalo Civil War Round Table by Mike McFarland of Rochester, New York. It was passed down verbally in his family. Since the remains of James McMahon were returned to Buffalo after the war, the sentiments regarding his reburial support the claim that the poem is from shortly after the conclusion of the war. Although James and John McMahon rested for many years in Holy Cross Cemetery, Lackawanna, New York, John's widow had the bodies moved to St. Agnes Cemetery in Utica, New York, where they were reinterred on Halloween 1905. My deep appreciation to all for allowing the poem to be used.

APPENDIX H

The Notre Dame Connection

Just about everyone knows that the athletic teams of the University of Notre Dame, located in South Bend, Indiana, are called the Fighting Irish. Most think this is because the university is run by a teaching order of the Roman Catholic Church. Ergo, it should have an Irish flavor about it, since Irish and Catholic are synonymous, are they not? Well not exactly. The Congregation of the Holy Cross was founded in France and the founder of Notre Dame was Father Edward Sorin, French-born and not exactly enamored of the Irish. He regarded them as not amenable to discipline, even though there were several Irish-born priests in the original foundation.

Seven priests of the faculty went off to serve as chaplains in the Union army during the Civil War. As we have seen, Fathers Corby and Dillon served with Meagher's and Corcoran's formations. After his army service, Father Corby served two terms as president of the university. He and the other former army chaplains formed a GAR post there that was somewhat unique, since there were no lay members. Early on he began to collect artifacts of the Irish Brigade and some are now on display in the school's library. Meagher's sword and spurs were placed in the custody of the university on March 4, 1914, to join the sword of James Shields and several of the colors of the New York regiments. At Father Corby's funeral, his pallbearers were not priests, as is usually the case, but Union army veterans. His coffin was covered with the American and Irish Brigade flags.

General St. Clair Mulholland conceived the idea of erecting a monument to Father Corby on the spot at Gettysburg where he had given general absolution to the brigade. This worthwhile project had the support of all the Sodalities of Philadelphia and the statue was unveiled in 1910, a few months after the death of Mulholland. A similar statue was placed on the

Notre Dame campus some decades later. It is usually known to Notre Dame students as "Fair Catch Corby" since the priest's right arm is extended upward as if signalling for a fair catch.

This association of Fathers Corby and Dillon undoubtedly led to the Notre Dame teams being called the "Fighting Irish," not due to the automatic linking of "Irish" and "Catholic." In the early days of Notre Dame football there were a host of non-Irish names: Rockne, Dorais, Eichenlaub, Harper, Gipp, Mohardt. Even the Four Horsemen only mustered one Irishman. In fact, so little was the school known when the team came east to play Army in 1913, that the Army coach told the New York press that the visitors were from "somewhere in Illinois." In 1931 when I first began to follow Notre Dame football, the backfield was Jaskwich, Sheeketski, Schwartz, and Banas. Not exactly a group of Gaelic-sounding names. So the start of the Notre Dame legend must come from the memory of men who played a much more serious game than football, the Irish regiments of the Civil War.

BIBLIOGRAPHY

Manuscripts

For anyone engaged in research on the Irish regiments, the Judge Charles Patrick Daly Collection of letters in the New York Public Library is a treasure trove of information about the early steps in organizing the 69th New York State Militia for the three-months service, and the formation of the Irish Brigade. Judge Daly was born in New York City in 1816, two years after his parents had emigrated from Ireland. From humble beginnings he rose to be a leader in many fields: a patron of the arts, philanthropist, Shakespearean scholar, and eminent jurist. Columbia University conferred the degree of Doctor of Laws on him in 1860 and engaged him, a man of almost no formal education, to lecture in the School of Law.

Judge Daly's active service on the bench is one of the longest in American jurisprudence. He was known as an incorruptible judge who fought Boss Tweed and his cohorts with vigor and success. A Tammany man in his early career, Daly became a Union Democrat during the Civil War and belonged to the reform element of the Democratic Party after the war.

Two minority groups were indebted to Judge Daly for his efforts—the Irish and the Jews. Author of *The History Of The Jews In North America*, he contributed generously to Jewish charities and was instrumental in founding the Jewish Orphans Home in the city.

The other manuscript material which is brought to light for the first time is the diary of Brig. Gen. Thomas A. Smyth. This covers the time period from January 1864 until he was fatally wounded at the Battle of Farmville on March 7, 1865, the last Union general officer to die in the war. This diary was

411

entrusted to me in 1965 by the grandson of General Smyth, Mr. Thomas Carswell of Chestertown, Maryland. General Smyth was an active and successful soldier and brought the Irish Brigade back from the verge of extinction to play a valiant part in the great Second Corps surge under Hancock in 1864.

Anthony McDermott, the adjutant of the 69th Pennsylvania during the Civil War, wrote the history of the regiment. He also corresponded with John Bachelder in the period of 1886-1889. These letters are in the New Hampshire Historical Society. I have drawn on the letter of June 2, 1886.

Newspapers

The availability on microfilm of the *New York Times* as well as its easy accessibility in the library of my alma mater, Widener University, has been a godsend to me. In addition, the *Irish American*, a newspaper published at that time, is a great source of information, although its over-enthusiasm must be filtered out in some cases. The Philadelphia newspapers are also available in various libraries and have been extremely useful. The National Archives have been an aid, especially for analysis of pension claims which throw much light on the everyday life of the people of the era. Several correspondents, Michael Kane, of Pittsburgh, and William Rose, the creator of the 69th Pennsylvania Skirmishers, have done a magnificent public service in bringing back the memories of this great fighting unit. Both have been of great help in furnishing material that was moldering in the dusty archives of time. Ben Maryniak of Buffalo, New York, has also been of great assistance in running down material concerning the 155th New York, the Western Irish in the Corcoran Legion.

Government Publications

Eighth Census of the United States, 1860, Population, Washington, 1864.

New York State Adjutant General's Reports, #22-1900, #27-1901, #28-1902, #31-1901, #39-1904, #40-1904, #41-1905, #42-1905.

Supreme Court of Pennsylvania. May Term, 1891. No's 20, 30. Middle District. Appeal of the Gettysburg Battlefield Memorial Association from the Decree of the Court of Common Pleas of Adams County, Paper Book of Appellants.

United States War Department, *The War of the Rebellion: A Compilation of the Official Records of the Union and Confederate Armies*. 70 vols. in 128 parts. Washington, D.C.: Government Printing Office, 1880-1901.

Books

Andrews, J. Cutler. *The North Reports the Civil War*. Pittsburgh: University of Pittsburgh Press, 1955.

Alexander, E. P. *Military Memoirs of a Confederate: A Critical Narrative*. New York: Charles Scribner's Sons, 1907.

Athearn, Robert G. *Thomas Francis Meagher: An Irish Revolutionary in America*. Boulder: University of Colorado Press, 1949.

Ballard, Colin. *The Military Genius of Abraham Lincoln: An Essay by Brigadier-General Colin R. Ballard*. London: Oxford University Press, 1926. Reprint. Cleveland: World Publishing Company, 1952.

Banes, Charles H. *History of the Philadelphia Brigade: Sixty-ninth, Seventy-first, Seventy-second, and One hundred and sixth Pennsylvania Volunteers*. Philadelphia: J. B. Lippincott, 1876.

Bates, Samuel P. *History of the Pennsylvania Volunteers, 1861-5*. 5 vols. Harrisburg, Pennsylvania: B. Singerly, State Printer, 1869-1871.

———— *Martial Deeds of Pennsylvania*. Philadelphia: T. H. Davis and Company, 1875.

Boatner, Mark M. *The Civil War Dictionary*. New York: D. McKay Company, 1959.

Burton, W. L. *Melting Pot Soldiers*. Ames: Iowa State University Press, 1988.

Catton, Bruce. *The Centennial History of the Civil War*. 3 vols. Garden City, New York: Doubleday and Company, 1961-65.

————— *Glory Road.* Garden City, New York: Doubleday and Company, 1952.

————— *Grant Takes Command.* Boston: Little, Brown, and Company, 1968.

————— *Mr. Lincoln's Army.* Garden City, New York: Doubleday and Company, 1951.

————— *A Stillness at Appomattox.* Garden City, New York: Doubleday and Company, 1953.

Campbell, J. H. *History of the Friendly Sons of St. Patrick.* Philadelphia: The Hibernian Society, 1892.

Cavanagh, Michael. *Memoirs of General Thomas Francis Meagher: Comprising the Leading Events of His Career.* Worcester, Massachusetts: The Messenger Press, 1892.

Coddington, Edwin B. *The Gettysburg Campaign: A Study in Command.* New York: Charles Scribner's Sons, 1968.

Cole, W., ed. *Folk Songs of England, Ireland, Scotland, and Wales.* Garden City, New York: Doubleday and Company, 1961.

Commager, Henry S., ed. *The Blue and the Gray: The Story of the Civil War as told by Participants.* Indianapolis: Bobbs-Merrill, 1950.

Conyngham, David P. *The Irish Brigade and Its Campaigns: With Some Account of the Corcoran Legion, and Sketches of the Principal Officers.* New York: William McSorley and Company, 1867.

Corby, William. *Memoirs of Chaplain Life.* Notre Dame, Indiana: Scholastic Press, 1894.

Cunliffe, Marcus. *The Royal Irish Fusiliers.* London: Oxford University Press, 1950.

Daly, Maria Lydig. *Diary of a Union Lady, 1861-1865.* Edited by Harold Hammond. New York: Funk & Wagnalls, 1962.

Dooley, John. *John Dooley, Confederate Soldier, His War Journal.* Edited by Joseph T. Durkin. Washington, D.C.: Georgetown University Press, 1945.

Dowdey, Clifford. *The Seven Days: The Emergence of Lee.* Boston: Little, Brown and Company, 1964.

————— *Lee's Last Campaign: The Story of Lee and His Men Against Grant, 1864.* Boston: Little, Brown and Company, 1960.

Emerson, Ralph W. *The Works of Ralph Waldo Emerson.* Boston: Black's Reader Service Company, 1947.

414

Foote, Shelby. *The Civil War: A Narrative.* 3 vols. New York: Random House, 1958-74.

Fox, William F. *Regimental Losses in the American Civil War, 1861-1865.* Albany, New York: Albany Publishing Company, 1889.

Freeman, Douglas S. *R. E. Lee: A Biography.* 4 vols. New York: Charles Scribner's Sons, 1934-35.

———— *Lee's Lieutenants: A Study in Command.* 3 vols. New York: Charles Scribner's Sons, 1942-44.

Galwey, Thomas F. *The Valiant Hours.* Harrisburg, Pennsylvania: Stackpole Company, 1961.

Grant, Ulysses S. *Personal Memoirs of U. S. Grant.* Edited by E. B. Long. Cleveland: World Publishing Company, 1952.

Guthrie, Sir Tyrone. *Shakespeare: Ten Great Plays.* New York: Golden Press, 1962.

Hanna, Charles. *The Scotch Irish.* Boston: C. P. Putnam, 1902.

Haskell, Frank A. *The Battle of Gettysburg.* Harvard Classics. New York: P. F. Collier and Company, 1910.

Hassler, Warren W. *General George B. McClellan: Shield of the Union.* Baton Rouge: Louisiana State University Press, 1957.

Headley, Phineas C. *Massachusetts in the Rebellion: A Record of the Historical Position of the Commonwealth, and the Services of the Leading Statesmen, the Military, the Colleges, and the People, in the Civil War of 1861-65.* Boston: Walker, Fuller and Company, 1866.

Hendrick, Burton. *Lincoln's War Cabinet.* Boston: Little, Brown and Company, 1946.

Hitchcock, Frederick L. *War From The Inside; or, Personal Experiences, Impressions, and Reminiscences of one of the "Boys" in the War of the Rebellion.* Philadelphia: J. B. Lippincott Company, 1904.

Hood, John Bell. *Advance and Retreat: Personal Experiences in the United States and Confederate States Armies.* Philadelphia: Press of Burke and McFetridge, 1880.

Humphries, Andrew A. *The Virginia Campaign of '64 and '65: The Army of the Potomac and the Army of the James.* New York: Charles Scribner's Sons, 1883.

Hyde, Thomas W. *Following the Greek Cross; or, Memories of the Sixth Army Corps.* Boston: Houghton, Mifflin and Company, 1894.

Johnson, Robert U. and Clarence C. Buel, eds. *Battles and Leaders of the Civil War.* New York: The Century Company, 1887-88.

Jones, J. D. *A Rebel War Clerk's Diary at the Confederate States Capital.* Philadelphia: J. B. Lippincott and Company, 1866. Reprint. Edited by Howard Swiggett. 2 vols. New York: n.p., 1935.

Jones, Paul. *The Irish Brigade.* Washington, D. C.: Robert Luce, 1969.

Lee, Robert E. *The Wartime Papers of Robert E. Lee.* Edited by Clifford Dowdey and Louis H. Manarin. Boston: Little, Brown and Company, 1961.

Leech, Margaret. *Reveille in Washington, 1860-1865.* New York: Harper and Brothers, 1941.

Lewis, Lloyd. *Sherman: Fighting Prophet.* New York: Harcourt, Brace and Company, 1932.

Lincoln, Abraham. *The Collected Works of Abraham Lincoln.* Edited by Roy P. Basler. 9 vols. New Brunswick, New Jersey: Rutgers University Press, 1953-55.

Livermore, Thomas L. *Numbers and Losses in the Civil War in America, 1861-65.* Boston: Houghton, Mifflin and Company, 1901.

Lonn, Ella. *Foreigners in the Union Army and Navy.* Baton Rouge: Louisiana State University Press, 1952.

Longstreet, James. *From Manassas to Appomattox: Memoirs of the Civil War in America.* Philadelphia: J. B. Lippincott Company, 1896.

McClellan, George B. *McClellan's Own Story: The War for the Union, the Soldiers Who Fought it, the Civilians Who Directed it and His Relations to it and to them.* New York: C. L. Webster and Company, 1887.

McDermott, Anthony. *A Brief History of the 69th Regiment Pennsylvania Veteran Volunteers, from its formation until final muster out of the United States service.* Philadelphia: D. J. Gallagher and Company, 1889.

MacNamara, Daniel G. *The History of the Ninth Regiment, Massachusetts Volunteer Infantry, Second Brigade, First Division, Fifth Army Corps, Army of the Potomac, June, 1861-June, 1864.* Boston: E. B. Stillings and Company, Printers, 1899.

Maull, David W. *The Life and Military Services of the Late Brigadier General Thomas A. Smyth.* Wilmington, Delaware: H. & E. F. James, Printers, 1870.

Meade, George G. *With Meade at Gettysburg.* Philadelphia: John C. Winston Company, 1930.

Muffly, J. W. *The Story of Our Regiment: A History of the 148th Pennsylvania Volunteers.* Des Moines, Iowa: Kenyon Printing and Manufacturing Company, 1904.

Mulholland, St. Clair A. *The Story of the 116th Regiment Pennsylvania Volunteers in the War of the Rebellion, the Record of a Gallant Campaign.* Philadelphia: F. McManus, Jr. and Company, Printers, 1903.

Murray, Thomas H. *History of the Ninth Regiment, Connecticut Volunteer Infantry, "The Irish Regiment," in the War of the Rebellion, 1861-65.* New Haven, Connecticut: Price, Lee and Adkins, 1903.

Nevins, Allan. *The War for the Union.* 4 vols. New York: Charles Scribner's Sons, 1959-71.

New York Monuments Commission for the Battlefields of Gettysburg and Chattanooga. *Final Report on the Battlefield of Gettysburg.* Edited by William F. Fox. 3 vols. Albany, New York: J. B. Lyon Company, Printers, 1900.

Nye, Wilbur S. *Here Come the Rebels.* Baton Rouge: Louisiana State University Press, 1965.

Osborne, William H. *The History of the Twenty-ninth Regiment of Massachusetts Volunteer Infantry, in the Late War of the Rebellion.* Boston: Albert J. Wright, Printer, 1887.

Palfrey, Francis W. *The Antietam and Fredericksburg.* New York: Charles Scribner's Sons, 1882.

Paris, Comte de. *History of the Civil War in America.* 4 vols. Philadelphia: Porter and Coates, 1875-1888.

Pennsylvania Gettysburg Battlefield Commission. *Pennsylvania at Gettysburg: Ceremonies at the Dedication of the Monuments Erected by the Commonwealth of Pennsylvania to Mark the Positions of the Pennsylvania Commands Engaged in the Battle.* Edited by John P. Nicholson. 2 vols. Harrisburg, Pennsylvania: E. K. Meyers, State Printer, 1893. Reprint. Harrisburg, Pennsylvania: W. S. Ray, State Printer, 1904.

Pennypacker, Isaac. *General Meade.* New York: D. Appleton and Company, 1901.

Philadelphia Brigade Association. *Reply of the Philadelphia Brigade Association to the Foolish and Absurd Narrative of Lt. Frank A. Haskell, which appears to be endorsed by the Military Order of the Loyal Legion Commandery of Massachusetts and the Wisconsin History Commission.* Philadelphia: Bowers Printing Company, 1910.

Pickett, George E. *Soldier of the South: General Pickett's War Letters to his Wife.* Edited by Arthur C. Inman. Boston: Houghton Mifflin Company, 1928.

Porter, Horace. *Campaigning With Grant.* New York: The Century Company, 1897.

Potter, George. *To The Golden Door.* Boston: Little, Brown and Company, 1960.

Priest, J. Michael. *Antietam: The Soldiers' Battle.* Shippensburg, Pennsylvania: White Mane Press, 1989.

Russell, William H. *My Diary North and South.* 2 vols. London: Bradbury and Evans, 1863.

Roche, J. J. *Life and Poems of John Boyle O'Reilly.* Boston: n.p., 1888.

Safire, William. *Freedom.* New York: Doubleday and Company, 1987.

Sandburg, Carl. *Abraham Lincoln: The War Years.* 4 vols. New York: Harcourt, Brace and Company, 1939.

Sears, Stephen W. *Landscape Turned Red: The Battle of Antietam.* New York: Ticknor & Fields, 1983.

———— *George B. McClellan: The Young Napoleon.* New York: Ticknor & Fields, 1988.

Shannon, Fred A. *The Organization and Administration of the Union Army, 1861-1865.* 2 vols. Cleveland: Arthur H. Clark Company, 1928.

Smith, J. L. *History of the Corn Exchange Regiment 118th Pennsylvania Volunteers, From Their First Engagement at Antietam to Appomattox.* Philadelphia: J. L. Smith, 1888.

Stewart, George. *Pickett's Charge: A Microhistory of the Final Attack at Gettysburg, July 3, 1863.* Boston: Houghton Mifflin Company, 1959.

Stewart, Robert L. *History of the One Hundred and Fortieth Regiment, Pennsylvania Volunteers.* Philadelphia: Printed by the Franklin Bindery, 1912.

Swinton, William. *Campaigns of the Army of the Potomac: A Critical History of Operations in Virginia, Maryland and Pennsylvania, from the Commencement to the Close of the War, 1861-1865*. New York: Charles Scribner's Sons, 1882.

Sypher, J. R. *History of the Pennsylvania Reserve Corps*. Lancaster, Pennsylvania: Elias Barr and Company, 1865.

Thomas, Benjamin. *Abraham Lincoln: A Biography*. New York: Knopf, 1952.

Townsend, George A. *Campaigns of a Non-Combatant, and His Romaunt Abroad During the War*. New York: Blelock and Company, 1866.

Tucker, Glenn. *Hancock the Superb*. Indianapolis: Bobbs-Merrill, 1960.

Wainwright, Charles S. *A Diary of Battle: The Personal Journals of Colonel Charles S. Wainwright, 1861-1865*. Edited by Allan Nevins. New York: Harcourt, Brace and World, 1962.

Walker, Francis A. *History of the Second Army Corps in the Army of the Potomac*. New York: Charles Scribner's Sons, 1886.

————— *General Hancock*. New York: D. Appleton and Company, 1894.

Ward, Joseph R. C. *History of the One Hundred and Sixth Regiment Pennsylvania Volunteers, 2d Brigade, 2d Division, 2d Corps, 1861-1865*. Philadelphia: Grant, Faires and Rodgers, 1883. Reprint. Philadelphia: F. McManus, Jr. and Company, 1906.

Webb, Alexander S. *The Peninsula: McClellan's Campaign of 1862*. New York: Charles Scribner's Sons, 1881.

Welles, Gideon. *Diary of Gideon Welles*. Edited by Howard K. Beale. New York: W. W. Norton, 1960.

Williams, Kenneth P. *Lincoln Finds a General: A Military Study of the Civil War*. 5 vols. New York: MacMillan, 1949-59.

Williams, T. Harry. *Lincoln and His Generals*. New York: Knopf, 1952.

INDEX

Page numbers in italics indicate maps. Page numbers in bold indicate photographs.

Aarons, Solomon 277
Adams house 103, 118
Alabama 21, 63
Alabama troops 100, 105, 192, 264
Albany, New York 33, 172
Alexander, Col. E. Porter 276
Alexander's Bridge 130
Alexandria, Virginia 69, 92, 176, 177
Allegany, New York 32
Allegheny, Pennsylvania 375
Amelia Court House, Virginia 383
Anderson, Maj. Gen. Richard H. 245, 272, 342
Andrew, Gov. John Albion 18, 36, 37, 71, 164
Angle *282*, 288, 293, 295
Annapolis, Maryland 30
Antietam, Maryland 183, *190*, 194-196, 199-201, 208, 219, 221, 233, 254, 262, 276, 315, 321, 327, 340, 364, 391, 392, 394, 396
Antietam Campaign 195
Antietam Creek 182-184, 186, 187, 192

Appomattox Court House, Virginia 390, 399
Appomattox River 367, 369, 371, 383
Aqueduct Bridge 31, 53, 78
Aquia Creek 176
Arlington Heights, Virginia 31, 51
Armistead, Brig. Gen. Lewis A. 104, 105, 106, 148, 288, 289, 291-294
Army of Northeastern Virginia 43, 50
Army of Northern Virginia 78, 85, 103, 114, 127, 143, 147, 176, 181, 184, 194, 209, 225, 239, 241, 243, 274, 340, 343, 351, 383
Army of the Cumberland 302
Army of the James 350, 364, 365, 372
Army of the Potomac 13, 16, 83, 84, 86, 91, 94, 111, 114, 115, 133, 134, 137, 138, 141, 144, 146, 147, 158, 159, 162, 163, 175, 178-181, 204, 209, 210,

212, 227, 230, 231, 235, 239, 245, 253, 254, 256, 258, 267, 274, 300, 302, 305, 307, 308, 311, 319, 321, 323, 324, 343, 349-351, 358-362, 365, 366, 368, 369, 376, 383, 388, 391

Army of the Potomac, First Corps 87, 94, 95, 97, 158, 184, 185, 195, 211, 233, 236, 256, 261, 262, 264, 299, 314

Army of the Potomac, Second Corps 93, 99, 102, 107, 136, 144, 151, 155, 162, 163, 177, 178, 181, 182, 184, 185, 192, 193, 201, 203, 208, 210, 211, 214, 218, 220, 222, 224, 227, 231, 238, 242, 243, 245, 247, 250, 256, 258, 262-265, 269, 272, 276, 277, 285, 299-302, 304, 305, 310, 312, 314, 317, 321, 322, 324, 325, 329, 330, 332-341, 343, 345, 346-353, 355, 357-362, 364, 365, 369, 370, 372, 374-377, 379, 381-383, 385-387, 396

Army of the Potomac, Second Corps hospital 386

Army of the Potomac, Third Corps 93, 99, 100, 104, 114, 138, 144, 151, 162, 211, 236, 254, 256, 263-265, 270, 272, 273, 299, 303, 314, 343

Army of the Potomac, Fourth Corps 93, 99, 104, 134, 138, 144, 155

Army of the Potomac, Fifth Corps 93, 95, 97, 113, 115-117, 122, 124, 126, 134, 144, 146, 148, 152,

162, 211, 236, 238, 243, 244, 256, 258, 272, 299, 302, 314, 324, 325, 327, 331, 337, 343, 350, 358, 368, 373, 380-383

Army of the Potomac, Sixth Corps 93, 113, 114, 115, 126, 134, 177, 182, 184, 193, 194, 211, 236, 245, 256, 281, 314, 324, 330, 331, 337, 343, 345, 350, 351, 360, 370, 375

Army of the Potomac, Ninth Corps 180, 181, 184, 194, 208, 211, 221, 358

Army of the Potomac, Tenth Corps 372

Army of the Potomac, Eleventh Corps 196, 236, 242-244, 256, 262, 263, 276, 299, 302, 315

Army of the Potomac, Twelfth Corps 181, 184-186, 195, 236, 242, 243, 247, 256, 275, 299, 302

Army of the Potomac, Eighteenth Corps 350, 351, 358, 365

Army of the Potomac, Cavalry Corps 382

Army of the Valley 114, 115

Army of Virginia 175, 178

Ashland, Virginia 96, 114-116

Ashland and Hanover Court House Roads 95

Astor house 254, 255

Athearn, Robert G. 206, 253

Atlanta, Georgia 319

Atlas, U.S.S. 33

Auburn Station, Virginia 303

Auburndale, Massachusetts 390

Ayres, Bvt. Maj. Gen. Romeyn B. 328

Bagely, Maj. Alderman 57, 61, 62

Bailey's Creek 370

Baker, Col. Henry 14, 72, 75, 76, 147, 163, 183

Ball's Bluff, Virginia 76, 84

Baltimore, Maryland 69, 169

Baltimore Pike 263

Bank's Ford 241, 242

Banks, Maj. Gen. Nathaniel P. 86

Bardwell, Maj. George H. 233

Barksdale, Brig. Gen. William 136, 272

Barlow, Brig. Gen. Francis 191, 315, 324, 334-336, 338, 342, 346, 348, 352, 353, 357, 358, 365, 372, 373, 385

Barnes, Lt. Col. Joseph H. 152, 183, 206, 208

Baxter, Col. De Witt C. 75, 258

Beauregard, Gen. P. G. T. 41, 44, 365

Beaver Dam Creek 115-119, 138, 146, 148

Beck, Col. Samuel 116

Belle Plain, Virginia 345

Benét, Stephen Vincent 324

Bentley, Maj. Richard C. 200

Berdan, Col. Hiram 125

Berdan's Sharpshooters 264

Bermuda Hundred, Virginia 350, 364, 365, 370

Berry, Brig. Gen. Hiram 89, 100

Bethesda Church, Virginia 391

Birney, Maj. Gen. David Bell 254, 264, 265, 324, 325, 335, 336, 343, 365

Blair, Frank 58, 72

Blair, Montgomery 58

Blake, Lt. John J. 221

Blenker, Brig. Gen. Louis 73

Block House Bridge 335

Bloody Angle 343, 357

Bloody Lane 190, 192, 194, 315

Blue Ridge Mountains 176, 180, 199, 203, 204, 209, 300

Boatswain's Creek 117, 122, 132

Boatswain's Hill 121

Boatswain's Swamp 117, 355

Bolivar Heights 196

Boonsborough, Maryland 180, 183

Boston Common 38

Boston, Massachusetts 36-38, 58, 65, 68, 72, 119, 120, 161, 208, 242, 368, 390

Bottom's Bridge 93

Boydton Plank Road 379, 381, 393, 394

Bradley, Cpl. Hugh 290

Brady, Judge 309

Brady, Lt. Eugene 376

Branch, Brig. Gen. Lawrence O'Bryan 94, 95, 96

Brandywine Cemetery [Wilmington, Delaware] 396

Breckinridge, Maj. Gen. John C. 355

Breslin, Capt. John 54

Bridgeport, Connecticut 65, 68

423

Bristoe Station, Virginia 392, 394

Brock Road 324, 325, 332

Brooke, Col. John R. 191, 224, 268, 270, 271, 334, 338, 353, 369, 372

Brown Lt. T. Fred 273, 280, 339

Brown house 338

Buchanan, Lt. Col. Robert C. 155

Buchanan, Pres. James 20

Buckingham, Brig. Gen. Catharinus P. 204

Bull Run 48, 50, 56, 78, 267

Burk, Adjt. B. H. 51

Burke, Lt. Col. Dennis 355, 381, 386

Burke, Col. John 32, 77, 148, 163, 189, 200, 398

Burkesville Station 386

Burns, Brig. Gen. William W. 136

Burnside, Maj. Gen. Ambrose 85, 176, 179-181, 194, 195, 205, 209-214, 220, 222, 224, 228, 229, 231, 370

Burton, Dr. William 39, 390

Busch, Captain 33

Butler, Maj. Gen. Benjamin F. 86, 345, 350, 364, 365, 370, 372

Butterfield, Brig. Gen. Daniel 152, 275

Byrnes, Col. Richard 207, 219, 220, 225, 253, 314, 316, 346, 354, 357, 359, 366, 396, 397

Byron, Lt. Col. John 373, 374

Cadwalader, Maj. Gen. George 34

Caldwell, Brig. Gen. John C. 191, 192, 219, 223, 230, 251, 265, 270, 271

California 75, 76

Calvary Cemetery [Long Island City, New York] 229, 307, 395

Cameron, Sec. of War Simon 58, 64, 67

Camp California 69, 72, 92, 164, 177

Camp Scott 172

Campbell, Lt. Murdoch 296, 297

Cartwright, Col. George W. 380

Casey, Brig. Gen. Silas 93, 99, 100, 106

Cass, Col. Edward 35, 38, 95, 96, 97, 99, 100, 106, 132, 145, 161

Cass, Col. Thomas 36, 121, 152, 397

Cassidy, Sgt. John 326

Catharpin Road 324

Cathedral Cemetery [Philadelphia, Pennsylvania] 311, 399

Catoctin Mountains 181

Cattaraugus County, New York 32

Cauldon, Captain 82

Cavanagh, Maj. James 103, 193, 219

Cavanagh, Michael 28, 29, 167

Cemetery Hill 261, 263, 264, 275, 276

Cemetery Ridge 261, 263-265, 271, 272, 274-277, 286-288, 294

Centerville Pike 43

Centerville-Warrenton Pike 43

Centreville, Virginia 42, 43, 50, 51, 303

Century Magazine 121, 133

Chambers, Sgt. Patrick 220

Chambersburg, Pennsylvania 34, 257

Champion, U.S.S. 81

Chancellor house 245, 247

Chancellorsville, Virginia 197, 239, 250, 256, 257, 262, 321, 322, 324, 327, 330, 337, 340, 391, 392, 394, 398, 399

Chantilly, Virginia 178, 254, 391, 394

Charles City Road 138

Charleston, South Carolina 21, 169, 277

Charleston Irish Volunteers 121

Charlestown, West Virginia 164, 203

Cheek's Ford 178

Cheseapeake Bay 81

Chester County, Pennsylvania 77

Chicago, Illinois 305, 380

Chickahominy River 13, 85, 92-94, 97, 101, 102, 104, 111, 113, 114, 115, 117, 118, 122, 124, 126, 129, 130, 134, 136, 145, 146, 160, 350, 351

Chickamauga, Georgia 302

Chilton, Asst. Adjt. Gen. Robert H. 149

Chisholm, Pvt. Daniel 327

City Point, Virginia 370, 371, 399

City Point Railroad 365

Clarke, Capt. William T. 33

Clarksburg, Maryland 181

Cleveland, Ohio 162

Clipp farm 189

Clooney, Capt. Patrick F. 193

Clump of Trees 278, 281

Cobb, Brig. Gen. Thomas R. R. 214

Cochrane, Capt. William 348

Codori house 273

Cold Harbor, Virginia 120, 197, 207, 253, 350, 351, 356, 360-362, 364, 366, 373, 377, 391-394, 397, 398, 405, 407

Columbia, U.S.S. 82

Columbian Artillery 36, 120

Conboy, Sgt. Martin 91

Condon, Capt. Patrick 217, 218, 219, 220, 223

Connacht Rangers 77, 137, 183, 243

Connecticut, 9th 73

Connecticut, 14th 251, 276

Connecticut troops 43, 235

Conroy, Col. Patrick W. 34

Conscription Act 308

Consolidated Brigade 373, 374

Conyngham, Capt. David Powers 15, 82, 107

Cooke, Brig. Gen. Philip St. George 127, 131

Corby, Father William 77, 104, 155, 191, 213, 237, 265, 266, 267, 268, 316, 380, 409

Corcoran, Brig. Gen. Michael 19, 21, 22-24, 30-32, 33, 41-43, 49, 50, 53, 57, 72, 168-171, 172, 174, 196, 201, 230, 305-307, 309, 345, 347, 354, 357, 359, 369, 379, 381, 386, 395, 409

Cordero, Capt. John 120
Corn Exchange Regiment 188
Cosslett, Lt. Charles 316, 326, 330, 348
Couch, Brig. Gen. Darius 93, 99, 103, 242, 251, 256
Courtney house 103
Cowan, Capt. Andrew 281
Crampton's Gap, Maryland 182
Crawford, Pvt. Daniel C. 339
Cronin, Jeremiah 121
Cross, Col. Edward E. 105, 268
Cub Run Bridge 51
Culp's Hill 275, 276, 299
Culpeper Court House, Virginia 209, 301
Cumberland Valley 178
Curtin, Gov. Andrew 71, 111, 171, 296, 297, 311
Cushing, Lt. Alonzo 277, 278, 280, 281, 286, 293
Cypress Hills Cemetery [Brooklyn, New York] 396

Dabney's Mills, Virginia 394
Daidy, Lt. Lawrence 220
Dale, Lt. Col. Richard 323, 325, 326, 332, 336, 340
Daly, Judge Charles 30, 32, 61, 62, 68, 169, 173, 200, 201, 306
Daly, Maria Lydig 61, 67, 201, 307
Dana, Charles 345
Dana, Brig. Gen. Napoleon 185
Danville Railroad 383
David's Island 66
Davis, Pres. Jefferson 89, 94, 103, 132

Davis, Thomas 36
Davis, Capt. William 277, 302, 311, 330
Deep Bottom, Virginia 370-372, 391-394
DeHaven, Pvt. William 215, 217
Delaware, 1st 311, 313, 396
Deserted House, Virginia 393
Devereux, Col. Arthur 295
Devil's Den 264
Dickinson, Sen. Edward 75
Diederichs, Capt. Otto 138
Dillon, Father James 77, 173, 409
Dinwiddie Court House, Virginia 381
Dix, Maj. Gen. John 86
Donovan, Capt. John 166
Dooley, Capt. John 287
Doran, Capt. Richard 33, 354
Douglas Guards 36
Douglas, Stephen 17, 36
Draft Act 310
Dublin, Ireland 70, 72
Duffy, Capt. Felix 131, 193
Duffy, Maj. James 277, 294, 311
Duffy, Capt. Michael 274, 277
Dunkard Church 185, 186
Dwyer, Lt. John 220

Eagan, Lt. John 294
Eagan, Capt. Michael 105
Early, Lt. Gen. Jubal 370
Edward's Ferry, Virginia 257
Edwards, Capt. John 125
Egan, Father Costney 302
Ellicottsville, New York 32
Ely's Ford, Virginia 322
Emacipation Proclamation 173

Emmet Guards 287
Emmet, Lt. Temple 152
Emmitsburg Road 263-265, 272-274, 276, 286
Enchantress, U.S.S. 169
Enright, Col. Richard C. 70, 76
Evans, Col. Clement A. 340
Evans, Brig. Gen. Nathan G. 43, 44, 76
Evelington Heights 159
Ewell, Lt. Gen. Richard S. 256, 264, 275, 303, 324, 325, 327, 329-331
Excelsior Brigade 237

Fair Oaks, Virginia 111, 129, 134, 136, 148, 391, 392, 394, 398
Fair Oaks Station, Virginia 99, 101, 106
Fairfax Court House, Virginia 305, 306
Fairfax Station, Virginia 305
Fallon, Pvt. Thomas 91
Falmouth, Virginia 212, 221, 239, 241, 256
Farmville, Virginia 313, 392, 396
Fenian Brotherhood 27, 38, 68, 70, 167
Finegan, Brig. Gen. Joseph 355
Fitzgerald, Lord Edward 36
Fitzpatrick, Lt. Charles 297
Five Forks, Virginia 382, 383
Five Points, New York 57, 388
Fleming, Capt. James 355, 359
Florida troops 355
Flynn, Lt. John 220

Fort Corcoran, Virginia 42, 51, 53, 69
Fort Monroe, Virginia 81
Fort Schuyler, New York 66, 71, 72, 77
Fort Shaw, Montana Territory 224
Fort Slocum, Maryland 172
Fort Stedman, Virginia 382
Fort Sumter, South Carolina 17, 21, 28
Fowler, Lt. Col. Henry 70, 154, 155, 183, 200
Fox's Gap, Maryland 181
Frailey, Lt. Peter H. 339
Frank, Col. Paul 237
Franklin, Brig. Gen. William B. 93, 137, 177, 182, 194, 195, 211, 213
Frayser's Farm, Virginia 138
Frederick, Maryland 178, 180-182, 258
Fredericksburg, Virginia 55, 85, 94, 95, 114, 176, 197, 199, 209-211, *216*, 222, 224, 226, 230, 233, 234, 237, 242, 245, 253-255, 267, 268, 276, 285, 294, 310, 312, 314, 345, 358, 372, 388, 391, 392, 394, 396, 398, 399
Fredericksburg Road 113
Freeman, Douglas Southall 138, 147, 180, 223
Fremont, Maj. Gen. John 58, 86
French, Brig. Gen. William H. 102, 104, 105, 127, 131, 186, 214, 215, 243, 248, 303
Frietchie, Barbara 178
Funk, George 107

Gaines' Mill 97, 116-118, 120, 121, *123*, 141, 145, 147-149, 154, 157, 160, 350, 391, 392
Galwey, Sgt. Thomas 162, 187
Garnett, Sgt. Joseph 289
Garnett, Brig. Gen. Richard B. 287, 288, 290, 292
Garrett, Maj. John 354
"Garry Owen" 54
Georgia 21, 176, 345
Georgia, 48th 274
Georgia troops 132, 214, 219, 220, 272-274, 283, 285, 286, 380
Germanna Ford, Virginia 312
Getty, Brig. Gen. George 324
Gettysburg, Pennsylvania 54, 61, 85, 195, 198, 259, 261, 269, *282*, 284, 296, 307, 308, 310-312, 314, 315, 321, 327, 331, 353, 358, 364, 372, 377, 381, 391, 392, 394, 396, 398, 399, 409
Gibbon, Brig. Gen. John 256, 257, 272, 273, 275, 278, 287, 324, 325, 335, 336, 345-347, 352, 353, 354, 355, 357, 359, 365, 374-377, 386
Gibson, Col. William 274
Gleason, Capt. John H. 220, 316, 327, 355, 381
Glendale, Virginia 138, *139*, 141, 146, 147, 162, 276, 285, 391, 392, 394
Gloucester Point, Virginia 87, 88
Gordon, Brig. Gen. John B. 331, 340
Gordonsville, Virginia 176
Gorman, Brig. Gen. Willis 185

Gosson, Capt. Jack 92, 152, 237, 238
Granger, Capt. Charles M. 301
Grant, Lt. Gen. Ulysses S. 85, 253, 317, 319, 323, 324, 329-332, 334, 336, 337, 339, 343, 348, 349-351, 353, 360-367, 369, 370, 373, 376, 379, 389
Grapevine Bridge 13, 102
Greeley, Horace 71, 239
Gregg, Brig. Gen. David M. 374, 381
Gregg, Brig. Gen. Maxcy 119, 120, 121, 122
Griffin, Brig. Gen. Charles 48, 117, 118, 122, 125, 129, 144, 145, 150, 327, 328, 329, 368
Grover, Brig. Gen. Cuvier 141
Guiney, Louise 390
Guiney, Col. Patrick Robert **128**, 129, 130, 132, 145, 162, 302, 327, 328, 368, 390, 397
Guiney's Station, Virginia 94, 349

Hagerstown, Maryland 38, 178, 181, 182
Hagerstown Pike 185, 186
Haggerty, Francis 157
Haggerty, Lt. Col. James 47, 53, 57, 157
Hall, Col. Norman J. 295
Halleck, Maj. Gen. Henry W. 175, 176, 177, 179, 210, 256, 257, 361
Halpin, Sgt. George 244
Hamilton, Captain 213
Hamilton's Crossing 213
Hampton, Virginia 81, 82

Hampton Roads, Virginia 84
Hancock, Maj. Gen. Winfield
  Scott 74, 193, 201, 203, 211,
  215, 217, 221, 222, 229-231,
  245, 247, 249, 256, 257, 259,
  261, 265, 266, 272, 275, 280,
  281, 304, 310, 322, 324, 326,
  330, 334, 335, 339, 340, 346,
  347, 348-351, 358, 364, 365,
  370-372, 374-376, 379, 381
Hanley, Lt. Col. Patrick T. 119,
  121, 145, 162, 328, 329
Hanover Court House, Virginia
  94, 95, 391
Hardie, Capt. William T. 223
Harmon, Capt. Luke G. 33
Harper's Weekly 63, 78
Harpers Ferry, Virginia 180,
  182, 196, 198, 199, 201, 202,
  203, 262, 300
Harrisburg, Maryland 178
Harrisburg, Pennsylvania 67,
  71
Harrison, L.F. 309
Harrison's Creek 365
Harrison's Landing 163, 164,
  175
Harron, John 113
Harrow, Brig. Gen. William 274
Hart, Capt. William G. 221
Haskell, Lt. Frank A. 287
Haskell, Capt. William T. 120
Hatcher's Run, Virginia 344,
  377, 391, 393, 394, 399, 406
Haverty, Quartermaster Patrick
  M. 200
Haw's Shop, Virginia 350
Hayman, Col. Samuel 33, 91,
  100, 101, 397

Hazzard, Capt. George W. 143
Heenan, Col. Dennis 171, 196,
  198, 233, 399
Heintzelman, Col. Samuel P. 42,
  93, 99, 151
Henry house 47, 48
Henry House Hill 46, 47
Henry, Judith 44
Heth, Maj. Gen. Henry 278,
  374, 375
Hibernian Guards 162, 187
Higgins, Lt. William H. 220
Higham, John 389, 390
Hill, Maj. Gen. A. P. 85, 115,
  119, 121, 124-26, 138, 141,
  146, 166, 256, 264, 272, 278,
  283, 303, 324-326, 329, 330,
  332, 336, 355, 374
Hill, Lt. Gen. Daniel Harvey 85,
  99, 126, 132, 133, 146, 149,
  150, 180, 182, 186-89
Hill, Capt. William 291, 293
Himmer, Cpl. George 126
Hitchcock, Ethan 84
Hitchcock, Frederick 183
Hobart Catholic Relief Army
  77
Holy Cross Cemetery [Lack-
  awanna, New York] 408
Holyhood Cemetery [Brook-
  line, Massachusetts] 397
Hood, Maj. Gen. John Bell 272
Hooker, Maj. Gen. Joseph 85,
  89, 93, 126, 138, 140, 142,
  144, 184, 185, 209, 211, 235,
  237, 238, 239, 242, 243, 245,
  250, 256, 324
Horgan, Captain 105
Horgan, Maj. William 223, 229
Howard, Brig. Gen. Oliver O.
  82, 104, 185

Huger, Maj. Gen. Benjamin 99
Hughes, Archbishop 68
Humphreys, Brig. Gen. Andrew A. 265, 325, 381
Hunt, Brig. Gen. Henry 276, 280, 281

Indiana, 27th 181
Ireland 29, 63, 77
Irish Brigade 15, 25, 53, 56, 60, 64, 65, 67-70, 73, 77, 82, 102, 107, 108, 111, 112, 132, 133, 137, 143, 146, 155, 162, 164, 165, 167, 177, 183, 184, 189, 191, 192, 194-196, 198, 200, 203, 206, 208, 212, 215, 216, 217, 223, 225, 227, 229-231, 239, 244, 245, 249, 251, 259, 262, 266, 267, 301-303, 307-309, 313, 314, 315, 322, 324-326, 332, 339, 342, 345, 346, 347, 352, 354, 357, 359, 364, 366, 369, 372, 373, 377-380, 386, 387, 390, 395-398, 409
Irish Legion 173, 305, 353, 364
Irish, 3rd 58, 60, 66

Jackson, Lt. Gen. Thomas J. 85, 94, 97, 114, 115, 134, 138, 143, 177, 178, 180, 182, 185, 195, 210, 243, 244, 245, 331, 340, 370
James Island, South Carolina 391
James River 81, 87, 116, 134, 137, 138, 143, 144, 159, 175, 176, 210, 319, *363*, 364, 365, 369-371
Johnson, Pres. Andrew 395
Johnston, Gen. Joseph E. 86, 89, 93, 94, 97, 99, 103, 106, 383
Joint Committee of the Conduct of the War 84
Jones' Wood 63
Joyce, Capt. John 193

Kavanagh, Capt. John 32, 33, 193
Kearny, Maj. Gen. Philip 89, 93, 100, 101, 126, 142, 144, 236, 254
Keedysville, Maryland 183
Kelly, Lt. Charles 274, 294
Kelly, Lt. Col. James 53, 183, 193, 253
Kelly, Col. Patrick D. 57, 58, 60, 105-107, 147, 148, 163, 190, 219, 220, 225, 241, 242, **252**, 253, 254, 265, 267, 268, 270, 271, 364, 366, 398
Kelly, Capt. Thomas 302, 303, 311
Kemper, Brig. Gen. James L. 138, 287, 288, 290, 292
Kershaw, Brig. Gen. Joseph B. 136, 268, 370
Keyes, Brig. Gen. Erasmus 87, 93, 99, 100
Kimball, Brig. Gen. Nathan 162, 183, 184, 186-188, 214
King, Sen. Preston 72
King, Lt. Rufus 147
Kings County Volunteers 316
Kirby, Lt. Edward 103
Knieriem, Capt. John 138

Lacy house 222
Landrum house 346
Lawlor, Maj. Andrew 348
Lawton, Brig. Gen. Alexander
  R. 132, 133
Lebroke, Cpl. James H. 247, 249
Lee, Brig. Gen. Fitzhugh 243
Lee, Gen. Robert E. 94, 115,
  126, 132, 134, 137, 143, 146,
  148, 151, 157, 159, 177, 180,
  181, 183-185, 194-196, 199,
  204, 209, 212, 239, 243-245,
  250, 256, 263, 264, 274, 276,
  279, 283, 299, 301, 319, 324,
  329, 331, 332, 334, 335, 336,
  338, 340, 343, 346, 349, 351,
  352, 355, 357, 360, 362, 364,
  365, 367, 369, 370, 373, 382,
  383, 385, 386
Leppine, Capt. George 247, 322
Leslie's Illustrated News 78
Libby Prison 159
Lieb, Capt. Frank R. 348, 359
Lincoln, Pres. Abraham 18, 31,
  33, 42, 43, 58, 72, 73, 75, 84,
  85, 87, 93, 144, 178, 179,
  195, 209-211, 235, 238, 239,
  251, 254, 257, 300, 309, 319,
  354
Little Round Top 264, 267, 272,
  280, 286, 304
Livermore, Lt. Thomas 192
London Times 22, 56, 163, 225
Long Bridge 51, 168
Long Bridge Road 138, 146
Long Island 36
Long Wharf 37
Longstreet, Lt. Gen. James 85,
  89, 115, 138, 183, 195, 204,
  209, 210, 256, 262, 263, 264,

265, 272, 278, 279, 301, 303,
  329-331, 387
Louisiana 21, 42, 214
Louisiana, 10th 156
Loundon Valley, Virginia 300
Lowe, Thaddeus 117
Lynch, Capt. James 247, 276,
  286, 348
Lynch, Maj. John 246
Lyon, Matthew 113

MacNamara, Sgt. Daniel G. 37,
  96, 113, 114, 119, 125, 130,
  144, 145, 150, 160
MacNamara, James 37, 38, 121
MacNamara, Michael 36, 38
Magner, Capt. James 348
Magruder, John B. 86, 87, 115,
  116, 134, 136, 149, 150
Mahone, Brig. Gen. William
  104, 105, 106
Maine, 5th 247
Maine troops 235, 322
Malin, Sgt. Francis 270
Malvern Hill, Virginia 35, 134,
  145, 146, *153*, 154, 157, 161,
  163, 166, 183, 195, 200, 310,
  364, 391, 392, 397, 398
Manassas, First 41, *45*, *46*, 53,
  58, 60, 62, 71, 76, 91, 157,
  163, 167, 191, 262, 299, 395,
  396
Manassas, Second 172, 177,
  179, 196, 206, 208, 233, 391
Manassas Gap, Virginia 300
Manassas Junction, Virginia
  43, 86, 256
Manhattan Island 32
Mansfield, Maj. Gen. Joseph
  K. F. 185

Marley, Sgt. John 217
Martin, Capt. Augustus P. 96, 122
Martindale, Brig. Gen. John H. 127
Martinsburg, West Virginia 180
Marye's Heights 216, 222, 225, 226, 230, 231, 242, 358
Maryland 176, 178, 179, 194, 204, 257, 261, 276, 387
Maryland Heights 182
Massachusetts 18, 36, 37, 71, 164, 368, 390, 403
Massachusetts, 1st 141, 142
Massachusetts, 9th 35-38, 58, 73, 78, 82, 94-96, 111, 113, 116, 117-122, 125, 128-132, 142, 144, 145, 150-152, 160-162, 208, 238, 301, 302, 327-329, 368, 380, 390, 391, 397, 401
Massachusetts, 13th 36
Massachusetts, 15th 273
Massachusetts, 16th 141
Massachusetts, 19th 291, 294, 295
Massachusetts, 28th 73, 207, 208, 215, 219, 220, 234, 241, 242, 314, 316, 325, 326, 339, 346, 348, 355, 358, 359, 369, 379, 380, 391, 397, 403
Massachusetts, 29th 111, 112, 133, 137, 143, 147, 152, 154, 163, 164, 177, 181, 183, 189, 193, 198, 206, 208
Massachusetts, 55th 172
Massachusetts, 101st 401
Massachusetts, 182nd 401
Massachusetts Air Defense

Regiment, 69th 401
Massachusetts National Guard 401
Massachusetts troops 235
Mattapony River 92
Mayre, Col. E. A. 211
McAnally, Capt. Charles 297, 341, 342, 381
McCafferty, Capt. James E. 119, 121
McCafferty, Pvt. Neal 294
McCahey, Sgt. Bernard 246
McCall, Brig. Gen. George 113, 115, 118, 122, 138, 140, 142, 144, 146
McCartan, Capt. John 136
McClellan, Gen. George B. 13, 36, 69, 76, 81, 84-89, 92-95, 99, 101, 113-117, 133, 134, 137, 144, 148, 154, 157, 159, 162, 171, 175, 176, 178, 179, 180-182, 184, 194-196, 199, 203-206, 209, 210, 239, 253, 274, 275, 300, 319, 343, 350, 364
McCunn, Col. John 31, 32, 33, 77, 397
McDermott, Anthony 81, 277, 278, 280, 283, 288, 289, 291, 294, 295, 303, 311, 341, 387
McDermott, Col. Peter 172, 173
McDougall, Col. Clinton D. 353, 369
McDowell, Gen. Irwin 41, 42-44, 47, 48, 87, 88, 94, 95, 97, 113, 158
McEvily, Col. William 172, 398
McGee, Capt. James 309
McHugh, Capt. Francis J. 33
McHugh, Mary 33

432

McIvor, Col. James P. 51, 381, **384**, 399
McKee, Father Edward 198, 316
McKeen, Col. H. Boyd 353
McKeever, Sgt. Hugh 294, 342
McKeever, Cpl. Joseph 279, 288
McLaws, Maj. Gen. Lafayette 182, 185, 245
McLean house 386
McMahon, Col. James P. 171, 174, 347, 354, **356**, 357, 359, 360, 398, 405, 407, 408
McMahon, Col. John 171, 172, 174, 398, 408
McMahon, Capt. Martin 360
McPherson's Ridge 262
McQuade, Col. James 95
Meade, Maj. Gen. George G. 195, 199, 244, 258, 261, 265, 274, 275, 278, 299, 301-304, 322, 324, 334, 365, 376, 377, 387
Meagher, Elizabeth Townsend 27, 57, 199, 395
Meagher, Brig. Gen. Thomas Francis 14, **25**, 27, 28-31, 36, 43, 53, 54, 56, 57, 58, 60-62, 63, 64, 65, 67, 68, 70-74, 76, 77, 82, 92, 102, 104, 106, 107, 108, 110, 111, 127, 129, 131, 132, 136, 142, 143, 146, 147, 152, 154-157, 162-167, 171, 176, 177, 181, 183, 188, 189, 191, 193, 196, 198, 199, 200, 201, 203, 205, 206, 208, 215, 217, 218, 220-223, 225-230, 234-239, 241, 244, 245, 246-248, 250, 251, 253-255, 305-307, 309, 386, 395, 409

Mechanicsville, Virginia 115, 146, 391
Medal of Honor 91, 197, 198, 248, 297, 303, 316, 342, 399
Mexican War 60, 75
Michigan, 3rd 100
Michigan, 4th 116, 117, 122, 151, 368
Michigan, 5th 89, 91, 100
Michigan troops 100
Middlebrook, Maryland 181
Miles, Col. John 34
Miles, Brig. Gen. Nelson 325, 326, 332, 338, 353, 354, 369, 374, 375, 382
Miller, Capt. John L. 120
Mine Run, Virginia 303, 324, 391, 394
Mineral Run 244
Minnesota, 1st 78
Mississippi 21, 175, 211, 266
Mississippi troops 194
Mitchel, John 60
Mitchel, Pvt. Willie 287
Moncrief, Judge 31
Monitor, U.S.S. 84, 87
Monocacy River 258
Montana Territory 244, 395
Monteith, Col. William 397
Montgomery Guards 38, 164
Mooney, Quartermaster Thomas 238
Moran, Capt. Patrick 277, 360
Morehead, Col. Turner G. 75, 258
Morell, Brig. Gen. George W. 93, 113, 117, 122, 124, 125, 127, 144, 152
Morgan, Col. Charles H. 351, 352, 361, 372, 373
Morgan, Gov. Edwin D. 64, 67

Moroney, Capt. Richard 255, 309, 354, 381

Morris, Col. Dwight 186

Morrisville, Virginia 300, 302

Mott, Brig. Gen. Gershom 324, 325, 338, 343, 372

"Mud March" 231

Mulholland, Lt. Col. St. Clair A. **197**, 198, 199, 203, 205, 212, 217, 218, 223, 224, 233, 236, 238, 244, 245-249, 256, 265, 268, 270, 271, 300, 302, 316, 322, 326, 327, 330, 332, 333, 340, 347-349, 371, 380, 399, 409

Mullin, Lt. Michael 294

Murphy, Col. Matthew 167, 172, 307, **344**, 345-347, 379, 381, 399

Murphy, Capt. Michael 33

Naglee, Brig. Gen. Henry M. 138

Napoleon 77, 85

National Road 181, 183

Nelson's farm 138

New Cold Harbor 118

New England 65, 112, 181, 206, 237, 283, 291

New Hampshire, 5th 104, 105, 192, 223, 224, 243

New Market, Virginia 345

New Orleans, Louisiana 44, 73, 211

New York 14, 23, 27, 31, 32, 49, 53, 56-58, 60-63, 65, 67, 70, 71-73, 77, 84, 88, 108, 162, 163, 165, 167-169, 171, 172, 183, 198, 208, 225, 226, 229, 234, 238, 241, 254, 255, 305, 307, 309, 359, 388, 392, 395, 396

New York, 5th 67

New York, 8th 369

New York, 7th 18, 20, 165

New York, 9th 212

New York, 13th 42, 48

New York, 14th 95, 116, 117, 122, 125

New York, 20th 237

New York, 37th [Irish Rifles] 26, 33, 38, 57, 73, 76, 77, 89, 91, 100, 101, 111, 162, 391, 397, 403

New York, 38th 50

New York, 42nd 73, 291, 294, 295

New York, 52nd 237

New York, 57th 193

New York, 61st 191, 375

New York, 62nd 369

New York, 63rd 70, 71, 76, 77, 103, 104, 152, 154, 155, 163, 189, 193, 200, 217-221, 223, 238, 241, 246, 325, 326, 327, 355, 377-379, 381, 392, 398, 403

New York, 64th 191

New York, 66th 339

New York, 69th 64, 69, 77, 103-105, 137, 152, 154-157, 163, 166, 189, 193, 199, 217, 219-221, 223-225, 241, 255, 259, 325, 326, 348, 354, 364, 379, 382, 392, 396, 398, 403

New York, 70th 237

New York, 71st 237

New York, 72nd 237

New York, 73rd 237

New York, 74th 237
New York, 79th 42, 48
New York, 82nd 273
New York, 88th 14, 68, 71, 72, 77, 104, 105, 107, 132, 136, 147, 148, 152, 154-156, 163, 183, 191, 193, 200, 217, 219, 229, 238, 241-243, 245, 252, 301, 307, 308, 326, 355, 364, 369, 373, 379, 381, 392, 398, 403
New York, 106th 382
New York, 111th 369
New York, 155th 171-173, 346, 347, 354, 359, 393, 395, 398, 403, 405
New York, 164th 172-174, 346, 347, 354, 356, 357, 359, 376, 377, 393, 395, 398, 403
New York, 170th 172, 173, 346, 347, 354, 381, 384, 393, 395, 399, 403
New York, 182nd 171, 344-347, 354, 357, 359, 393, 395, 399, 403, 392, 398, 403
New York Artillery, 1st 93
New York Artillery, 10th 67
New York Circle of the Brotherhood 24
New York City, New York 20, 21, 22, 26, 30, 65, 181, 229, 239, 309, 379, 395, 396, 401
New York Corn Exchange 167
New York Excelsior Brigade 73
New York Heavy Artillery, 7th 379
New York Heavy Artillery, 8th 354, 376, 377, 408

New York *Herald* 13, 14, 107, 110, 129
New York Independent, 1st 281
New York Irish-American 111
New York Light Artillery 15
New York Light Artillery, 1st 327
New York Militia, 69th 19, 20, 21, 23, 24, 26, 27, 30, 31, 38, 41, 44, 47-49, 51, 53, 54, 58, 60-63, 65, 66, 68, 70, 167, 168, 170, 171, 183, 395, 401
New York National Guard Artillery, 69th 171
New York State Militia, 7th 172
New York Sun 225
New York Times 31, 32, 54, 56, 62, 64, 70, 165, 168, 307
New York troops 89, 110, 172, 174, 181, 193, 208, 209, 234, 255, 310, 315, 369, 373, 409
New York Veteran Volunteers, 69th 55
New York Zouaves, 75th 32, 33
Newport News, Virginia 172, 174
Nine Mile Road 99, 103
Norfolk, Virginia 87, 367
North Anna River 85, 349, 350, 354, 355, 392
North Carolina 94, 96, 181, 192, 367, 373, 383
North Carolina troops 283, 325
North River 33
Nowlen, Capt. Garret 247, 270, 375, 376
Nugent, Lt. Col. Robert 28, 53, 54, **55**, 56, 58, 63, 65, 105, 106, 121, 148, 155, 156, 163,

435

166, 183, 199-201, 219, 253, 309, 379, 382, 387, 396, 398

Nye, Gov. James Warren 255

O'Connor, Capt. Charles 31, 33

O'Dowd, Lt. Frank 121

O'Driscoll, Sgt. Maj. 309

O'Ganlon, Quartermaster 14, 15

O'Grady, Lt. William L. 77, 229, 253

O'Hagan, Father Joseph B. 237

O'Hanlon, Quartermaster Philip 103

O'Kane, Col. Dennis 201, 202, 258, 276, 283, **284**, 289, 294, 310, 390, 399

O'Leary, Capt. Timothy 96, 119, 162

O'Mahony, James 60

O'Mahony, John 24, 26, 28

O'Meagher, Surg. William 33

O'Neil, Maj. Joseph 155, 218

O'Neill, Capt. James 200

O'Neill, Maj. Thomas 132

O'Reilly, Father 54

O'Reilly, Capt. James 277

O'Reilly, John Boyle 223

O'Reilly, Pvt. Miles 309

Oak Grove, Virginia 114

Occoquan Creek 256

Ocean Queen, U.S.S. 82

Ohio, 8th 162, 187

Old Cold Harbor, Virginia 118, 124

Old Tavern 114

Opdyke, Mayor 254

Orange & Alexandria Railroad 305, 345

Orange Plank Road 242, 324

Orange Turnpike 243, 325, 327

Osborne, William 133, 163

Otis Guards 36

Otis, Harrison 36

Ouellette, Father Thomas 77, 104, 316, 380

Overland Campaign 319, *320*, 364, 368

Owen, Brig. Gen. Joshua T. 15, 34, 75, 110, 111, 140, 141, 201, 202, 212, 257, 353, 355, 399

Owen, William Miller 223

Palmer, Col. Oliver H. 215

Pamunkey River 85, 92, 349

Parrott guns 247, 249

Patterson, Robert 34, 58

Payne, Cpl. John N. 223

Peach Orchard 107, 264, 268, 270-272, 274, 285

Peckham, Capt. Erasmus W. 33

Pegram, Brig. Gen. John 340

Peninsula 86, 114, 116, 134, 145, 146, 157, 166, 167, 180, 195, 210, 230, 236, 254, 258, 262, 274, 312, 319, 321, 327, 396

Peninsular Campaign 77, 85, *98*, 116, 157, 159, 167, 175, 319, 364

Pennsylvania 71, 73, 76, 111, 117, 171, 195, 198, 248, 261, 276, 283, 285, 296, 316, 326, 332, 336, 387

Pennsylvania, 24th 33, 34, 38, 58, 198, 276, 312,

395

Pennsylvania, 53rd 223, 224, 271

Pennsylvania, 62nd 116, 117, 122, 125, 151, 327, 368

Pennsylvania, 63rd 148, 315, 316

Pennsylvania, 69th [2nd California] 15, 73, 75, 76, 81, 110, 111, 131, 136, 138, 140, 141, 148, 162, 198, 201, 205, 238, 257, 273, 274, 276-280, **282**, 283-293, 295-297, 302-304, 306, 309, 310, 311, 330, 355, 369, 381, 387, 394, 399, 403

Pennsylvania, 71st [1st California] 75, 272-274, 278, 286-290, 292, 369

Pennsylvania, 72nd 75, 272, 289, 291, 295

Pennsylvania, 81st 105, 243

Pennsylvania, 106th 75, 205, 272-274, 276, 281, 286

Pennsylvania, 116th 171, 172, 196-200, 203, 215, 217-220, 233, 234, 270, 303, 316, 325, 332-335, 339, 348, 354, 359, 366, 369, 375, 379, 380, 394, 399, 403

Pennsylvania, 118th 188

Pennsylvania, 132nd 182, 189

Pennsylvania, 140th 230, 231, 236, 248, 267

Pennsylvania, 148th 230, 231, 380

Pennsylvania Railroad 277

Pennsylvania Reserve Corps 113, 117, 119, 124, 138, 142, 143, 258

Pennsylvania troops 113, 115, 177, 187, 196

Petersburg, Virginia 116, 175, 252, 319, 362, 364-367, 369, 370, 373, 375, 377, 379, 380, 383, 391-394, 398

Petersburg Mine 369, 370

Petersburg Railroad 374

Petersburg & Richmond Railroad 367

Pettigrew, Brig. Gen. J. Johnston 278, 285, 292

Pettit, Capt. Rufus 15, 16, 143

Peyton, Maj. Charles 292, 293

Philadelphia, Pennsylvania 15, 34, 58, 71, 110, 169, 171, 196, 198, 199, 202, 203, 258, 302, 303, 310, 312, 316, 399, 409

Philadelphia Brigade 76, 111, 136, 140, 141, 186, 205, 256-258, 272, 273, 274-276, 286, 287, 292, 295-297, 353, 355, 369

Philadelphia County Militia 34

Phoenix Brigade 24, 27, 28

Pickett, Maj. Gen. George E. 104, 106, 278, 283, 285, 286, 288, 292, 294, 322, 358, 382, 383

Pierce, Col. Ebenezer 112, 143, 164

Pittsburgh, Pennsylvania 116, 316

Pitzer Run 283

Plank Road 211, 214

Po River 334, 335, 394, 399

Pope, Maj. Gen. John 85, 175, 176, 177, 178, 179, 195, 228, 229, 239, 300

Porter, Col. Andrew 47, 48, 49
Porter, Maj. Gen. Fitz John 93-
95, 113-116, 117, 121, 122,
126, 127, 131, 134, 148, 151,
154, 350, 364
Porter, Horace 353
Post Road 93
"Potomac Circle" 70, 316
Potomac Railroad 94
Potomac River 41, 51, 76, 81,
176-178, 180, 182-184, 204,
212, 231, 257, 299, 368, 370,
380
Poughkeepsie, New York 172
Powell, Dr. Francis 222
Powhite Creek 94, 117, 120,
124, 355
Price, Capt. Henry 380
Princeton, New Jersey 170

Quaker Road 138, 143, 144,
146
Quinlan, Maj. James 148
Quirk, Lt. William 220

Raccoon Ford, Virginia 301
Radford, Col. Richard C.W. 51
Randol, Lt. Alanson 141
Rapidan River 301, 312, 321,
322, 337, 342, 352, 358,
359
Rappahannock River 85, 86,
94, 176, 209, 221, 239, 241,
244, 250, 301, 303
Rappahannock Station, Virginia 314
Reams' Station, Virginia 374,
376, 391-394

Rectortown, Virginia 204
Reid, Lt. Thomas 354
Reynolds, Maj. Gen. John F.
138, 262, 299
Reynolds, Surg. Lawrence 70,
238, 316, 327, 377, 379, 386
Rhode Island troops 273
Richardson, Brig. Gen. Israel
92, 93, 102-104, 107, 111,
131, 136, 147, 171, 183, 184,
191, 193, 203
Richmond, Virginia 13, 53, 56,
83, 84, 85, 87, 89, 92, 93, 94,
95, 97, 99, 107, 113-115, 116,
117, 133, 135, 138, 157, 159,
161, 165, 167, 168, 175, 176,
209, 287, 319, 345, 349, 350,
354, 362, 364, 366, 367, 373,
383
Richmond & Fredericksburg
Railroad 349
Richmond and York River Rail-
road 94
Ricketts, Capt. James B. 48, 49
Ripley, Brig. Gen. Roswell S.
186
Rob Wheat's Tigers 44
Roberts, Col. R. Biddle 142
Robertson farm 303, 311
Robinson house 47
Robinson, Brig. Gen. John C.
331
Rockville, Maryland 181
Rodes, Brig. Gen. Robert E. 100,
186, 192
Rodgers, Commodore John 144
Rose, William 270
Roulette farm 188

Round Tops 261, 262
Rowanty's Creek 373
Royal Marines Light Infantry
    Battalion 77
Russell, William Howard 22,
    23, 27, 30, 41, 42, 56, 78, 163
Ryan, Lt. John 294

Sacriste, Lt. Louis 248, 303
Sailor's Creek, Virginia 392
Sandford, Maj. Gen. Charles W.
    22, 26
Savage's Station, Virginia 100,
    101, 136, 147, 148, 161, 394
Schouler, William 368
Schurz, Maj. Gen. Carl 253
Scott, Maj. George Winfield 41,
    42, 247
Scott, Thomas A. 63, 65
Scott's Mills 244
Scully, Father Thomas 160, 161
Sedgwick, Maj. Gen. John 93,
    102, 103, 104, 178, 184-186,
    299, 337
Seminary Ridge 272, 276, 279,
    283, 293
Semmes, Brig. Gen. Paul J. 136
Seneca Mills, Maryland 181
Seven Days 114, 134, 138, 146,
    157, 195, 350
Seven Pines, Virginia 13, 93,
    99, 101, 111, 113, 114, 391,
    392, 394
Seward, Sec. of State William
    31
Seymour, Gov. Horatio 171
Seymour, Brig. Gen. Truman
    118, 124
Shady Grove Church 324
Shady Grove Road 335

Shanley, Capt. Tim 193
Sharpsburg, Maryland 183
Sharpsburg Road 181
Sharpsburg-Hagerstown Road
    183
Sharpsburg-Keedysville Road
    184
Shenandoah Valley 34, 94, 97,
    114, 162, 180, 203, 204, 209,
    256, 300, 345
Sherfy farm 264
Sheridan, Maj. Gen. Philip H.
    382
Sherman, Maj. Gen. William
    Tecumseh 42, 43, 44, 47-51,
    53, 345, 389
Shields, Maj. Gen. James 59,
    60, 61, 62, 68, 72-75, 76, 94,
    162
Sickles, Maj. Gen. Daniel E. 73,
    253, 264, 265, 309
Sigel, Maj. Gen. Franz 253, 345
Slocum, Brig. Gen. Henry W.
    93, 126
Smith, Gen. Gustavus W. 99,
    103, 106
Smith, Col. James 61
Smith, Cpl. J. L. 188
Smith, Penn 258
Smith, Maj. Gen. William F. 93,
    365
Smyth, Amanda Pounder 395
Smyth, Col. Thomas A. 34, 311,
    312, **313**, 314-316, 322, 326,
    327, 332, 333, 342, 346, 353,
    362, 369, 375, 377, 378, 379-
    381, 385, 386, 395, 396
Snickersville, Virginia 205
Sorin, Father Edward 409
South Bend, Indiana 77, 409
South Carolina, 1st 119-121

439

South Carolina, 4th 44
South Carolina, 12th 120
South Carolina troops 119, 120, 211, 268
South Mountain 181, 391
Southside Railroad 381
Spangler's Wood 283
Spaulding, A. F. 309
Spotsylvania County 322
Spotsylvania Court House, Virginia 297, 331, 334, 336, 345, 351, 357, 361, 368, 373, 377, 381, 391-394, 399
St. Agnes Cemetery [Utica, New York] 398, 408
Stafford County, Virginia 212, 221, 222
Stannard, Brig. Gen. George J. 287
Stanton, Sec. of War Edwin M. 74, 79, 84, 85, 87, 94, 211, 234, 235, 236, 251, 319, 345, 378
Star of the West, U.S.S 21
State of Maine, U.S.S. 82
Staten Island 172
Stephens, James 27
Steuart, Brig. Gen. George 339
Stevensburg, Virginia 305
Stewart, George 257, 292
Stewart, Pvt. Robert Laird 267
Stone, Brig. Gen. Charles 84
Storrs, Father 68
Strawberry Plains, Tennessee 391
Stuart, Maj. Gen. J. E. B. 85, 159, 180, 182
Sudley Springs, Virginia 47
Sudley Springs Road 48
Suffolk, Virginia 305, 393

Sullivan, Capt. John 220
Sully, Brig. Gen. Alfred 227
Sumner, Brig. Gen. Edwin Vose 69, 89, 93, 99, 101, 102, 104, 107, 136, 137, 138, 140, 148, 151, 155, 156, 162, 176, 177, 178, 185, 194, 195, 208, 211, 214, 222
Sunken Road 187-189, 192
Susquehanna River 182
Sutherland Station, Virginia 394
Sweeney, Private 54
Sweitzer, Col. Jacob B. 271, 327, 328, 329
Sykes, Maj. Gen. George 93, 122, 124-126, 132, 144

Taggart, Capt. Samuel 316, 333, 375
Tammany Hall 31, 66, 254
Taney, Chief Justice Roger B. 17
Taneytown Road 262, 271
Taneytown, Pennsylvania 258
Telegraph Road 115, 211, 212, 214
Tenallytown, Virginia 178
Tennessee 302, 303
Tennessee troops 283
Terry, Capt. William R. 51
Thomas, Adjt. Gen. Lorenzo 74, 75
Thompson, Capt. George C. 277, 290, 294
Thoroughfare Gap, Virginia 256
Tidball, Capt. John C. 119
Timon, Bishop John 171

440

Tipping, Sgt. George 174, 405, 406
Tissot, Father Peter 33, 91
Todd's Tavern 324, 332, 334
Totopotomoy Creek 115, 197, 350, 391, 392, 394, 399
Touhey, Maj. Thomas 327
Townsend, George Albert 13-15, 16, 107, 111, 129
Trent farm 132
Trimble, Maj. Gen. Issac 279, 292
Tschudy, Lt. Col. Martin 274, 277, 289, 294
Turkey Hill 131, 132, 136
Turner, Captain 111
Turner, Lt. James 143
Turner's Gap, Maryland 181, 183, 186
Tyler, Brig. Gen. Daniel 43
Tyler, Brig. Gen. Robert O. 354
Tyrrel, Color Sgt. William 219

United States 19, 22, 24, 29, 30, 60, 75, 84, 85, 199, 251, 253
United States Army 58, 63, 69, 77, 309, 396, 398
United States Artillery, 1st 103
United States Artillery, 3rd 125
United States Artillery, 4th 147
United States Artillery, 5th 117
United States Cavalry, 5th 208
United States Congress 17, 42, 78, 84, 168, 206, 234, 256, 295
United States Constitution 22, 66, 170
United States Field Artillery, 4th 277

United States Ford 241, 245, 248
United States Government 307
United States Infantry, 7th 33
United States Infantry, 13th 309
United States Infantry, 14th 49
United States Military Academy 397
United States Navy 116
United States Senate 60, 74
United States War Department 18, 26, 31, 57, 64, 65, 74, 84, 168, 177, 179, 196, 200, 234, 238, 250, 255, 308, 364, 377, 403
University of Notre Dame 77, 409, 410
Upton, Brig. Gen. Emory 354
Utica, New York 398, 408

Vegesack, Col. Ernest 237
Vermont Brigade 78, 308
Vermont troops 137, 287, 308
Vicksburg, Mississippi 331
Virginia 15, 31, 41, 42, 57, 85, 138, 149, 180, 182, 257, 276, 283, 307, 310, 311, 316, 323, 331, 345, 358, 383, 387, 407
Virginia, 1st 287
Virginia, 19th 292
Virginia, 43rd 106
Virginia, 47th 143
Virginia, 53rd 106
Virginia, C.S.S. 84, 87
Virginia Cavalry, 30th 50
Virginia Central Railroad 96, 114, 176, 373

Virginia troops 51, 105, 278, 283, 285, 287-291, 293, 331, 339

Wadsworth, Brig. Gen. James S. 84, 86
Waggaman, Lt. Col. Eugene 156
Wainwright, Maj. Charles 88, 89, 93
Walker, Lt. Col. Francis A. 102, 155, 224, 245, 347, 352-354, 359, 371-373, 383
Walker, Brig. Gen. John 182
Walton, Col. James B. 225
Ward, Joseph 205, 258
Warren, Maj. Gen. Gouverneur K. 125, 303, 304, 324, 331
Warrenton, Virginia 204, 205, 209
Warrenton Junction, Virginia 300
Warwick River 87, 88, 116
Washington, D.C. 31, 38, 43, 51, 53, 57, 58, 60, 61, 64, 65, 67, 68, 69, 73, 75, 77, 78, 84, 85, 157, 159, 161, 168, 169, 170, 171, 172, 175-179, 196, 199, 203, 204, 209, 228, 237, 267, 302, 305, 306, 311, 319, 338, 350, 354, 362, 368, 371, 388, 397
Washington, Lt. J. Barroll 99
Washington Artillery 211, 214, 223, 228
Washington Garrison 343
Watts' house 118
Webb, Gen. Alexander Stewart 257, 259, 273, 274, 285, 286, 288, 289, 291, 295, 296, 297, 304, 353, 381
Weber, Brig. Gen. Max 186
Weldon Railroad 364, 367, 373, 394
West house 152
West Point Military Academy 31, 41, 42, 58, 99, 103, 113, 126, 257, 299, 354
West Wood 185
Wheatfield 268-271
White House 17, 53, 92, 113, 116
White Oak Church, Virginia 248
White Oak Road 394
White Oak Swamp 99, 101, 134, 138, 143, 145, 147, 157, 160, 164
White's Ford 178
Whiteford, Lt. Edward 248
Whittick, Robert 289
Whittier, Lieutenant 248, 249
Wilderness 128, 197, 243, 244, 321, 323, 329-331, 335, 337, 354, 361, 368, 390-392, 394, 397, 398
Willard, Col. George C. 272
Willard's Hotel 73, 77, 168
Willcox, Brig. Gen. Orlando 221
William's farm 394
Williamsburg, Virginia 89, *90*, 91, 92, 391
Williamsburg Road 93, 99, 100, 103, 136
Williamsburg-Hampton Road 89
Williamsport, Maryland 300
Wilmington, Delaware 34, 312, 395, 396

Wilson, Lt. William P. 249
Windmill Point 364
Winn, William 121
Wisconsin 49
Wisconsin, 2nd 42, 48
Wisconsin, 36th 377
Wistar, Isaac 75
Wofford, Brig. Gen. William T. 271
Wright, Brig. Gen. Ambrose 149, 272, 274, 275, 286
Wright, Brig. Gen. Horatio 337, 360

York River 81, 86-88, 92, 113, 319, 350
Yorktown, Virginia 87-89, 92, 149, 394
Young, Adjt. John R. 223
Young's Branch 48, 50

Ziegler's Grove 263
Zook, Brig. Gen. Samuel 218, 223, 230, 265, 267, 268